THE VARIETIES OF REFERENCE

THE VARIETIES OF REFERENCE

Gareth Evans

EDITED BY

JOHN McDOWELL

CLARENDON PRESS · OXFORD
OXFORD UNIVERSITY PRESS · NEW YORK

1982

Oxford University Press, Walton Street, Oxford OX2 6DP

London   Glasgow   New York   Toronto
Delhi   Bombay   Calcutta   Madras   Karachi
Kuala Lumpur   Singapore   Hong Kong   Tokyo
Nairobi   Dar es Salaam   Cape Town
Melbourne   Auckland

and associates in
Beirut   Berlin   Ibadan   Mexico City   Nicosia

Published in the United States by
Oxford University Press, New York

British Library Cataloguing in Publication Data

Evans, Gareth
    The varieties of reference.
    1. Reference (Philosophy)
    I. Title   II. McDowell, John
    149'.946   B105.R25

ISBN 0-19-824685-4
ISBN 0-19-824686-2 Pbk.

Library of Congress Cataloging in Publication Data

Evans, Gareth.
    The varieties of reference.

    Bibliography: p.
    Includes index.
    1. Reference (Philosophy)   I. McDowell, John Henry.   II. Title.
B105.R25E9   1982   160   82-8052
ISBN 0-19-824685-4   AACR2
ISBN 0-19-824686-2 (pbk.)

Typeset by
Butler & Tanner Ltd, Frome and London
Printed in Great Britain
at the University Press, Oxford
by Eric Buckley
Printer to the University

Editor's Preface

Gareth Evans, who died, aged 34, in August 1980, had been working for years on a book about reference. But he was constantly rethinking both his ideas on the subject and his strategies of exposition; each successive draft is not so much a polishing of its predecessors as a first version of a substantially new work. In his last months he undertook an attempt to prepare his book for publication, and he managed to write or dictate new versions of the Introduction and chapters 1, 2, and (in part) 3. For the rest of the book he left drafts from various earlier dates (very occasionally only in note form); these were more or less heavily annotated, with indications of footnotes, intended additions, and criticisms of the material as it stood. In the case of chapter 7, and, to a lesser extent, chapter 6, the later material is more substantial: in the Trinity Term of 1980 Evans offered a course of graduate classes on self-identification and self-reference, and in his preparation for this he arrived at improved formulations of many of the arguments of those chapters, and some thoughts that were altogether new. It is clear that he intended a radical revision of those two chapters.

It would have been possible simply to transcribe Evans's words as they stood. But even with a quite extensive commentary, the result would have been very difficult reading, except perhaps for people already partly familiar with Evans's ideas through hearing his lectures. It seemed clear that the overriding aim of this publication should be to make his thoughts as accessible as possible, and that this aim would not be best served by an excessively reverent approach to the draft. Accordingly, where his intention seems clearly expressed in notes, I have worked them up into prose. Similarly, where there is a subsequent expression of dissatisfaction with the original draft, and amendment is possible without disruption to the flow of the argument, I have simply recast the material to reflect the later

view. In chapters 6 and 7, I have added extensively to the basic
drafts, and sometimes replaced parts of them, with material
taken from the lectures. (Much of 4.3 is from this source too,
replacing a version Evans was dissatisfied with.) Throughout—
bearing in mind that what we have is essentially a first draft—
I have recast some sentences and paragraphs in the interest of
clarity. When it seemed to help the exposition, I have incorporated material from lecture-notes or earlier drafts into the text or
the footnotes. I have corrected anything that seemed to be a
mere slip. In all this, it seemed best to effect changes without
remarking on them, rather than to burden the text with a
complex apparatus of brackets and editorial footnotes.

The Appendices contain material which for various reasons
resisted this silent incorporation into the book. The Appendix
to chapter 3 stands in for a planned final section for which there
are only brief notes; although the material is all taken from
writings by Evans, its conformity to his plan for the section is to
some extent a matter of guesswork, and it seemed best not to
pretend otherwise by including it in the body of the chapter. In
assimilating material into chapters 6 and 7, I have adhered (as
everywhere) to Evans's own articulation of the chapters into
sections: the Appendices to those chapters preserve some relevant material which does not readily fit into those frames.
Elsewhere in the Appendices, I have tried to convey the character of some doubts and afterthoughts which could not be dealt
with by minor emendations of the chapters. The substance of
all the Appendices, and most of the writing, are due to Evans.
But in some places he clearly has to figure in the third person
rather than the first; and I have adopted the convention that
that is so throughout the Appendices. Square brackets round
footnotes and parts of footnotes, elsewhere in the book, mark off
either references to the Appendices or comments of mine on the
arguments.

The latest draft contains no indication of an intended title.
However, in notes for a lecture course on the theory of reference,
Evans remarked that whereas some years previously he would
have been tempted to call such a course 'The Essence of Reference', now he would prefer to call it 'The Varieties of Reference';
and this idea appears also in some notes for a Preface to an
earlier version of the book. What he meant in the lectures was

probably connected with his having become convinced that 'descriptive names' are a perfectly good category of referring expressions. Earlier he would have insisted that all genuine singular reference is, in the terminology of this book, Russellian. Now that struck him as unwarrantedly essentialistic: a theoretically well founded conception of genuine singular terms could embrace both Russellian and non-Russellian varieties. But the title is appropriate to this book in another way as well. It fits the conviction—manifested especially in chapters 6, 7, and 8— that a simple general theory even of one of those two varieties, the Russellian, is no substitute for a detailed and specific investigation of how each of its sub-varieties functions.

In his final attempt on the book, Evans contracted its plan, in the hope of being able to work through the whole in the time that was left to him. Earlier plans had involved a more complex treatment of the different kinds of demonstrative expressions, to be interwoven with the discussions of different modes of identification which form the bulk of the present Part Two. And he had intended to reinforce the chapter on proper names with a partly parallel chapter on natural-kind terms; and to discuss testimony at much greater length. Even discounting the contraction, moreover, this volume obviously constitutes at best a remote approximation to what would have resulted from a complete revision by its author. Nevertheless, I believe that the brilliance and depth of his thinking about reference emerge from these pages with sufficient clarity to make generally accessible a lively appreciation of how much philosophy has lost by his early death.

Acknowledgements

I am very grateful to Antonia Phillips for entrusting to me the task of preparing this book for publication, and for much help and encouragement in its execution. I have to thank the Master and Fellows of University College, Oxford, for granting me a leave of absence to work on the book. I am most grateful to the British Academy for a grant, originally to Evans and then to me, which made the work possible; thanks are due to Richard Wollheim for his good offices in securing this beneficence. I have had help and advice from Ronald Dworkin, J. A. Gray, I. L. Humberstone, Christopher Peacocke, Galen Strawson, P. F. Strawson, and David Wiggins. Andrea McDowell prepared a beautiful typescript from what became a very messy original, and helped in many other ways too. I should like to acknowledge also the helpfulness of the staff of the Oxford University Press.

Chapter 1 draws on Evans's article 'Understanding Demonstratives', in Herman Parret and Jacques Bouveresse, eds., *Meaning and Understanding* (De Gruyter, Berlin and New York, 1981), pp. 280–303. He seems also to have intended some of this material to appear in chapter 6, and I have incorporated the relevant part of the article, slightly amended, into the Appendix to that chapter. Chapter 2 draws on Evans's article 'Reference and Contingency', *The Monist* lxii (1979), 161–89. Thanks are due to the original editors and publishers for permission to use this material.

J. McD.

Many people have helped to bring this book to publication, with advice, practical assistance and encouragement. I want to take this opportunity to express gratitude to all of them, on Gareth's behalf as well as my own: Katherine Backhouse, Arnold Cragg, Ronald Dworkin, Andrea McDowell, David Pears,

Galen Strawson, Sir Peter Strawson, David Wiggins and Richard Wollheim; Peter Brown and the British Academy for their speedy and flexible support; University College, Oxford, for the use of its photocopying facilities and for releasing John McDowell from his teaching duties; and, of course, John McDowell himself.

Antonia Phillips

Contents

Introduction

Things which appear similar to ordinary observation, and which behave similarly for ordinary purposes, are frequently called by the same name. When people acquire the methods for more detailed observation, and an interest in the construction of theories, many of these groupings have to be revised. Whales do not really belong with the fish they superficially resemble, since the similarity of form and behaviour conceals radical differences of structure and function. Now it may well be that our intuitive semantic classifications stand in need of a similar revision. 'What do you *mean*?', 'Who are you *talking about*?', 'That's not what you *said*', 'That's not *true*'. These are the rough and ready semantic concepts of the market-place, which have been used and refined by the many different people—philosophers, grammarians, teachers—who have been obliged to reflect on the operations of their own language. And, despite this refinement, they continue to reflect those similarities in linguistic form and function which are particularly striking. It is the aim of this book to examine whether one such grouping of intuitive semantics—that of the singular terms or referring expressions[1]—has a place within a developed semantic theory of natural language, and if so, what place it has.

The class of referring expressions has traditionally been taken to include proper names; definite descriptions ('the tallest man in the world'); demonstrative terms ('this man', 'that woman'); and some pronouns. The similarities underlying this traditional classification are partly similarities of (grammatical) form and partly similarities of function. Each of the kinds of expressions I have mentioned comprises noun phrases, capable of filling the traditional subject-position in a subject–predicate sentence; each of these expressions will couple with a (monadic) predicate like 'smokes' to yield a complete sentence. Quantifier expressions,

[1] These two phrases will be used interchangeably throughout.

like 'a man', 'no girl', or 'every boy', also occupy this position, but these have not, or at least not consistently, been
regarded as referring expressions. This is where the intuitive
conception of role or function comes in. In coupling a referring
expression with a predicate, say 'smokes', a speaker intends to
be taken to be making a remark about just one particular
thing—a remark that is to be determined as true or false according to whether some one indicated individual smokes. So it is
said that the role of a referring expression is that of indicating to
the audience which object it is which is thus relevant to the
truth-value of the remark. For instance, A. N. Prior wrote:

By a *name* logicians generally understand an expression that we use to
indicate *which* individual we are talking about when we are making a
statement.[2]

And P. F. Strawson writes in a similar vein:

The task of forestalling the ... question ['What (who, which one) are
you talking about?'] is the referring ... task.[3]

The point is not that 'A so-and-so smokes' will always be true,
if it is true, in virtue of the smoking of more than one thing, for
there may be only one so-and-so; rather, the fact that there is, if
there is, just one thing whose smoking will render the remark
true is not something conventionally indicated to the audience.
This second, functional aspect of the classification could be
captured by this formulation: if t is a referring expression understood in the same way in its occurrences in both of the
sentences 't is F' and 't is G', then it follows logically from the
truth of these sentences that there is something which is both F
and G.

It is undeniable that all the expressions traditionally regarded
as referring expressions can be said to play this role. But our
question concerns the significance of this fact. Does this similarity conceal deep differences? Even if this function is one which
semantic theory should recognize, are there radically different
ways in which different expressions perform it?

---

[2] *Objects of Thought*, edited by P. T. Geach and A. J. P. Kenny (Clarendon Press,
Oxford, 1971), p. 155. (I assume that Prior is using 'name' to cover all singular terms.)
[3] 'On Referring', in *Logico-Linguistic Papers* (Methuen, London, 1971), pp. 1–27, at p.
17. (Reprinted from *Mind* lix (1950), 320–44.)

These questions are not new, and the extensive discussion they have received in the philosophical literature makes some historical preliminaries almost inevitable. Although systematic semantic theory can be said to have started with Frege, in a sense the theory of reference, conceived as a theoretical examination of the questions I have posed, began with Russell, for it was he who first challenged the validity of the traditional grouping, and thereby forced those questions into the centre of philosophical attention. Frege, on the other hand, despite the enormous sophistication of his semantic theory, was content to place at its heart the category of terms intuitively regarded as referring expressions. Nevertheless, I shall begin with Frege, because he was the author of a model of the communicative situation which is of the greatest importance for our investigation. At some points we shall be able to use his model, at others we must reject it; but at all points it serves as a clear and effective benchmark, and we shall be dealing with Fregean ideas throughout the book.

I have tried to consider all the main kinds of referring expressions, so that the functioning of one can be compared with, and so cast light upon, the functioning of others; and although I am conscious of how many things remain unclear, I have tried to make this work a pretty comprehensive investigation of the phenomenon of reference. However, there is one important limit that I have observed: I have ignored questions of *ontology*. I have not enquired into what it means to say, or how one might establish, that speakers of a language have an ontology which comprises this or that kind of object.[4] I have supposed myself to be working within a scheme of interpretation for the language which fixes the interpretation of, and hence fixes the objects capable of satisfying, its predicates; the questions which I want to discuss arise after these decisions have been made. In fact, I have followed most of my predecessors in concentrating upon reference to spatio-temporal particulars, though at various points in the argument I have tried, like a cautious builder, to have a thought for the constructions which must at some later time be added.

---

[4] For some discussion of these matters, see my 'Identity and Predication', *Journal of Philosophy* lxxii (1975), 343–63.

Part One

Historical Preliminaries

Chapter 1

Frege

1.1 INTRODUCTORY

Frege was the first to formulate a systematic theory of meaning for a fragment of natural language; systematic in that it sought to provide an explanation of how the significance of complex expressions, particularly sentences, depends upon the significance of their parts. Unsurprisingly, given Frege's larger purposes in investigating the foundations of mathematics, the fragment which concerned him was free of many of the characteristic features of natural language; in particular, indexical expressions like 'I', 'now', 'here', etc. However, Frege did offer suggestions as to how his apparatus could be brought to bear upon such devices, and we shall consider these in due course.

His entire semantic theory was built around an account of the functioning of atomic sentences—sentences in which one or more singular terms are concatenated with a 'concept-expression' or predicate of corresponding degree. It will be this, the most elementary part of his theory, which will concern us, though the heights of Frege's genius are more fully revealed in the account of quantified, especially multiply quantified, sentences which he built upon this basis.[1]

Frege himself divided his theorizing about language into two phases: the phases before and after the discovery of the distinction between sense and Meaning.[2] (We may date the discovery around 1890.) After the discovery, Frege held a two-level semantic theory—a theory which attributed to each significant expression of the language two different but intimately related

---

[1] I have discussed Frege's treatment of quantification in 'Pronouns, Quantifiers, and Relative Clauses' (I), in *Canadian Journal of Philosophy* vii (1977), 467–536.

[2] *Sinn* and *Bedeutung*; '*Bedeutung*' has standardly, at least since the appearance of P. T. Geach and Max Black, *Translations from the Philosophical Writings of Gottlob Frege* (Blackwell, Oxford, 1952), been rendered 'reference', but 'meaning' is adopted in the translation of the *Nachlass* (Gottlob Frege, *Posthumous Writings*, edited by Hans Hermes,

kinds of semantic property; whereas previously he had worked
with only one. Although this division in his thought has been
widely recognized, it should not be exaggerated. Frege's theory
of Meaning for the fragment of language he was concerned with
after 1890 corresponds exactly to the theory that was implicit in
the earlier works, the *Begriffschrift* and the *Grundlagen*. The analysis of singular sentences, and the analysis of quantified sentences
based upon the analysis of singular sentences, did not alter with
the discovery of sense; rather, Frege saw more clearly what kind
of analysis he had provided, and saw the need for something
more. In later works, Frege was grafting on to this enduring
semantic theory his new conception of sense. (It is not clear that
he succeeded in doing this in an entirely satisfactory way.)

1.2 MEANING (*Bedeutung*)

Frege's idea of a theory of Meaning was roughly this. He took
as his starting-point the idea that the significance of a complete
sentence consisted in its being true or false. Now it is natural to
think of each significant expression of a language as having
what one might call a *semantic power*; and, given Frege's
starting-point, it is natural to think of this as the power to affect
the truth-value of the sentences in which it occurs. Frege was
distinctive in supposing that the semantic power of an expression was determined by that expression's being associated with
some extra-linguistic entity. He called such an entity the expression's Meaning; given the multiplicity of use of the word 'meaning', one might follow Michael Dummett and call this entity the
expression's *semantic value*.[3]

Originally concentrating exclusively upon extensional frag-
ments of language, and later feeling able to lay aside non-
extensional contexts as special or abnormal (i.e. as contexts in

---

Friedrich Kambartel, and Friedrich Kaulbach, and translated by Peter Long and
Roger White (Blackwell, Oxford, 1979)): this practice will be followed in this book (but
with a capital letter as a reminder that we are dealing with a technical use of the word).
It is a good idea not to use 'reference' for Frege's concept, given that reference is the
topic of this book. As Montgomery Furth observes (in Gottlob Frege, *The Basic Laws of
Arithmetic* (University of California Press, Berkeley and Los Angeles, 1967), p. xx), the
greater part of Frege's essay 'Über Sinn und Bedeutung' is devoted to defending the
application of the concept of *Bedeutung* to *sentences*.

[3] See Michael Dummett, 'Frege's Distinction between Sense and Reference', in *Truth
and Other Enigmas* (Duckworth, London, 1978), pp. 116–44.

which expressions do not have their normal semantic value), Frege was drawn to the identification of the Meaning (semantic value) of a singular term with what would normally be regarded as that term's referent. The idea that the semantic power of a singular term consists in its being associated with an object in the world as its referent makes evident good sense, once the decision to lay aside non-extensional contexts for special treatment has been made, since, given that decision, any two co-referring expressions can be intersubstituted anywhere *salva veritate*. However, this consideration by no means forces the identification of a singular term's semantic value with its referent; and the consequence that all empty singular terms have no semantic value, and hence no semantic power, is not one which is obviously acceptable. Frege's later willingness to ascribe sense to terms with no semantic value is only dubiously coherent. I shall consider this at much greater length below (1.6).

The choice of a truth-value as the Meaning (semantic value) of a complete sentence was made inevitable by the starting-point of Frege's theory of Meaning (the thesis that significance in a complete sentence amounts to its possession of one of the values, the True and the False); the decision to regard semantic power as always consisting in an association with an extra-linguistic entity; and the laying aside of non-extensional contexts for special treatment. Once these two anchors—the assignment of truth-values to sentences, and the assignment of objects to singular terms—have been lowered, the kind of entity that constitutes the semantic value of an expression of any of the various other kinds is more or less determined by its grammatical category.

If we use the notation of 'categorial grammar', the correspondence between grammatical category and kind of semantic value is very striking. A description of a given grammatical category in categorial grammar is either primitive or derived. The two *primitive* notions of a Fregean categorial grammar would be that of a sentence, S, and that of a Proper Name or singular term, N.[4] Categorial descriptions for *derived* categories take the form of a description of a grammatical category,

---

[4] 'Proper Name' is here used as Frege used 'Eigenname', to apply to singular terms generally, rather than the particular kind of singular term that is the concern of chapter 11. This Fregean use will be signalled by initial capitals.

followed by a slash, followed by one or more descriptions of a grammatical category, e.g. 'S/N' or '$S/S,S$'. To say that an expression is of the form S/N is to say that it is an expression which, when concatenated with a Proper Name, yields a sentence; to say that an expression is of the category $S/S,S$ is to say that it is an expression which, when concatenated with two sentences, yields a sentence; and so on. So 'S/N' is a derived description of the category of monadic concept-expressions, while '$S/S,S$' is a derived description of a category into which the binary propositional connectives, e.g. 'and', 'or', etc., fall. The semantic value of any derived category in this grammar, with a description of the form $\alpha/\beta_1, \ldots, \beta_n$ $(n \geqslant 1)$, will be a function from n $(n \geqslant 1)$ semantic values of the sort appropriate to a β to a semantic value of the sort appropriate to an α. Thus the semantic value of a monadic concept-expression (S/N) is a function from N-values to S-values, i.e. a function from objects to truth-values. The semantic value of a binary connective like 'and' $(S/S,S)$ is a function from pairs of S-values to S-values, i.e. a function from pairs of truth-values to truth-values. A simple unary quantifier expression, such as 'every boy' $(S/(S/N))$, has as its semantic value a second-level function from S/N-values to S-values, i.e. a second-level function from a function from objects to truth-values, to truth-values.[5]

1.3 EMPTY SINGULAR TERMS: PRELIMINARY REMARKS

An analysis provided by the theory of Meaning for a singular sentence such as 'John is wise'—an account of the mechanism whereby a truth-value for the sentence is determined—is implicit in these assignments of Meanings (just as, indeed, a full definition of well-formedness is implicit in the assignments of expressions to syntactic categories made by a categorial grammar). The Proper Name 'John' has the role of introducing an *object*, which is to be the argument to the function introduced by the concept-expression 'ξ is wise'—a function which maps all and only wise objects on to the value True. Thereby, and only thereby, is the sentence determined as having a truth-value, and, therefore, as having the significance of a complete

---

[5] The importance of the 'two anchors' is seen very clearly by Hans D. Sluga in section II of his review of Frege's *Nachgelassene Schriften*, in *Journal of Philosophy* lxviii (1971), 265-72.

sentence—something capable of being used alone to make an assertion.

It follows very directly that there are two parallel defects of a radical kind to which Proper Names and concept-expressions are liable, and these Frege very often treated together.

In the first place, a Proper Name may fail to have an object as its Meaning, and hence fail to provide any singular sentence in which it occurs with an argument to the function associated with the concept-expression. The consequence for any such sentence is that it is not determined to have a truth-value. Frege registered this by saying that the sentence is neither true nor false, and his reason for saying this makes it absolutely clear that he meant that the sentence fails to have any truth-value at all; he was not thinking of a third truth-value (a member of the class of undesignated values), as Dummett has suggested.[6] Were Frege to have recognized such a third value, then his concepts would have mapped objects on to a larger category of entities; but we would still have been left with the possibility that a sentence may have no truth-value, because no argument is presented to the appropriate function.[7]

In the second place, a concept-expression may fail to introduce a function which yields a truth-value for each object of the domain. Concept-expressions whose functions are partial—i.e. not everywhere defined—simply do not have a Meaning of a kind that fits them to serve *generally* in a language used for making serious assertions about the world. If such concept-expressions are allowed, some singular sentences will fail to have a truth-value, as will many quantified sentences, especially universally quantified sentences.[8]

[6] *Frege: Philosophy of Language* (Duckworth, London, 1973), ch. 12.

[7] See John McDowell, 'Truth-Value Gaps', forthcoming in the Proceedings of the Sixth International Congress for Logic, Methodology, and Philosophy of Science. I do not deny that Dummett has good reason for *offering* Frege the proposal of a third, undesignated truth-value—at least so long as Frege includes definite descriptions as singular terms. But this is an inadequate basis for the *interpretation*.

[8] 'It can be objected that such words are used thousands of times in the language of life. Yes; but our vernacular languages are not made for conducting proofs. And it is precisely the defects that spring from this that have been my main reason for setting up a conceptual notation. The task of our vernacular languages is essentially fulfilled if people engaged in communication with one another connect the same thought, or approximately the same thought, with the same proposition. For this it is not at all necessary that the individual words should have a sense and meaning of their own, provided only that the whole proposition has a sense. Where inferences are to be drawn

Before the distinction between sense and Meaning, Frege
quite explicitly embraced the consequences, as regards empty
singular terms, of his view of the Meaning of singular terms.
Proposition 9 of Frege's unpublished 'Seventeen Key Sentences
on Logic' runs:

A sentence can be true or untrue only if it is an expression for a
thought. The sentence 'Leo Sachse is a man' is the expression of a
thought only if 'Leo Sachse' designates something. And so too the
sentence 'this table is round' is the expression of a thought only if the
words 'this table' are not empty sounds but designate something
specific for me.[9]

Again, in the dialogue with Pünjer on existence (from before
1884), Frege wrote:

The rules of logic always presuppose that the words we use are not
empty, that our sentences express judgements, that one is not playing
a mere game with words. Once 'Sachse is a man' expresses an actual
judgement, the word 'Sachse' must designate something, and in that
case I do not need a further premise in order to infer 'there are men'
from it.[10]

These passages, with many others which may be found in the
Grundlagen, make it clear that Frege was perfectly familiar with,
and at one time certainly embraced, a view of singular terms
which is commonly regarded as much more Russellian than
Fregean: namely, the view that someone who uttered a sentence
containing an empty singular term would fail to say anything,
in the sense that he would fail to express a thought. This fact
makes my use of the expression 'Russellian singular term' to
mean a singular term whose significance depends upon its having a referent—a use I shall adhere to throughout this book—
somewhat unhistorical, though I shall offer a defence of it later
(2.3). This fact also refutes Dummett's claim that 'Frege *never*
lapsed so far from plausibility as to maintain that to utter a

---

the case is different: for this it is essential that the same expression should occur in two
propositions and should have exactly the same meaning in both cases. It must therefore
have a meaning of its own, independent of the other parts of the proposition.' Gottlob
Frege, *Philosophical and Mathematical Correspondence* (Blackwell, Oxford, 1980), p. 115.

[9] *Posthumous Writings*, p. 174. I am accepting the dating of this passage, by the editors
of the *Nachlass*, as contemporary with the dialogue with Pünjer, though my case would
be much strengthened if the dating, by Scholz, of around 1906 could be substantiated.

[10] *Posthumous Writings*, p. 60.

sentence containing a name lacking a bearer is to fail to say anything in the sense of failing even to express a thought.'[11] This was a view of singular terms with which Frege was familiar, though in no way do I mean to deny that after making the distinction between sense and Meaning, Frege felt himself able to say much more tolerant things about empty names, and sentences containing them, than before.

Although the introduction of the distinction between sense and Meaning did have this consequence, the issue which prompted the distinction had nothing at all to do with the issue of empty terms. As is well known, the point of the distinction has to do with the need to take account of the *cognitive* aspects of language use. We can think of the theory of Meaning, very generally, as concerned with relations between expressions of the language and entities in the world. Now, Frege came to see the need for another level of description and theory which is concerned, we might with equal generality say, with relations between expressions of the language and the understanding that competent speakers have of them. He found it necessary to recognize the possibility of an objective semantic difference between two expressions not distinguishable by the theory of Meaning (two expressions with the same Meaning)—this difference having to do with the different ways in which the expressions are to be understood by competent speakers, these different ways in turn ultimately resting upon the different thoughts and propositional attitudes that competent speakers will have on hearing and understanding sentences containing the two expressions. If we look at matters in this way, there can be no more question of regarding the theory of sense as quite independent of the theory of Meaning than there is of regarding the semantic relations between words and the world as quite independent of the thoughts and propositional attitudes associated by competent speakers with those words. I shall try to say more about the relation of the theory of sense to the theory of Meaning below (1.4).

The motive, then, was originally to understand how certain sentences can be informative when other sentences, composed of expressions with the same semantic values, were uninformative. The point was much more to see how two sentences with

---

[11] *Frege*, p. 403: my italics.

the same semantic value, put together in the same way out of expressions which likewise had the same semantic values, can express *different* thoughts than it was to show how a sentence containing an expression which altogether lacked a semantic value might nevertheless express a thought.

However, as I said earlier, with two levels of significance to work with, Frege apparently felt able to reconcile a defect at one level with adequacy at the other; there are many passages in which he states that empty singular terms may have a sense, and that sentences containing them may express thoughts.[12] Although I believe these statements are very much more equivocal than at first appears, it seems difficult to deny that Frege felt some relief at being able to offer these verbal formulations. For we must remember that his category of Proper Names included both definite descriptions and names whose reference is fixed by descriptions, and in both cases it is indeed a very serious lapse from plausibility to hold that nothing is said, no thought is expressed, by someone who utters a sentence containing an empty term of either category. (I shall try to defend this later (2.1).)

It is far from clear that Frege's new notion, the notion of sense, allowed him consistently to ascribe sense to empty singular terms while the basic theory of Meaning remained unaltered. This no doubt explains why the comforting formulations which he offered were usually embedded in a context which made them both qualified and equivocal. To get clear about these matters we must turn directly to Frege's notion of sense.

1.4 SENSE: PRELIMINARY REMARKS

A good brief introduction to Frege's notion of sense is found in a letter Frege wrote to Philip Jourdain around 1914.

... Let us suppose an explorer travelling in an unexplored country sees a high snow-capped mountain on the northern horizon. By making inquiries among the natives he learns that its name is 'Aphla'. By sighting it from different points he determines its position as exactly as possible, enters it in a map, and writes in his diary: 'Aphla is at least 5000 metres high'. Another explorer sees a snow-capped mountain on the southern horizon and learns that it is called Ateb. He enters it in his map under this name. Later comparison shows that both explorers saw the same mountain. Now the content of the proposition 'Ateb is

[12] e.g. *Translations*, pp. 62–3; *Posthumous Writings*, pp. 191, 225.

Aphla' is far from being a mere consequence of the principle of identity, but contains a valuable piece of geographical knowledge. What is stated in the proposition 'Ateb is Aphla' is certainly not the same thing as the content of the proposition 'Ateb is Ateb'. Now if what corresponded to the name 'Aphla' as part of the thought was the meaning of the name and hence the mountain itself, then this would be the same in both thoughts. The thought expressed in the proposition 'Ateb is Aphla' would have to coincide with the one in 'Ateb is Ateb', which is far from being the case. What corresponds to the name 'Ateb' as part of the thought must therefore be different from what corresponds to the name 'Aphla' as part of the thought. This cannot therefore be the meaning which is the same for both names, but must be something which is different in the two cases, and I say accordingly that the sense of the name 'Ateb' is different from the sense of the name 'Aphla'. Accordingly, the sense of the proposition 'Ateb is at least 5000 metres high' is also different from the sense of the proposition 'Aphla is at least 5000 metres high'. Someone who takes the latter to be true need not therefore take the former to be true. An object can be determined in different ways, and every one of these ways of determining it can give rise to a special name, and these different names then have different senses; for it is not self-evident that it is the same object which is being determined in different ways. We find this in astronomy in the case of planetoids and comets. Now if the sense of a name was something subjective, then the sense of the proposition in which the name occurs, and hence the thought, would also be something subjective, and the thought one man connects with this proposition would be different from the thought another man connects with it; a common store of thoughts, a common science would be impossible. It would be impossible for something one man said to contradict what another man said, because the two would not express the same thought at all, but each his own.

For these reasons I believe that the sense of a name is not something subjective [crossed out: in one's mental life], that it does not therefore belong to psychology, and that it is indispensable.[13]

In the original article Frege spoke of sense as a 'mode of presentation' of Meaning, and elsewhere he pictured expressions with the same Meaning but different senses as illuminating the Meaning from different sides. None of these metaphors makes the relation between sense and Meaning entirely clear. But it seems to me to be possible to dispense with them.

Let us focus upon the case of singular terms for the moment.

[13] *Philosophical and Mathematical Correspondence*, p. 80.

Someone who hears and understands an utterance of a sentence
containing a singular term, such as 'Aphla is over 5000 metres
high', must at least think of the mountain—in having, precisely,
this thought: that what the speaker is saying is true if and only
if that mountain is over 5000 metres high. Now, it is not possible
to think of a mountain save in some particular way. If you gave
the way in which our subject was thinking of it, you would be
giving what Frege calls the sense he attaches to the name
'Aphla'.[14] Frege's idea was that it may be a property of a
singular term as an element of a public language that, in order
to understand utterances containing it, one must not only think
of a particular object, its Meaning, but one must think of that
object *in a particular way*: that is, every competent user of the
language who understands the utterance will think of the object
in the same way. 'The sense of a proper name is grasped by
everybody who is sufficiently familiar with the language or
totality of designations to which it belongs.'[15]

   Although the notion of sense is frequently illustrated by the
behaviour of singular terms, Frege applies it to all Meaningful
expressions of the language, and the simple explanation of the
notion which I have given can also be applied quite generally
(perhaps giving Frege his pinch of salt).[16] For we can equally
say that someone who understands an utterance of the sentence
'Aphla is over 5000 metres high' must think of, or in some way
or other have in mind, the concept (function) associated with
the expression 'ξ is over 5000 metres high'. And since, for Frege,
functions are extensional entities, it becomes not merely possible
but mandatory to insist that someone who understands the
sentence must grasp the function *in a particular way*, namely as
that function which maps on to the True precisely those things

---

[14] The principle that it is not possible to think of an object except in some particular
way corresponds to Dummett's principle that it is not possible to have a bare knowledge
concerning some object that it is the referent of a term. Either principle will yield the
conclusion that for any term t and any person p, there is a sense s such that if p
understands t, he attaches s to it. But what is needed for any singular term to have an
objective sense, as an element of a public language, is that for any term t there is a sense
s such that for any person p, if p understands t, he attaches s to t. Sliding between these
was the fallacy in Dummett's defence of Frege in *Frege* (e.g. ch. 5); this is acknowledged
in the later paper 'Frege's Distinction between Sense and Reference' (in *Truth and Other
Enigmas*): see especially pp. 130 ff.

[15] *Translations*, p. 57: 'familiar with' might be glossed by 'competent in'.

[16] Cf. *Translations*, p. 54.

which are over 5000 metres high, and not, for example, as the function which maps the following objects ... (imagine here a list of mountains) on to the value True. Finally, once it is remembered that truth-values, like entities of any other kind, can be thought of in a myriad different ways, and not merely as the True and the False, we can even see how someone who understands a complete sentence will be thinking of its truth-value *in a particular way*. It is not sufficient for understanding 'Aphla is over 5000 metres high' that one think of it as having the value True, identified as such (supposing the sentence is true); but one will have understood the sentence if one thinks of it as having the truth-value of the thought that Aphla is over 5000 metres high, as one would if one thought that the sentence is true if and only if Aphla is over 5000 metres high.[17]

To summarize, then, I suggest that we take Frege's ascription of a sense to a Proper Name to mean that not only must one think of an object—the referent of the term—in order to understand a sentence containing it, but also anyone who is to understand the sentence must think of the referent *in the same particular way*. It is therefore, for Frege, as much a public and objective property of a term that it imposes this requirement, as that it has such and such an object as its referent.

[17] Though I owe a great deal in my interpretation of Frege to Michael Dummett, the account I am offering of the relation between sense and Meaning is rather different from his. We do not diverge importantly over the conception of a theory of Meaning; indeed my account of this derives almost entirely from his (see, e.g., 'Frege's Distinction between Sense and Reference', in *Truth and Other Enigmas*, at pp. 119-20). But we differ over how sense relates to Meaning. Dummett's view starts from the observation that there is no question of making it a requirement, for understanding a sentence, that one know its truth-value. This leads him to think generally that the sense of an expression is (not a way of thinking about its Meaning, but) a method or procedure for determining its Meaning. So someone who grasps the sense of a sentence will be possessed of some method for determining the sentence's truth-value. It will be derived from a grasp of the senses of the constituent expressions, since the sense of a Proper Name, for Dummett, is a criterion for, or means of, identifying its referent, and the sense of a concept-expression is a way of determining whether or not something satisfies it; and if we put these two procedures together, we shall have a procedure for determining the truth-value of a sentence. The procedures in question cannot necessarily be effective procedures, or even procedures we ourselves are capable of following. Dummett's interpretation of sense thus commits Frege to a form of what we may call 'ideal verificationism' (on which see further 4.2). Now I do not mean to say that there are no traces of verificationism in Frege's thought (particularly in his early work). But Dummett's ideal verificationism is a very strong doctrine with many exceptionable features, and there is scant evidence for attributing it to Frege. So I have gone back to the beginning of Dummett's line of thought; and I have felt able to grasp the nettle—to suppose that in understanding a sentence one *would*, in one way, be thinking of its truth-value.

1.5 SENSE AND THOUGHT

Frege never said much about particular ways of thinking of objects; he provided no analysis of what it is to think of an object demonstratively, for example, and while he was confident that there is a particular way in which each of us thinks of himself, he said hardly a word about it.[18] It is fairly clear that he supposed that the way in which we think about a great many objects is, as Russell would say, 'by description'. But it should be stressed that there is absolutely nothing in the texts to support the claim that he held that the way of thinking of any object *must* exploit the subject's knowledge of some description uniquely true of it. (Indeed such a generalized 'descriptivism' is extremely implausible.) In fact, all that Frege said about the way in which we think of ourselves, when we think of ourselves self-consciously, was that it is primitive and available to no one else, and neither of these things would be true on a generalized 'descriptive' theory of thought.

It does not appear to me that it was incumbent upon Frege to undertake detailed investigations of different particular ways of thinking of objects, although they are of great independent interest, and must be undertaken by anyone who wishes to investigate specific kinds of singular terms, in order to determine what kind of sense they have. Frege said little enough about the idea of a mode of presentation, or a way of thinking of an object, in general. He did, however, link them to notions employed in ordinary propositional-attitude psychology, and this, while it does not by any means uniquely fix the interpretation of those ideas, imposes a considerable constraint upon it. The link between the notion of sense and the ordinary notions of propositional-attitude psychology was extremely direct. The sense of a sentence, which is of course a function of the sense of its parts, is (in Frege's terminology) a thought; and the single constraint Frege imposed upon his notion of thought was that it should conform to what we might call 'the Intuitive Criterion of Difference', namely, that the thought associated with one sentence S as its sense must be different from the thought associated with another sentence S' as *its* sense, if it is possible

[18] See 'The Thought' (translated by A. M. and Marcelle Quinton), in P. F. Strawson, ed., *Philosophical Logic* (OUP, Oxford, 1967), pp. 17–38, at pp. 25–6 (reprinted from *Mind* lxv (1956), 289–311).

for someone[19] to understand both sentences at a given time while coherently taking different attitudes towards them, i.e. accepting (rejecting) one while rejecting (accepting), or being agnostic about, the other. This is made perfectly clear in the passage from the letter to Jourdain quoted earlier:

Accordingly, the sense of the proposition 'Ateb is at least 5000 metres high' is also different from the sense of the proposition 'Aphla is at least 5000 metres high'. Someone who takes the latter to be true need not therefore take the former to be true.[20]

To give one of a thousand other places where Frege employed this Criterion: in a letter to Russell in 1902, Frege wrote:

... The thought that *all thoughts belonging to Class M are true* is different from the thought that *all thoughts belonging to Class N are true*; for someone who did not know that *M* coincided with *N* could hold one of these thoughts to be true and the other to be false.[21]

Frege needed this connection between his theoretical notion of sense and ordinary propositional-attitude psychology if that theoretical notion was to help him solve the original puzzle about how sentences composed out of expressions with the same Meanings can have different cognitive values. For the notion of cognitive value is a notion partially defined in terms from propositional-attitude psychology: a sentence S has a different cognitive value from a sentence S' just in case it is possible to understand S and S' while taking different attitudes towards them.[22]

It follows from this that if the notion of 'a way of thinking

---

[19] Not 'anyone'. The thought expressed by 'Hesperus is F' is different from the thought expressed by 'Phosphorus is F', but it is not true that *anyone* who understands the two sentences can take different attitudes to them. For example, it is not true of someone who knows that Hesperus is Phosphorus. I owe my awareness of the need for care on this point to Paul Benacerraf.

[20] *Philosophical and Mathematical Correspondence*, p. 80. (In the second sentence, 'therefore' might be read as 'on that account'; this would avert the risk of reading the second sentence as an inference from the first—whereas it is in fact a reason given for accepting the first.)

[21] *Philosophical and Mathematical Correspondence*, p. 153. See also *Posthumous Writings*, p. 197.

[22] Given that Frege's senses do link up with the concepts of ordinary propositional-attitude psychology, it is open to him to offer his analysis of idioms used in expressing that theory (e.g. of 'X believes that a is F'), according to which in such contexts the sentence 'a is F' has as its Meaning its customary sense (a thought).

about something' is to be elucidatory of Frege's notion of sense, ways of thinking about things must be identified and distinguished in harmony with the Intuitive Criterion of Difference for thoughts. We must not discriminate ways of thinking of things so finely that no difference of epistemic attitude can rest upon the discrimination. To take an example of Frege's, we must say that someone who thinks of a horse as the horse ridden by the Queen is thinking of the horse in the same way as someone who thinks of it as the Queen's steed, for the difference in poetic colouring could never be the basis, for someone who fully grasped both senses, for taking different attitudes towards the two thoughts.[23] (If we found different senses here, then Frege's explanation of the difference in cognitive value of two sentences, in terms of their possessing different senses, would not be generally acceptable.) Equally, we must not make our discrimination of ways of thinking of objects so coarse that we reckon a subject to be thinking about an object in the same way in two episodes of thinking about it, when it would be perfectly possible for the subject coherently to take different attitudes towards the thoughts thus entertained.

At this point it is necessary to take account of some features of the use of the expression 'a way of doing something'. It is possible to say that two subjects are V-ing in the same way, provided that there is some one adverb of manner which can provide a true answer to the question 'How did he V?' raised with respect to each of them. Thus, it is perfectly legitimate to say that two men are thinking of something in the same way, provided that they are both thinking of it 'by description', no matter how different the descriptions may be. But this is obviously not the notion of a 'way of thinking about an object' which Frege wants. I suggest that the desired notion can be explained in terms of the notion of an account of what makes it the case that a subject's thought is a thought about the object in question. Imagine such an account written out. 'S is thinking about the object a in virtue of the fact that ... S ...': what follows 'that' is an account in which references to the subject and the object thought about appear, possibly at several places. Now I suggest that another subject, S', can be said to be thinking about the object a in the same way if and only if we get a true

---

[23] See 'The Thought', p. 23.

statement when we replace reference to S with reference to S' throughout the account provided for S, deriving 'S' is thinking about a in virtue of the fact that ... S' ...'.

Some people have objected to my account of Fregean sense, in terms of the notion of a way of thinking of something, on the following ground. Surely it is very natural to say that two men who are located at different places, but who both think about their immediate vicinity in a way they would naturally express using the word 'here', are thinking about a place *in the same way*. But if this is so, then this way of thinking about a place can hardly be equated with a Fregean sense, since, if it were so equated, the sense would not even determine the referent.[24] But this is just to misunderstand my proposal. To say that a sense is a way of thinking about an object is to say that the sense of a given singular term corresponds to an answer to the question 'How did S V?', when the relevant substitution for 'V' is, e.g., 'think of Vienna', or 'think of position P', or 'think of Winston Churchill'. Since there is no one place that the two subjects in the envisaged case are both thinking of, there is obviously no place that they are both thinking of in the same way. (Of course we can register the similarity between them, because they are doing *something* in the same way, namely 'thinking of a place'; that is to say, satisfying the predicate '$(\exists x)$ (x is a place and ξ is thinking of x)'.)

The Intuitive Criterion of Difference for thoughts cannot by itself fully determine the identity and distinctness of thoughts—questions of identity and distinctness arise in the case of thoughts of different subjects, or of a single subject at different times, while the Intuitive Criterion can be brought to bear only when the same subject is entertaining the thoughts at the same time. Consequently, the connection between sense and thought leaves considerable latitude for answering questions about the identity and distinctness of senses, or ways of thinking of things. But it imposes a tight restriction on acceptable answers.

We may derive from these reflections the following Fregean model of successful communication using a sentence containing a Proper Name. The speaker, S, utters the sentence 'a is F',

---

[24] This phrase (which Frege also used) can give rise to confusion. I use it (and believe that Frege used it) to mean that Meanings correspond one-many with senses; not that sense is a route to, or means of determining, the Meaning of an expression.

having in mind the thought whose content is determined by the senses he attaches to the expressions 'a' and 'ξ is F'. This thought will be about the referent of the term 'a', but he will be thinking of it in the particular way which constitutes the sense he attaches to the name. The hearer, A, will, in understanding the sentence, also entertain a thought, understood to have the same truth-value as S's utterance. The content of A's thought will likewise be determined by the senses he attaches to the constituent expressions. If we assume, with Frege, that it is an objective property of expressions of the language which S and A speak that they have a definite sense, and further that S and A are competent speakers of their language, then we shall be assured that A will have the very same thought that S was expressing, or making as if he was expressing. (Actually, the whole content of this assurance amounts to no more than this: A will not have a thought distinct, by the Criterion of Difference, from S's. Or at least it amounts to no more than this until we have further constraints on the notion of 'same thought'.)

1.6 EMPTY SINGULAR TERMS: SENSE WITHOUT MEANING?

Some suspicion that all is not well with Frege's willingness to ascribe sense to empty singular terms (1.3) emerges from trying to cash the metaphor with which Frege introduces the idea of sense. It is really not clear how there can be a mode of presentation associated with some term when there is no object to be presented. On my interpretation of the metaphor the difficulty remains acute: it certainly does not appear that there can be a way of thinking about something unless there is something to be thought about in that way. But it may be said that the metaphors are unimportant, and perhaps, that I have misinterpreted Frege's intentions.

Deeper difficulties emerge if we ask: what, on Frege's view, is the meaning of assigning an entity to an expression as its semantic value? What, for example, is meant by the fundamental choice of truth-values as the Meanings of sentences? Surely the choice of entities of a given type as appropriate semantic values for expressions of a given category must mean that the functioning of any member of that category as a viable element of language depends upon its being associated with such an entity.

So if we find sentences which we accept as intelligible and yet of which we are prepared to say that they have no truth-value,[25] then we must simply revise our estimate of what the appropriate semantic values of sentences are.

Let me put this point another way. The central fact from which semanticists start is that a certain body of discourse is significant: it is effectively used for the expression and transmission of thoughts. The semanticist seeks to account for this remarkable fact. Following Frege, as a part of his procedure he decides to construct a theory of Meaning, the main aim of which is to help to explain how the significance of sentences depends upon the significance of their parts. But then it is just not open to the semanticist to say 'There is a gap in my theory; here is a group of viable sentences which might be used to express and transmit thoughts, but to which my theory just does not apply. Since they do not have semantic values of the kind I have deemed appropriate for sentences, my theory of how the semantic value of a complex expression depends upon the semantic values of its parts does not apply to them.' Rather than say this, the semanticist must go back and adjust his theory, specifically the assignments he deemed appropriate as the semantic values of sentences.

Yet it appears that Frege was prepared to allow that there were perfectly meaningful sentences of the language, which could be used to express and convey thoughts, but to which his theory of Meaning would not apply. And he was apparently prepared to allow that parts of such sentences (specifically, empty Proper Names) could make a regular and systematic contribution to the thoughts expressed by sentences containing them, without having a semantic value of the kind he deemed appropriate for such expressions. This position seems barely intelligible.

To this it might be replied that after the distinction between sense and Meaning, Frege had no such global notion as that of 'significance' or 'semantic viability', which I have been attempting to use in this criticism. Why could he not say that empty Proper Names, and sentences containing them, have one kind of meaning and not another? But this does not appear to me to be a tenable position. There just *is* a pre-theoretical notion of a sentence's being significant—a sentence's being so constructed

---

[25] Remember: *no* truth-value; not a third, undesignated value. (See 1.3.)

that it is capable of expressing or conveying a thought to, and
perhaps inducing a belief in, anyone sufficiently familiar with
the language.

'Yes,' it might be said, 'but there remains this deficiency still
to be registered at the level of the theory of Meaning: that the
thoughts associated with these sentences are, according to
Frege, one and all without truth-values.' Here it seems to me
that we finally come to the great fault-line in Frege's mature
philosophy of language. What can it mean on Frege's, or on
anyone's, principles, for there to be a perfectly determinate
thought which simply has no truth-value? Remember that the
notion of thought that Frege was intending to use had strong
links with notions embedded in ordinary propositional-attitude
psychology—the notions of belief, knowledge, memory, information, judgement, and so on. If someone understands and
accepts a sentence containing an empty name, then, according
to Frege, he thereby forms a belief; not a belief about language,
but a belief about the world. But what sense can be made of a
belief which literally has no truth-value—which is neither correct nor incorrect? It is precisely this incomprehension, so effectively voiced by Dummett,[26] that makes Frege's choice of
truth-values as the semantic values of sentences so apposite.

Really, it is another way of making the same point to say
that, given Frege's views, his proposal to ban empty singular
terms from any scientific language cannot be justified. By 'a
scientific language' Frege meant a language used exclusively for
the pursuit of truth, and he felt himself justified in purging
empty Proper Names from any such language, presumably
because no truth could be expressed with their use. But if a
sentence 'Fa', containing the empty Proper Name 'a', expresses
a thought which is at least definitely not true, how can it be
ruled out that a scientific language should contain a 'global' or
wide-scope negation operator, 'Neg', such that, for any sentence
S, 'Neg'$\cap S$ expresses a truth provided that S does not have the
value True? Then in 'Neg(Fa)' we appear to have the possibility
of expressing a true thought with the use of 'a'—perhaps a
thought that can be expressed only with the use of 'a'. (The
prospect of an entire Free Logic opens up before us.) Now it is
true that anyone who holds that a given singular term, 'b', is

[26] See Dummett, *Frege*, especially ch. 12.

Russellian must, like Frege, regard such Free-Logical man-oeuvrings as quite out of place; he too will subscribe to the principle Frege here upholds, namely that if *S* has no truth-value, no embedding of *S* can be true. But the Russellian has something to say to defend his use of the principle. In his case, 'failing to have a truth-value' amounts to 'failing to express any thought at all', and since no complex sentence can express a thought if a constituent sentence (used, not mentioned) fails to do so, it follows that no embedding of a sentence without a truth-value, even within the scope of 'Neg', can be true, failing as it does to express a thought. Frege, as far as I can see, had nothing with which he could defend his use of this principle.

I said that this was essentially the same point, because it rests upon the incomprehensibility of the idea that the thought that *p* and the thought that *it is not true that p* can both fail to be true. Surely the thought that it is not true that *p* is true just when the thought that *p* is not true. So resistance to the idea that both thoughts may fail to be true is, once again, resistance to the idea of a gap between a determinate thought's failing to have the value True and its having the value False. Where thoughts, or beliefs, are concerned, surely failing to have the value True *just is* having the value False.

I have been objecting to Frege's attempt to discern sense where there is no semantic value, essentially on the ground that it deprives a theory of semantic value of any obvious place in the general theory of language. It might be said that Frege thought of the theory of semantic value as needed for the purpose of investigating logical inference. But the theory which Frege offered is adequate for this role only if we assume that the language under study contains no empty singular terms. This is a restriction for which we could find no justification.

Quite apart from what Frege says about the sense of this or that expression, he seems to have envisaged a systematic theory of sense—a theory which shows how the sense of complex expressions is dependent upon the sense of their parts—as being built on, or derived from, the theory of Meaning. Frege nowhere appears to have envisaged a theory which would entail, for any sentence of the language, *S*, a theorem of the form

The sense of *S* is . . . ,

derived from axioms which would state the sense of the primitive words of the language. Frege had no more idea of how to complete a clause like

The sense of 'and' is . . .

than we do.

Dummett explains this point, which lies at the basis of the relationship between Fregean theory of sense and theory of semantic value, very clearly.

Indeed, even when Frege is purporting to give the sense of a word or symbol, what he actually *states* is what the reference is: and, for anyone who has not clearly grasped the relation between sense and reference, this fact makes his hold on the notion of sense precarious. The sense of an expression is the mode of presentation of the referent: in saying what the reference is, we have to choose a particular way of saying this . . . In a case in which we are concerned to convey, or stipulate, the sense of an expression, we shall choose that means of stating what the referent is which displays the sense: we might here borrow a famous pair of terms from the *Tractatus*, and say that, for Frege, we *say* what the referent of a word is, and thereby *show* what its sense is.[27]

If sense is a mode of presentation of semantic value, we should hardly expect to be introduced to the sense of an expression save in the course of being given, or being presented with, its semantic value. In view of this, the closest we shall get to a systematic theory of sense is a systematic theory of semantic value which, however, identifies the semantic values of expressions, including whole sentences, in the way in which the competent speakers of the language identify them. Thus the clauses

(1) The semantic value of 'Aphla' = Aphla

and

(2) The semantic value of 'Aphla' = Ateb

are equivalent in any theory of semantic value, given that Aphla = Ateb, but only (1) identifies the semantic value of the name in a way which *shows*, or *displays*, its sense. When a theory of semantic value meets this condition quite generally, we may say that it can *serve* as a theory of sense, and if someone knows that it meets this condition, he may *use* it as a theory of sense.

This conception of the relation between Fregean theories of

[27] *Frege*, p. 227.

sense and of semantic value is attractive, both because it makes the form of a theory of sense so unmysterious, and because it explains the central place of a theory of semantic value in the global theory of a language. We can see how the need to have one formulation of the theory of semantic value which is capable of serving as a theory of sense (and hence one formulation which specifies the semantic value of every sentence of the language in a way which displays the thought expressed by that sentence) is the source of considerable empirical constraints on the theory of semantic value. But it is clear that if we suppose that expressions without semantic value may still have a sense, we cannot avail ourselves of this conception. In fact we simultaneously lose our grip both on the point of the notion of semantic value and on the nature of sense.

Given all of this, it becomes impossible to regard Frege as an early adherent of the doctrine, later associated with A. J. Ayer and John R. Searle among others, that the possession of a referent by a singular term is simply irrelevant to the question whether or not it has a sense.[28] The passages in which Frege says that empty names may have a sense cannot be interpreted to support such an attribution, counterbalanced as they are by equally many views and doctrines which are hostile to, or straightforwardly inconsistent with, the position of these later philosophers. These later philosophers have no motive for purging a language of these names, no motive for denying that truths may be expressed with their use, no motive for rejecting the development of a Free Logic. They have no conception of a theory of sense which would be undermined by the doctrine. They do not habitually explain the difference between concept-expressions and singular terms by reference to the question whether or not a term's viability depends on there being an object suitably related to it.[29] They do not habitually explain the difference between the kind of sense a whole sentence has (a thought), and the kind of sense any sub-sentential expression has, by saying that the senses of sentences are true or false.

So on this matter of the senses of empty singular terms Frege

---

[28] Ayer, 'Names and Descriptions', in *The Concept of a Person* (Macmillan, London, 1964), pp. 129–61; Searle, *Speech Acts* (CUP, Cambridge, 1969), pp. 162–74 (note especially pp. 164–5).

[29] Cf., e.g., *Translations*, pp. 83, 106.

was inconsistent. Why did he not see the inconsistency? Why did he continue to adhere to a basically Russellian view of singular terms in all his serious theorizing, despite his willingness to contemplate empty singular terms with a sense? The answer, I think, is that Frege found a convenient mat under which he could sweep the problem posed for his theory by his assigning sense to empty singular terms, a mat we might label 'Fiction'. This line of thought does not present Frege in a very good light, but it seems clearly present in many places in his work.

The first stage in the cover-up is when Frege quite unjustifiably treats any use of an empty singular term as a fictional, or sometimes a poetical, use of language. Frege was well aware that language can be used in fiction, story-telling, and drama, and he quite rightly wished to set this use of language aside for special treatment. Perhaps nourished by an unbalanced diet of examples of empty singular terms, almost all of which were associated with this special use of language ('Odysseus', 'Nausicaa', 'Scylla', etc.), Frege assimilated perfectly serious uses of empty definite descriptions ('the least rapidly convergent series') and empty demonstratives ('that lime tree') to fictional uses of language. In 'The Thought', for example, he says:

But if my intention is not realized, if I only think I see without really seeing, if on that account the designation 'that lime tree' is empty, then I have gone astray into the sphere of fiction without knowing it or wanting to.[30]

This is no momentary aberration; at almost every place where Frege discusses empty singular terms, the idea of myth or fiction, sometimes even poetry, is close at hand.[31]

However much we may deplore this assimilation, this, in my view, is the way Frege felt able to live with the inconsistency in his position. Having quite rightly reserved the fictional use of language for special treatment, he needed to make only the slightest emendation, and apparently a justifiable one, to his pre-sense-and-Meaning position, in order to seem to allow for a more liberal view about the sense of empty singular terms. Whereas the ninth Key Sentence on Logic said 'The sentence

[30] 'The Thought', p. 28.
[31] See, e.g., *Translations*, pp. 62–3, 104, 167; *Philosophical and Mathematical Correspondence*, pp. 63, 80; *Posthumous Writings*, pp. 130, 191, 225.

"Leo Sachse is a man" is the expression of a thought only if "Leo Sachse" designates something',[32] he could now say that 'Leo Sachse is a man' is the expression of a thought *outside the sphere of fiction* only if 'Leo Sachse' designates something. Whereas previously he would have said 'Thoughts are true or false, *tertium non datur*',[33] he could now say '*Myth and fiction apart*, thoughts are true or false, *tertium non datur*'.

If we look at what Frege says about fiction, we shall see that it in fact implies a much less tolerant view of the 'sense' of empty singular terms than is suggested by the simple statements on which so much attention is focused by those who regard Frege as a forerunner of Ayer and Searle.

Names that fail to fulfil the usual role of a proper name, which is to name something, may be called mock proper names. Although the tale of William Tell is a legend and not history, and the name 'William Tell' is a mock proper name, we cannot deny it a sense. But the sense of the sentence 'William Tell shot an apple off his son's head' is no more true than is that of the sentence 'William Tell did not shoot an apple off his son's head'. I do not say that this sense is false either, but I characterize it as fictitious...

Instead of speaking about fiction we could speak of 'mock thoughts'. Thus, if the sense of an assertoric sentence is not true, it is either false or fictitious, and it will generally be the latter if it contains a mock proper name. (Footnote: We have an exception where a mock proper name occurs within a clause in indirect speech.) Assertions in fiction are not to be taken seriously, they are only mock assertions. Even the thoughts are not to be taken seriously as in the sciences: they are only mock thoughts. If Schiller's *Don Carlos* were to be regarded as a piece of history, then to a large extent the drama would be false. But a work of fiction is not meant to be taken seriously in this way at all: it's all play...

The logician does not have to bother with mock thoughts, just as a physicist, who sets out to investigate thunder, will not pay any attention to stage-thunder. When we speak of thoughts in what follows we mean thoughts proper, thoughts that are either true or false.[34]

In this passage it is clear that Frege is prepared to speak of sentences containing Proper Names used fictionally (i.e., of

[32] *Posthumous Writings*, p. 175.
[33] Cf. 'Compound Thoughts', in Frege, *Logical Investigations*, ed. by P. T. Geach (Blackwell, Oxford, 1977), pp. 55-77, at p. 56.
[34] *Posthumous Writings*, p. 130. (Cf. *Philosophical and Mathematical Correspondence*, p. 152.)

sentences containing any empty singular terms) as expressing
mock thoughts, and not real thoughts. Such a description may
be apt for some cases, but it is quite inadequately defended by
Frege in the passage quoted, where the only argument appears
to be a slide from the fact that story-tellers are only pretending
to make assertions—only pretending to express thoughts—to
the conclusion that they are expressing only pretend-thoughts.
In any case, this passage makes me reluctant simply to say that
Frege was inconsistent and leave matters there. The unqualified
passages ascribing sense to empty singular terms and sentences
containing them do induce an inconsistency. But when they are
interpreted in the light of Frege's views on fiction the inconsistency disappears, for we may gloss those passages in which Frege
says that a sentence containing an empty singular term may
express a thought as follows. Yes: a sentence containing an
empty singular term may have a sense, in that it does not
necessarily have to be likened to a sentence containing a
nonsense-word. But no: it does not *really* have a sense of the kind
possessed by ordinary atomic sentences, because it does not
function properly, it is only *as if* it functions properly. Frege's
use of the notion of fiction wrongly directs our attention to just
one case in which it is *as if* a singular term refers to something,
namely when we are engaged in a pretence that it does, but
there are others, and if we think of them, we might speak of
apparent, rather than mock or pretend, thoughts.

1.7 EMPTY SINGULAR TERMS: SENSE WITHOUT REFERENT

We may, therefore, justifiably regard Frege as having departed
very little from the 'Russellian' model of the functioning of
singular sentences which he had embraced before 1890. The
main changes were just these. First, the notion of sense was
beneficially grafted on to the model, so that singular terms now
had a sense as well as a Meaning (= their referent). Second,
Frege pointed in the direction in which we should look for a way
of understanding the case where a singular term is empty,
namely as involving some sort of *pretence* or *appearance* of
thought-expression rather than the real thing. (Anyone who is
attracted by a Russellian view of a class of singular terms must
always attempt this further task: the task of explaining why,

when a member of the class is empty, there is such a strong *impression* of understanding, communicating, and thinking. I shall return to this in chapter 10.)

However, given that Frege was content to deal with the *intuitive* category of singular terms or referring expressions, this general model of the functioning of singular sentences cannot be accepted. For, although I should (and shall) defend the idea that there are many kinds of singular term (paradigmatically, genuine demonstratives) such that, when they are empty, there can be nothing but the *illusion* of thought-expression and of understanding, it seems to me impossible to maintain this position for all the expressions in the rag-bag intuitive category. I agree with Russell that someone who sincerely utters a sentence containing a perfectly intelligible definite description which applies to nothing may thereby express a thought, and convey this thought to his audience. (I shall defend this view below: see 2.1.) And even if we follow Russell, and hive off definite descriptions for separate treatment as quantifiers, there still remain terms which would intuitively be regarded as singular terms, but for which the 'no referent—no thought (sense)' position seems quite incorrect. A particularly clear example can be produced by introducing a name into the language by some such 'reference-fixing' stipulation[35] as this:

(3) Let us call whoever invented the zip 'Julius'.

I call such names, whose reference is fixed by a description, 'descriptive names'. Here, as with definite descriptions, it seems impossible to deny that someone speaking, and known to be speaking, 'within the scope of' this stipulation could express a thought, and convey that thought to another person, by uttering

(4) Julius was an Englishman,

even if the name is empty. Talk of 'mock' or 'apparent' thoughts seems to be as much out of place in this case as it is in the case of empty descriptions, and for much the same reasons. And it is not very plausible to deny that 'Julius' is a member of the same semantical category as other proper names.

[35] See Saul A. Kripke, 'Naming and Necessity', in Donald Davidson and Gilbert Harman, eds., *Semantics of Natural Languages* (Reidel, Dordrecht, 1972), pp. 253-355, at pp. 290-1.

Both of these claims require some argument, which I shall give in the next chapter. My present concern is not to discuss descriptive names, but to clarify what has been argued for in the previous section. I have *not* argued that the entire structure of a Fregean semantic theory would break down if one insisted upon ascribing a Fregean sense to an empty singular term. What I have claimed is that dire consequences follow from the ascription of a Fregean sense to any expression that has no *Meaning* or *semantic value*; hence the consequences ensue for Frege because he selected, as appropriate semantic values for singular terms, the objects that would be regarded as their *referents*. But the equation between semantic value and referent is by no means mandatory. In fact it has to be given up if empty singular terms are to be ascribed a sense.[36]

If we wished to incorporate significant but empty Proper Names within a Fregean framework, one formally adequate possibility would be to regard the semantic value of each singular term as a *set*, which would be either the singleton of the referent or the empty set, according to whether or not the term has a referent. If no one person invented the zip, the name 'Julius' would have a *semantic value*, namely the empty set, but it would have no *referent*. Its sense would then be a mode of presentation of its semantic value, the empty set, and its *semantic power* would be quite plausibly represented as consisting in the fact that it is associated with the empty set—that no object is determined as its referent. Appropriate adjustments would have to be made to the semantic values of concept-expressions, which would now have to map singletons on to the values True and False, but always map the empty set on to the value False.[37] The proposal may seem strange, and there may be other proposals which are better. But a version of the proposal, expressed in a neo-Fregean semantic theory in the style of Davidson, is in fact quite familiar to philosophers and logicians.

[36] The possibility of giving up the equation would have been much more clearly perceivable if 'Meaning' (or 'semantic value') had been favoured over 'reference' as the translation of '*Bedeutung*'. Dummett (*Frege*, pp. 93–4) tries to express the relevant distinction by means of the difference between 'referent' and 'reference'. But although these two words do differ in meaning, the meaning of 'reference' is not really what is wanted. (On the word 'reference', see John McDowell, 'On the Sense and Reference of a Proper Name', *Mind* lxxxvi (1977), 159–85, at pp. 162–3.)

[37] This seems better than the alternative proposal (to meet the same need) that we should regard concepts as functions from name-*senses* to truth-values.

I shall now spend some time trying to elaborate the relationship between High Fregean semantic theories, with their rich ontology of extra-linguistic entities serving as the Meaning of words, and the much less committed neo-Fregean theories of recent times. I shall then transpose the discussion of Russellian and descriptive singular terms to this lower key.

1.8 INTERPRETATIONAL SEMANTICS AND TRUTH THEORIES

A semantic theory of Frege's type, in which entities are assigned to the various significant expressions of the language in an ontologically quite profligate way, is by no means the only kind of semantic theory there is, or the only kind in which Frege's fundamental ideas may be expressed.

We may see Frege's original semantic theory as a species of what I have elsewhere called *interpretational semantics*.[38] The interpretational semanticist seeks to characterize the notion of an admissible interpretation of a language, or language-fragment, considered as made up of expressions of certain definite semantic categories; expressions of the same category receive, upon any admissible interpretation, an assignment of the same kind. Thus typical statements of interpretational semantics will be that on any admissible interpretation each expression of a certain category (those called 'proper names') will be assigned an object in the domain, and that on any admissible interpretation each expression of another category (those called 'predicates of degree n') will be assigned a function from n-tuples of objects of the domain on to the truth-values. We have recently considered a variant proposal on which proper names would, on any admissible interpretation, be assigned sets: either singletons of objects in the domain or the null set.

This enterprise differs from model theory, as understood by logicians, both in its ultimate purpose and by including, within the categories of expressions for which assignments are to be sought, *all* the categories of expressions of the language: the logical words are not assumed to have a constant interpretation. Furthermore, the interpretational semanticist's job will not be

[38] See my 'Semantic Structure and Logical Form', in Gareth Evans and John McDowell, eds., *Truth and Meaning* (Clarendon Press, Oxford, 1976), pp. 199–222; cf. also Dummett, *Truth and Other Enigmas*, p. 123.

complete until he has specified, or shown how to specify, the
actual or *designated* interpretation—the particular assignments
which the expressions of a language must be seen as possessing,
given the significance which those expressions actually have.
Thus in addition to the general remark (say) that expressions in
a given language of the category $S/\mathcal{N}$ are assigned (on admissible
interpretations) functions from objects to truth-values, we
should expect the statement that on the actual interpretation of
that language the expression 'ξ is blue' is assigned that function
from objects to truth-values which yields truth just in case the
argument is *blue*.

I believe the enterprise of interpretational semantics to be of
some importance, since I believe that questions about the nature
and boundaries of semantic categories are unavoidable. However, there are less ontologically committed approaches to semantics: theories in which some favoured semantic predicate of
sentences or utterances (such as 'true' or 'warrantedly assertible'
or 'provable') is characterized recursively for the language in
question, without regard to the possibility of alternative interpretations. Many of the points and distinctions which philosophers of language wish to make may be effectively stated or
explained in terms provided by these theories. But we can rely
upon such 'direct theories' only to the extent to which we regard
them as adequate—as dealing with all the members of each real
underlying semantic category in the same way. In using a
particular direct semantic theory for a natural language, therefore, one must have in mind the possibility of its being validated
by being shown to be *in harmony with* some coherent interpretational semantic theory. So, the rather cumbersome theories in
which entities are assigned to expressions as their semantic
values seem ultimately unavoidable, if interpretational semantics has the role I have described, since an interpretation just is
such an assignment. However, it may help to increase the clarity
and appeal of the points I have been making if I express them
in terms provided by one of these more familiar and less cumbersome theories. I shall use a truth theory of the kind made
popular by Donald Davidson, which stands the greatest chance
of being *in harmony with* a full Fregean semantic theory.[39]

In a way we can go on regarding a truth theory as corres-

[39] See Davidson, 'Truth and Meaning', *Synthese* xvii (1967), 304–33.

ponding to a theory of semantic value. For, even though a truth theory does not assign Meanings or semantic values to concept-expressions, logical words, etc., one can more or less derive, from what it *explicitly* states about the primitive expressions of the language, the assignment of Meanings (from the appropriate elements of Frege's ontology) which would be made to those expressions upon the *distinguished* or *actual* interpretation; but one can in no way derive the *senses* which they actually have. Applied to the case of (Russellian) proper names, the point is obvious enough. The typical truth-theoretic clause

(5) The referent of 'Aphla' = Aphla

can be no truer as a statement of the Meaning of 'Aphla' than the clause

(6) The referent of 'Aphla' = Ateb.

But here we can again make use of the idea of a single theory being used to show or display facts not explicitly stated (cf. 1.6). Obviously, only (5) can occur in a theory of truth which is to *serve as a theory of sense*, for it alone identifies the referent of the name in a way which shows or displays its sense.[40]

Such a theory is quite capable of stating the referent, and displaying the sense, of a Russellian singular term, '*a*'. The axiom dealing with '*a*' will be of the familiar form

(7) The referent of '*a*' = α,

where 'α' is '*a*' when the theory is stated in an extension of the language under study, or a term of another language with the same sense.[41] In the event that a term appropriate for treatment in this way lacks a referent, no such clause can truly be stated, so that truth-conditions for sentences containing the term cannot be derived. This is a formal representation of the fact that such a term has no sense, and that sentences containing it express no thought.

If we are persuaded that there is such a thing as a non-Russellian singular term, as was suggested in 1.7, we shall

---

[40] See the passage from Dummett, *Frege*, p. 227, quoted in 1.6 above; cf. also McDowell, 'On the Sense and Reference of a Proper Name'.

[41] These remarks are restricted to members of the intuitive category of singular terms other than definite descriptions (whose status as singular terms is *sub judice*: see further 2.1, 2.4).

therefore have to contemplate clauses of a quite different form. For example, where '*a*' is a name whose reference is fixed by the description 'the ϕ', we shall expect a clause of the form

(8) (x) (The referent of '*a*' $= \underline{x}$ iff x is ϕ).[42]

Clauses like these give truth-theoretical expression to the alternative semantic values contemplated for names in 1.7. If my view of the role of interpretational semantic theories is at all on the right lines, appeal would have to be made to the possibility of this variant assignment of semantic values in order to defend the claim that descriptive names and Russellian names both belong to the same semantic category.

Clauses like (8) will yield correct but non-homophonic truth-conditions for sentences containing descriptive names. But this failure of homophony is quite inessential to the approach.

We noted, in 1.6, that once singular terms are admitted which can have a sense whether or not they have a referent, there can be no objection to allowing that complex sentences containing such terms may be *true* when the term is empty. I focused then on the case of a negated sentence, but similar true sentences can be constructed with the use of any truth-functional connectives, given other constituents with appropriate truth-values. It is thus an immediate consequence of recognizing names like 'Julius' in a language that classical logic must be modified. As it stands, the classical rule of Existential Generalization allows us to infer

$$(\exists x)\ (x = a\ \&\ (\ldots x \ldots))$$

from any sentence '$(\ldots a \ldots)$', no matter how '*a*' is embedded in the sentence. Equally, the rule of Universal Elimination allows us to go from any sentence of the form

$$(x)\ (\ldots x \ldots)$$

to an instantiation with *any* name '*a*',

$$\ldots a \ldots$$

---

[42] Underlining is used to indicate uniqueness. The short vertical stroke is necessary so that we can distinguish $\underline{R(x,y)}$ from $R(x,y)$. Thus in general $\ulcorner \underline{A(t_1 \ldots t_i \ldots t_n)} \urcorner$ (where $n \geqslant 1$) abbreviates $\ulcorner A(t_1 \ldots t_i \ldots t_n)\ \&\ \underline{(z)}\ (A(t_1 \ldots z \ldots t_n) \rightarrow z = t_i) \urcorner$, where '*z*' is distinct from all the terms in $\ulcorner t_1 \ldots t_n \urcorner$.

Neither of these rules remains valid once names like 'Julius' are in the language. Unmodified, the rules would permit us to pass from the true premiss '$\neg (F(\text{Julius}))$' to the possibly false conclusion '$(\exists x)(\neg(F(x)))$', and from the true premiss '$(x)(x=x)$' to the false conclusion 'Julius = Julius'.[43] Logics with the appropriate restrictions on the rules of Existential Generalization and Universal Elimination (Free Logics) have been extensively studied.[44] I shall suppose that we are working with a language possessing a device for indicating the scope of a name, similar to Russell's parallel device for descriptions, so that we can simply express both

$$[a] \neg F(a)$$

and

$$\neg[a](F(a)),$$

and distinguish

$$[a]P \vee (F(a))$$

from

$$P \vee [a](F(a)).$$

The revised rule of Existential Generalization would permit

$$(\exists x)(\ldots x \ldots)$$

to be inferred only from

$$[a](\ldots a \ldots),$$

while

---

[43] Remember that all atomic sentences containing empty names are false. Free Logicians draw upon themselves legitimate criticism only when they step beyond this line—whether, with Dana Scott or Richard E. Grandy, they regard 'Julius = Julius' as true even when 'Julius' is empty, or, with Karel Lambert, they regard statements about fiction, like 'Odysseus slept on the shore', as both straightforward atomic sentences and true. (See Dana Scott, 'Existence and Description in Formal Logic', in Ralph Schoenman, ed., *Bertrand Russell: Philosopher of the Century* (George Allen and Unwin, London, 1967), pp. 181–200; Richard E. Grandy, 'A Definition of Truth for Theories with Intensional Definite Description Operators', *Journal of Philosophical Logic* i (1972), 137–55; Karel Lambert, 'Existential Import Revisited', *Notre Dame Journal of Formal Logic* iv (1963), 288–92, at p. 290.)

[44] For an excellent text, see Rolf Schock, *Logics without Existence Assumptions* (Almquist and Wiksell, Stockholm, 1968).

$$[a] \ (\ldots a \ldots)$$

could be inferred from

$$(x) \ (\ldots x \ldots)$$

by the revised rule of Universal Elimination only if we are given the further premiss

$$(\exists x) \ (x = a).$$

With this in mind, we can see that there is no obstacle to using a name like 'Julius' to state its own semantic contribution, in the way which is characteristic of truth theories formulated in the language under study. We can replace axiom (8) with

(9) (x) (The referent of 'Julius' $= x$ iff [Julius] $(x = $ Julius)).

Using a clause like this, we shall be able to derive homophonic truth-conditions for sentences containing the name 'Julius'. But, since the name has narrow scope in (9), and in the resulting statement of truth-conditions, the semantic theorist himself will not be committed to the existence of a referent for the name.[45]

1.9 CONCLUSIONS

We leave our study of Frege's treatment of singular terms with the following claims and conclusions:

(i) Frege held, both before the distinction between sense and Meaning and, despite appearances, after it, a highly Russellian view of singular terms. Frege's later apparent willingness to ascribe sense to certain empty singular terms was equivocal, hedged around with qualifications, and dubiously consistent with the fundamentals of his philosophy of language.

(ii) Whether or not it is correct to claim, as (i) does, that for Frege, all singular terms were and remained really Russellian, it must be admitted that there was absolutely nothing in his semantic theory to preclude his recognizing Russellian singular terms, and regarding them as having a Fregean sense as well as a referent. Frege nowhere said that absolutely *any* kind of singular term could have a sense whether or not it has a referent, nor did he say anything from which this may be derived.

[45] For more about 'Julius', see 2.3.

(iii) However, there was equally nothing to prevent Frege from recognizing non-Russellian singular terms; indeed, so long as he regarded definite descriptions as singular terms, such a recognition was absolutely imperative. The recognition of non-Russellian singular terms would require some alteration, in that Frege's global identification of the semantic value of a singular term with its referent would have to be given up.

There is a clear possibility of an eclectic Fregean theory—one which recognizes both kinds of singular term, making use of clauses like (9) as well as clauses like (7), and, of course, ascribing sense to both kinds of term. We therefore leave Frege with *two* simplified models of the functioning of referring expressions in hand: simplified in that they are fashioned for immediate application to a formal language of restricted scope, such as one for dealing with arithmetic or geometry. Obviously, amendments would have to be made in order to find applications for either model in the case of a natural language, with its characteristic feature of context-dependence. Indeed, some philosophers have argued that the sheer phenomenon of context-dependence precludes the application of either Fregean model to natural language.[46] But in fact the difficulty of finding an application for either model in any living language goes much deeper.

While we may have a verbal understanding of what a Russellian singular term is, and of how it may yet have a sense, no basis has yet been provided for thinking that such terms are so much as possible. We have, and convey, thoughts about a myriad particular objects—objects which we can currently perceive, or which we can remember, however faintly; or of whose existence we are aware by the testimony of others; or in whose existence we have reason to believe in other ways. But to which features of these ways of thinking about objects are we to appeal, in order to defend the claim that where there is no object referred to, no thought is expressed? (In almost all cases it will seem to a sincere speaker and a suitably deluded hearer that the case is exactly as normal, with thoughts being entertained and communicated; and, in so far as we put ourselves imaginatively

---

[46] e.g. David Kaplan in his unpublished monograph 'Demonstratives'.

in their position, this will strike us as the right thing to say too.)
We have so little understanding of the complex details of the
many ways in which human thought can concern particular
objects that we do not know how it could be correct to say that
a subject is thinking about an object in such a way that, were
there to be no object thought about, he would not even have a
thought.

I do not believe that we shall be able to force all varieties of
reference in natural language into a development of one or
other Fregean model, both of which require that for successful
communication speaker and hearer do not have thoughts cer-
tifiable as distinct by the Intuitive Criterion of Difference. When
one comes to examine most proper names in use in the market-
place, it seems impossible to force them into this mould. It seems
possible that the introduction to the name '*a*' which one subject
is given (perhaps ostensively) may be adequate to make him
competent with that name, while at the same time leading him
to associate with sentences containing it thoughts which may be
judged, by the Intuitive Criterion, to be distinct from the
thoughts associated with these same sentences by another subject, who has been given an adequate but different (perhaps
verbal) introduction to the name '*a*'. Frege takes this as a
sloppiness in ordinary language, and Dummett essentially
agrees when he takes the Fregean model of communication as
an *ideal* (for this must mean that in a certain sense we do not
really communicate, do not *perfectly* understand one another).[47]
But it is the actual practice of using the name '*a*', not some ideal
substitute, that interests us; it is obviously viable and effective
as a medium of communication, in that it provides speakers
with a means of transmitting knowledge, and it is its functioning
that we seek to account for. In view of this, Frege's and Dummett's way out of the difficulty is not open to us.[48]

However, even if the Fregean model of sense and of communication has no role to play in an account of the functioning of
our ordinary name-using practices, this hardly provides us with
a reason for despairing of its having any application to natural
language at all. The diversity of ways of thinking of the referent
permissible between speaker and hearer when using ordinary

[47] See Dummett, *Frege*, pp. 105–6.
[48] Ordinary proper names are discussed in chapter 11 below.

proper names does not at all appear to be the general case with referring expressions. Many indexical expressions, like 'here' and 'now', many demonstrative expressions, like 'this man' or 'that Russian we had dinner with last week', at least appear to require the audience to think of the referent in a quite specific way, not obviously allowing room for counter-examples to the principle that communication requires that a speaker and his audience have the same thought. So Frege's model of referential communication may still have extensive, if not unlimited, application.

A great deal of the remainder of this book will be concerned with the questions I have raised here—trying to understand what would justify the application of the Fregean models to natural language, and with that understanding, trying to come forward with a better view of the functioning of ordinary English referring expressions. But before turning to these investigations I wish to pursue the history of the theory of reference a little further.

Chapter 2

Russell

I wish to discuss Russell's work from a highly limited perspective. My interest is exclusively in Russell's theory of reference and some of its philosophical underpinnings; I am not interested in tracing connections between Russell's philosophy of language and his epistemology and metaphysics. I am concerned with the views Russell held on reference for a relatively brief period of his life—the views he expressed in 'On Denoting', 'Knowledge by Acquaintance and Knowledge by Description', and *The Philosophy of Logical Atomism*.[1]

As I said in the Introduction, Russell challenged the unity of the intuitive category of referring expressions, and in so doing he really aroused the debate about the nature of reference which continues to the present day.

Russell had just one model of genuine singular sentences in mind—basically the same model which Frege elaborated before 1890. A genuine referring expression has as its sole function the identification of an object such that if it satisfies the predicate, the sentence is true, and if it fails to satisfy the predicate, the sentence is false. But if the expression fails to identify an object at all, then the truth-evaluation of the sentence cannot get started, and the whole sentence is an aberration. (Russell, perhaps rather unwisely, said that the sentence is 'nonsense'. What he meant by this was that someone who uttered the sentence would be like someone who uttered nonsense in that he would have said nothing at all.) The only way in which Russell's model differed from the basic model that Frege redefined after the distinction between sense and Meaning was retrograde; it simply made no provision for sense:

---

[1] The first and third of these can be found in Bertrand Russell, *Logic and Knowledge*, ed. by R. C. Marsh (George Allen and Unwin, London, 1956); the second in Russell, *Mysticism and Logic* (George Allen and Unwin, London, 1917).

... for the name itself is merely a means of pointing to the thing, and does not occur in what you are asserting, so that if one thing has two names, you make exactly the same assertion whichever of the names you use, provided they are really names and not truncated descriptions.[2]

With this single conception of the functioning of singular sentences and of genuine reference in mind, Russell had a sharp criterion against which to test the terms intuitively classified as referring expressions. We can call it 'Russell's criterion':

Whenever the grammatical subject of a proposition can be supposed not to exist without rendering the proposition meaningless, it is plain that the grammatical subject is not a proper name, i.e. not a name directly representing some object.[3]

Russell was convinced, in the case of all expressions of the form 'the ϕ', that they did not pass this test, and I have already said (1.3, 1.7) that in this we have to follow him. Where 'ϕ' is a coherent description, perfectly clear conditions for the truth of the sentence 'The ϕ is F' (and thereby equally clear conditions for its non-truth) have been laid down: the absence of a satisfier of the description is no obstacle to someone's correctly understanding an utterance of the sentence as having these truth-conditions. A thought may be conveyed; and a belief (that the conditions are satisfied) may be induced. I do not believe it is open to us to hold, with Strawson,[4] that someone who utters a sentence containing an empty description has said nothing (expressed no proposition), or to liken an utterance of 'The Queen of Germany is beautiful' to an utterance of 'This butterfly is beautiful' when there is no object being referred to.

Furthermore, Russell was convinced that the same reasoning applied to almost all other singular terms, including the mass of names for historical characters and even acquaintances. He

[2] *The Philosophy of Logical Atomism*, p. 245 in *Logic and Knowledge*.

[3] A. N. Whitehead and Bertrand Russell, *Principia Mathematica*, vol. i (CUP, Cambridge, 2nd edn. 1927), p. 66. (Note, and guard against, the slide between things and expressions.) 'Directly' is not merely metaphorical. Most 'reference by description' will involve descriptions of the form 'the *x* which is *R* to *a*', in which the 'referent' is identified by reference to something else, and so indirectly.

[4] 'On Referring', in *Logico-Linguistic Papers*, pp. 1–27.

held a theory of thought which incorporated the principle that
it is not possible for a person to have a thought about something
unless he knows which particular individual in the world he is
thinking about. Russell also held that there are only two ways
of discharging this requirement: one is to be, or to have a
memory of being, 'acquainted' with the object concerned, and
the other is to think of the object as the unique satisfier of some
description. Since the range of Russell's special relation of acquaintance between subject and object is extremely limited—
extending mainly to private sensory items of immediate experience and (at certain periods) oneself—thought about all physical objects was held to be 'by description'. It follows that
apparent singular terms in sentences apt for expressing such
thoughts would fail Russell's test.

Russell never took much account of the distinction between
thinking something and saying something in a public language,
and interested himself but little in formulating the consequences
of his theory of thinking for an analysis of the idioms of natural
language. But had he done so, I suppose he would have regarded
a name like 'Julius' (1.7, 1.8) as a paradigmatic example of a
grammatical proper name masquerading as a genuine referring
expression. This case represents an ideal to which most ordinary
proper names would not fully approximate, because of differences in the descriptions associated by people with ordinary
proper names.

2.2 RADICAL REFERENCE-FAILURE

It is clear that the restriction Russell imposed upon the epistemological relation which could sustain genuine reference gives
that semantical relation application only to a private language,
and many philosophers have rightly deemed this absurd. But
few have understood Russell's reasons for the restriction.

All the items with which a subject may be acquainted have
what may be termed the Cartesian property: it is not possible
for a subject to think that there is an item of the relevant kind
with which he is acquainted (and hence to think that it is
possible to essay a thought about it) without there being such
an item. The importance of this fact is as follows. Given Russell's
restriction, a situation can never arise in which a subject thinks
that he is having or expressing a thought about an object while

failing to do so; and this was a possibility which Russell very much wished to rule out, because it seemed to him incoherent. Russell worked with a conception of the mind which was thoroughly Cartesian: it would not make sense for a subject to be in error as to whether or not he satisfied the mental predicate 'ξ is thinking about some thing'.

This point needs careful statement. Russell would have been perfectly happy to acknowledge the existence of composite predicates with a mental component, such as 'ξ knows that P', or 'ξ is thinking that Bismarck is F'; and a subject is clearly not possessed of infallible knowledge as to whether he satisfies these predicates. But Russell, like any Cartesian, would wish to decompose such predicates into strictly mental and non-mental components, the claim about infallibility extending only to the former. So, for Russell, the predicate 'ξ is thinking about Bismarck' would break down into the conjunction of some purely mental predicate 'ξ is thinking that the ϕ is F' and the non-mental statement 'Bismarck is uniquely ϕ'.

Russell was as aware as anyone else that not everything can be thought of by description, on pain of the whole system of identification failing to be tied down to a unique set of objects, in the circumstances which Strawson has called 'massive reduplication'.[5] So he was aware that some thought-relations between the subject and objects in the universe must be incapable of decomposition in the style of the Bismarck example. But his Cartesian theory of the mind, embodied in his aversion to the idea that a subject may essay a thought and literally think nothing at all, ensured that the anchorage for the whole system of descriptive identification was to objects for which this falling into the abyss was not a possibility.

We shall meet many times with hostility to this possibility, not always for Russell's reasons. However, there does not seem to me to be anything incoherent in the idea that it may be, for a subject, exactly as though he were thinking about a physical object (say) which he can see, and yet that, precisely because there is no physical object he is seeing, he may fail to have a thought of the kind he supposes himself to have. It is not part of this proposal that his mind is wholly vacant; images and words

[5] *Individuals* (Methuen, London, 1959), p. 20.

may clearly pass through it, and various ancillary thoughts may even occur to him. The claim is simply that there is a kind of thought we sometimes have, typically expressed in the form 'This *G* is *F*', and we may aim to have a thought of this kind when, in virtue of the absence of any appropriate object, there is no such thought to be had. Obviously to defend this way of looking at things will require a full account of the nature of demonstrative identification of physical objects, and the rebuttal of several alternative proposals, but it does not appear to me that the proposal can be faulted on grounds of coherence alone.

A. N. Prior, who in his works on reference explored Russell's ideas in a way which casts great illumination on them, thought that he had an argument to bolster Russell on just this point. What sense, Prior argued, can it make to say that a subject thinks he has a thought when in fact he does not? Surely if a subject can think that he has the thought that *a* is *F*, he must be able to have the thought that *a* is *F*? For is not entertaining the thought that *a* is *F* part of what is involved in having the compound thought 'I am thinking that *a* is *F*'?[6]

The answer to these questions is 'Yes, of course'. But Prior was quite unjustified in assuming that those who hold that a person may wrongly think he has a thought of the form '*a* is *F*' need be committed to the view that such a subject has a thought of the form 'I am thinking that *a* is *F*'. All that is being credited to such a subject is the intention of thinking a thought of a certain particular kind, and the belief that he is thinking such a thought. Obviously if there is no thought of the appropriate kind available, then there is no possibility, either for the subject or for anyone else, of giving the content of the thought he wishes, but fails, to entertain.

2.3 RUSSELLIAN SINGULAR TERMS AND DESCRIPTIVE NAMES

By labelling singular terms whose sense depends upon their having a referent 'Russellian', I have given Russell credit for the recognition of the possibility that such terms might exist. I

[6] See *Objects of Thought*, pp. 153-4.

feel able to do this despite the fact that, in my view, Frege's conception of singular terms made them one and all Russellian, both because the clarity of the conception was smudged by Frege's apparent willingness to ascribe a sense to empty singular terms, and because Frege does not seem to have been fully aware of the consequences of treating a term as Russellian. Otherwise how could Frege have been willing to treat definite descriptions, and names whose referents he held to be fixed by description, as Russellian singular terms?

Of course many modifications have to be made to Russell's original conception of genuine singular terms before anything viable emerges: notably the ascription of sense to such terms, understood as Frege understood it, and the abandonment of the Cartesian conception of thinking to which the restriction of genuine reference to private languages can be traced. Nevertheless, I think the resulting conception remains distinctively Russell's, incorporating as it does the idea of an opposition between (Russellian) singular terms and any term whose reference or denotation is determined by a description. For Russell held, and I think he was entirely right to hold, that where a clear descriptive condition exists for something's being the referent or denotation of a term, a quite determinate truth-condition is associated with sentences containing the term, whether or not it is empty; the sentence is true just in case there exists something which uniquely satisfies the condition, and which satisfies the sentence's predicate.[7]

Russell was clearly right to hold that there is an important difference between Russellian singular terms on the one hand, and those members of the intuitive category of referring expressions which are associated with a clear descriptive condition for something's being their referent on the other. But was he right to deny that terms of the latter kind are referring expressions, are—at some suitably high level of description—members of the same category as Russellian singular terms? I shall discuss his treatment of definite descriptions separately (2.4), and so the present discussion concerns a class of expressions which occur rather rarely in natural language, the best examples of which

---

[7] I do not deny that if the term were discovered to be empty it would almost certainly be withdrawn from circulation; but I regard this as a sign of its *uselessness* in those circumstances, not of its lack of *sense*.

are what we may call 'descriptive names', such as 'Julius' (1.7,
1.8).[8] I have already indicated my disagreement with Russell's
refusal to regard these terms as referring expressions, but it is
now time to expand the argument that they are referring expressions, as promised in 1.7.

In the case of descriptive names there is a public, semantical
connection between the name and the description: the sense of
the name is such that an object is determined to be the referent
of the name if and only if it satisfies a certain description.
Anyone who understands the name must be aware of the
reference-fixing role of the description.

Very few names which naturally occur in ordinary language
can be regarded as descriptive names. It is difficult to hold, of
ordinary proper names, that there is some particular description
semantically associated with the name. It is more plausible to
hold the view which David Wiggins put as follows:

> The sense of a proper name simply consists in its having been assigned
> whatever reference it has been assigned: to know the sense of *n* is to
> know to which entity *n* has been assigned, a single piece of knowledge
> which may be given in countless different ways by countless different
> descriptions.[9]

Even when there is a community-wide association between a
name and one description, as perhaps 'Homer' is now associated
with the description 'the author of the *Iliad* and the *Odyssey*', it
is more plausible to regard the association as constituting a bit
of information, or misinformation, inherited from people who
purported to use the name as an ordinary proper name, rather
than as manifesting a general intention to use the name to refer
to whatever in fact satisfies the description.[10] A natural example
of a descriptive name will occur only when a name is *introduced*
in connection with some description. Kripke mentions 'Jack the
Ripper' and 'Neptune' as examples of such names;[11] another
example might be 'Deep Throat', used as a name for whoever
in the White House was the source of the Watergate-related

[8] There are other members of the class: for instance, certain expressions used in
connection with deferred ostension, and—if my theory is correct—what I have called
'E-type' pronouns; see 'Pronouns, Quantifiers, and Relative Clauses' (I), and 'Pronouns', *Linguistic Inquiry* xi (1980), 337–62.

[9] 'Identity, Designation, Essentialism and Physicalism', *Philosophia* v (1975), 1–30, at
p. 11.

[10] See chapter 11 (especially 11.4).   [11] 'Naming and Necessity', pp. 291, 347–8.

information of Woodward and Bernstein. But no matter how rare examples may be, it would appear to be always possible to create descriptive names by stipulation, as we envisaged 'Julius' to have been introduced into the language.

It seems to me reasonable to hold that the semantical relation of reference (between singular terms and objects in the world) is empirically anchored by its connection with the concept of truth as applied to atomic sentences (sentences in which an n-place concept-expression is combined with n singular terms). The most elementary form of the principle connecting reference with truth is

(P) If S is an atomic sentence in which the n-place concept-expression R is combined with n singular terms $t_1 \ldots t_n$, then S is true iff $\langle$ the referent of $t_1 \ldots$ the referent of $t_n \rangle$ satisfies R.

Satisfaction is also whatever relation makes (P) true. (P) may be regarded as simultaneously and implicitly defining reference and satisfaction in terms of truth. Do not think that the use of (P) presupposes a prior identification of the singular terms (referring expressions) of the language. Think rather of (P) as inviting the semantic theorist, confronting some fragment of natural language, to try to identify a class of sentences in which he can discern expressions of two characteristic types, and to deal with expressions of each type by means of two different semantic relations which fit together according to (P) to yield the truth-conditions of those sentences. This is all you know, and all you need to know, by way of a *definition* of reference (or of satisfaction). (This 'holistic' characterization no doubt provides the basis for considerable indeterminacy.)

Given this characterization of reference, it seems to me to be correct to regard as a referring expression any expression whose contribution to the truth-conditions of sentences containing it is stated exclusively by means of the relation of reference which is found in (P).

Obviously clauses suitable for Russellian singular terms, like

(1) The referent of 'Aphla' = Aphla,

use the relation of reference in the most direct possible way, so that we are assured not only that 'Aphla' is a referring expression, but also that 'Aphla' refers to Aphla. But it is equally true that a clause of a different kind, like

(2) (x) (The referent of 'Julius' $= x$ iff x uniquely invented the zip),

or equivalently

(3) (x) (The referent of 'Julius' $= x$ iff [Julius] $x =$ Julius),

uses only the relation of reference to state the semantic contribution to sentences of the expression 'Julius'. From (2) or (3), taken together with the normal satisfaction clauses for atomic concept-expressions, and principle (P), we shall be able to derive truth-conditions, for sentences containing 'Julius', of the form

(4) 'Julius is F' is true iff the inventor of the zip is F;

or equivalently

(5) 'Julius is F' is true iff [Julius] Julius is F.

Consequently, it seems to me that if there is a unique inventor of the zip, then 'Julius' *refers to* that person, and in exactly the same sense as that in which a Russellian name refers to its bearer.

In saying that the thought expressed by 'Julius is F' may equivalently be expressed by 'The inventor of the zip is F', I think I am conforming to common sense. Someone who understands and accepts the one sentence as true gets himself into exactly the same belief state as someone who accepts the other. Belief states are distinguished by the evidence which gives rise to them, and the expectations, behaviour, and further beliefs which may be derived from them (in conjunction with other beliefs); and in all these respects, the belief states associated with the two sentences are indistinguishable. We do not produce new thoughts (new beliefs) simply by a 'stroke of the pen' (in Grice's phrase)[12]—simply by introducing a name into the language.

It is true that the two sentences embed differently inside modal operators, and this is a fact which must be explained later (2.5). But I deny that it follows that they express different

---

[12] H. P. Grice, 'Vacuous Names', in Donald Davidson and Jaakko Hintikka, eds., *Words and Objections* (Reidel, Dordrecht, 1969), pp. 118–45, at p. 140.

thoughts. Furthermore, if one gives, as the truth-condition for 'Julius is F', that *the inventor of the zip is F*, this does not force one, incorrectly, to give, as the truth-condition for 'It is possible that Julius is F', that *it is possible that the inventor of the zip is F.* (Much more on this below: 2.4, 2.5.)

2.4 DEFINITE DESCRIPTIONS

In 'On Denoting', Russell presented three arguments against regarding definite descriptions as referring expressions.

One of these (the argument which depends on George IV's knowledge that Scott = Scott and his ignorance that Scott = the author of *Waverley*) depends upon Russell's unfortunate incapacity, or refusal, to see that referring expressions (even Russellian referring expressions) can have different senses despite having the same referent.

In another argument, he argued that if 'The ϕ is F' is treated as an atomic sentence, then its negation must be 'The ϕ is not-F', and so adherence to the Law of the Excluded Middle would enable us to assert

(6) (The ϕ is F) or (The ϕ is not-F),

both of the disjuncts of which entail that the ϕ exists.

Now, for Russellian singular terms, there is no difference between narrow-scope and wide-scope negation. They could come apart only if ' $\neg$ (a is F)' were *true* where 'a' does not refer; whereas 'a is F', and, hence, ' $\neg$ (a is F)', are unintelligible (say nothing) if 'a' does not refer. But for *non*-Russellian singular terms an important difference opens up between what we should represent in a Free Logic as

(7) $\neg [a] F(a)$

and

(8) $[a] \neg F(a).$[13]

In English we do have the ability to distinguish wide-scope from narrow-scope negation, for we distinguish

(9) It's not the case that (The ϕ is F)

[13] See Dummett, *Frege*, p. 115: '... so long as it is allowed that there may be proper names which are meaningful and yet not guaranteed a reference, and that the possession or lack of a reference by a proper name will in general affect the truth-value of a sentence in which it occurs, the question of scope may arise for a proper name.'

from

(10) The ϕ is not-*F*.

And obviously when Russell was aiming to construct an instance of the Law of the Excluded Middle, he should have chosen the wide-scope negation, thus:

(11) (The ϕ is *F*) or It's not the case that (The ϕ is *F*).

Naturally, the second disjunct is true if there is no unique ϕ.

I have tried to show (2.3) that there can be non-Russellian referring expressions. This means that, even when they are empty, atomic sentences containing such expressions are perfectly intelligible. It is therefore unavoidable, if there exists a global negation operator 'N' in the language, that

(12) N(*a* is *F*)

will be intelligible, and *true*, when '*a*' is empty. To insist that *the* negation of '*a* is *F*' must be formed by attaching the operator to the predicate is to insist, question-beggingly, that all singular terms must be Russellian.

By far the most important argument that Russell gave was this: if we treat definite descriptions as referring expressions, then we shall be obliged to conclude that, in the absence of a referent, sentences containing them would not be meaningful— i.e. would fail to express a thought.[14]

---

[14] In view of Russell's concerns, I must conclude that Strawson (in 'On Referring'; and see *Subject and Predicate in Logic and Grammar* (Methuen, London, 1974), for the latest expression of his view) failed to join issue with Russell in any effective way. No doubt Russell's claim that, if a description was empty, an 'atomic' sentence containing it would be *nonsense* on the 'referential' view requires sympathetic interpretation. But Russell's worry was obviously not one about a failure on the part of the description as an expression *type* to have a conventional meaning. It was a worry about what, if anything, would be *said*, on the 'referential' view, by an *utterance* of the sentence. And Strawson seems to have thought it acceptable to say that *nothing* would have been said— precisely the conclusion from which Russell rightly recoiled. (In fairness to Strawson, it should be pointed out that a great deal of his opposition to Russell's Theory of Descriptions resulted from a global opposition to the enterprise of using translation into the restricted syntax of *Principia Mathematica* to determine the 'logical form' of English sentences, with the consequent butchering of which I speak below. In this hostility Strawson has been entirely vindicated by recent work in semantics.) Equally irrelevant to the issues of this section is the discussion in Keith S. Donnellan's 'Reference and Definite Descriptions', *Philosophical Review* lxxv (1966), 281–304. The issue between Frege, Strawson, and Russell concerns what I call 'pure' uses of definite descriptions, where there is no question of aiming to invoke antecedently existing identificatory knowledge of some object. That descriptions may, as Donnellan points out, be used in this latter way is an important observation (see 9.3), but irrelevant at this point.

Russell was quite right to be appalled by such a consequence; but we have just seen (2.3) that Russell's criterion *for being a referring expression* simply will not stand up. Obviously, definite descriptions, if they were referring expressions, would be non-Russellian. We should not expect a semantic theory to comprise a clause for each description, of the form

(13) (x) (the referent of 'The author of *Waverley*' $= x$ iff x uniquely wrote *Waverley*).[15]

For there are infinitely many descriptions, and anyway we shall need to show how their reference depends upon the significance of the words embedded in the description. Rather, a theory which treated definite descriptions as referring expressions would contain a single recursive clause on these lines:

(14) (ϕ) (x) (The referent of 'The' $^\cap\phi = x$ iff Satisfies (x, ϕ)).

Such a theory would enable us to derive truth-conditions for any sentences containing a definite description, whether or not the description was empty.[16]

We are therefore unable to extract from Russell's writings any acceptable argument against those who wish to treat definite descriptions as members of the category of referring expressions, and as referring to things, so long as they hold the eclectic theory I have offered them, and do not treat descriptions as members of the sub-category of *Russellian* referring expressions.

Nevertheless, I believe that Russell's opposition to this position was correct, and that his intuition that descriptions belong to a quite different category of expressions (the quantifiers) was sound. But we have to appeal to considerations he never remarked upon. We shall find that the axiom (14) is not adequate to explain the behaviour of definite descriptions in all contexts.

The feature of the behaviour of descriptions which cannot be captured in this way comes out most clearly in modal contexts,

[15] This clause uses a metalinguistic definite description ('the referent of "The author of *Waverley*"') as a referring expression. Strictly speaking we should need to signal that it occurs with narrow scope, thus:

(x) ([The referent of 'The author of *Waverley*'] (the referent of 'The author of *Waverley*' $= x$ iff x uniquely wrote *Waverley*)).

[16] Semantic theories for definite descriptions on these lines have been constructed: see Tyler Burge, 'Truth and Singular Terms', *Nous* viii (1974), 309–25.

and in order to explain it, we must work with some semantic theory adequate to deal with those contexts. Since possible-worlds semantic theories are both familiar and easy to work with, I shall put my points in their terms, but my points should be capable of translation into any semantical framework. I certainly do not wish my use of possible-worlds semantics to be taken to indicate either that I believe it to be the correct semantical framework for modal sentences of natural languages, or that I believe it to be immune to philosophical objection.[17]

A possible-worlds semantic theory states the truth-conditions of sentences of a language containing modal operators in a metalanguage which dispenses with such operators in favour of explicit quantification over possible worlds. For each n-place predicate, R, of the object language, there is in the metalanguage an $n+1$-place predicate, R'; the additional argument-place being occupied by terms referring to, and variables ranging over, possible worlds. These pairs of predicates are connected via satisfaction-clauses of the form

$$(x_1) \ldots (x_n) \; (\text{Satisfies}_w(`R', \langle x_1 \ldots x_n \rangle) \text{ iff } R'(x_1, \ldots x_n, w)).^{18}$$

For example, an object satisfies 'Bald' *with respect to* a world w if and only if it is bald in w. The theory is so constructed that we are able to derive, for each sentence S, a theorem of the form

$$(w) \; (\text{True}_w \, (S) \text{ iff} \ldots);$$

with which the clauses for the modal operators connect in the familiar way:

$$(S)(w)(\text{True}_w \, (`\text{It is possible that' } \frown S) \text{ iff } (\exists w')(\text{Alt } (w,w') \, \& \, \text{True}_{w'} \, (S))).$$

('Alt' is some suitable 'alternativeness relation', defined over the set of possible worlds; its properties need not concern us.) A

[17] For an alternative approach to the semantics of modality, see Christopher Peacocke, 'Necessity and Truth Theories', *Journal of Philosophical Logic* vii (1978), 473–500.

[18] I subscript the satisfaction relation thus ('Satisfies$_w$'), and similarly with 'True$_{w'}$', partly for ease of comparison with classical clauses, but also to emphasize that these relativized semantical relations are not got by the same process that gives us '$F'(x,w)$' from '$F(x)$'. The statement that a is bald in w ('Bald'(a,w)') can be understood as equivalent to the simple counterfactual 'If w had been actual, a would have been bald'. But the statement that S is true with respect to w ('True$_w(S)$') is not equivalent to the simple counterfactual 'If w had been actual, S would have been true'. See my 'Reference and Contingency', *The Monist* lxii (1979), 161–89, at p. 181.

sentence is true *simpliciter* if and only if it is true$_{w*}$, where '$w*$' refers to the actual world.

In the context of this semantic theory, the principle (P) must be modified to (P′), which connects reference with the notion of truth$_w$.

> (P′) If $R(t_1 \ldots t_n)$ is atomic, and $t_1 \ldots t_n$ are referring expressions, then $R(t_1 \ldots t_n)$ is true$_w$ iff ⟨the referent of $t_1 \ldots$ the referent of t_n⟩ satisfies$_w$ R.

(From this principle, the principle (P) can be derived as a special case.) Once this change has been made, no other is required, so long as definite descriptions are not treated as referring expressions. Even for a modal language, all that is necessary in order to state the significance of names and other referring expressions is to state what, if anything, they refer to; the truth-with-respect-to-a-situation of a sentence containing a singular term depends simply upon whether or not its referent satisfies the predicate with respect to that situation. But, notoriously, this is not the case with definite descriptions. If we assign them a reference by means of a principle like (14), and connect this assignment with truth by means of (P′)—if, in short, we treat them as referring expressions—then we capture only one of the readings of a sentence like 'The first man in space might have been an American', namely that on which it is equivalent to the claim that Gagarin might have been an American. The whole sentence is determined as true if and only if there is a possible world with respect to which the referent of the description, i.e. Gagarin, satisfies 'American'. In order to capture the other reading of this sentence, on which it is true if and only if there is a possible world in which the man who is first in space in *that* world is an American (in that world), some changes have to be made.

The only way of making those changes, while still attempting to treat descriptions as referring expressions, is by relativizing the relation of reference to a possible world. (14) must become

(15) $(\phi)(x)(w)$ (Refers to$_w$ ('the' $^\cap\phi$, x) iff $\underline{\text{Satisfies}}_w\ (\phi, \underline{x})$);

and (P′) must become:

> (P″) If $R(t_1 \ldots t_n)$ is atomic, and $t_1 \ldots t_n$ are referring expres-

sions, then $R(t_1 \ldots t_n)$ is true$_w$ iff $\langle$the referent$_w$ of $t_1 \ldots$ the referent$_w$ of $t_n\rangle$ satisfies$_w$ R.

This can be done.[19] But at a high price, owing to the fact that we must now relativize the relation of reference—defined as it is by (P''), our descendant of (P)—in *all* cases. Simply in order to assimilate descriptions to referring expressions, we introduce a major change in the semantic apparatus in terms of which we describe the functioning of referring expressions in general. As a consequence of this change, we ascribe to names, pronouns, and demonstratives semantical properties of a *type* which would allow them to get up to tricks they never in fact get up to; since their reference never varies from world to world, this semantic power is never exploited.

A similar point can be made when we take account of the existence of ambiguities which definite descriptions generate in tensed sentences, like 'The leader of the Conservative Party will be courageous'. To deal with this essentially similar ambiguity, the relation of reference must also be relativized to a time. Once again, this enrichment of the type of semantical assignment made to singular terms is unnecessary for all terms other than descriptions.

Finally, the fact that a position inside a description can be bound by a higher quantifier, as in the sentence 'The father of each girl is good to her', requires a relativization of the relation of reference to a sequence, or an assignment, π, to the empty singular term positions which the description may contain.[20]

Thus, if we are to include definite descriptions in the category of referring expressions, we are forced to describe the behaviour of all the members of that category in terms of the relation

[19] It has been done, e.g. by Richmond H. Thomason and Robert C. Stalnaker, 'Modality and Reference', *Nous* ii (1968), 359–72. 'An expression like $["(1x)\phi(x)"]$ is assigned a referent which may vary from world to world' (p. 363). On such a view, the first reading considered is captured by giving the descriptive singular term wide scope with respect to the modal operator.

[20] This point is made in Benson Mates's paper, 'Descriptions and Reference', *Foundations of Language* x (1973), 409–18. In fact the objection can be dealt with if one uses 'Fregean' rather than 'Tarskian' treatments of the quantifiers; for this distinction, see my 'Pronouns, Quantifiers, and Relative Clauses' (I), at pp. 471–7. It should be stressed that the relativity to a time required to deal with the temporal flexibility of descriptions is quite different from that introduced by context-dependence; so that treating descriptions as referring expressions imposes on the relation of reference a double relativity to a time.

'Refers to$_{w,t,\pi}(t,x)$', rather than the simple relation 'Refers to (t,x)', which is otherwise perfectly adequate. This certainly does not constitute a knock-down argument against treating descriptions as referring expressions, but it rather strongly suggests that the grouping that results on this treatment may not correspond to any natural semantical kind.

The case is strengthened when we look at the other side of the story, and examine alternative approaches to descriptions. One approach looks especially promising. Every semantical theory must recognize the category of quantifiers, members of which occur in the sentences 'Every ϕ is ψ', 'Some ϕ is ψ', 'No ϕ is ψ', etc. We find that if we suppose the sentence 'The ϕ is ψ' to be built up in exactly the same way, out of exactly the same type of semantic elements, as the quantified sentences which it so closely resembles, we achieve a remarkably good fit with the behaviour it is observed to display. Even on a theory which attempts to treat descriptions as singular terms, we could introduce, with no complication of theory, a quantifier 'The', and the resulting sentences would be indistinguishable from those containing the supposed singular term. Such a theory could then be considerably simplified if it made do with just the quantifier 'The', and allowed the relation which deals with referring expressions to revert to its simple, unrelativized form. In other disciplines, such a consideration would strongly recommend the resulting theory, and I am not sure why the theorist of meaning should be unmoved by it.[21]

To treat 'The ϕ is F' as built up out of the same sort of elements as 'Some ϕ is F', 'No ϕ is F', 'Every ϕ is F', still leaves room for disagreement over what kind of treatment all these quantified sentences should receive. One thing is sure: there is absolutely no need for the butchering of surface structure in which Russell so perversely delighted; the analysis of 'The ϕ is F' into the form

(16) $(\exists x)(\phi x \mathbin{\&} (y)(\phi y \rightarrow x = y) \mathbin{\&} Fx)$

is entirely an artefact of his determination to arrive at a quantificational sentence expressible in the notation of *Principia Mathematica*.

---

[21] I discuss the aspect of the methodology of semantic theories on which I am here relying in my paper 'Semantic Structure and Logical Form'.

One different proposal would be to regard all natural-language quantifiers as *binary quantifiers* (unlike the two unary quantifiers of *Principia Mathematica*), taking *two* open sentences (or two simple or complex concept-expressions) to make a sentence. Then the Meaning of each quantifier would be a function from a *pair* of concept-expression values (functions from objects to truth-values) to the truth-values. 'The' would be associated with the function from concept-expression values which yields *truth* if and only if (i) there is exactly one object which the first concept-expression value maps on to the True, and (ii) that object is also mapped by the second concept-expression value on to the True. A regimented notation might represent 'Most ϕs are F' as

(17) $\text{M}x\ [\phi(x); F(x)]$,

and 'The ϕ is F' as

(18) $\text{I}x\ [\phi(x); F(x)]$.

But even this degree of regimentation is avoidable, if we take seriously the fact that English does not make use of the variable-binding construction in every quantified sentence, and, in particular, indicates which place in a concept-expression is being quantified upon by which quantifier by actually inserting the quantifier-expression into that place. Thus the one-place concept-expression 'ξ is F' can be completed either by a singular term to yield

a is F,

or by a quantifier-expression to yield

The ϕ is F.[22]

These two sentences, however, have different grammatical structures. One is the concatenation of an N with an S/N; the other is the concatenation of an $S/(S/N)$ with an S/N. Both yield an S, but different categories are involved. And the categorial notation makes clear how in the one case, the function

[22] There is therefore no basis for the charge of *clumsiness* with which Russell's proposal has so often been greeted: see, for example, Richmond H. Thomason, 'Modal Logic and Metaphysics', in Karel Lambert, ed., *The Logical Way of Doing Things* (Yale University Press, New Haven and London, 1969), pp. 119-46, at pp. 128-9.

associated with the S/N is supplied with an argument, while in the other that function is itself the argument to a higher-level function.

For the language fragment Russell studied, there is in fact no need to regard 'The' even as a binary quantifier. We can think of 'The' as an expression which takes a simple or complex one-place concept-expression ('man who broke the bank at Monte Carlo') to yield a unary quantifier ('The man who broke the bank at Monte Carlo').[23] This is to regard 'The' *not* as an $S/(S/N)$, (S/N), but as a 'unary quantifier former' (an $(S/(S/N))/(S/N)$. This view would make Russell wrong even in his claim that 'the ϕ' does not form a logical unit in 'The ϕ is F'. However, once again Russell has ultimately turned out to have been right, but for the wrong reasons. For there are sentences such as

(19) The only man who owns a donkey beats it,

in which the quantifier-expression and the main concept-expression 'ξ beats it' cannot be independently constructed, so the binary approach is actually forced upon us by more complex sentences.[24]

Although I am fairly sure that it is better to treat 'The ϕ' as a quantifier than as a referring expression, it is possible that I have not presented the best version of the quantifier option. Noam Chomsky has made a very interesting suggestion designed to unify the use of 'The' with singular and plural concept-expressions—'the man who broke the bank' and 'the men who robbed your wife'.[25] He regards 'The' as a form of *universal* quantifier (but one carrying existential commitment)— the implication of *uniqueness* in the singular case arising from the singular form of the concept-expression. To my knowledge, no philosophical semantic theory has taken serious account of the manifestly important phenomenon of *number* in natural language, and it may well be that when a larger range of facts is

[23] The Meaning of this quantifier is a function which maps concept-expression values on to the True just in case there is one and only one man who broke the bank at Monte Carlo and the concept-expression value maps him on to the True. (Or, homophonically: just in case the man who broke the bank at Monte Carlo is mapped by the concept-expression value on to the True.)

[24] I deal with these matters in much greater detail in my paper 'Pronouns, Quantifiers, and Relative Clauses' (I).

[25] See 'Questions of Form and Interpretation', *Linguistic Analysis* i (1975), 75-109.

taken into account, a proposal like Chomsky's will prove far superior to the one suggested here.[26] Nevertheless, all uses of definite descriptions in this book, both formal and informal, are intended to be understood according to the proposal I have tentatively put forward.[27]

2.5 'RIGID DESIGNATION' AND FREGEAN SENSE

In my argument against treating descriptions as referring expressions, I assumed that it is just a feature of the way proper names, pronouns, and demonstratives are used in English that, in evaluating the truth with respect to a possible situation of a sentence containing one of these terms, we are exclusively concerned with whether or not the referent of the term (if any) satisfies (with respect to that situation) the relevant predicate. And I assume that this holds good of those expressions whether or not they have their reference fixed by description. We would not accept such claims as

> (20) If Haldeman had released the information to the reporters, he would have been Deep Throat,

or

> (21) If Haldeman had released the information to the reporters, Deep Throat would have had an extremely high position in the Administration.

Equally, we would not say

> (22) If you had invented the zip, you would have been Julius.

These facts should come as no surprise. The agreement by which 'Julius' was introduced was this: 'Let us call whoever invented

[26] It is one of the deficiencies of this book that I have not included work on plural reference.

[27] The argument presented here for denying that definite descriptions are singular terms is related to Geach's view that genuine singular terms are scopeless. See *Logic Matters* (Blackwell, Oxford, 1972), p. 144: a similar view is put forward by Christopher Peacocke in 'Proper Names, Reference, and Rigid Designation', in Simon Blackburn, ed., *Meaning, Reference and Necessity* (CUP, Cambridge, 1975), pp. 109-32. However, the observation that referring expressions are scopeless in *modal* and *temporal* contexts certainly fails to show that they are absolutely scopeless. And if descriptive names are to be treated as referring expressions, the claim is obviously not true, since scope differences will show up even with simple truth-functional connectives. In fact I do not believe even that all *Russellian* singular terms meet this condition; this turns on complex questions about the semantics of belief-sentences.

the zip "Julius".' The use of 'Julius' in the sentence (22) is a use quite unallowed for by that agreement: an utterer of (22) cannot be represented as using the name to refer to whoever invented the zip. On the contrary, he would have to be using the name as an abbreviation for a description—a quite different matter.

Both this observation about the behaviour of proper names in modal contexts, even such odd names as 'Julius', and the distinction between a reference-fixing stipulation and an abbreviatory convention were made by Saul Kripke in his seminal lectures 'Naming and Necessity'. He chose to describe terms which function in this way in modal contexts as 'rigid designators'. But if we adopt the viewpoint of the previous section, they are better described simply as 'designators' or 'referring expressions'. For if we use a semantic theory which has an unrelativized relation of reference or designation, we shall not say that a referring expression 'designates the same thing with respect to each possible situation'; it simply designates, and the truth-value of any sentence containing it, including any modal sentence, depends upon what, if anything, it designates. The term 'rigid designator' carries with it the suggestion, or the thought, of '*non*-rigid designation', and hence only belongs in a theory in which the designation or reference relation is relativized to possible worlds, and used in the treatment of both names and descriptions.[28]

I hope that the little theory for modal sentences offered in 2.4 suffices to show that there is no inconsistency whatsoever between, on the one hand, a singular term's being associated with a clear descriptive criterion for something's being its referent, and its functioning as a 'rigid designator' on the other. If this is true in the case where the Fregean sense of a singular term is purely descriptive, how much more clearly must it be true that behaviour as a rigid designator is consistent with possession of a Fregean sense when that sense must be explained in terms of some way of thinking of an object which has nothing to do with any description—for example, the Fregean sense of demonstrative singular terms. Yet at least one prominent philosopher, David Kaplan, has repeatedly argued that this or that

---

[28] However, the phrase 'behaves as a rigid designator' is a useful one with an agreed meaning, and I shall continue to use it.

singular term cannot possess a Fregean sense simply on the ground that it behaves as a rigid designator.[29] Kaplan describes what he calls 'the semantics of direct reference':

By this I mean theories of meaning according to which certain singular terms refer directly without the mediation of a Fregean *Sinn* as meaning.[30]

(Those who have appreciated the conception of Fregean sense which I put forward in 1.5 will wish to object in the strongest possible terms to the idea that the possession by a singular term of a Fregean sense must render thought about the referent somehow indirect. Perhaps such talk can be justified in the case of descriptive names, for one can think of the reference as mediated by the grasp of some description—an intermediary stage which can occur whether or not an object is actually being thought of. But when we realize that the possession by a singular term of a Fregean sense can depend upon nothing more than its being associated with a proprietary way of thinking about an object, the idea that thought about an object which depends upon grasp of a Fregean sense must somehow be indirect will seem absurd. The fact that one is thinking about an object in a particular way can no more warrant the conclusion that one is not thinking of the object in the most direct possible fashion, than the fact that one is giving something *in a particular way* warrants the view that one's giving is somehow indirect. However, it may well be that Kaplan's terminology of 'direct reference' is intended to convey no such implications about the nature of thoughts.)

It becomes clear that Kaplan's notion of 'directly referential' expressions is to be explained in terms of behaviour in modal contexts:

---

[29] In taking this line, Kaplan is certainly not following Kripke. While Kripke does suppose that Frege's notion of sense *can* be interpreted so as to have the consequence that a singular term with a Fregean sense would behave non-rigidly, he is equally prepared to allow that it can be interpreted so as not to have this consequence. (Indeed, he criticizes Frege for not making it clear which of these interpretations is correct.) Dummett (in the Appendix to ch. 5 of *Frege*) does take the view that singular terms with Fregean sense would behave as non-rigid designators, while (heroically) denying that this is the ground for any objection. But I doubt that he would argue that the thesis of non-rigidity is forced on one by the sheer use of the notion of sense.

[30] 'Demonstratives' (unpublished): Draft no. 2, UCLA mimeo, 1977, p. 1.

... I intend to use 'directly referential' for an expression whose referent, once determined, is taken as fixed for all possible circumstances...[31]

Unless these two characterizations of 'direct reference' generate
an ambiguity, Kaplan must suppose that the possession by a
singular term of a Fregean sense rules out its behaving as a rigid
designator. But I cannot understand why he supposes this to be
so. Frege himself never spoke about modal contexts, so there
can be no support in Frege's actual writings. What other support for the position there can be, I simply do not know. I
suspect that Kaplan, like many others, has derived his Frege
from Carnap, and is prepared to ascribe many of Carnap's
views to Frege. Carnap explicitly worked with a background
modal metalanguage, and thought of the 'intension' of a term
as something like a function from possible worlds to extensions.
If a Fregean *Sinn* is thought of as a Carnapian intension, then
some of Kaplan's criticisms and comments become explicable.

[31] 'Demonstratives', p. 12.

Chapter 3

Recent Work

3.1 GOING BEYOND RUSSELL: SINGULAR THOUGHTS

Many philosophers today look at the theory of reference through essentially Russellian eyes. They have the idea that fundamental differences in the ways in which referring expressions of ordinary language function ultimately rest upon fundamental differences in the ways in which it is open to us to *think* about particular objects. Like Russell, they recognize the possibility, perhaps as a limiting case, of thinking of an object by description: as one may think of a man, some African warrior perhaps, when one thinks that the tallest man in the world is thus and so. But, again like Russell, they cherish the idea of a more 'intimate', more 'direct' relation in which a subject may stand to an object (a situation in which the subject would be '*en rapport* with' the object), and the idea that when a subject and his audience are both situated *vis-à-vis* an object in this way, there exists the possibility of using singular terms to refer to, and to talk about, that object in a quite different way—expressing thoughts which would not have been available to be thought and expressed if the object had not existed. They have even taken over from Russell the idea that the central case of a situation which gives rise to the possibility of this 'more direct' way of thinking and talking about an object arises when we can perceive the object concerned.

A considerable amount of work has been done in trying to push these Russellian ideas further, and many interesting observations have been made. But the difficulty has always been that of providing a principled way of proceeding beyond the demonstrative paradigm.[1] To be sure, there are analogies

---

[1] Russell himself made an attempt to allow the notion of (Russellian) reference a wider field of application, but he did this by trying to assimilate the situation in which one thinks about oneself, and the situation in which one thinks about a remembered item, to the *perceptual* situation—a distortion which his use of the term 'acquaintance' to cover all non-descriptive modes of identification must have encouraged.

between a situation in which a subject knows of the existence of an object on the basis of his current perceptions, and a case in which he knows of the existence of an object because of perceptions which he received in the past and can remember. Analogies exist even between the central case and a case in which the subject knows of the existence of an object as a consequence of the observations and testimony of others, perhaps transmitted through a long chain. But are the analogies of the right kind, or sufficiently strong, to justify extending the model of 'direct reference'?

Some present-day philosophers, for example Strawson, have stayed with an essentially Russellian bifurcation between 'demonstrative identification' (knowledge by acquaintance) and 'descriptive identification' (knowledge by description).[2] However, Strawson adopted this bifurcation not out of deference to Russell but because he was moved, I think, by an argument which had moved Russell also. Russell held the view that in order to be thinking about an object or to make a judgement about an object, one must *know which* object is in question—one must *know which* object it is that one is thinking about.[3] (I call this principle Russell's Principle; it is the topic of chapter 4.) Russell took this Principle to require that someone who was in a position to think of an object must have a *discriminating conception* of that object—a conception which would enable the subject to distinguish that object from all other things. And it is quite easy to get oneself into a frame of mind in which it seems that where this discriminatory conception does not reduce to a capacity to locate the object in one's vicinity, it must somehow or other rest upon knowledge of some distinguishing feature of the object concerned. (Actually, to be fair to Strawson, he expressly allows for cases in which the subject can be said to know which object he is thinking of simply in virtue of having a capacity to recognize the object,[4] and I think this is genuinely a third possibility, which we shall be considering in a later chapter: see chapter 8.)

Adherence to Russell's Principle certainly makes the task of a principled generalization beyond the demonstrative paradigm

---

[2] See, e.g., *Individuals*, pp. 18–20.
[3] See *The Problems of Philosophy* (OUP, London, 1912), p. 58.
[4] See *Subject and Predicate in Logic and Grammar*, p. 47.

much more difficult, though I do not say that this provides the whole explanation of why work in pursuit of this Russellian programme has been, until fairly recently, stalled.

It should be mentioned, as something of a historical accident, that a good deal of the work carried out in this tradition has not been immediately concerned with distinguishing different kinds of *singular terms*. Rather, the concern has been to draw a distinction between two different kinds of *beliefs* about objects: beliefs on the one hand that are reportable *de re*, and beliefs on the other that are reportable only *de dicto*.[5] Nevertheless, it was implicit in much of the discussion that the condition of being '*en rapport* with' an object which would sustain beliefs about that object reportable *de re* would also provide the condition for making and understanding references in the appropriately 'direct' style.

Several philosophers working on this problem have concluded that really there is no genuine unity to the class of cases where we wish, intuitively, to say that the subject is related to the object of his thought in a sufficiently direct way for his thought to be reportable *de re*. Tyler Burge has recently given expression to this pessimistic view:

The lead role of *de re* attitudes is sponsored by a contextual, not purely conceptual, relation between thinkers and objects. The paradigm of this relation is perception. But projections from the paradigm include memory, many introspective beliefs, certain historical beliefs, beliefs about the future, perhaps beliefs in pure mathematics, and so on. There is no adequate general explication of the appropriate non-conceptual relation(s) which covers even the most widely accepted projections from the perceptual paradigm.[6]

(By 'conceptual' I think we may safely take Burge to mean 'descriptive'.) Such an attitude is perhaps tolerable when the issue concerns a distinction (which is in fact highly questionable) between kinds of belief, ultimately resting upon intuitions about correct English usage. But a distinction to which such an attitude is appropriate is obviously quite inadequate as a basis for the establishment of a theoretical distinction which is to be of some importance in the theory of language.

[5] This concern derives from W. V. Quine, 'Quantifiers and Propositional Attitudes', *Journal of Philosophy* liii (1956), 177–87.

[6] 'Belief *De Re*', *Journal of Philosophy* lxxiv (1977), 338–62, at pp. 361–2.

I think it is fair to say that work in the tradition most directly influenced by Russell had, until recently, ground to a halt upon the difficult questions I have been mentioning. It has been the impact of work of a very different style, with quite different presuppositions, by Saul Kripke which has stimulated further progress. How this has come about I shall try to explain below.

3.2 RUSSELLIAN SAYINGS: THE TWO STRATEGIES

Russell's sole interest in natural language was as a guide to the structure of human thought. He was accustomed to go straight from remarks about 'the thought in the mind of the man who utters a certain sentence' to remarks about the nature of the statement he was making, the proposition he was putting forward, and so on.[7]

For Russell language was not an intrinsically social phenomenon. But contemporary work in the philosophy of language has quite abandoned Russell's egocentric viewpoint. Once one's interest is in the phenomenon language itself, one must be concerned with the way in which it functions as a means of communication among members of a community. One will then regard the utterances of individual speakers of the language as exploitations of a linguistic system which exists independently of anyone's exploitation of it. One must be able to think in terms of the possession of semantic properties by expressions of the language independently of any particular occasion of use, as well as in terms of the significance of particular utterances. There immediately opens up the possibility of a gap between what a speaker means to say by uttering certain words—what thought he wishes to express—on the one hand, and what he strictly and literally says, according to the conventional meanings of the words he utters, on the other.

It is easiest to see the gap which arises by reflecting on the fact that uttering certain words with the intention of expressing the thought that p is not sufficient for saying that p. For a person to say that p, it is at least required that the thought that p is one of the things which the words he utters may, in the circumstances of use, be conventionally used to express. And we are all familiar with cases in which, through carelessness or ignorance

---

[7] See, e.g., *The Problems of Philosophy*, p. 54.

of the language, the speaker selects words unsuitable to his thoughts.

Natural language is full of ambiguity, and when an audience or a theorist confronts an utterance of an ambiguous sentence, the only sensible direction in which he may look for information enabling him to disambiguate the utterance is towards facts which bear on the speaker's intentions. This might lead one to think that it is at least a *necessary* condition for saying that p that the subject have the intention to express the thought that p; and as this would ordinarily be understood, it would require the subject to have, or at least to be capable of having, the thought that p. This principle would thus seem to legitimize delving into the half-baked ideas and misconceptions people have associated with at least the more specialized words of the language, in order to decide what a speaker is saying when he utters the words

(1) This ship is veering to port.

However, the sheer fact that the intentions of the speaker are uniquely relevant to disambiguating utterances of sentences like (1) by no means forces one to embrace this rather alarming conclusion. The contemporary approach to the philosophy of language highlights an analogy which holds in some respects between linguistic moves and moves in a game, a board game perhaps. The pieces are endowed with powers and potentialities by the basic rules of the game, just as the words and modes of composition of a language are endowed with a significance by the conventions of the language.[8] Now in a board game, a move by a player has certain consequences, determined as ensuing quite independently of the purpose he may have had in making the move. There does not normally exist in board games anything analogous to ambiguity in natural language, but this does not force us to abandon the analogy altogether. For it is not unreasonable to think that where we have a sentence type with several distinct meanings, we really have several distinct linguistic pieces or counters, which may be moved in this or that way. So when we wish to establish what a person is saying in

---

[8] No particular weight is to be placed on this use of the concept of convention. What the claim means is that the meanings of words are supervenient on social practices; but the relation is not a simple one.

uttering certain words, we must get clear exactly which linguistic counter, so to speak, the speaker is putting forward. Here the speaker's intentions are indeed paramount. But, once it is clear which linguistic counter he is putting forward, the content of what he says is determined by the significance which that counter has in the game, and not by whatever half-baked and ill-informed conception he may have of its meaning.

So we can think of English as containing at least two linguistic counters associated with the word type 'port'—one signifying the side of a boat opposite to starboard, the other signifying a town with a fairly serious commercial harbour. In order to determine what was said by someone who uttered (1), we should have to determine which of these two linguistic counters he was using, and it is upon this question that his thoughts, intentions, and background beliefs would bear. But once it became clear, for example, that he was using the linguistic token signifying the side of a boat, the content of what he said would be determined by the meaning with which that linguistic counter is endowed in the community, and not by the conception which he, the speaker, associates with the term. It can be perfectly clear both that a speaker intends to use just this linguistic counter, and that he does not know what it means; and in such a case it is the conventional significance of the term which determines what he says, not the thought in his mind.

The distinction between what a subject says and the thought he intends to express holds good even when there is no question of the speaker's being under some misapprehension about the conventional significance of his words. I remarked in 1.9 that it is not only coherent but actually quite plausible to maintain, in the case of ordinary proper names, that they are not associated with any particular way of thinking of their referents. Full competence with such an expression would seem to be exhausted by knowing which object it is the name of; 'a single piece of knowledge', as Wiggins says, 'which may be given in countless different ways'.[9] In the context of such a view of the functioning of an ordinary proper-name-using practice, it is just as vital to distinguish between the thought in the mind of the speaker, or

[9] 'Identity, Designation, Essentialism and Physicalism', p. 11.

hearer for that matter, and what the speaker is saying when he utters a sentence containing a name. For all I have said, this view about how proper names work could be—indeed it has been[10]—combined with the most orthodox and conventional 'descriptivist' views about the way human thought may relate to its objects. A philosopher who held the combined view would hold that the thought in the mind of the speaker can be specified by mentioning some individuating property true of the referent; but that that is certainly not what he *says*, since he may be understood by someone who makes no association between the name and that property. In fact, on this view, the content of a singular belief or thought is categorially distinct from the content of any singular statement.[11] (Which does not mean, of course, that no explanation can be given of the locution '*A* believes what *S* said'.)

It is important to notice that, in a sense of 'Russellian' slightly different from that which we have encountered before (1.3, 2.3), this composite theory regards ordinary proper names as Russellian singular terms. For, according to this theory, ordinary names have the following property: if a name has no referent, nothing is *said* by someone who utters a sentence containing it. If nothing counts as understanding what is said, then it must be the case that nothing is said. But, according to this theory, the only general way to describe what is required for understanding a sentence, '*a* is *F*', involving an ordinary proper name, '*a*', is this: one must think of the referent, in whatever way one is accustomed to think of it, and take the remark to be true just in case that object is *F*. It is all very well to allow diversity in the various states of mind that count as understanding a given remark, but it is not the case that anything goes; and the only principle capable of determining what does go must make essential reference to a particular object. The only thing that unifies these disparate states of mind is that they all embody ways of thinking about one particular object. If there is no one

[10] N. L. Wilson, 'On Semantically Relevant Whatsits: A Semantics for Philosophy of Science', in Glenn Pearce and Patrick Maynard, eds., *Conceptual Change* (Reidel, Dordrecht, 1973), pp. 233-45.

[11] The only appropriate way of reporting *what is said*, on this view, is in a transparent style—'*S* said of *x* that it is *F*'. (Since there is no privileged way of identifying the referent involved in the speech situation, there is no basis for an opaque style of reporting what is said.) This will not be so in the case of belief reports.

object to which appeal can be made, then there is no principle of unity; so there is no state of understanding, and hence no saying.

This example clearly illustrates that the recognition of Russellian singular terms, in the now slightly more precise sense of singular terms of a kind such that any utterance of a sentence containing an empty member of that kind fails to say anything, need not necessarily be the result of any searching examination of the nature of the relation between human *thought* and its objects. Indeed, it might well be thought that the Russellian strategy mentioned in 3.1, which does depend upon an investigation into the nature of that relation, is itself somewhat undermined if we maintain a very sharp distinction between what a person says and what thought he has in mind. Generally speaking, the strategy described in 3.1 was to defend the status of certain singular terms as Russellian by showing that no *thought* of the kind 'typically associated with' sentences containing such singular terms could exist, or be entertained, in the absence of an object the thought is about. (It is a convenient extension of terminology, which should generate no confusion, to speak of *thoughts* as being Russellian: a thought is Russellian if it is of such a kind that it simply could not exist in the absence of the object or objects which it is about.)

It is true that the formulation of the strategy has so far been inadequately precise, particularly as a consequence of neglecting the distinction between what is said and what is thought or meant. Even the definition of 'Russellian' that I have been using so far (1.3, 2.3) suffers from this defect. But I have no doubt that the general strategy—that of founding a linguistic distinction upon a distinction at the level of thought—can be formulated in a way which is immune to criticism on this score.

In the first place, we should adopt, as the single definition of a Russellian singular term, the definition in terms of 'saying': a term is a Russellian singular term if and only if it is a member of a category of singular terms such that nothing is said by someone who utters a sentence containing such a term unless the term has a referent—if the term is empty, no move has been made in the 'language-game'. To say that nothing has been said in a particular utterance is, quite generally, to say that nothing constitutes *understanding* the utterance.

Now we have seen, above, one way in which the claim that nothing constitutes understanding a particular utterance may be made out, a way which need involve no penetrating investigation into the relation between thought and its objects. To pursue the alternative strategy mentioned in 3.1, one would need to proceed as follows. First, one would need to show that in order to understand sentences involving terms of the category in question, it is required that the audience have a particular kind of *thought*. And, secondly, one would need to show that thoughts of the required kind are Russellian—that they simply are not available to be thought in circumstances in which there is no object (no referent).

Let me illustrate this by very briefly outlining the strategy I shall be pursuing in the case of demonstrative singular terms: expressions such as 'this cup', uttered when a particular cup is in full view of both speaker and hearer; or 'that man under the tree', uttered when a man is similarly salient for both speaker and hearer; and so on.

I shall claim that English contains a category of linguistic counters, which we may call genuine demonstrative singular terms, such that, if anyone uses such a counter, say 'that cup', with the intention of using a genuine demonstrative singular term, then it is a necessary condition for understanding what is said that one have what I shall call a *demonstrative thought* about the referent. (Unfortunately the classes of linguistic counters and of word types do not match perfectly here; as we shall see (5.5, 9.1), there are many uses of 'that ϕ' that are obviously not intended to evoke a demonstrative thought on the part of the hearer.) Now, what a demonstrative thought about an object is will be the subject-matter of a great deal of work that lies ahead,[12] but the general idea is that thinking about an object demonstratively is thinking about an object in a way which crucially depends upon the subject's currently *perceiving* that object. Thus one simply will not have understood a normal use of the sentence 'That cup is F', unless (i) one can perceive the cup, and (ii) one thinks, in a way that depends on that perception, 'That cup is F, that's what the speaker is saying' (or something along those lines).

The second stage of the strategy is to show that demonstrative

---

[12] See chapter 6.

thoughts are Russellian thoughts. This is not merely the trivial point that when, for example, a person has a hallucination and essays a thought about the object he takes himself to be perceiving, his thought will not permit of a description in relational style: '*S* is thinking about *x*, to the effect that it is *F*.' The point is rather that, in the case where the subject *does* perceive an object, there is available to him a thought with a *content* of a certain type, and no thought with a content of this type is available when there is no object which the subject is perceiving. Since it is a thought with this type of content which is required for understanding a sentence containing a genuine demonstrative singular term, we may put the two points together, and conclude that when such a term, as used, is empty, nothing counts as understanding what the speaker said. Consequently, the term, as used, is Russellian.

3.3 KRIPKE: SINGULAR THOUGHT WITHOUT DISCRIMINATING KNOWLEDGE?

Saul Kripke devoted a section of his seminal 'Naming and Necessity' to arguing against the 'Description Theory of Names' which he found in Frege and Russell. I do not now want to discuss the success or failure of Kripke's arguments against that theory; the extent to which I think they are correct will become clear from subsequent material in this book, especially chapter 11. My present concern is to trace the considerable influence which Kripke's lectures have had, in a curious way, upon recent philosophical discussion of the nature of human thought about objects.

At several points during his lectures, Kripke adverts to the possibility of someone being able to use a proper name to refer to something when he himself is not able to provide any individuating description of that thing. There are two kinds of case. In one kind of case, the subject does not associate with a name anything which purports to provide an individuating description of the referent. Suppose a child is introduced to the name 'Socrates' by hearing simply that Socrates was a Greek philosopher. According to Kripke, the child may then go on to use the name, and on his lips it has to refer to a particular historical philosopher, whom he has not the resources to distinguish from any other Greek philosopher.[13] In the second kind of case, the subject has associated with the name a description he takes to be individuating, but which is not true of the object to which we would naturally take the name, on his lips, to be referring.

It is not clear who should be troubled by these possibilities, since they seem to be straightforward instances, in the field of singular reference, of the gap which opens up (3.2) between what a speaker says and what thoughts he may have in his mind. In both kinds of case, there is enough material to indicate which 'name-counter' the speaker intends to be using; and it is commonplace to suppose that what the speaker says should be determined by the referent which that 'name-counter' has in a community.

Of far greater significance, as a subversion of traditional ways of thinking about reference, though quite inessential to Kripke's argumentative purposes, and so little distinguished by Kripke, was the claim, endorsed in one or two places, that not only were subjects capable of *referring* to—*saying* things about—individuals which they could not distinguish from others, but, further, they could hold *beliefs* about—be *thinking* of—those same individuals. To my knowledge, this is the first explicit challenge to what I have called Russell's Principle (3.1): the principle that in order to have a thought about a particular object, you must *know which* object it is about which you are thinking.[14] It must surely be agreed that, had Kripke genuinely demonstrated Russell's Principle to be false, he would have shown something of even greater importance than the unacceptability of the Description Theory of Names, or than any of the many other fascinating conclusions contained in the lectures. But I think it fair to say that Kripke did not refute Russell's Principle.

The only evidence that Kripke explicitly marshalled against Russell's Principle is the observation that in certain cases of these ignorant speakers, we might find it quite *natural to say* that

---

[13] One might wonder why the child's ability to use the name does not constitute his possession of such resources. (In general it is not clear whether Kripke is best understood as challenging Russell's Principle or as proposing acceptance of a specially exiguous way of conforming to it. See n. 14 below, and 11.5.)

[14] Strictly, the challenge need not be to Russell's Principle as such; it may be taken as a challenge to the interpretation of it as requiring a *discriminating conception* of an object of thought. (See 4.1.) The challenge can be interpreted as conceding Russell's Principle, as here formulated, but pressing a different interpretation of the *knowing which* that it requires.

they held or expressed a belief about the referent of the name.
But, in the first place, as Kripke himself points out, the circumstances under which we are inclined to say this are rather
special. If the ignorant child has got hold of the widely disseminated piece of information (or misinformation) 'Socrates was
snub-nosed', we might well be inclined to say that the child has
a true or false belief about Socrates, or at least has acquired
information (or misinformation) about him. But the inclination
to say that the child has, and is expressing, a belief about
Socrates is far less strong when we envisage the child not merely
repeating a widely disseminated piece of information, but uttering the words 'Socrates was fat' (say), perhaps as the result of
some confusion. Indeed, the circumstances required to produce
the supposed counter-example clearly undermine its status as
such. If we are to say that the sheer introduction of a subject to
a name which has a referent in the community may suffice to
enable that subject to have thoughts about the referent—not
merely beliefs but presumably the whole range of propositional
attitudes—in contravention of Russell's Principle, then we are
committed to saying that the subject has thereby acquired a
capacity to entertain indefinitely many thoughts about the referent; one, in fact, for each simple or complex property of which
the subject has a conception. For we cannot avoid thinking of
a thought about an individual object x, to the effect that it is
F, as the exercise of two separable capacities; one being the
capacity to think of x, which could be equally exercised in
thoughts about x to the effect that it is G or H; and the other
being a conception of what it is to be F, which could be equally
exercised in thoughts about other individuals, to the effect that
they are F.[15] In order to overthrow Russell's Principle, one
would have to show that this general capacity to think of an
object, and grasp indefinitely many hypotheses about it, can be
possessed entirely in the absence of any discriminating conception of the object. And it is far from clear that when we bring
our linguistic intuitions, in the case of the ignorant name-user,
to bear on this larger question, the issue goes against Russell.[16]

[15] I call this the Generality Constraint: see 4.3.

[16] The cases where we are inclined to attribute beliefs can be easily accounted for in
terms of the well-attested 'quotational' or *oratio recta* use of the constructions '*S* believes
that …' and '*S* thinks that …'. (See Alonzo Church, 'Intensional Isomorphism and
Identity of Belief', *Philosophical Studies* v (1954), 65–73.)

In any case, it should be clear that the truth or falsity of Russell's Principle is not to be decided by evidence as to the pattern of ordinary English usage with respect to propositional-attitude words. It seems to me that in order either to attack or to defend Russell's Principle, one needs at least something in the way of a *theory* of thought, judgement, belief, etc.; and while it is true, of course, that these terms are anchored to psychological phenomena by the ordinary linguistic practices with the words 'thought', 'belief', 'judgement', it is not for me to remind Kripke that the deliverances of untutored linguistic intuition may have to be corrected in the light of considerations of theory.[17]

3.4 THE PHOTOGRAPH MODEL

None of the above can properly be regarded as a criticism of Kripke. He did not trumpet himself as having overturned that venerable Principle; on the contrary, where *belief*, as opposed to *saying* and *referring*, is concerned, he expressed his views with great tentativeness. In any case, the point seems to me to lie somewhat off Kripke's main argumentative track. However, those parts of Kripke's lectures with which we have been concerned have had an enormous influence on subsequent work on thought, belief, etc.—work in a field which we may follow others in calling the study of mental representation—and I think it is reasonable to have misgivings about the form that this influence has assumed. I shall mention two misgivings.

The first is implicit in what has gone before (3.3). Although, as we have seen, it is far from being the case, many philosophers have simply assumed that Kripke showed Russell's Principle to be false. A really revolutionary change in our way of thinking about how thoughts and other mental states represent particular objects has thus been quietly assumed, with none of the general or theoretical arguments that one would have expected the acceptance of such a change to require.[18]

My second misgiving will take longer to state, because it will require me to say a brief word about Kripke's positive proposal

---

[17] On Russell's Principle, see further chapter 4, and 11.5.

[18] The abandonment of the principle of identification at the level of saying is a trivial consequence of the distinction between what one says and what thought one intends to express. Its abandonment at the level of *belief* or *thought* would be an extremely significant move. What has happened is that the former has been mistaken for the latter.

on the question of what makes it the case that a saying—and, contentiously, a belief—of an ignorant name-user concerns a particular object. I shall present no necessary and sufficient conditions here, but the general idea is this: a name-user refers to an object *x* by his use of the name *a* at time *t* if one can trace a continuous causal route from an event, perhaps far in the past, in which the name was originally assigned to the object *x* (most characteristically, a dubbing), through a series of reference-preserving links, as one speaker passes on his competence with a name to another, to an event whereby the subject first acquired the use of the name—an event which is one of the causal antecedents of his use of it at time *t*. (It is unfortunate that Kripke chooses to analyse the notion in this way, because it collapses two questions which are usually distinguished: 'What is it for there to exist in a given community *C* at time *t* a name-using practice in which *a* refers to *x*?', and 'What is it for a speaker to be participating in one of the name-using practices in existence in a community involving the name *a* and not another, when he utters a sentence containing the name *a*?' I shall try to explain, in chapter 11, the merits of keeping these questions separate.)

Speaking abstractly, then, we may say that what Kripke proposes is that the 'representational properties' of the ignorant name-user's *utterance* depend upon the existence of a causal relation between that utterance and an object. And, going on to the more contentious part of his proposal, while still speaking equally abstractly, we may say that, for Kripke, the representational properties of the ignorant name-user's *thought*—the thought he expresses in using the name—depend upon the existence of a causal relation between a psychological state and the object it represents.

Now it was this idea—the idea that the representational properties of the *thought*, or *belief*, depend upon its causal qualities—which inspired those who were working on the nature of belief or thought. For, quite independently of Kripke, the idea had been emerging that causality had some important role to play in determining what objects our thoughts and beliefs are about.[19] Very often, our thoughts about objects rest upon

---

[19] See, e.g., David Kaplan, 'Quantifying In', in Donald Davidson and Jaakko Hintikka, eds., *Words and Objections*, pp. 206-42.

information which is causally derived from an individual: for
instance, a demonstrative thought rests upon perceptual information derived from something perceived; and another kind of
thought may rest upon information acquired via the testimony
of others, which ultimately derives from the doings and condition of some particular object. It was becoming clear that
nothing can sensibly be regarded as the object of such an
'information-based' thought unless it is in fact the source of the
information on which the thought rests. Perhaps over-impressed
by the fact that the word 'causality' was involved in both cases,
many working in the field tended to believe that the phenomenon Kripke claimed to have noticed was essentially the same as
the phenomenon they had been concerned with. Thus, among
philosophers emboldened by Kripke's willingness to allow the
existence of a certain appropriate causal relation between a
mental state and an object to be *sufficient* for that state to represent that object, there emerged a theory which one might call
'The Photograph Model of Mental Representation', in which
the causal antecedents of the information involved in a mental
state, like the causal relation Kripke was concerned with, are
claimed to be sufficient to determine which object the state
concerns. (The name 'Photograph Model' is apt, because we do
speak of a photograph's being a photograph *of* one object rather
than another solely on the basis of which object was related in
the appropriate way to its production.) For example, there may
have been two Polish grocers in my home town, although I now
retain only the dimmest recollection of one of them. In this
situation, I may think 'I wonder what happened to that nice
Polish grocer'. Suppose it is further discovered that, although
both grocers were well known to me as a child, the information
I retain is exclusively derived from grocer *A*. The Photograph
Model will have the consequence that I am thinking of grocer
A, even though I have no means by which to distinguish the
object of my thought from grocer *B*.[20]

I am now in a position to state my second misgiving about
the nature of the influence that Kripke's lectures have had upon
subsequent work in the theory of mental representation.
Kripke's model of how a thought may, at least in special cases,
concern an object in virtue of a causal link with an object, the

[20] The Photograph Model will be further discussed in chapter 4.

tracing of which requires the tracing *of the history of a name*, is, however formally analogous to the Photograph Model, completely distinct from it. The Photograph Model applies in a very large range of cases where there simply is no relevant name, and when it is applied in cases where there is both name and information to be traced, it is clear that the two theories may give conflicting results.[21] Yet it has been a consequence of the fact that Kripke's lectures were the inspiration for much of the recent work on the relation between thoughts and objects that there has been a persistent tendency to attempt to unify the two models, whether this be by taking Kripke's model as somehow a special case of the Photograph Model,[22] or, more amazingly, by seeing the Photograph Model as a special case of Kripke's.[23] From the synthesizers and bandwagon performers in the philosophical profession, there have come names for the unified theory: 'The Causal Theory of Reference' and 'The Historical Explanation Theory of Reference'. But these names have no reference; the bandwagon is going nowhere.

[21] See Kripke's remarks on 'Santa Claus', 'Naming and Necessity' pp. 300, 302; my paper 'The Causal Theory of Names', *Aristotelian Society Supplementary Volume* xlvii (1973), 187-208; and Kripke's supplementary remarks in *Semantics of Natural Languages*, at pp. 768-9.

[22] e.g. Michael Devitt, 'Singular Terms', *Journal of Philosophy* lxxi (1974), 183-205.

[23] e.g. Gilbert H. Harman, 'How to Use Propositions', *American Philosophical Quarterly* xiv (1977), 173-6.

Appendix[1]

What has emerged is a distinction between two ways in which one can argue for the Russellian status of a given category of singular terms.

One way, briefly outlined in 3.1 and illustrated in 3.2 by an anticipation of the strategy to be adopted later in the book with demonstrative singular terms, is founded on work in the philosophy of mind. This is Russell's own way with the Russellian singular terms which he countenanced (their claim to be Russellian being based on their amenability to what might be described as the model of acquaintance, as opposed to the model of description, for thoughts which concern objects).[2] Any attempt to extend the class of Russellian singular terms in the first way, beyond Russell's own narrow limits, while respecting Russell's Principle, requires careful exploration of the possibility that there may be non-descriptive modes of identification (ways in which a thought may concern an object otherwise than 'by description') which are less restrictive than Russell's model of acquaintance.

The second way, illustrated in 3.2 by the case of proper names, does not require arguments in the philosophy of mind directed towards extending the class of Russellian *thoughts*. For, as 3.2 makes clear, a cogent argument to the effect that ordinary proper names (excluding, that is, names like 'Julius': 1.7, 1.8, 2.3) figure in (so to speak) Russellian *sayings* can be constructed even if we believe that there are no Russellian *thoughts* at all—even if we believe that thoughts can concern particular objects only 'by description'.

Kripke's work on names, apart from some tentative asides about thought and belief, is pretty clearly an example of the second way of proceeding: Kripke's argument is for a non-descriptive account of what a speaker *says* by uttering a sentence containing a name, and his argument exploits considerations relating to the social and communicative function of language, rather than considerations relating directly to the thoughts in the minds of speakers.[3] But, partly because the tentative asides made it seem that Kripke was rejecting Russell's Principle as a constraint on thought about objects, and partly because

[1] Evans projected a final section for chapter 3, which was to deal with the consequences of the conflation discussed in 3.4. I have tried here to give some idea of how it might have gone, using material from earlier drafts and lecture notes.

[2] For the two models, see 2.1.

[3] Note Kripke's stress on the predominantly social character of naming (e.g. at pp. 299, 301). It should be remarked that Kripke himself is not primarily interested in the question of Russellian status (the dependence of a saying for its existence on the existence of its object); though if a saying is Russellian, it will certainly be (what Kripke is primarily concerned to establish for the sayings that interest him) non-descriptive.

Kripke's stress on causation struck a chord in the minds of philosophers already inclined to believe (correctly enough) that causal relations are important in giving an account of ways in which thought can concern particular objects otherwise than 'by description', Kripke's work has encouraged a position (the Photograph Model of mental representation of particular objects) which has implications for the first sort of approach to the question of Russellian status: implications, that is, for the philosophy of mind. According to the Photograph Model, a mental state can represent a particular object simply in virtue of that object's playing a suitable role in its causal ancestry. Such a particular-representation will certainly be Russellian: there will be no possibility of a mental state possessing the representative character in question in the absence of a suitably related object. But such particular-representation need not conform to Russell's Principle. Thus, the Photograph Model holds out the promise of extending the class of Russellian singular terms beyond the constricting limits imposed by Russell's model of acquaintance, with an argument of the first kind (an argument in the philosophy of mind), but without the severe constraint imposed by the principle that thought about a particular object requires the subject to have discriminating knowledge of that object.

A pernicious result of this seepage of considerations properly belonging to arguments of the second sort into arguments of the first sort is that it encourages the idea that there cannot be two Russellian singular terms for the same object which differ in Fregean sense. One way of putting this idea, which is very widely accepted, is that the content of a Russellian thought involving the ascription of a monadic property to an object can be appropriately represented as the ordered couple of the object and the property.[4] (Obviously this generalizes to cover relational thoughts.)

It is true that this idea—the idea that the very notion of a Russellian singular term leaves no room for use of the concept of sense—goes back to Russell himself (see 2.1). Russell's own conception of genuine reference had two strands: first, the thesis that genuine reference requires an object, in the sense that nothing constitutes understanding an utterance containing an expression of one of the relevant kinds if it lacks a referent (because no thought or proposition is expressed by such an utterance); and second, the thesis that 'if one thing has two names, you make exactly the same assertion [express exactly the same thought] whichever of the two names you use'.[5] The use made of the

---

[4] See, e.g., Keith S. Donnellan, 'Speaking of Nothing', *Philosophical Review* lxxxiii (1974), 3–31, at pp. 11–12.

[5] *The Philosophy of Logical Atomism*, at p. 245 in *Logic and Knowledge*. (Russell's own practice justifies this free interchange between what is said and what is thought, as noted at the beginning of 3.2.)

notion of a Russellian singular term throughout this book connects the notion to the first of these two strands, and ignores the second as an error (as a retrograde step on Russell's part).

It is certainly an error to suppose that the second strand is a corollary of the first. The first strand registers the idea that there are things which we say and believe whose content cannot be faithfully represented without the reporter himself making a reference to an object in the world which those utterances and beliefs concern—so that, were there no such object, there would be no such content available to be faithfully represented. And it certainly does not follow, from the fact that the only accurate report of what is said or thought involves reference to a particular thing, that *any* report which involves reference to that particular thing would be equally accurate, so long as it was otherwise unaltered. For it may be that an accurate report requires a coincidence or harmony between the way in which the reporter's reference is made and the way in which the object is identified in the reported saying or thought.

Russell may have deceived himself into supposing that the second strand had to accompany the first by the rather pictorial way in which he liked to formulate the first strand, namely, in terms of the idea that the object in question actually *occurs in* the thought or proposition expressed by an utterance in which genuine reference is made. For if we say that the object itself is actually *in* the thought—like a pea in a pod—then we seem to have made no provision for a distinction between different thoughts in which the same property is ascribed to the same object. But the pictorial formulation is quite inessential to the insight embodied in the first strand. (We saw in chapter 1 that there is nothing to prevent the attribution of Fregean sense to singular terms which are Russellian in a sense determined by the first strand.)

Russell himself had an excuse for his espousal (in effect) of the ordered-couple conception of monadic Russellian thoughts, in that he restricted the objects of such thinking mainly to items which were conceived to be so fleeting and insubstantial that it seemed unintelligible to suppose a person might identify the same one twice without knowing that it was the same. But this excuse is not available to those who extend the ordered-couple conception of Russellian thoughts outside the sphere of thoughts about objects of Russellian acquaintance.

The fact that the Photograph Model encourages the ordered-couple conception is intimately connected with the fact that it purports to free us from any obligation to respect Russell's Principle when we seek to extend the class of Russellian thoughts beyond Russell's model of acquaintance. If we are seeking the extension in conformity to Russell's Principle, then the task takes the form of looking for further non-descriptive modes of identification—further ways in which the subject may *know which* object it is that his thought concerns. And, given the connection between the concept of a mode of identification and the subject's awareness, it is clearly reasonable to conceive the *content* of the thoughts in question, not as determined simply by the identity of the relevant object (together with what is thought about it), as on the ordered-couple conception, but rather, as partly determined by the way in which the subject knows which object is the relevant object—so that, theoretically at least, there can be room for two thoughts to ascribe the same property to the same object while differing in content, because they differ in the ways in which the object is identified. According to the Photograph Model, on the other hand, what determines which particular object a mental state represents is facts about the mental state's causal ancestry, quite independent of anything we could recognize as discriminating knowledge, on the subject's part, of the object in question—facts, indeed, of which the subject himself may be quite unaware. And it is quite obscure how, if one mental state represents a particular object in virtue of one sort of causal relation to it, and another mental state (of the same subject) represents that object in virtue of another sort of causal relation to it, the sheer difference between the causal relations could generate a difference in *content* between the two mental states, given that it need not in any way impinge on the subject's awareness. Thus, precisely by disavowing the need, consequent upon acceptance of Russell's Principle, to investigate modes of identification, the Photograph Model seems to exclude any more fine-grained conception of the identity and difference of Russellian thoughts than that afforded by the ordered-couple conception.

But this is disastrous for the whole project of trying to extend the class of Russellian singular terms beyond Russell's own limits.

It seems coherent to maintain that there can be *sayings*—moves in a public language-game—which can be accurately reported *only* in a transparent style ('He is saying, of such-and-such, that it is thus and so'). Transparent reports commonly involve a retreat back from some notional report that could be given ('He is saying that such-and-such is thus and so'), with some loss of information consequent upon the retreat, since the transparent report gives the object which the saying concerned, but not the way it was identified in the saying. But if a saying can be accurately reported only in the transparent style, then there is no more informative notional report, from which the transparent report represents a retreat: the transparent report is the fundamental description. It would follow that the content of the saying can be appropriately represented in the ordered-couple way. Perhaps this is the right position to adopt for sayings involving ordinary proper names (see 3.2, and 11.5); at any rate the position is coherent.

But it does not seem to be coherent to adopt this position quite generally about the content of Russellian *thoughts*—not, at any rate, if we wish to extend the class of Russellian thoughts beyond Russell's own limits. The ground for this claim is not merely the thesis that, if someone has a thought about a particular object, then there must be some specific way in which he identifies the object of his thought, respect for which would then generate the possibility of a more informative notional report of the thought. (Although this thesis is extremely plausible, it would be question-begging simply to assume it at this point.) But if our only conception of Russellian thoughts is the ordered-couple conception, then we shall have no coherent characterization to give, in Russellian terms, of a variety of situations which are perfectly possible.

Suppose a person can see two views of what is in fact one very long ship, through two windows in the room in which he is sitting.[6] He may be prepared to accept 'That ship was built in Japan' (pointing through one window), but not prepared to accept 'That ship was built in Japan' (pointing through the other window). Now suppose we try to describe this situation in terms of the ordered-couple conception of Russellian thought. We have a single proposition or thought-content—⟨the ship in question, the property of having been built in Japan⟩ to which the subject both has and fails to have the relation corresponding to the notion of belief. Not only does this fail to give any intelligible characterization of the subject's state of mind; it appears to be actually contradictory. By constructing cases of this kind, it is not difficult to argue, given the assumption that Russellian thoughts must be representable in the ordered-couple way, that there is very little applicability, and perhaps no applicability at all, for the notion of Russellian thoughts outside Russell's own narrow limits. But this line of argument simply lapses if the assumption is discarded.

Of course the ordered-couple conception of Russellian thought, on the one hand, and the orthodox conception of the Fregean sense of a singular term as something in no way dependent on its actual possession of a referent (see 1.6), on the other, are two sides of the same coin. Only the concept of Fregean sense (or something to the same effect) will permit us to distinguish pairs of thoughts which ascribe the same property to the same thing; and if Russellian thoughts have to be representable in the ordered-couple way, then thoughts which admit of such a distinction cannot be Russellian.

Adherence to Russell's Principle is fundamental to the view of

[6] This case is similar to one considered by John Perry, in 'Frege on Demonstratives', *Philosophical Review* lxxxvi (1977), 474–97, at p. 483.

Russellian reference to be advanced in this book. (See chapter 4.) Ironically, the proponents of the Photograph Model, in their flouting of Russell's Principle, seem to show an excessive respect for the *structure* of Russell's own position. Convinced, like Russell, that not all thought about objects is 'by description', and convinced that Russell's only alternative, the model of acquaintance, is too restrictive, they seek another single model, equally monolithic but more comprehensive, to replace the model of acquaintance—hence the Photograph Model. Although there is indeed an important unifying feature common to the Russellian thoughts which are recognized in this book, the class is internally heterogeneous, and an appreciation of the differences is as vital to a proper understanding of the theory of reference as is the appreciation of the unity of the class. Faithfulness to Russell's Principle is crucial here: what unifies the different modes of identification recognized is conformity to the requirement which the Principle imposes; but the important differences between them are revealed by always pressing the question 'How is it, in this case, that the subject can be said to know which object his thought concerns?'

A major aim of this book is the same as one which is characteristic of proponents of the Photograph Model: namely, to argue (against Russell himself) that many of the referring expressions of natural language are Russellian—that their significance depends on their having a referent. (Many, not all: we must remember 'Julius'.) This is argued in both of the legitimate ways distinguished in this chapter. The chapters on specific modes of identification (chapters 6, 7, and 8) argue for the Russellian character of several kinds of particular-*thoughts*; given the thesis (for which see 9.1) that various uses of singular terms require thoughts of this kind for their understanding, this yields an argument of the first kind for the Russellian status of those singular terms. And the argument about proper names given in 3.2, which is an argument of the second kind, stands.

What is not countenanced anywhere in the book is the sort of defence of a Russellian position about a certain category of singular terms which the Photograph Model purports to provide. The Photograph Model, and the generalized Causal Theory of Reference which is its counterpart in the philosophy of language, originated in a confusion, as 3.4 explains. Against them stand the powerful attractions of Russell's Principle. And once they are detached from their dubious genesis, the only positive reason appearing to be in their favour is the naturalness of various psychological locutions which seem to flout Russell's Principle (3.3); but this naturalness will be explained, without any deviation from Russell's Principle, in 5.3 and 11.5.

Part Two

Thought

Chapter 4

Russell's Principle

4.1 ITS MEANING AND IMPORTANCE

The difficulty with Russell's Principle has always been to explain what it means. The principle is that a subject cannot make a judgement about something unless he knows which object his judgement is about.[1] Perhaps this will be conceded, even by adherents of the Photograph Model; the real dispute concerns what it is to have such knowledge.

If the principle is interpreted as appealing to the colloquial use of the expression 'knows which', then it is surely incorrect, since a subject may make a judgement about an object which he sees, or about himself, even when it would be correct to say that he does not know which item he is seeing, or who he is. If, on the other hand, no restriction is placed upon the kind of answers the subject may be able to give to the question 'Which item are you thinking about?', then the principle appears trivial, since anyone who is prepared to ascribe to a subject the thought that *a* is *F* in the first place will also be prepared to ascribe to him the thought, and presumably the knowledge, that it is *a* that he is thinking about.

In order to make Russell's Principle a substantial principle, I shall suppose that the knowledge which it requires is what might be called *discriminating knowledge*: the subject must have a capacity to distinguish the object of his judgement from all other things. This makes things only a little clearer, but it is enough to get along with. We have the idea of certain sufficient conditions for being able to discriminate an object from all other things: for example, when one can perceive it at the present time; when one can recognize it if presented with it; and when one knows distinguishing facts about it.[2] And we can easily

---

[1] See Russell, *The Problems of Philosophy*, p. 58.

[2] I am not the first to have noticed this trichotomy. See Strawson, 'Identifying Reference and Truth-Values', in *Logico-Linguistic Papers*, pp. 75–95, at p. 77: '... a

think of cases in which a subject does not have the capacity to distinguish an object from all other things. Suppose, for example, that on a certain day in the past, a subject briefly observed two indistinguishable steel balls suspended from the same point and rotating about it. He now believes nothing about one ball which he does not believe about the other. This is certainly a situation in which the subject cannot discriminate one of the balls from all other things, since he cannot discriminate it from its fellow. And a principle which precludes the ascription to the subject of a thought about one of the balls surely has a considerable intuitive appeal. Certainly, if one imagines oneself in this situation, and attempts to speculate about one of the balls rather than the other, one finds oneself attempting to exploit some distinguishing fact or other.

On the other hand, there is a conflicting intuition. Let us tell the story of the steel balls rather differently, so that our subject briefly sees one ball rotating by itself on one day, and the other on a later day. And let us further suppose that the subject retains no memory of the first episode, because of a localized amnesia produced by a blow to the head. Suppose, finally, that many years later our subject reminisces about 'that shiny ball' he saw many years earlier. If asked which ball he is thinking about, our subject cannot produce any facts which would discriminate between the two. (I assume, as I think I am entitled to, that he would not think of distinguishing the ball he is thinking of as the one from which his current memory derives.)

On the one hand, this subject will certainly behave as though *he* subscribed to Russell's Principle, interpreted as requiring discriminating knowledge; when appraised of the fact that there were two balls which he saw, he will hardly go on reminiscing about 'that ball', consoling himself with the thought that he knows which ball he means, since only one of them is *that* ball. On the other hand, it would certainly be quite natural, in view of the facts, to say that he was *thinking of* the second ball, or that he had the second ball *in mind*, or, if he spoke, that he *meant* the second ball.

---

person may be able to pick a thing out in his current field of perception. Or he may know there is a thing (not in his current field of perception) to which a certain description applies which applies to no other thing ... Or he may know the name of a thing and be able to recognize it when he encounters it ...' (But knowing a thing's name does not appear to be particularly important to recognition-based identification.) A similar trichotomy is found in Dummett, *Frege* (see 4.2 below).

Our situation, then, is this. We have, on the one hand, a fundamental principle with a certain intuitive appeal, and, on the other, some apparent counter-examples.[3] What we do not yet have, on either side, is a theoretical argument, either for imposing the requirement of discriminating knowledge, or for attaching the importance to the facts of causality which the counter-examples encourage us to do. We cannot be content to rest the Photograph Model upon the observation that our ordinary usage of propositional-attitude expressions appears to be in conformity with it, in the way we have recently been encouraged to do.[4] But equally, we cannot accept a principle as fundamental as Russell's simply because it *seems* correct.

In fact, the use to which I propose to put Russell's Principle, interpreted as requiring discriminating knowledge, means that for me it stands in need of a theoretical defence quite independently of the necessity of convincing myself of its truth. For, however persuaded one was of the truth of the Principle, one would not really know, in the absence of a theoretical defence, what it means. Our intuitive idea of being able to distinguish an object collects together several different relations in which subjects may stand to objects, but we have as yet no idea of what unifies them. We cannot rest content with a purely disjunctive understanding of the concept of discriminating knowledge; but a more adequate understanding can be provided only by giving a theory in which the concept of discriminating knowledge is linked to the concepts of thought and judgement by way of Russell's Principle. Only a theoretical defence of Russell's Principle will provide us with an account of what common thing it is which descriptive, demonstrative, and recognition-based identification enable a subject to do, by showing us why it is that thought about a particular individual requires the subject to be able to do it.

Again, we need a defence of Russell's Principle in order to answer questions about the boundaries of demonstrative

---

[3] I am restricting myself here to apparent counter-examples in which the naturalness of saying that the subject is thinking of a certain object, in the absence of any ability to discriminate it from all other objects, is not supposed to turn on his having been introduced to a *name* for that object—i.e. I am leaving aside counter-examples of the sort that Kripke produced (see 3.4). I reserve the latter for discussion in 11.5.

[4] See, e.g., Keith S. Donnellan, 'Proper Names and Identifying Descriptions', in Davidson and Harman, eds., *Semantics of Natural Languages*, pp. 356-79.

identification. The idea of demonstrative identification may seem clear enough, but on reflection it is difficult to understand what is involved, and where its boundaries lie. Does perception of an object always provide one with discriminating knowledge of it? Can one demonstratively identify an object seen in a photograph or heard on the radio, or must one rather think about such objects descriptively? These are genuine questions, rather than merely terminological questions, precisely because the concept of identification or discriminating knowledge is linked, via Russell's Principle, to the ascription of thoughts. Only a theoretical defence of Russell's Principle will yield a basis on which to proceed (in chapter 6) to an attempt to return theoretically-motivated, as opposed to merely intuitive, answers to such questions. (For this reason, I do not want to place any weight in what follows on an unexplained notion of demonstrative identification.)

Why does the investigation of the requirements for thought and judgement about particular individuals matter? It matters because the concept of thought about an individual is tied to the concept of *understanding* a statement about an individual. I hold that it is in general a necessary condition for understanding an utterance of a sentence containing a Russellian referring expression, say '*a* is *F*', that one have a thought, or make a judgement, about the referent, to the effect that it is being said to be *F*. This is not a necessary condition for making such an utterance in such a way as to say of the referent that it is *F*. The divergence arises because of the possibility that a subject may exploit a linguistic device which he does not himself properly understand (cf. 3.2). Given the divergence between the requirements for *understanding* and the requirements for *saying*, it would be absurd to deny that our primary interest ought to be in the more exigent conditions which are required for understanding.[5]

---

[5] There is a principle parallel to Russell's Principle, to the effect that in order to have the concept of a given natural kind one must have some way of distinguishing its members from all other things. (This could perhaps be regarded as an application of the same principle.) A challenge, similar to that mounted against Russell's Principle on the basis of the Photograph Model, has been mounted against this principle about natural kinds: see Hilary Putnam, 'The Meaning of "Meaning" ', in *Mind, Language and Reality* (CUP, Cambridge, 1975), pp. 215–71. I think this challenge, which rests on rather different considerations, should also be resisted.

4.2 VERIFICATIONISM AND IDEAL VERIFICATIONISM

There is one theoretical account of our thinking which would sustain a version of Russell's Principle (and in doing so tell us what discriminating knowledge is), namely verificationism. For a verificationist, the fundamental mode of identification of an object is the demonstrative mode; other forms of identification count as such because they constitute effective procedures for determining, of an object identified demonstratively, whether or not it is the relevant object. And one will be in a position to identify an object demonstratively just in case one is in a position, without further preliminary, to determine the applicability to that object of some basic range of decidable properties. Thus, for a verificationist, there are two very different kinds of thought which one can have about an object: those for which a one-step verification procedure is appropriate, and those for which a two-step verification procedure is appropriate. In the case of demonstrative thoughts—thoughts about items identified demonstratively—the subject's knowledge of what is in question will consist simply in his disposition to regard certain events, whose occurrence he is immediately in a position to recognize, as decisive of the truth or falsity of the thought. (Even if there are many objects with respect to which the subject is in a deciding position, the particular thought in question may nevertheless have this dispositional connection to one rather than another of them.) On the other hand, when the subject is not in a deciding position *vis-à-vis* an object, his knowledge of what is in question when he entertains the thought *that a is F* will consist partly in his capacity to recognize, when confronted (in a deciding position) with an object, that it is *a*. Hence for thoughts of this latter kind, a two-stage verification procedure will be appropriate: one stage would issue in the judgement 'This is *a*', and the other stage would issue in the judgement 'This is *F*'. Furthermore, there appear to be just two ways of being able to decide the truth-value of propositions of the form 'This is *a*'. Either the subject is in possession of a formula or criterion for determining whether a given object is *a*—an employment of this formula or criterion would manifest what others have known as 'descriptive identification'; or else he possesses, in Dummett's phrase, a mere 'propensity for recognition'.[6]

---

[6] *Frege*, p. 488.

Thus not only does a verificationist provide us with an account of what discriminating knowledge amounts to, but he does so in a way which appears to capture precisely the three kinds of discriminating knowledge which we intuitively identified (4.1).

Now it is of course highly unlikely that Russell's Principle is a verificationist one (though I fear that it has to a certain extent been caught up in the stampede away from verificationism). Knowledge of an individuating fact would count as possession of discriminating knowledge, for Russell and for most later subscribers to the Principle, even if its being true of an object was not effectively decidable. Nevertheless, I believe Dummett would argue that this verificationist account of the notion of discriminating knowledge still has a certain validity within the realistic framework accepted by most subscribers to Russell's Principle. For Dummett thinks that a realist is obliged to base his theory of thought upon verificationist foundations, accommodating the higher flights of human thought (or fancy) by allowing us to form a conception of the carrying out of procedures of verification appropriate to our thoughts by beings with powers greater than our own. Realism, according to Dummett, sustains itself by appealing to a sort of ideal verificationism. (For instance, the realist supposes that the link between an existentially quantified proposition and the idea of a *search* of a domain can be retained, even in the context of quantification over infinite totalities, provided we are allowed to imagine a search of the domain by a being with infinite powers.)

In this ideal verificationist spirit, Dummett is prepared to regard as more or less conforming to the views of Frege—surely a realist—the following model of knowledge of the sense of a sentence containing a singular term, and hence of grasping or having a thought about a particular object:

... a rough model for the sense of a proper name of a concrete object: to grasp the sense of such a name is to have a criterion of identification of an object as the referent of the name. In many cases the phrase 'criterion of identification' is too ponderous, and it would be preferable to substitute something like 'propensity for recognition'; but the general idea was that a grasp of the sense of the name consisted in a capacity to say, of any given object, whether or not it was the referent or bearer of the name. Here again qualification is needed: particularly when the name is a complex one, it may be impossible to determine from mere inspection whether some object presented is that for which the name stands ... At least from Frege's standpoint, there cannot even be a requirement of effective decidability: as long as I can recognize something as settling the question, it is unnecessary that I should be able in all cases to employ some procedure which will lead to a settlement of it.

In offering this account, we are faced with the difficulty of explaining the notion of an object's being 'given' or 'presented' ... In the case of concrete objects, we supposed that this would be done by the use of a demonstrative. On this account, therefore, the understanding of the sense of a name amounts to an ability to determine the truth-value—more properly to know what would determine the truth-value—of a sentence containing the name in question, of a quite particular kind, viz. one of the kind we called a 'recognition statement': a sentence of the form 'This is X' ...[7]

This account fits into an account of what is involved in knowing what is in question where the whole thought is concerned:

... the determination of the truth-value of any given sentence goes via the identification of an object as the referent of each proper name occurring in the sentence: guided by the senses of these names, we first identify certain objects as their referents, and after that, we neglect all special features of those senses save the fact that they determine those objects as their referents; all that remains is to decide whether or not the predicate or relational expression applies to that object or those objects.[8]

This ideal verificationist model incorporates many fundamental aspects of our thinking, and it undeniably has a certain appeal; but I do not think that a realist should be seduced into accepting it. For, first, there are equally important aspects of

---

[7] *Frege*, p. 488.

[8] *Frege*, p. 229. The context rather suggests that Dummett is here giving a Fregean model of what it is to know the sense of a singular term in general (a Proper Name), not just a model of what it is to know the sense of a proper name in the ordinary sense. If this is correct, it is remarkable that Dummett does not observe that at least some singular terms, namely the demonstrative expressions themselves, must have a different kind of sense—i.e. not a matter of their being associated with a criterion for recognizing an object as their bearer—on pain of a vicious regress. In view of this, I hope I am justified in thinking that Dummett would endorse the bipartite account given above, and even the explanation of demonstrative identification in terms of the idea of a 'deciding position' with respect to an object.

our thought which can be incorporated in it only with extreme
artificiality. And, second, those aspects of our thought which it
does take account of can be accommodated by other models.
This model appeals to us because it finds an echo in the imaginings with which we are prone to accompany our reflections
about the spatial world, but it profoundly misrepresents their
significance.

To elaborate the first of these points, we have only to consider
the ease with which our thought extends to microscopic objects,
like atoms, molecules, and the like, which we conceive to be
located in space in just the same way as the larger objects we
can perceive. To apply the model to these microscopic objects
would force us to try to make sense of a possible *encounter* with
one of these objects—if not by ourselves, then by a being either
very much smaller or very much more sharp-sighted than we
are.

It is true that Dummett is prepared to recognize (on Frege's
behalf, so to speak) that many objects of which we speak are not
possible objects of demonstrative identification (however widely
that concept is applied). He supposes that in these cases a merely
analogous model of sense will apply.

... for names of abstract objects of certain kinds, it is possible to
preserve the structure of the account of the sense of a name as consisting in a criterion for identifying its bearer. We have to find, for a given
category of abstract objects, some preferred range of names for them:
e.g., in the case of natural numbers, we might select the numerals
from some particular system of notation; or in the case of abstract
objects forming the range of some functional expression, such as
'the shape of ξ', whose arguments are possible objects of ostension, we
might choose the use of that functional expression completed by a
demonstrative.[9]

It is true, also, that Dummett supposes that the idea of
demonstrative ('ostensive') identification can be extended far
beyond the range of cases in which any talk of a perceptual
encounter would be appropriate, so as to include, for example,
cases in which a person identifies a city or solar system as 'this
city' or 'this solar system', simply by virtue of being in it, and
cases in which a person identifies an object as the one which is

[9] *Frege*, p. 499.

making an impact upon some instrument which can detect its presence.[10]

The objection to this is not that it is unprincipled, for Dummett states a principle (in terms of the object's being a possible cause of change), but rather that it is impossible to see what part ostensive identification, thus understood, has to play in any version of the original model of sense, or thought, connected as the latter was with the idea of *a procedure by which the thought could be determined as true or false.* For, once we have made this extension, being in a position to identify an object demonstratively has no particular connection with being in a position to decide, or to set about deciding, the truth-value of propositions about it. When ostensive identification is thus understood, it ceases to be true that a determination of the truth-value of the thought proceeds via the identification of objects as the referents of the names. So a capacity to decide, or to know what would decide, the truth-value of identifications of the form 'This is *a*' has no particular status in an account of the capacities upon which thought about an object depends.

Taking the verificationist character of the original model seriously enables us to make a motivated decision upon the boundaries of demonstrative identification, but they do not reach far enough for the model to cover all thought about objects. When we abstract the notion of demonstrative identification from a verificationist context, then we can certainly stretch it as far as we like, but the model of sense then rests upon an unexplained primitive notion, whose only justification seems to be that it coincides, more or less, with the propensity of English speakers to use 'this' and 'that'.

A similar difficulty arises when we try to apply the model to our understanding of reference to abstract objects. Dummett considers this point:

. . . we have already noted that certain objects, of a kind most naturally called 'abstract', cannot be considered as possible objects of ostension. For names of such objects, the account of what it is to grasp the sense

---

[10] *Frege*, p. 490-1. (It is extraordinary that Dummett allows detection by means of instruments. After all, this is possible in the case of objects which are also available to ordinary perception. Would Dummett want 'This is Mrs *Y*', said in the presence of an X-ray photograph of a broken leg, to have the same status—that of a 'recognition statement'—as 'This is Mrs *Y*' said in the woman's presence?)

of such a name must be revised so as to consider the ability to recognize an object as the referent of the name as relative to some other standard method of being given or presented with such an object.... We have to find, for a given category of abstract objects, some preferred range of names for them: e.g. in the case of natural numbers we might select the numerals from some particular system of notation ... Thus on such an account, the sense of an arbitrary numerical term v would consist in the criterion for deciding the truth-value of any sentence of the form $\ulcorner v = x \urcorner$, where x is a numeral: the criterion for determining such an identity-statement as true would here play the role which was played, in the case of the name of a concrete object, by the criterion for determining the truth of a recognition statement.[11]

The trouble with this is that we have no idea of a principle upon which we may select the 'preferred' or 'standard' method of being given the object. Once again, in a strictly verificationist context, the principle would be clear: the mode of identification is that in which the subject, given the object in that way, is then able to determine the applicability to the object of the properties that may be ascribed to it. Indeed, it is possible that such a criterion would yield the numerals as providing a privileged mode of identification of the natural numbers, for we can think of mastery of some predicate of numbers, 'ϕ', as being the ability to decide the truth-value of '$\phi(n)$' for arbitrary numeral 'n', and then think of the procedure for determining the truth-value of thoughts about numbers not identified by numerals—thoughts to the effect that $\phi(a)$—as running through two stages issuing respectively in '$a = n$' and '$\phi(n)$'. But the idea cannot be generalized, and this leaves the choice of preferred or standard means simply arbitrary.

There is another difficulty that Dummett does not dwell on, specifically about past-tense propositions such as 'Julius Caesar was bald'. Dummett's model would seem to require that the determination of the truth-value of this proposition proceed— in this case as in others—via the *present* identification of an object as Caesar, followed by establishing of it whether or not it satisfies the past-tense predicate 'was bald'. (The two-stage verification procedure would yield 'This is Caesar' and 'This was bald'.) Thus we are brought to contemplate the possibility of a *current*

---

[11] *Frege*, pp. 489, 499.

identification of something as Caesar, and to think of our idea of Caesar as something that would assist us in effecting this extraordinary discovery. The model forces us to make sense either of our returning to the past, or of Caesar's surviving to the present.[12]

As for the second of the two points I mentioned above: if we restrict our attention to thoughts about concrete objects, there may seem to be something profoundly correct about the idea that someone who entertains a thought about a particular object which he cannot at the time demonstratively identify—say, 'The man who made this table is a good carpenter'—is thereby conceiving of a state of affairs in which his thought homes in upon one particular man—a man with a bank account and a drunken wife, as Russell might have said. Here perhaps we think of the subject as imagining, from a sufficiently lofty perspective, all the men in the universe laid out before him, and appreciating that his thought homes in on just one of them, and that its truth or falsity is determined by whether or not *he* is a good carpenter. And then we might think that he has encapsulated in his imagination just the procedure of verification which Dummett suggests is canonical.

Who can deny, with his hand on his heart, that such imaginings play a part in both his ordinary and his philosophical thinking? But it is not the imaginings that need to be denied; only the interpretation placed upon them. Evidently what is essential for a subject's conception to involve a spatio-temporal object is his conceiving that *somewhere* there exists an object which his thought concerns, and these imaginings are no more than the reflection of this idea. Our thought about the spatial world is, perhaps necessarily, accompanied by models or maps.[13] Most of us have, for example, such a model of the solar system, with the sun in the centre, and the planets revolving at

---

[12] This application of the model is strongly suggested by what Dummett says about the assertion that Frege was a great philosopher (pp. 235 ff.). Although 'questions about whether some aged man really was to be identified as the author of those works would be a distraction and an irrelevance' for us, trying to determine whether the assertion is true (p. 236), Dummett implies that they would *not* be a distraction and an irrelevance in the *direct* verification of the assertion, in terms of which it is understood.

[13] A subject's capacity to think about the spatial world in this way explains his capacity to *perceive* spatially (though I should immediately want to insist on the blind man's capacity to engage in this form of imagery). See, further, 6.3.

differing distances around it. The mistake—one which renders some form of ideal verificationism almost inescapable—is to suppose that, in constructing these models, we are thinking of *the content of a possible experience*. If we conceive our model of the solar system in these terms, then we seem to be forced to agree with Berkeley:

... the question of whether the earth moves or no amounts in reality to no more than this, to wit, whether we have reason to conclude from what hath been observed by astronomers, that if we were placed in such and such circumstances, and such and such a position and distance, both from the earth and sun, we should perceive the former to move among the choir of the planets, and appearing in all respects like one of them ...[14]

In a similar way, we seem to be forced to suppose that the model we might form of the DNA molecule—a model which might certainly be in the background of any quantified or particular thought about its constituents—commits us to the idea of a being for whom such constituents are perceptible. It is not that I want to deny the importance of these imaginings to our reflections, or to deny that they contain important philosophical clues. But what they point to is not ideal verificationism, but the crucial role of our conception of the spatial world in much of our thinking.

4.3 THE GENERALITY CONSTRAINT

In discussing the nature of our conceivings we have little enough to go on, but there is one fundamental constraint that must be observed in all our reflections: I shall call it 'The Generality Constraint'.

It seems to me that there must be a sense in which thoughts are structured. The thought that John is happy has something in common with the thought that Harry is happy, and the thought that John is happy has something in common with the thought that John is sad. This might seem to lead immediately to the idea of a language of thought, and it may be that some of the proponents of that idea intend no more by it than I do here. However, I certainly do not wish to be committed to the idea

---

[14] *Of the Principles of Human Knowledge*, §LVIII; p. 141 in *A New Theory of Vision and Other Writings* (Dent, London, 1910).

that having thoughts involves the subject's using, manipulating, or apprehending *symbols*—which would be entities with non-semantic as well as semantic properties, so that the idea I am trying to explain would amount to the idea that different episodes of thinking can involve the same symbols, identified by their semantic and non-semantic properties. I should prefer to explain the sense in which thoughts are structured, not in terms of their being composed of several distinct *elements*, but in terms of their being a complex of the exercise of several distinct conceptual *abilities*.[15] Thus someone who thinks that John is happy and that Harry is happy exercises on two occasions the conceptual ability which we call 'possessing the concept of happiness'. And similarly someone who thinks that John is happy and that John is sad exercises on two occasions a single ability, the ability to think of, or think about, John.[16]

Although I think the cases are quite different (for reasons I shall give shortly), we can shed some light on what it means to see a thought as the result of a complex of abilities by appealing to what is meant when we say that the understanding of a sentence is the result of a complex of abilities. When we say that a subject's understanding of a sentence, 'Fa', is the result of two abilities (his understanding of 'a', and his understanding of 'F'), we commit ourselves to certain predictions as to which other sentences the subject will be able to understand; furthermore, we commit ourselves to there being a common, though partial, explanation of his understanding of several different sentences. If we hold that the subject's understanding of 'Fa' and his understanding of 'Gb' are structured, we are committed to the view that the subject will also be able to understand the sentences 'Fb' and 'Ga'.[17] And we are committed, in addition, to holding that there is a common explanation for the subject's understanding of 'Fa' and 'Ga', and a common explanation for his understanding of 'Fa' and 'Fb'. Each common explanation

---

[15] Cf. P. T. Geach, *Mental Acts* (Routledge and Kegan Paul, London, 1957), especially chs. 5, 14.

[16] When two thought-episodes depend on the *same* ability to think of something, we can say that the thing is thought about *in the same way*; cf. the explanation of Frege's notion of sense in 1.5.

[17] With a proviso about the categorial appropriateness of the predicates to the subjects; but the substantive point is not affected. A similar proviso is needed at various places below.

will centre upon a state—the subject's understanding of '*a*', or his understanding of '*F*'—which originated in a definite way, and which is capable of disappearing (an occurrence which would selectively affect his ability to understand all sentences containing '*a*', or all sentences containing '*F*').

Similar commitments attach to the claim that the thought that *a* is *F* and the thought that *b* is *G* are structured. If we make that claim, then we are obliged to maintain that, if a subject can entertain those thoughts, then there is no conceptual barrier, at least, to his being able to entertain the thought that *a* is *G* or the thought that *b* is *F*. And we are committed in addition to the view that there would be a common partial explanation for a subject's having the thought that *a* is *F* and his having the thought that *a* is *G*: there is a single state whose possession is a necessary condition for the occurrence of both thoughts.

The language case is useful also for illustrating this point: each of the abilities involved in the thought that *a* is *F*, though they are separable, can be exercised only in a (whole) thought—and hence always together with some other conceptual ability. This is the analogue of the fact that the understanding of a word is manifested only in the understanding of sentences, and hence always together with the understanding of other words.[18]

Although the language case yields these useful analogies, there is a crucial difference, which we might put like this: while sentences need not be structured, thoughts are *essentially* structured. Any meaning expressed by a structured sentence could be expressed by an unstructured sentence. (Think of a one-word sentence introduced by stipulation to have such-and-such a meaning.) But it simply is not a possibility for the thought that *a* is *F* to be unstructured—that is, not to be the exercise of two distinct abilities. It is a feature of the thought-content *that John is happy* that to grasp it requires distinguishable skills. In particular, it requires possession of the concept of happiness—

---

[18] Waiving qualifications about one-word sentences. Notice that it follows from the point in the text that it is not sufficient, for the claim that a given thought is structured, that it should admit of separate descriptions on the lines of 'John is thinking of Harry' and 'John is thinking of happiness'. It would follow from the applicability of those descriptions that John has the ability to think of Harry and the ability to think of happiness; but it would not follow that he has separate abilities to think of those things.

knowledge of what it is for a person to be happy; and that is something not tied to this or that particular person's happiness. There simply could not be a person who could entertain the thought that John is happy and the thought that Harry is friendly, but who could not entertain—who was conceptually debarred from entertaining—the thought that John is friendly or the thought that Harry is happy. Someone who thinks that John is happy must, we might say, have the idea of *a happy man*—a situation instantiated in the case of John (he thinks), but in no way tied to John for its instantiation.[19]

This is a point that Strawson emphasized when he wrote:

The idea of a predicate is correlative with that of a range of distinguishable individuals of which the predicate can be significantly, though not necessarily truly, affirmed.[20]

It is perhaps easier to see the point I am making in the sort of context Strawson was concerned with. We should surely be reluctant to assign the content 'I am in pain' to any internal state of a subject unless we were persuaded that the subject possessed an idea of what it is for someone—not necessarily himself—to be in pain, and unless we were persuaded that the internal state in question involved the exercise of this idea.

What we have from Strawson's observation, then, is that any thought which we can interpret as having the content *that a is F* involves the exercise of an ability—knowledge of what it is for something to be *F*—which can be exercised in indefinitely many distinct thoughts, and would be exercised in, for instance, the thought that *b* is *F*. Similarly for the thought that *a* is *G*. And this of course implies the existence of a corresponding kind of ability, the ability to think of a particular object. For there must be a capacity which, when combined with a knowledge of what it is in general for an object to be *F*, yields the ability to entertain the thought that *a* is *F*, or at least a knowledge of what it is, or would be, for *a* to be *F*. And this capacity presumably suffices to yield a knowledge of what it is, or would be, for *a* to be *G*, when

[19] It cannot, therefore, represent any conceptual advance to move to the thought that *some* man is happy—a thought in which the same conceptual ability is exercised in a different thought.

[20] *Individuals*, p. 99.

combined with a knowledge of what it is for an object to be G, for any arbitrary property of being G.[21]

Thus, if a subject can be credited with the thought that a is F, then he must have the conceptual resources for entertaining the thought that a is G, for every property of being G of which he has a conception. This is the condition that I call 'The Generality Constraint'.[22]

Using what I hope is a harmless piece of convenient terminology, I shall speak of the Ideas a subject has, of this or that particular object, on the model of the way we speak of the concepts a subject has, of this or that property.[23] And I shall allow myself to say that this or that particular thought-episode comprises such-and-such an Idea of an object, as well as such-and-such a concept. This is simply a picturesque way of rephrasing the notion that the thought is a joint exercise of two distinguishable abilities. An Idea of an object, then, is something which makes it possible for a subject to think of an object in a series of indefinitely many thoughts, in each of which he will be thinking of the object in the same way.[24]

It is not difficult to find work which infringes the Generality Constraint.[25] There is a danger of infringing it whenever atten-

[21] We thus see the thought that a is F as lying at the intersection of two series of thoughts: on the one hand, the series of thoughts that a is F, that b is F, that c is F, ..., and, on the other hand, the series of thoughts that a is F, that a is G, that a is H, ...

[22] Even readers not persuaded that *any* system of thought must conform to the Generality Constraint may be prepared to admit that the system of thought we possess— the system that underlies our use of language—does conform to it. (It is one of the fundamental differences between human thought and the information-processing that takes place in our brains that the Generality Constraint applies to the former but not the latter. When we attribute to the brain computations whereby it localizes the sounds we hear, we *ipso facto* ascribe to it representations of the speed of sound and of the distance between the ears, without any commitment to the idea that it should be able to represent the speed of light or the distance between anything else.)

[23] The terminology is borrowed from Geach (see *Mental Acts*, pp. 53 ff.). What are here called 'concepts' will also sometimes be called 'Ideas'. I capitalize the initial letter as a reminder that we are dealing with a technical use of the term.

[24] We cannot *equate* an Idea (a particular person's capacity) with a Fregean sense, since the latter is supposed to exist objectively (independently of anyone's grasp of it). But there is a very close relation between them. Two people exercising their (numerically different) Ideas of an object may thereby 'grasp' the same Fregean sense. What this means is that they may think of the object in the same way. (And the way of thinking would be available even if no one ever thought of the object in that way.)

[25] Note that it is a merit of Dummett's model of sense that it clearly conforms to the Generality Constraint. (See, e.g., *Frege*, p. 238: '... to give an account of the sense expressed by such a phrase as "the author of these works" must be to give a uniform

tion is focused exclusively upon the question 'What makes it the case that a person's *belief* is about such and such an object?' For example, Keith S. Donnellan has proposed an answer to that question along these lines: a belief state naturally expressed in the words '*a* is *F*' is about the object *x* if and only if *x* is the object causally responsible—in an appropriate way—for this belief of the subject's that something satisfies '*F*'.[26] Presumably a thought expressive of this belief state would also be about the object the belief is about; and this might clearly yield a violation of Russell's Principle, interpreted as requiring discriminating knowledge. However, if we take Donnellan's line, we shall have treated only of a very restricted class of thoughts, namely those expressive of beliefs; and this in itself is an infringement of the Generality Constraint. Whenever we consider putative counter-examples to Russell's Principle, we must remember that we are concerned not with a single thought, still less with a single belief, but with an Idea of an object which is to be capable of yielding indefinitely many thoughts about it, entertained in other modes than as expressive of belief.[27]

Perhaps it ought to be conceded that the Generality Constraint is an ideal, to which our actual system of thoughts only approximately conforms. But the possibility of vagueness and indeterminacy is not important for present purposes.

4.4 THE FUNDAMENTAL LEVEL OF THOUGHT

We may begin our search for a non-verificationist defence of Russell's Principle, truistically enough, with the idea that, in order for a subject to be credited with the thought that *p*, he must know what it is for it to be the case that *p*. This, like the unrestricted version of Russell's Principle with which we began,

---

means by which the contribution of that phrase to the determination of the truth-conditions of a sentence in which it occurs can be construed. This will be ... to fix some route to the determination of the truth-value of any such sentence as in some way preferred ...')

[26] See 'Proper Names and Identifying Descriptions'.

[27] Thoughts not expressive of belief are particularly evident in prudential or moral reasoning. Consider, for instance, a situation in which one contemplates the state of affairs of so-and-so's going around in ignorance of such-and-such, and realizes that one cannot stand the idea. It is worth remembering also that Russell's Principle would apply to desire: one cannot desire that *a* be *F* unless one has a way of distinguishing *a* from all other things.

is a form of words which, perhaps, no one will deny; the difficulty, as Dummett has remarked on many occasions,[28] is to give
any substance to the notion of knowing what it is for a proposition to be true, when this is not to be equated with an ability
to determine whether or not it is true. However, some substance
it must have, if the requirement of discriminating knowledge is
to be justified outside a verificationist framework. I should
explain at the outset that I am quite unable to give a general
account of this notion. (Even if I could, such an account would
involve us at once in an extensive discussion of the most fundamental aspects of the philosophy of language.) My strategy,
rather, will be this: to make as precise as possible what notion of
knowing what it is for a proposition to be true one is committed
to by a denial of Russell's Principle; when this commitment is
laid bare, I hope it will seem very unattractive, since it appears
to involve the idea that there may be no difference, in respect of
what they can do, between a thinker who knows what it is for
some proposition to be true, and one who does not.

With the Generality Constraint in mind, we may take a small
step from our truistic starting-point, and say that in the case of
a proposition of the form 'a is F', knowledge of what it is for it
to be true must be the result of two pieces of knowledge, one of
which can be equated with an Idea of an object, and the other
with an Idea of a property, or more familiarly, a concept. I now
want to explain—initially quite independently of Russell's Principle—what I take an Idea of an object to involve.

An Idea of an object is part of a conception of a world of such
objects, distinguished from one another in certain fundamental
ways. For every kind of object, there is a general answer to the
question 'What makes it the case that there are two objects of
this kind rather than one (or three rather than two)?' For
example, we may say that shades of colour are distinguished
from one another by their phenomenal properties, that shapes
are distinguished from one another by their geometrical properties, that sets are differentiated from one another by their
possessing different members, that numbers are differentiated

---

[28] See, e.g., 'What is a Theory of Meaning?', in Samuel Guttenplan, ed., *Mind and
Language* (Clarendon Press, Oxford, 1975), pp. 97-138; and 'What is a Theory of
Meaning?' (II), in Gareth Evans and John McDowell, eds., *Truth and Meaning*, pp. 67-
137.

from one another by their position in an infinite ordering, and that chess positions are distinguished from one another by the positions of pieces upon the board. There cannot be two indistinguishable shades of colour, two different shapes with the same geometrical properties, two numbers with the same position in the ordering, two sets with the same members, or two chess positions with the same arrangement of pieces.

In the case of temporal objects—objects which exist in time and which change—we must replace the absolute notion of what differentiates an object from others with the notion of what differentiates an object from others *at a time*. It is tempting to say of objects which exist in space that what differentiates them from others at a time is their occupancy of a particular spatial position at that time. But this is not quite right, since although two *G*s may not be able to share a position at a time, a *G* may be able to share a position with a thing of a different kind: for instance a statue and a piece of clay.[29] The answer to the question what differentiates a statue from every other thing at a time is given by citing (i) the position which it occupies at that time and (ii) the fact that it is a statue.

For any object whatever, then, there is what may be called *the fundamental ground of difference* of that object (at a time). This will be a specific answer to the question 'What differentiates that object from others?', of the kind appropriate to objects of that sort. For example, the fundamental ground of difference of the number *three* is being the third number in the series of numbers; the fundamental ground of difference of the shape *square* is having four equal sides joined at right angles; and so on.

Let us say that one has *a fundamental Idea* of an object if one thinks of it as the possessor of the fundamental ground of difference which it in fact possesses. (Such an Idea constitutes, by definition, distinguishing knowledge of the object, since the object is differentiated from all other objects by this fact.) Evidently, we do very often employ such fundamental Ideas of objects in our thinking about them,[30] but even when we do not,

[29] See David Wiggins, 'On Being in the Same Place at the Same Time', *Philosophical Review* lxxvii (1968), 90–5.

[30] This is especially clear with abstract objects. (Proper names of abstract objects are typically such that understanding them requires a fundamental Idea of the referent; this is not so with proper names of material objects.)

I want to suggest that such Ideas play a very central role in our thinking.

It seems to me that the idea of how objects of a given kind, Gs, are distinguished from each other and from all other things must enter our every conception of a state of affairs involving a G. For there is no thought about objects of a certain kind which does not presuppose the idea of *one* object of that kind, and the idea of one object of that kind must employ a general conception of the ways in which objects of that kind are differentiated from one another and from all other things. A conception of a state of affairs involving a G is such in virtue of its being a conception of a state of affairs involving an object conceived to be distinguished from other objects by some fundamental ground of difference appropriate to Gs, and hence as distinguishable, or differentiable, by citing a fact of this kind. Thus the conception of a G's being F is the conception of a state of affairs involving an F thing which is differentiated from all other objects by a ground of difference appropriate to Gs. Consequently, the proposition that some G is F is a proposition which is conceived to be such that it would be rendered true by the existence of just such a state of affairs. That is to say, the proposition that some G is F is conceived to be such that it would be rendered true by the truth of some proposition of the form $\ulcorner \delta$ is $F \urcorner$, where δ is a fundamental Idea of a G.[31] The thought that some G is F just is the thought that some singular proposition of this kind is true.

I am not here merely giving expression to the idea that an existential statement is conceived to be true in virtue of the truth of some singular proposition. Rather, I am saying that we conceive the existential statement 'Some G is F' to be true in virtue of the truth of a member of a *special sub-class* of singular propositions, namely, those entertainable with the use of a *fundamental Idea* of a G. I do not mean that the general statement is understood as equivalent to a disjunction of the members of this sub-class, since one can obviously grasp the thought that

---

[31] I shall quite generally use 'δ' as schematic for fundamental Ideas of objects. Talk of an Idea δ *occurring* in a proposition of the form $\ulcorner \delta$ is $F \urcorner$ must be understood as a mere *façon de parler;* more strictly, we should think of the Idea as a capacity exercised (by a particular individual: see n. 24 above) in a thought—the entertaining of a proposition (entertainable also by other individuals)—to the effect that the object of the Idea is F. Corner-quotes will be used throughout as a reminder of this.

some G is F without having fundamental Ideas of all the Gs that there are. One's grasp of the relevant series of particular-propositions[32] is constituted, not by an ability to enumerate them, but by one's general conception of the way in which Gs are distinguished from one another, and from all other things.

If this is correct, then we can say very generally what kind of knowledge is required for possession of a concept of being F, applicable to Gs: it is knowledge which, when conjoined with that knowledge which constitutes possession of a fundamental Idea, $\delta*$, of a particular G, yields knowledge of what it is for the proposition $\ulcorner\delta* \text{ is } F\urcorner$ to be true. I shall call this, slightly inaccurately, knowledge of what it is for an arbitrary proposition of the form $\ulcorner\delta \text{ is } F\urcorner$ to be true. What this term brings out is something I have attempted to capture from the very beginning: the idea people express by saying that one cannot possess the concept of being F, and be able, for example, to entertain the thought that some G is F, without knowing what it is for a particular G to be F. Although such conceptual knowledge relates in the first instance to a specific class of particular-propositions about Gs—propositions involving fundamental Ideas of Gs—it suffices, nevertheless, for a grasp of other thoughts involving the exercise of the concept, because they are understood in such a way that they are determined as true or not true by the truth of propositions of that specific class.

We have seen how this is so in the case of quantificational propositions about Gs. And we can appreciate how the same point applies in the case of particular-thoughts about Gs which do not involve fundamental Ideas of them—and which, therefore, involve *non-fundamental Ideas* of them. Such a thought must equally involve the idea of the fundamental ground of difference of Gs. After all, it too comprises the idea of a G's being F, and so it too must be conceived to be true (if it is true) in virtue of the truth of some proposition of the form $\ulcorner\delta \text{ is } F\urcorner$.

What distinguishes a particular-proposition, say $\ulcorner a \text{ is } F\urcorner$, involving a non-fundamental Idea-of-an-object, a, from the

---

[32] Particular-propositions are propositions the specification of whose content involves the use of a singular term (e.g. the thought that Winston Churchill is F, which might be called, following Goodman, a Winston-Churchill-representation: see *Languages of Art* (OUP, London, 1969), ch. 1). 'Particular-thoughts', below, is to be understood analogously (in the light of n. 31 above).

merely existential proposition $\ulcorner$Some G is $F\urcorner$ is this: as a matter of the nature of the thought-elements involved, there is at most one proposition of the form $\ulcorner\delta$ is $F\urcorner$ whose truth is capable, as things stand, of making the particular-proposition true.[33] Which fundamental proposition is uniquely relevant to the truth of the particular-proposition must be determined in advance by the Idea a: the Idea a will determine some proposition $\ulcorner\delta^*$ is $F\urcorner$ as uniquely relevant to the truth of the proposition $\ulcorner a$ is $F\urcorner$ in virtue of the fact that $\ulcorner\delta^* = a\urcorner$ is the only true proposition of the form $\ulcorner\delta = a\urcorner$. Evidently a subject cannot be credited with such an Idea a unless he knows what it is for a proposition of the form $\ulcorner\delta = a\urcorner$ to be true. So we can take the subject's Idea-of-the-object, a, to consist in his knowledge of what it is for an arbitrary proposition of the form $\ulcorner\delta = a\urcorner$ to be true.

Such knowledge is formally of the same kind as the knowledge in which possession of a concept of a property of Gs consists, but it does not begin to follow that a non-fundamental Idea of an object can be regarded as always embodying the concept of some property—not, at any rate, if we wish to argue that properties are always graspable, whether or not anything falls under them.[34]

So far, I have been concentrating upon the simpler case of non-temporal objects. For spatio-temporal objects, we must think in terms of time-relative fundamental Ideas and time-relative properties, which I shall indicate, respectively, in the style δ_t and F_t. We shall surely want to say that, *in the first instance*, possessing a concept of the property of being F_t is knowing what it is for arbitrary propositions of the form $\ulcorner\delta_t[\text{is}]F_t\urcorner$ to be true.[35] (It is these propositions which may be

---

[33] When I say 'as a matter of the nature of the thought-elements involved', I mean to give expression to the view that the particular-thought and the existential thought are different in *content*: the thought that some G is F does not become a particular-thought simply because there happens to be only one G. The point of the qualification 'as things stand' is this. We are characterizing a purely formal difference between thoughts which will allow the thought that Julius is F (see 1.7, 1.8, 2.3) to be a particular-thought. If the object of the Idea δ^* invented the zip, then only the truth of the proposition $\ulcorner\delta^*$ is $F\urcorner$ is capable, as things stand, of making it true that Julius is F (though of course, since many individuals might have invented the zip, there are many propositions of the form $\ulcorner\delta$ is $F\urcorner$ that might, in some absolute sense, have made it true that Julius is F).

[34] This conception of properties rules out counting as a property what is ascribed by the concept-expression '$\xi = a$', where 'a' is a Russellian singular term. These remarks look ahead to what I shall say (chapter 8) about knowledge of what it is for $\ulcorner\delta = a\urcorner$ to be true based upon a recognitional capacity for an object.

[35] The square brackets indicate that the verb is tenseless.

regarded as 'barely true' in Dummett's sense.) In the case of a proposition of the form $\ulcorner \delta_{t'}$ [is] $F_t \urcorner$, where $t' \neq t$, we can discern some articulation in what makes it true—some structure in the knowledge of what it is for it to be true. For this knowledge plainly rests upon the subject's knowledge of the identity-conditions of the object through time, as well as his knowledge of what it is for an object to possess the property. Thus we may say that such a proposition is true in virtue of the joint truth of some pair of propositions of the forms $\ulcorner \delta_t = \delta'_{t'} \urcorner$ and $\ulcorner \delta_t$ [is] $F_t \urcorner$, and that it is his general knowledge of the identity-conditions of such objects through time that constitutes his knowledge of what it is for propositions of the first of these two forms to be true.

Non-fundamental Ideas of objects must be considered in a similar light. The subject will know what it is for $\ulcorner a$ [is] $F_t \urcorner$ to be true for arbitrary t because he knows what it is for $\ulcorner \delta_t = a \urcorner$ to be true for arbitrary t. We may wish to see *this* knowledge as articulated in its turn, with the subject knowing, in the first instance, what it is for propositions of the form $\ulcorner \delta_{t'} = a \urcorner$ to be true, for some particular t', and using his knowledge of the identity-conditions of the object concerned to make the link with t. In this case, we shall see the proposition $\ulcorner a$ [is] $F_t \urcorner$ as true in virtue of the truth of three propositions, of the forms $\ulcorner \delta'_{t'} = a \urcorner$, $\ulcorner \delta'_{t'} = \delta_t \urcorner$, and $\ulcorner \delta_t$ [is] $F_t \urcorner$.) This will certainly be the case if, for example, the subject distinguishes the object by means of the property of being $\phi_{t'}$.

This account of what constitutes a non-fundamental Idea of an object advances us very little. The problematic idea of knowing what it is for a proposition to be true remains unclarified. (By the same token, there is little here with which the opponent of Russell's Principle is required to disagree.) But the proposal does at least enable us to see how our thinking can conform to the Generality Constraint. When our Idea of an object is a *fundamental Idea*, the knowledge which constitutes our possession of the concept of being F can apply directly, to yield a knowledge of what it is for the proposition $\ulcorner \delta^* $ is $F \urcorner$ to be true. When our Idea of an object is of a *non-fundamental* kind, we know what it is for a proposition of the form $\ulcorner a$ is $F \urcorner$ to be true, because we know that it is true (if it is) in virtue of the truth of some pair of propositions of the forms $\ulcorner \delta = a \urcorner$ and $\ulcorner \delta$ is $F \urcorner$; and our Idea of the object and our concept of the property constitute, respectively, knowledge of what it is for propositions of these forms to be true. Provided a subject knows what it is for identifications like $\ulcorner\delta = a\urcorner$ to be true, a link is set up between his Idea, a, and his entire repertoire of conceptual knowledge, and he will be able to grasp as many propositions of the form $\ulcorner a$ is $F\urcorner$ as he has concepts of being F. His Ideas make contact with his concepts, so to speak, at the fundamental level, and hence there is no need, or possibility, of accounting for his knowledge of what it is for propositions about the object to be true one by one. (We have seen how this is true of tensed propositions.) But, correlatively, it will not be possible to pick upon this or that proposition, $\ulcorner a$ is $F\urcorner$ or $\ulcorner a$ is $F'\urcorner$, and claim that the subject knows what it is for *this* proposition to be true, perhaps because he seems to be responsive, or to have been responsive, to evidence germane to its truth, while conceding that he does not have a clue about what would make an arbitrary identification $\ulcorner\delta = a\urcorner$ true.

4.5 COMPARISON WITH VERIFICATIONISM

I have attempted to emphasize the importance, to *all* our thoughts about Gs, of a level of thought which is fundamental in a strict sense: every thought about Gs which is not of this level is conceived to be made true by the truth of thoughts which are of this level. In so doing, I have captured, within a realistic framework, some of the structure of the verificationist models of thought which we considered earlier (4.2). Perhaps what I have said can thereby inherit some of the appeal which those models had.[36] Corresponding to the distinction between particular-thoughts which do not involve a criterion of identification (demonstrative thoughts) and particular-thoughts which do, we have the distinction between thoughts which involve fundamental Ideas of objects and thoughts which do not. And this correspondence is more than just structural. It is open to us to

---

[36] Indeed Dummett almost certainly had this model in mind, but dismissed it because of the obscurity of the notion of knowing what it is for propositions of the forms $\ulcorner\delta = a\urcorner$ and $\ulcorner\delta$ is $F\urcorner$ to be true. See *Frege*, p. 231: 'If we do not invoke this thesis [viz. that for every true statement, there is something which we could know and which, if we knew it, would establish conclusively for us the truth of the statement], then we should be forced to say something like: To grasp the sense of a name is to understand what has to be the case, for any given object, for it to be the bearer of that name; and to grasp the sense of a predicate is to know what has to be the case, for any given object, for the predicate to apply to it. The trouble with this formulation is that we can give little content to the notion of possessing knowledge of this kind unless it be verbalizable knowledge...'

introduce a notion of canonical verification, such that a canonical verification of a proposition proceeds by establishing the fundamental propositions in whose truth the truth of the given proposition is understood to consist. For example, an existential proposition, $\ulcorner$Some G is $F\urcorner$, would be canonically verified by the demonstration of the truth of some instance of the form $\ulcorner\delta$ is $F\urcorner$. (A verification which proceeded by demonstrating that the negation of the proposition leads to a contradiction would not be canonical.) Equally, a canonical verification of a non-fundamental particular-thought, $\ulcorner a$ is $F\urcorner$, would involve establishing the truth of a pair of propositions of the forms $\ulcorner\delta = a\urcorner$ and $\ulcorner\delta$ is $F\urcorner$, and would therefore have a component lacking in the canonical verification of a particular-thought involving a fundamental Idea.

I have not taken as a primitive the notion of *demonstrative* identification (compare 4.2), or the notion of any other preferred mode of identification. It remains something of an open question how our intuitive notion of demonstrative identification fits into the picture, and so also where its boundaries should properly be regarded as falling. (This is the subject-matter of chapter 6.)[37]

Equally, the idea of a present confrontation with an aged Frege need not be taken to play a role in our grasp of the thought that Frege was a great philosopher (compare 4.2). The non-fundamental Idea we have of Frege, we may suppose, equips us to know what it is for propositions of the form $\ulcorner\delta_t = \text{Frege}\urcorner$ to be true (where t is earlier than now), and hence, to know what it is for propositions of the form $\ulcorner\text{Frege [is]} F_t\urcorner$ to be true. The truth of a proposition of the form $\ulcorner\delta_{\text{now}} = \text{Frege}\urcorner$ need play no part (unless, of course, the non-fundamental proposition in question is of the form $\ulcorner\text{Frege [is]} F_{\text{now}}\urcorner$).

Finally, we can perhaps appreciate the significance of those

---

[37] Non-reliance on the notion of demonstrative identification pays off when we apply the model to abstract objects. When Dummett comes to think about numbers, he asks himself (on Frege's behalf) what way of thinking about a number comes closest to being 'presented with' it, in order to find a preferred mode of identification. He chooses thinking about the number as the nth in the series of numbers—i.e. the way of thinking that is involved in the grasp of a specification of a number via a numeral. This corresponds with my idea of a fundamental identification of a number; but my idea is not based upon a possibly incoherent speculation about what it would be like to be 'presented with' a number.

pervasive imaginings in connection with our thought about the spatio-temporal world (see 4.2). When we represent material objects in the imagination, we *ipso facto* represent them as located and differentiated in space. We imagine the carpenter, in the example of 4.2, as located at a particular position in space, though, of course, there is no particular position we imagine him as having. Such representations of objects in the imagination are just like *arbitrary* fundamental Ideas (to be understood on the model of the arbitrary names of certain formal systems).

4.6 THE COUNTER-EXAMPLES

It will not be difficult to see, on this account, what unifies the various situations in which a person is supposed to have distinguishing or identifying knowledge of a thing (see 4.1). In chapter 6, I shall try to make clear how demonstrative identification relates to the fundamental identification of material objects. The two other sorts of situation, in which a subject can recognize an object and in which he can cite some fact uniquely true of the object, can both be regarded as different species of non-fundamental identification of an object—of knowledge of what it is for an arbitrary proposition of the form $\ulcorner \delta = a \urcorner$ to be true. The first kind of knowledge must be regarded as involving (but not as constituting—see chapter 8) a practical capacity to decide the truth of propositions of the form $\ulcorner \delta = a \urcorner$. (A realist anyway must acknowledge this sort of thing as a species of knowing what it is for a proposition to be true in cases such as the possession of the concept of red, or magenta.) It will therefore constitute an (adequate) Idea of an object—a capacity to think of it—provided the subject is disposed to identify just one object as that object. As for the other kind of case: provided that being ϕ is a property of which the subject has a conception, then, by our account of what it is for him to have such a conception, he does know what it is for an arbitrary proposition of the form $\ulcorner \delta$ is $\phi \urcorner$ to be true; and if not more than one object can be ϕ, he thereby knows what it is for an arbitrary proposition of the form $\ulcorner \delta$ is the $\phi \urcorner$ to be true.[38]

The question whether there are other sorts of non-fundamental Ideas brings us back to Russell's Principle.

---

[38] This needs to be generalized to cover the possibility of tensing in the predicate.

Let us return to the case of the subject supposedly thinking about a steel ball he encountered many years earlier, and which he can no longer distinguish. We have reduced the question whether he has an adequate Idea of the ball to this: can he be said to know what it is for an arbitrary proposition of the form $\ulcorner\delta = \text{that ball}\urcorner$ to be true? Thus we envisage him contemplating some object (a ball) as the occupant, at a given time, of some position in space; and we envisage him raising the question, of an object thus fundamentally identified, 'Is this ball *that* ball?' Does he really know what it would be for the answer to this question to be 'Yes', or for it to be 'No'? His Idea corresponding to 'that ball'—if he has one—does contain some 'descriptive' ingredients: he can exploit the fact that he encountered the ball on an occasion when it was rotating, etc. But *ex hypothesi* these elements do not exhaust his Idea, since they fail to distinguish between the two balls, while his (supposed) Idea does not. So let us suppose that our subject is satisfied that this ball is ϕ, for any predicate 'ϕ' that expresses one of those elements. Now supposedly there remains for him the further question 'Is this ball that ball?' Of course he cannot decide whether or not this ball is that ball, but the idea is that he can, for example, *suppose* that it is. But what is it that he supposes?[39]

The reason we find a certain amount of difficulty with this question is that our subject's supposed Idea of that ball is completely independent, not only from any possible experience, but also from everything else in his conceptual repertoire. There is no question of his recognizing the ball; and there is nothing else he can do which will show that his thought is really about one of the two balls (about *that* ball), rather than about the other. The supposed thought—the supposed surplus over the *ex hypothesi* non-individuating descriptive thought—is apparently not connected to anything.

R. M. Chisholm has argued that if a human brain were divided, and the parts placed in different bodies in such a way as to yield two persons, the original person would survive as *one* of the resulting persons, even though it would be quite impossible

---

[39] It is a point that I have already made (4.1), but one which is worth repeating here, that our subject will certainly not *take* himself to have a conception of the kind that is being attributed to him; that he will not take it to be a determinate further question which ball is *that* ball, on the discovery that there are the two balls meeting all the conditions which he can think of laying down.

for anyone to tell which, since no fact of the kind normally relevant to judgements of identity can discriminate between the two resulting persons.[40] Chisholm takes himself to be able to grasp the supposition '*This* one, not that one, is the original person'. I mention this case not merely because it bears a striking resemblance to the one we are considering, but also because it seems to be a very good example of a spurious or illusory supposition. It reminds us of the need to place *some* empirical restrictions upon what it is to grasp a supposition, or to know what would make it true, however difficult they may be to formulate. A philosopher who is content to believe that the notion of knowing what it is for a proposition to be true is purely formal and insubstantial is powerless in the face of the most arrant nonsense. To avoid this, we must be prepared to raise the question 'What is the difference between someone who has and someone who has not the capacity to make this supposition?'[41]

Now it is true that those who wish to credit our subject with the capacity to make the supposition that this ball is that ball do have an answer to this question (unlike Chisholm with the corresponding question about his supposition). They will say that the subject's knowledge of what it would be for his supposition to be true is, at least partly, constituted by the fact that his Idea is causally derived from an encounter with a particular ball. But the fact that they say this surely makes their case worse rather than better. For the suggestion entirely subverts the very logic or grammar of the concept of knowing what it is for it to be true that *p* (or for an object to be *F*). The concept is one of a *capacity*, and the proof of its being possessed at a given time must surely reside in facts about what the subject can or cannot do at that time.[42]

---

[40] 'Identity Through Time', in Howard E. Kiefer and Milton K. Munitz, eds., *Language, Belief, and Metaphysics* (SUNY Press, Albany, N.Y., 1970), pp. 163–82; for an especially clear expression, see 'Reply to Strawson's Comments', in the same volume, at pp. 188–9.

[41] There must be some difference between knowing the meaning of an expression and not knowing it (a difference which is made by *learning* the meaning of the expression).

[42] Contrast Devitt, 'Singular Terms', p. 205: '... identification depends not on anything [the speaker] *could or would do* but on what he *did* ...' (Remember the Generality Constraint. Our subject has to be able to entertain such thoughts as that that ball was sold for scrap or that that ball is now in Czechoslovakia; not merely the thoughts which encourage adherents of the Photograph Model, such as the thought that that ball was shiny.)

This answer reminds us of another divergence from Chisholm's case. It is a singular aspect of the doctrine we are considering that its proponents are prepared to say quite simply what in fact would make the supposition $\ulcorner \delta^* = \text{that ball}\urcorner$ true—namely, that δ^* should be a fundamental Idea of that object from which the subject's current conception ('that ball') causally derives. When we concentrate upon this aspect of the doctrine, the case seems much less mysterious than Chisholm's. (Chisholm is able to offer no parallel explanation, but must suppose the identity judgement barely true.) We see perfectly well why there is, in the situation described, one and only one object which *could* correctly be identified as 'that ball'. But then the difficulty emerges at another place: how can we suggest that the subject knows what it is for the identification $\ulcorner \delta^* = \text{that ball}\urcorner$ to be true, when he has not an inkling of the kind of consideration that in fact would *make* it true? (It is an assumption of the case that the subject would not have any notion of appealing to these causal considerations; otherwise the case ceases to be a counter-example to Russell's Principle.)[43]

The contradiction here is not immediate. It is consistent to hold, for example, that the proposition 'This is water' is true in virtue of the truth of 'This is H_2O', without being forced to equate someone's Idea 'water' with his Idea 'H_2O'. But this kind of situation can arise only because there is a characterization of the one proposition which explains how it is capable of being true *in virtue of* the other. We give the explanation by explaining that the thought that something is water is the thought that it is of the same character as the stuff which is found in lakes, rivers, and seas, and which falls as rain. That is, the thought that this is water involves the thought that there is some fundamental characterization of *this* which also applies to the stuff cited. 'H_2O' is then the instantiation which makes this existential thought true. But I cannot see how we can, in a parallel way, permit our subject's supposed thought to be one which is rendered true by the truth of some proposition $\ulcorner \delta^* = \text{the}$ object from which the subject's current conception causally derives$\urcorner$. The idea of the relevant causal connections, *ex hypothesi*, does not enter into the subject's thinking in the way in which the idea of a fundamental characterization of the stuff in ques-

---

[43] It is surely correct to assume that thinkers (among whom we have to include very young children) will not in general resort to this way of identifying the object of their thought. I shall make this assumption throughout the book.

tion enters into the thinking of someone who judges that something is water.

Anyone who has followed recent work in the philosophy of
language will know that the question 'What does knowledge of
the truth-conditions of a proposition amount to?' is the subject
of a lively, and as yet quite unresolved, debate. The verificationist gives us a clear answer, but it is one that we do not want,
for we take ourselves to have a grasp of the truth-conditions of
certain propositions which are 'verification-transcendent'. Now
we can make a rough division among the concepts which are
problematic from the verificationist point of view. On the one
hand, there are the concepts that make up our ordinary realistic
conception of space, time, and matter. On the other hand, there
are the concepts which are embedded in specific empirical
theories. But it seems to me that neither of these classes of
concepts yields a model to be followed by the opponents of
Russell's Principle. Granting that verificationism has failed to
deal satisfactorily with these concepts, and that it is difficult to
provide a different substantial characterization of what our
possession of them amounts to, it would be quite superficial to
conclude from this that in the conceptual domain anything
goes—that the search for empirical constraints on the attribution of this or that conceptual capacity simply can be abandoned. If the opponents of Russell's Principle are to draw any
comfort from these considerations, they must attempt to show
some connection or analogy between the conceptions they wish
to allow, and one or other of the sorts of conceptual capacity
concerning which, in the general dispute, it has seemed that we
must reconcile ourselves somehow to verification-transcend-
ence. And this they surely cannot do.

Our subject's supposed knowledge of which ball is in question
cannot be understood on the model of our grasp of theoretical
concepts, for the simple reason that in his case there is no theory.
There is no set of interconnected propositions which connect his
supposed Idea to other members of a set of theoretical concepts,
and which face the tribunal of experience together.[44] No one
could suggest that the subject had to learn, or at least come to
understand, a theory in order to have his supposed Idea. What
would this theory be? What is it supposed to explain?

[44] Cf. W. V. Quine, 'Epistemology Naturalized', in *Ontological Relativity and Other
Essays* (Columbia U.P., New York, 1969), pp. 69–90, at p. 89.

Nor is there a model for the subject's supposed knowledge in our admittedly verification-transcendent grasp of the fundamental concepts that make up our realistic conception of space, time, and matter. If and when the realist justifies his view that we can coherently be supposed to possess such a conception, it will not be by his simply freeing the ascription of conceptual capacities from all empirical constraints, but rather, by the construction of a transcendental argument, demonstrating how the idea of an objectively existing world—which is a precondition of the possibility of experience—can be possessed only by someone whose conception of space, time, and matter has a verification-transcendent character. Such considerations will surely be very remote from the case of our subject allegedly thinking about the ball.

So the case must stand on its own; it cannot be seen as an instance of some general phenomenon whose existence is undeniable. To accept it as a case of knowing what it is for a proposition to be true seems to be inconsistent, not just with this or that particular theory of what it is to have such knowledge, but with any theory which places substantial restrictions, in terms of what a subject must be *able* to do, upon the use of that notion. The kind of consideration which must be regarded, by defenders of the case, as sufficient for possessing such knowledge is simply not a restriction of the right kind.[45]

Insistence on such cases involves an overthrow of our notion of what it is to possess a concept, and of what it is to know the truth-conditions of a proposition, which would be difficult to accept even if it were recommended by very weighty considerations. It is surely out of the question when it rests upon no more than 'what we would say' in the description of certain cases.

I have not denied that it would be natural to say that our subject 'had' one of the balls 'in mind', or that he 'meant' one of the balls. It is our next task to find out why this should be so.[46] Execution of this task will also enable me to explain why I do not feel that Russell's Principle allows us to deal with a thought on the model of thought by description, simply on the ground that the subject's knowledge of which thing is in question rests upon his capacity to cite individuating facts.

I hope I have said enough to explain why I wish to adhere to

[45] See n. 42, and associated text, above.
[46] See 5.3.

Russell's Principle. Even if the argument has not carried conviction, it should be of interest to see, in what follows, how few
of the fundamentally correct doctrines about reference which
have been based on the rejection of Russell's Principle have
needed to be so based.

Chapter 5

Information, Belief, and Thought

5.1 INFORMATION-BASED THOUGHTS: INTRODUCTORY

Our particular-thoughts are very often based upon information which we have about the world. We take ourselves to be informed, in whatever way, of the existence of such-and-such an object, and we think or speculate about it. A thought of the kind with which I am concerned is governed by a conception of its object which is the result neither of fancy (see chapter 10) nor of linguistic stipulation (as in the case of 'Julius': 1.7, 1.8, 2.3), but rather is the result of a belief about how the world is which the subject has because he has received information (or misinformation)[1] from the object.

When I speak of a subject's thinking being governed by a conception of its object, I mean that the way he entertains the thoughts (as probable, improbable, true, or false) and the significance he attaches to them (the consequences he is prepared to draw from them) are determined by the content of this conception. Thus, to take a very central example, a person may be thinking of an object which he can perceive—for example, a black and white cat sleeping on a mat. Assuming that we are dealing with a pure case for the moment, so that the subject does not recognize the cat, and has no information about it other than that which he is acquiring by current perception, the conception governing his thought will be determined simply by the content of his perception. For instance, he will be able to entertain the thought that the cat is ginger, but he will, of course, grasp it as false; whereas the thought or speculation that the cat is a favourite of Queen Elizabeth will be grasped as having the (probable) consequence that Queen Elizabeth likes black and white cats; and so on. Thus, even when the particular thought concerned is not itself a belief, but is, for example, a

[1] I shall drop this qualification in future; henceforth information includes misinformation.

speculation, or a thought grasped, via speech, as the thought of someone else, nevertheless, the thought-episode will manifest a belief about the world on the subject's part.[2] Since this belief is due to the subject's possessing certain *information*, I shall say that the information 'saturates' the thought, or that the thought is based on the information.

Slightly more precisely, we can say that a bit of information (with the content Fx) is in the controlling conception of a thought involving a subject's Idea of a particular object if and only if the subject's disposition to appreciate and evaluate thoughts involving this Idea as being about an F thing is a causal consequence of the subject's acquisition and retention of this information. Notice that the conception controlling a thought may be very extensive; and that the information does not at all have to be 'in mind' for it to be controlling a thought.[3]

At this point it becomes necessary to say a little about the notion of information.

5.2 THE INFORMATIONAL SYSTEM

When a person perceives something, he receives (or, better, gathers) information about the world.[4] By communicating, he may transmit this information to others. And any piece of information in his possession at a given time may be retained by him until some later time. People are, in short and among other things, gatherers, transmitters and storers of information. These platitudes locate perception, communication, and memory in a system—the informational system—which constitutes the substratum of our cognitive lives.

A traditional epistemologist would have recast these platitudes in terms of the concepts of *sensation* and *belief*. In both sorts of information-acquiring transaction, the subject would have been regarded as receiving data, intrinsically without objective content, into which he was supposed to read the appropriate

[2] This may seem doubtful; it may seem that it is necessary only for one to *have* the perception, not to believe that it is *veridical*. I shall argue in 9.3 that this is not true.

[3] Notice also that the disposition must be assumed not to be conditional on intervening identity discoveries. There are interesting issues here, which I shall not stop to consider. (For instance, after an identity discovery a subject may simply fail to pool the two bits of information in his thinking—although when asked whether the thoughts relate to a single object he will agree that they do.)

[4] See J. J. Gibson, *The Senses Considered as Perceptual Systems* (George Allen and Unwin, London, 1968).

objective significance by means of an (extremely shaky) inference. And in the case of testimony, the inference would have
been taken to proceed to information about the world through
an intermediate stage involving the belief of the informant. This
is not the place to explain and develop the criticism which this
reconstrual has received in recent times. At least as regards
perception, it is now widely realized that the traditional conception gets things impossibly the wrong way round. The only
events that can conceivably be regarded as data for a conscious,
reasoning subject are *seemings*—events, that is, already imbued
with (apparent) objective significance, and with a necessary,
though resistible, propensity to influence our actions. A parallel
reorientation of traditional views about testimony has not yet
taken place, though it is equally necessary, both to a sound
epistemology and to a sound philosophy of language.[5]

In general, it seems to me preferable to take the notion of
being in an informational state with such-and-such content as a primitive
notion for philosophy, rather than to attempt to characterize it
in terms of belief. In the first place, such a characterization
could not be simple, because of a fundamental (almost defining)
property of the states in the informational system, which I shall
call their 'belief-independence': the subject's *being* in an informational state is independent of whether or not he believes that
the state is veridical. It is a well-known fact about perceptual
illusions that it will continue to appear to us as though, say, one
line is longer than the other (in the Müller–Lyer illusion) even
when we are quite sure that it is not. Similarly, it may still seem
to us as though such-and-such an episode took place in the past,
even though we now believe our apparent experience of it to
have been hallucinatory. And our being placed in the appropriate informational state by someone telling us a story does not
depend upon our believing the story to be true.

---

[5] For the analogy between testimony and the senses, see Thomas Reid, *An Inquiry into
the Human Mind*, ed. Timothy Duggan (University of Chicago, 1970), ch. 6; see especially
pp. 240 1. On the importance for epistemology of a proper picture of the role of
testimony, see Wittgenstein, *On Certainty* (Blackwell, Oxford, 1969), *passim*. See also
C. A. J. Coady, 'Testimony and Observation', *American Philosophical Quarterly* x (1973),
149 55. I am aware that the parallel between testimony and the senses needs defence;
and of course there are important differences, notably in respect of the kind of information concerned (the senses yield non-conceptual information, whereas language
embodies conceptual information: on this distinction, see 6.3, 7.4). This is one of the
many places in this book where my position depends upon further work.

The belief-independence of the states of the informational system is not merely a curiosity, not even merely a suggestive curiosity. Upon it depends the whole of representational art, and, connectedly, it is productive of the most subtle and complicated phenomenon which the theory of reference must explain—the conniving use of empty singular terms. (See chapter 10.)

If we wish to define the states which the normal operation of the informational system produces in terms of belief, we shall have to adopt, quite generally, the manœuvre undertaken by several philosophers in the theory of perception, and make the connection via some such phrase as '*prima facie* inclination to believe'.[6] But—and this is the second objection—I cannot help feeling that this gets things the wrong way round. It is as well to reserve 'belief' for the notion of a far more sophisticated cognitive state: one that is connected with (and, in my opinion, defined in terms of) the notion of *judgement*, and so, also, connected with the notion of *reasons*. The operations of the informational system are more primitive. Two of them, after all, we share with animals; and I do not think we can properly understand the mechanism whereby we gain information from others unless we realize that it is already operative at a stage of human intellectual development that pre-dates the applicability of the more sophisticated notion.[7]

We can speak of a certain bit of information being of, or perhaps from, an object, in a sense resembling the way in which we speak of a photograph being of an object. It will be useful to have this sense made precise, both because it is a notion which we shall need, and because it may have become subliminally confused in some quarters with the notions of belief about an object, or thinking about an object, which we want to examine.

The sense in which a photograph is of an object is as follows. A certain mechanism produces things which have a certain informational *content*. I shall suppose for the moment that this content can be specified neutrally, by an open sentence in one or more variables (the number of variables corresponding to the

---

[6] See, e.g., D. M. Armstrong, *A Materialist Theory of the Mind* (Routledge and Kegan Paul, London, 1968), ch. 10.

[7] See Wittgenstein, *On Certainty, passim* (especially §§141, 143, 144, 160).

number of objects in the photograph).[8] Thus if we are concerned with a photograph of a red ball on top of a yellow square, then the content of the photograph can be represented by the open sentence

$$\text{Red}(x) \ \& \ \text{Ball}(x) \ \& \ \text{Yellow}(y) \ \& \ \text{Square}(y) \ \& \ \text{On Top Of}(x,y).[9]$$

The mechanism is a mechanism of information storage, because the properties that figure in the content of its output are (to a degree determined by the accuracy of the mechanism) the properties possessed by the objects which are the input to it. And we can say that the product of such a mechanism is *of* the objects that were the input to the mechanism when the product was produced. Correspondingly, the output is *of* those objects with which we have to compare it in order to judge the accuracy of the mechanism at the time the output was produced. Notice that I have explained the sense in which a photograph is of an object, or objects, without presupposing that a specification of its *content* must make reference to that object, or those objects.[10]

Now this structure can be discerned whenever we have systems capable of reliably producing states with a content which includes a certain predicative component, or not, according to the state of some object. (The structure is of course discernible even if, on some particular occasion, the system malfunctions.) The informational system constituted by several intercommunicating agents is just such a system.

A simple model of a social informational system might be represented diagramatically by Fig. 1. *A*, *B*, and *C* are persons; the left–right dimension stands for the temporal dimension; unbroken diagonal lines symbolize perceptual intake, dotted

---

[8] What gives a photograph its content is, of course, something quite different from what gives states of our brains their content. (The former is parasitic on the latter.)

[9] Of course the content of even the simplest photograph will be much more complex than this. (It will be something that can be specified *conceptually* only with some loss.)

[10] In fact I do not believe that a specification of the content of a photograph should make reference to the object or objects that it is of. A photograph should not be said to represent, e.g., that *a* and *b* are such that the former is *R* to the latter—at least, not in the way in which a painting may be said to represent, e.g., that Christ is on the cross. We see, here, the need for a distinction between, on the one hand, an *a*-representation (i.e. a species of particular-representation, in a specification of whose content mention of *a* would figure: something which represents, or misrepresents, *a*), and, on the other, something which, without being an *a*-representation, is a representation *of a*.

lines symbolize the retention of information in memory, and broken lines symbolize the transmission of information in communication.[11]

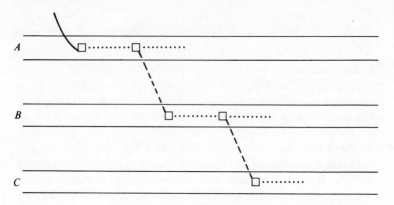

Notice that I shall be ignoring, for the time being, what is perhaps the central feature of our system of gathering information from individuals: namely the fact that we group pieces of information together, as being from the same object—that we collect information lines into bundles. It will be convenient to have a term for the process which leads to the formation of bundles: I shall call it *re*-identification (italicizing the prefix to stress the etymology, and to keep my use of the term distinct from Strawson's,[12] which is restricted to a special case of *re*-identification in my sense). Once we take note of *re*-identification, we make room (even without singular terms in the system of communication) for the following simple cases of controlling conceptions that are *mixed*:

(a) cases in which an object is recognized: an object currently perceived is *re*-identified as the same as one perceived at some earlier time;

(b) cases in which an object being perceived is *re*-identified as one of which the subject has heard.

If we lift the simplifying assumption—which I shall also be making for the time being—that there are no singular terms in

[11] A three-dimensional model would be better (allowing, e.g., the possibility of representing a direct testimony-link between *A* and *C* as well as the indirect one through *B*); but harder to represent in a diagram.

[12] See *Individuals*, pp. 31–8.

the communication system we are considering, then we make room, in addition, for the following simple species of mixed cases:

- (c) cases in which an object being perceived is *re*-identified as an object of which the subject is now hearing;
- (d) cases in which an object remembered is *re*-identified as an object of which the subject is now hearing;
- (e) cases in which an object which the subject is now hearing about is *re*-identified as an object that he heard about on an earlier occasion.

It is the essential significance of referring expressions that they require link-ups of just these last three kinds. Nevertheless, it will be useful initially to concentrate on *pure* cases, as in the diagram.[13]

Note that memory and testimony are, in a sense made clear by the diagram, *recursive* elements of this structure. It is a consequence of this fact that it would be quite wrong to make any generalization to the effect that all thoughts based on memory, or all thoughts based on testimony, are information-based thoughts in the sense I am concerned with. For it is clearly possible for a subject to *deduce* that there is a unique ϕ, and tell his friend so. His later thoughts 'based on memory', expressible in the form 'The ϕ is F', and his friend's thoughts of that form 'based on testimony' will not be information-based thoughts in my sense.

A social informational system manifests the structure discernible in the case of the photograph-producing mechanism, even if all the output states have a propositional content which is purely existential. Thus, suppose a party of people visits a foreign country, and one of their number sees a native, x, with a spike through his nose. He tells another 'I saw a man with a spike through his nose', and the information ends up with a subject S, who hears (and perhaps accepts) that there is a native with a spike through his nose. Now the *content* of this piece of information is purely existential. Still, it can be said to embody information from x. It is with x that the predicative material in the informational state has to be compared if we are to evaluate

---

[13] Given the simple species of mixed cases, we can obviously construct mixed cases of any degree of complexity. Mixed Ideas will be discussed in 8.6.

how successfully the system has worked. Equivalently, it is with *x* that the information has to be compared in order to establish whether any belief which *S* bases on this information constitutes a case of knowledge.

Any such belief would embody information from *x*; but I hope it will be generally agreed that it would not constitute a belief *about x*, in the sense of a particular-belief that represents *x*:[14] in accepting it, *S* could not be said to be having a thought *about* something.[15] (Consider my belief that swans are to be found in Uganda: is this a belief about some particular birds, long since deceased, that occasioned the report in the travel book from which I derived the belief?)

It is true that *if S reflects on the process of information-transmission*, he may, so to speak, aim a thought (a particular-thought) at 'that native'. But the object of the thought will be individuated, in this case, *by reference to its role in the operations of the informational system*.[16] This is a different kind of thought from the kind of particular-thought which it is the aim of this chapter to discuss.

An informational state may be of an object even though its content fails to fit the object at all well—because of malfunction in the system, either at source, or in transmission, or in memory. And an informational state may be of *nothing*: this will be the case if there was no object which served as input to the informational system when the information was produced. Information can fail to be information from anything, of course, even if there is an object which the content of the informational states that embody it *fits* closely.

The last sentence introduces a use of the notion of the same (bit or piece of) information which deserves explanation, even though it is common.[17] We want to be able to say that two informational states (states of different persons) embody the same information, provided that they result from the same

---

[14] Cf. n. 10 above, on the distinction between an *a*-representation and a representation *of a*.

[15] Observe, however, that even in these cases the 'have in mind' idiom can get a grip. 'I wonder who he can be thinking of', one might say. See 5.3.

[16] Suppose I hear a report to the effect that, contrary to what was hitherto supposed, there are still some Aborigines living in a certain region of Australia. If I begin now to entertain thoughts about *those Aborigines* (and mean by this something other than merely *the Aborigines in that region*), then I must be using the fact of information-transmission to individuate them.

[17] We do speak of certain information decaying (becoming garbled).

initial informational event (via informational transactions of the sorts we have described), even if they do not have the same *content*: the one may represent the same information as the other, but *garbled* in various ways. Conversely, and obviously, it is not sufficient, for two informational states to embody the same information, that they have the same content. When two states embody *the same information*, they are necessarily such that if the one is of an object *x*, then so is the other. (We shall discover later (9.2) that there are uses of singular terms such that it is necessary, for them to be understood, that we have *the same information* as the speaker.)

5.3 INTERPRETATION AND PSYCHOLOGICAL ATTRIBUTIONS

Our task is to understand the use of certain relational psychological statements, in apparent conflict with Russell's Principle (4.6). I am not suggesting that the notion of thinking of something, or having something in mind, as it figures in the apparent counter-examples to Russell's Principle, is the same notion as the notion of information from something. (Although the nature of the counter-examples makes it clear that they are connected, and I do think that in some cases 'belief *of x*' means no more than 'belief embodying information from *x*'.) However, it is as well to be aware that not every relational psychological idiom need involve a willingness to ascribe to the subject a judgement about the object. We have seen this exemplified in the case of the idiom '*S* has information from *x*'; and we shall see that the same holds for the idioms that figure in the counter-examples.

We were discussing Russell's Principle in connection with a case (4.1) in which a supposed thought was based upon information whose content the subject believed to be individuating, whereas in fact it was not individuating. The subject certainly did *essay* a particular-thought, although I have suggested that he should be regarded as having failed. Now we need to understand why we are inclined to say, in this and in similar cases, that the subject is thinking of ... —always citing, here, the object from which the relevant information derives. (The second steel ball, in the example of 4.1.)

I think we should realize, first, that these idioms (and, perhaps, all ordinary cognitive idioms) have their home in the activity of interpreting, or making sense of, the speech of others. We envisage our subject uttering a sentence: 'That ball was *F*'; we ask ourselves 'What can he be thinking of?', and answer 'He has the second ball in mind', or—making the concern with interpretation explicit—'He means the second ball'. Now when we interpret the remarks of another person, we aim to *make sense* of his act of uttering them, rather in the way that we aim to make sense of his other acts. We try to fit them into a pattern, to find the project to which they belong. We attribute a purpose to the speaker. When we say 'He means *x*', or 'He must be thinking of *x*', we are attributing to the speaker a purpose which explains his linguistic act: his purpose is to be referring to *x*.

It has been widely thought that statements of the purpose behind a linguistic act are true in virtue of a thought that the speaker has in his mind, or at least that a thought on the speaker's part is presupposed: the thought 'I shall say that *p*' for the attribution of the purpose of saying that *p*, and correspondingly the thought 'I shall refer to *x*' for the attribution of the purpose of referring to *x*. If either of these two contentions were correct, then the use of these idioms, in the cases we are considering, would involve attributing a thought to the speaker in violation of Russell's Principle. But neither of them seems to me to be correct.

Consider the following case. A young student is reading out an ill-prepared essay to his class. It contains the sentence 'A spark is produced electrically inside the carburettor'. 'That's not right', the teacher says. 'What does he mean, class?' And here someone may say 'He means the cylinder, sir'. In saying this, the second student is *not* committed to the idea that the subject had the thought, or even has the capacity to have the thought, 'I shall say that a spark is produced in the cylinder'. But nor is what he says independent of the subject's goals and beliefs. The point is rather something like this: to be saying that a spark is produced in the cylinder is what, given his general plans and his situation, the subject should be doing; that is, doing that is what would conform best with the subject's plans at this moment. The truth which he should have been trying to express at this point is that a spark is produced in the cylinder. (There is a similar use of 'want'. I go to a radio station and say that I want to register a complaint; I am told 'Then you want to see Mr *X* of our legal department'.)

It is true that such ascriptions of purpose to individuals are consequential upon ascriptions of purpose they would make to themselves. But it is not at all correct to suppose that when a singular term is employed in such a 'consequential' ascription, it occurs as the result of substitution for some singular term which might occur in an avowal of such a self-ascribed purpose. (I wanted to do what was necessary to register a complaint; I need not have realized that there was a particular person one had to see.)

When a person intends to give expression to an information-based thought, we can safely ascribe to him (in this extended sense) the purpose of referring to the object from which the information derives (provided, at least, that this does not conflict with other purposes). Only if he succeeds in referring to that object will his linguistic performance be *well-grounded*. This is so whether or not the particular sentence concerned gives expression to a belief of his: in either case he is talking in a way which requires a basis, and he has that basis only if he is talking about the object from which his information derives. Consequently, the purpose of talking about that object can be attributed to him, in virtue of a presumed desire that his activities be well-grounded. But there need be no avowable intention on his part—'I intend to refer to . . .'—from which we derive our interpreting statements ('He means the second ball', etc.) by substitution. In particular, it is quite unnecessary to attribute to him the intention to refer *to the object from which his information derives*; and unnecessary even to suppose that he can form such a concept.[18]

This explanation of the idioms that figure in the counter-examples to Russell's Principle requires us to realize that not everything which counts as *interpreting* (*making sense of*) the linguistic acts of a speaker involves the ascription to him of judgements or beliefs. Surely it is some sort of support for this conten-

---

[18] It is this which gets around the difficulty which many people have had with this kind of case. Surely (they say), when the facts are in, the subject will acknowledge the justice of the claim that it is the object which is the source of his information to which he intends to refer. (This is correct.) And therefore (they go on), there *is* a distinguishing property by which he individuates the object of his thought—namely, he individuates it *as* the source of his information. (This is *not* necessarily correct.)

tion that we find extreme difficulty, in the cases in question, in providing a *notional* report of what the subject is supposed to be judging—in *giving* the thought he is supposed to have.[19]

When our subject utters the words 'That ball was *F*', just as we can say, in this interpretational way, that he means to be speaking of the second ball, so we could say—though we would have less need to say this—that it is the second ball that he means to be making a judgement about. But, as before, this ascription of intention, properly understood, does not commit us to the view that the subject has the capacity to make such judgements.

5.4 THE RISK OF ILL-GROUNDEDNESS

There are many different modes of identification—ways of knowing which object is in question—and the next three chapters attempt to clarify some of them. But I have already endorsed the idea that one way of conforming to Russell's Principle is constituted by knowledge of individuating or distinguishing facts about an object; and even at this stage, while we are still being unspecific about the other modes of identification, we can use this relatively simple case to get clear about some (general) consequences of the fact that a thought is information-based.

Our explanation of the relational psychological idioms that figure in the counter-examples (5.3) drew attention to the fact that a *linguistic performance* involving the purported expression of an information-based thought would not be *well-grounded* unless reference was made to the object from which the information derived. Now, there is an entirely parallel point to be made about *thoughts*. Someone essaying an information-based particular-thought will employ some purported mode of identification of an object; and his attempt at a thought will evidently not be well-grounded unless the object (if any) which that mode of identification would identify is the object (if any) from which the information derives.

There are several main cases to consider; we can represent them diagrammatically by Fig. 2. (Unbroken lines represent

---

[19] It might be claimed that the subject's thought, in these examples, admits only of a relational specification. Either the suggestion is that all thoughts about objects admit only of relational specifications (which is absurd); or else we can probably let the opponents of Russell's Principle have these 'thoughts', and restrict the application of the Principle to thoughts which do admit of notional specification.

derivation of information; broken lines represent purported modes of identification.)

We have been considering cases of type (1). Here there is a unique object from which the information derives, but there is no object identified by the purported mode of identification. In the case of the steel balls (4.1) this is because of lack of uniqueness; in another kind of type-(1) case, the failure would be

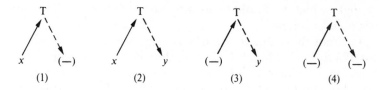

simply because there was nothing whatever which fitted the content of the purported mode of identification (because of considerable garbling and distortion).

Garbling and distortion of information can also produce cases of type (2); these differ from type-(1) cases only in that there happens to be something which would be distinguished by the exercise of the subject's purported discriminating knowledge.[20]

In cases of types (3) and (4) there is no object from which the information derives. (In our simple model, this would be due either to hallucination or to lying, somewhere in the system.) In (3) there happens to be something which would be distinguished by the exercise of the subject's purported discriminating knowledge; (4), where there is no such object, is of course more likely.

Now, we have an extreme reluctance to allow, in either (2) or (3), that the object *y*, which happens to be such that it would be distinguished by the exercise of the subject's purported discriminating knowledge, is the object of a thought on the subject's part. I am not appealing here to some linguistic intuition about the proper use of relational psychological terminology; I am appealing to a notion of the object of a thought which is straightforwardly connected with the notion of *truth*. Suppose a

[20] We could have used a case of this kind in considering the challenge posed by the Photograph Model to Russell's Principle. For if it was decided (as the Photograph Model would have it) that the subject in a case of this kind was making judgements about *x*, then this would be, contrary to Russell's Principle, a case in which he was making judgements about something without possessing a way of distinguishing it from everything else.

subject hears about a unique ϕ from someone whose aim is to deceive him; but, unknown to the deceiver, there is in fact such an object. The subject essays an information-based thought which he would express by saying 'That ϕ is F', and in fact the ϕ happens to be F. In this case (type (3)) we should be extremely reluctant to say that he had thought something true. And we can detect in ourselves a similar reaction to the case (type (2)) in which the subject essays an information-based thought which he would express by saying 'That ϕ is F', when y is F and x is not.

I do not think this reaction is an expression of adherence to the Photograph Model. If it were, then in a case of type (2), or type (1), in which (i) the subject's attempt at an information-based thought which he would express by saying 'That ϕ is F' is based on information which is derived from x, but which constitutes a wholly inaccurate conception of it; and (ii) x is in fact F, we ought to have an equally strong conviction that our subject thought something true. And I do not think we would wish to say that the subject thought something true in this kind of case, because we would be extremely embarrassed if we had to provide an account of what it was that he thought.[21]

Our reaction, it seems to me, is an expression of the idea that the thought-episode in question is ill-grounded. We know perfectly well which object the subject *wishes* to distinguish in thought. (We know this in the same way that we know which object he wishes to refer to, if he attempts to give linguistic expression to his purported thought: 5.4.) But he fails to distinguish that object in thought; and hence his essaying of a particular-thought about it is based upon a mistake. In such a situation I shall say that the thought-episode is not well-grounded.[22]

Essayings of information-based thoughts, then, are liable to a quite distinctive failing: that of being ill-grounded. (The clearest examples of this always come when the information on which the episode is based has no source.) It follows that *even when the mode of identification employed exploits individuating facts about*

[21] There is some degree of incorrectness in a subject's conception of an object that makes it pointless to ascribe thoughts about it to him.

[22] We can say that there is something at which the subject is *aiming* when he essays his particular-thought. So there is room for failure in this aim—even though, when there *is* failure, the subject cannot himself identify the object he was aiming to identify.

an object, an information-based thought cannot be regarded as
working like a descriptive thought (of which thoughts that
would be expressed with the name 'Julius' were our paradigm
examples: 1.7, 1.8, 2.3). An information-based thought has a
liability which corresponds to nothing in the case of a pure
descriptive thought. There is a logical gap between a thought
that can be expressed in the words 'The ϕ is F' and an
information-based thought such as would be expressed in the
words 'That ϕ is F', *even if the mode of identification employed in the
latter exploits the fact that its object is uniquely ϕ.*[23]

We shall see that this fact about information-based thoughts
has considerable consequences for the theory of reference; for
there are many uses of referring expressions for the understanding of which an information-based thought is required. As we
shall see in chapter 9, an argument for the Russellian status of
those referring expressions can be based on this fact. It is for this
reason that I have been quite happy to accept Russell's Principle, with its apparent consequence that there is an important
category of identification by description; given the central importance of information-based thoughts in an account of the
understanding of referring expressions, the consequence gives
little comfort to a 'description theory' of referring expressions
(apart from the special case of referring expressions like 'Julius').

5.5 PREVIEW

The picture of the theory of reference which emerges from the
following chapters is pretty complex, although I hope it is
coherent and unified. It would be desirable, therefore, to give a
preliminary sketch of the position I shall end up with.

The argument I alluded to in the preceding section is certainly the most general argument that can be offered in support
of a broadly Russellian conception of singular terms. A great
many sentences containing referring expressions do require
information-based thoughts for their understanding. Included
here are sentences containing ordinary demonstratives, referring to an object in the shared perceptual environment; sentences containing what I call 'past-tense demonstratives', referring to an object earlier observed and now remembered; and

---

[23] The reason is that there is no descriptive proposition a grasp of which can guarantee
the right sort of link-up with one's informational processes.

sentences containing what I call 'testimony demonstratives', which advert to information presumed to be in common possession through testimony. (See 9.1.) This general argument is given in chapter 9. It generates an obvious counter-argument, based on the apparently significant use of such expressions when they are empty; and this counter-argument is countered, with equal generality, in chapter 10.

If any line of thought in this book could be said to be its main plot, it is, on account of its generality, this one. But there are several sub-plots.

I think we have a fairly clear idea of what description-based identification amounts to. But we have a much less clear idea about the other kinds of identification, which cluster around two broadly distinguished kinds: the demonstrative and the recognition-based. I examine these in chapters 6 and 8, respectively. On examination, these kinds of identification turn out to have a character quite unlike that of description-based identification. In the case of description-based identification, a subject may have a fully *coherent* Idea-of-an-object, *a*, even if there is nothing that would be identified by that Idea. We can know what that Idea is, at least in the sense of knowing the way in which the subject knows what is in question in propositions of identification of the form $\ulcorner \delta = a \urcorner$—knowing what knowledge he has of what would make such propositions true.[24] But this is not so in the case of either of the other two modes of identification. In those cases, if there is no object that would be identified by the purported mode of identification, then there is no coherent Idea-of-an-object, even in this sense. In these cases it is therefore true, in the strictest sense, that where there is no object, *there is no thought*. Consequently, there is an extremely powerful argument which can be mounted for the Russellian status of those singular terms for whose understanding these modes of identification are required; and this is a major sub-theme of the book. It has the consequence that the Russellian status of certain singular terms is *over*-determined. But this second argument also applies in some cases in which the first does not; there are modes of identification, which may vaguely be considered demonstrative, which do not necessarily give rise to information-based

---

[24] Though I have warned (5.4) against taking this as a ground for regarding thoughts involving description-based identification as necessarily simply descriptive.

thoughts (those associated with 'here'—6.3—and 'I'—chapter 7).

Chapter 7, on 'I', represents something of a detour from the main line of argument. To a certain extent all the chapters on modes of identification are the result of an interest in them for their own sake; but I wish it to be clear that, in chapter 7, it is this interest, rather than a concern to exemplify the general picture, that predominates. I regard the chapter as a presumptuous, and obviously incomplete, first attempt on a very difficult topic.

Up to chapter 10, I shall have been considering referential devices which may be regarded as 'one-off'. (A referential device is one-off if its use is not necessarily part of a practice of using that device to refer to that object.) In chapter 11, I devote some attention to the other main kind of referential device— proper names. The fact that a use of such a device is part of a practice introduces quite novel elements.

Appendix[1]

The notion of an information-based particular-thought involves a duality of factors: on the one hand, the subject's possession of information derived from an object, which he regards as germane to the evaluation and appreciation of the thought; and, on the other hand, the subject's satisfaction of the requirement imposed by Russell's Principle—his identification of the object which his thought concerns. This duality is perhaps especially clear in a case of the kind mentioned at the end of 5.4, in which the subject employs a *descriptive* identification of the object; this might be the case with a thought which the subject might express by means of a past-tense demonstrative ('That ϕ was F'). But the duality is present in all cases of information-based particular-thoughts.

In all cases, the overriding point or purpose of the subject's thinking is to be thinking of the object from which the information derives. (This is an ascription of purpose of the 'interpretational' sort discussed in 5.3: it does not imply that the subject entertains thoughts in which the object is identified *as* the object from which the information derives. Not that that is not possible for a subject who reflects on the operations of the informational system: see 5.2. But it is not the normal case, and thoughts of this kind are not our present concern.)

Given this overriding purpose, we can make sense of the idea that the subject's thought-episode *aims at* a particular object, in such a way that—as with literal aiming—it is possible to miss the target object: as happens when the mode of identification employed does not identify that object. (This notion of a thought-episode having a target, with a possibility of missing it, makes no sense in the case of thoughts which would be expressed by sentences containing 'Julius': 1.7, 1.8, 2.3.) When we say that a thought-episode misses its target, we do not imply that the subject independently identifies the target: the *aiming* relation is determined to obtain between the subject and the object that is his target by truths of the 'interpretational' kind, and so it does not of itself involve the subject's *thinking of* that object. (Thus when a thought-episode does miss its target, we are left with nothing but the 'interpretational' relation between the subject and that object, and no relation involving the subject's thinking of that object except in the

---

[1] Evans was dissatisfied with the clarity with which the fundamental structure of his view of information-based thoughts had emerged in chapter 5. In this Appendix, I have tried to elaborate some subsequent notes of his; and entered what seems to be a consequential *caveat*.

non-strict sense involved in the 'interpretational' idioms—'He must be thinking of *y*'.)

Finding the *target* of an information-based particular-thought would involve tracing back the causal routes by which the relevant information is derived from the relevant object. Finding its *object* would involve employing the mode of identification which the subject employs in the thought (exploiting the answer to the question 'In virtue of what does the subject know which object his thought concerns?'). Only if these two procedures locate the same object can the subject be credited with an information-based particular-thought about that object. Notice that the causal connections which would be traced in the first procedure are not part of the *content* of the particular-thought which is ascribable to the subject if that condition is met. The content is determined by the subject's mode of identification (the second factor in our duality); the fact that the thought-episode is causally related to the object in question (the first factor) serves, not as a determinant of content, but as a necessary condition for the possibility of ascribing an information-based particular-thought with the content in question to the subject. In giving the content of the thought, we need to specify the object in a way which mirrors the mode of identification which the subject employs; hence, *not* as the object which bears the appropriate causal relations to the information on which the thought is based.[2]

Even so, it seems to be impossible to give a correct specification of content which does not specify an object standing in the right causal relations to the information. (This reflects the fact that we are dealing with a kind of thought which is not ascribable at all unless there is a coincidence or harmony between the two factors in the duality.) When, in the description-based case mentioned above, we say that the subject believes that that ϕ was F, we use 'that ϕ' in such a way that nothing could be that ϕ unless it was the source of the retained information on which the thought is based.

This last point suggests that we ought to enter a *caveat* about the interpretation of the distinction, briefly drawn in 5.5, between those modes of identification such that, where there is no object, there is in the strictest sense no thought, on the one hand, and those in which that is not so, on the other. What is said in 5.5 is that in the former sort of case (demonstrative and recognition-based identification) there is no thought at all, because, in the absence of an object, the subject has no coherent Idea-of-an-object which could be combined with a concept to yield a knowledge of what it would be for the supposed thought to

---

[2] This is not to deny the possibility of a different kind of thought, in which the subject exploits the object's connections with his informational system in the *content* of the thought. (See n. 16, and associated text, in chapter 5.)

be true; whereas in the latter sort of case (our case of descriptive identification employed in an information-based thought) that is not so. The implication might seem to be that in the latter sort of case there is, so to speak, a thought-content available, of which we can say that it would have been the content of the information-based thought which the subject would have liked to have ascribable to him, had such a thought been ascribable to him. No such thought is ascribable, not because there is nothing which could constitute its content, but simply because the thought-episode aims at what is, in fact, nothing. (In the former sort of case we have two reasons for refusing to ascribe an information-based particular-thought: not only does the thought-episode aim at nothing, but also there is nothing which could constitute its content. Hence, as remarked in 5.5, the Russellian status of the relevant singular terms is over-determined.)

But if this is the position, then we must ask: what is this thought-content, thinkable as things are (in the absence of an object), which would have been the content of the particular-thought which the subject would have liked to be able to express by 'That ϕ was F', had such a thought only been ascribable to him? The only answer seems to be: the content which the subject can express, as things are, by 'The ϕ was F'. But does this position sufficiently respect the distinction, insisted on at the end of 5.4, between the purely descriptive (i.e. not information-based) thought that the ϕ is (or was) F and any information-based thought? Surely the difference between the thought that the ϕ was F and the thought that *that* ϕ was F is a difference of *content*, and not a difference which can be wholly shunted off into some sphere of considerations external to the determination of content. (Recall that the notion of thought-content, as it is used in this book, is anchored to the notion of the subject's knowledge of what it is that he is entertaining—his knowledge of what it would be for the proposition in question to be true. No one would be counted as knowing what it would be for the proposition that that ϕ was F to be true—in the case we are considering—if he supposed that the proposition would be rendered true by the F-ness of something unique in being ϕ, even if the object in question had never been encountered by him.)

If this is correct, it suggests the following: if an Idea of an object is capable of employment in information-based thoughts about that object, then that fact is partly constitutive of the identity of the Idea; an information-based thought and a thought which is not information-based cannot employ the same Idea. (If the thought that the ϕ was F and the thought that that ϕ was F differ in content, then, given that they match in respect of the concept employed, they can differ only in the Ideas employed.) It cannot, then, be correct to suppose that the mode of identification (the Idea) employed in an information-based thought can be *exhaustively* given by a definite description 'the ϕ'. (Nor does 5.4 say that it can; but that thesis might have seemed to be implicit in the notion of an information-based thought which exploits a descriptive mode of identification.)

We can still make sense of the distinction of 5.5, provided that we can make sense of the notion of a kind of information-based particular-thought whose mode of identification is, as it were, *all but* exhausted by a definite description. (This will be how we should think of our initial example.) If a subject essays a particular-thought of this kind in the absence of an object, then it is not correct to say—as our initial crude interpretation of the distinction suggested—that there is a thought-content available which would have been the content of his information-based thought, had an information-based thought been ascribable to him. But there is a thought-content, thinkable as things are, which is very similar to what would have been the content of the information-based thought if there had been an information-based thought (namely the content of the purely descriptive thought); and nothing analogous can be said in the other cases. Thought-content is, as it were, more comprehensively *missing* in the case of purported demonstrative or recognition-based identification. (At any rate that is the doctrine; of course its defence is yet to come, in the chapters which deal with the relevant modes of identification.)

The duality of factors retains its importance: what we have seen is simply that, in all cases of information-based particular-thoughts (including those which exploit descriptive identification), we need to take account of the fact that a thought is information-based in considering both factors, and not only in considering the first. (The fact that the thought is information-based must be registered in a full account of the Idea employed.) It remains the case that a detailed description of the causal relations between the information on which the thought is based and the object which it is about is foreign to a specification of the *content* of a thought of the kind we are concerned with. We must distinguish the correct content-specification 'He thinks that that ϕ is F' (where the use of the past-tense demonstrative, as opposed to the pure definite description 'the ϕ', reflects the presence, in a full account of the Idea employed, of the fact that the thought is information-based in the way it is) from the incorrect content-specification 'He thinks that the ϕ from which his current memory-information is derived is F'.

These considerations bear on the question when two people can be said to have the same particular-thought. (See 1.5, on the Fregean model of communication.) If we conceive the content of information-based thoughts in the wrong way, then it can seem impossible for two people to share an information-based particular-thought. One person will be regarded as thinking that the object which is causally responsible in the appropriate way for *his* possession of such-and-such information is thus and so; and the other will be regarded as thinking that the object which is causally responsible in the appropriate way for *his* possession of such-and-such information is thus and so; and no matter how well the consignments of information (and the kind of causal responsibility in question) match, this will look, because of the references to the thinkers themselves, like a specification of two different thought-contents (even though the object specified is the same). If, on the other hand, we respect the duality of factors, we can continue at least to hold open the possibility of finding a match in thought-content between two people who can be credited with information-based thoughts which ascribe the same property to the same object, provided that each employs the same mode of identification (see 1.5): and we can (perhaps) count them as employing the same mode of identification when (say) each identifies the object in question demonstratively.

These questions will be considered in more detail later: see 9.2, 9.5, and the Appendix to chapter 9. For the present the point is that unless we properly understand, at this stage, the way in which the fact that a thought is based on certain information is reflected in its content, *without* its being correct for a specification of the content to include a spelling out of the causal relations involved, there will not even seem to be a possibility of applying the Fregean model of communication in the case of information-based thoughts, to be looked into in more detail at a later stage.

Chapter 6

Demonstrative Identification

6.1 DEMONSTRATIVE IDENTIFICATION AND PERCEPTION

Russell introduced us to the idea that demonstrative identification is a mode of identification quite unlike descriptive identification, and to the idea that it is apt to underlie the use of Russellian singular terms. Certainly, as we concentrate upon the standard cases, in which we identify objects in our immediate vicinity, his first contention seems plausible. But in order to go further we must discover what exactly demonstrative identification involves.

It is natural to think that it involves perception. Strawson writes that a subject can identify an object demonstratively if he 'can pick out by sight or hearing or touch, or otherwise sensibly discriminate' that object.[1] There must be something correct in what Strawson says, but I do not think we can regard it as a complete account of the notion of demonstrative identification.

In the first place, we need an explanation of exactly how it is that perceiving something makes a thought of a certain kind possible. And as I have urged before (4.1), such an explanation

---

[1] *Individuals*, p. 18. John Wallace has recently challenged this connection. He writes: 'Most of us are inclined to suppose that there are close connections between demonstration and perception; some of these could be brought out by principles of the form:

If conditions are C, then if a person makes a statement which demonstrates an object, the person perceives that object.

But I do not know how to spell out the conditions. One has to remember that one can point out distant objects with eyes closed and ears plugged, that blind people can point out the moon, etc.' ('Only in the Context of a Sentence do Words have any Meaning', in Peter A. French, Theodore E. Uehling, Jr., and Howard K. Wettstein, eds., *Contemporary Perspectives in the Philosophy of Language* (University of Minnesota Press, Minneapolis, 1979), pp. 305–25, at p. 319.) But the connection between demonstrative singular terms and perception comes out if we ask what is required in order to *understand* an utterance accompanied by one of these pointing gestures. It is necessary to perceive the object pointed out (to make it out), and to have the thought, about the object thus distinguished, that the speaker is saying of it that it is thus and so. Here again (cf. 4.1), the central concept is not that of *making* a reference of such-and-such a kind, but that of *understanding* one.

must enable us to understand what unifies demonstrative identification with other modes of identification.

But, secondly, even if we were incurious about this theoretical
unification, we should still need to go beyond Strawson's formulation, because the ordinary concept of perception is vague.
The core idea is clearly that of an information-link between
subject and object, which provides the subject with (non-conceptual)[2] information about the states and doings of the object
over a period of time.[3] But it is quite undetermined by the
ordinary concept what kinds of spatial circuitousness and
time-lags in the information channel are consistent with the
subject's being said to perceive the object. We speak of seeing
someone on the television, or hearing him on the radio. We
speak of seeing someone in a mirror as well as of seeing his
reflection—but only of seeing someone's shadow, not of seeing
him in a shadow. We speak without qualification of seeing stars,
despite the long delay that the channel involves; but we could
not speak without qualification of hearing Caruso when we
listen to a record.

There is another continuum, one which worried G. E.
Moore.[4] Moore was fairly sure that if someone pointed in the
direction of a beach from a little way offshore, and said 'This
island is uninhabited', he would have to be understood as referring to the island of which the beach is a part. Continuing this
line of thought, Moore arrived at the position that an ordinary
demonstrative like 'this chair' would have to be understood as
referring, 'by description', to the chair of which something one
could strictly refer to as 'this' is a part. The idea was that pure
demonstrative identification is possible only of something of
which one is aware; and that one cannot, strictly speaking, be
aware of something unless one is aware of all of it. Although
Moore never gave a very compelling argument for this latter
principle, he certainly raised a difficulty, and demonstrative
identification must be located on this continuum. Can a person

[2] For the distinction between conceptual and non-conceptual information, see 5.2,
6.3, 7.4.
[3] See J. L. Austin, *Sense and Sensibilia* (Clarendon Press, Oxford, 1962). Austin seems
to make it a necessary condition of perceiving an object that the link be continuous over
a period and be capable of yielding information about changes in the object.
[4] See 'Some Judgments of Perception', *Proceedings of the Aristotelian Society* xix (1918-
19), 1–29.

demonstratively identify the room or house in which he is sitting, or the city in which he lives?

When we consider the vagueness of the ordinary concept of perception, we may be unclear what the deliverances of Strawson's formulation are (what its content is). But when we bear in mind the complexity and variety of information-links, we may cease to be sure even of its truth. We do certainly use demonstrative expressions of natural language when watching television or listening to the radio together, but are they to be taken at face value? After all, we use demonstrative expressions very widely to effect what Quine calls 'deferred ostension',[5] as when we indicate a man by pointing to his car. 'That man is going to be sorry', we say, pointing to a car burdened with parking tickets. Here, surely, the identification is 'by description'. Is this the model we should follow in the case of the radio and television? It cannot be right, in answering this question, to be content to allow the concept of demonstrative identification to follow wherever the ordinary concept of perception, for whatever obscure reason, leads. The concept of identification is a theoretical concept, connected, via Russell's Principle, to the concepts of thought and judgement. A decision on its extension must take account of these ties. So we are brought back to the question 'How does perception make a thought possible?'[6]

6.2 INFORMATION-LINKS ARE NOT SUFFICIENT

I think that an information-link between a subject and an object is a crucial necessary condition of the mode of identification we are trying to characterize. A demonstrative thought is clearly an information-based thought (one might say, the mother and father of all information-based thoughts); the subject's thinking is governed by a controlling conception[7] he derives from the

---

[5] See *Ontological Relativity and Other Essays*, at pp. 40–1.

[6] I find little in recent work on the theory of reference which can assist us with this question. Some philosophers have thought to look to the notion of pointing; but this produces a notion of demonstrative identification of extreme heterogeneity and of questionable theoretical interest. Other philosophers have been content to rest upon an unexplained notion of 'demonstration'; but this can hardly be satisfactory.

[7] On the idea of a controlling conception, see 5.1. Remember (5.2) that we are concentrating on pure cases for the moment: we should think of cases in which the subject's identification of the object of his thought is wholly demonstrative (he neither recognizes it, nor identifies it as something of which he has heard).

object. If the question were raised 'How do you know there is such a thing as the thing you take yourself to be thinking about?', he would answer 'I can see' (or 'hear', or 'taste', or 'feel') 'that there is.' More distinctively, demonstrative thoughts take place in the context of a *continuing* informational link between subject and object: the subject has an evolving conception of the object, and is so situated *vis-à-vis* the object that the conception which controls his thinking is disposed to evolve according to changes in the information he receives from the object. This already imports an element of discrimination, and it rests upon certain very fundamental perceptual skills which we possess: the ability to keep track of an object in a visual array, or to follow an instrument in a complex and evolving pattern of sound.[8]

It is a consequence of this necessary condition that a subject who has a demonstrative Idea of an object has an *unmediated* disposition to treat information from that object as germane to the truth and falsity of thoughts involving that Idea. (When I say that his disposition is unmediated, I mean that it is not the product of any more general disposition to treat as germane to the truth and falsity of those thoughts information received from an object satisfying some condition, together with a recognition that the object satisfies that condition.)[9] To put this in the context of the interpretation of utterances (where it is anyway destined to belong), we can say that a subject who interprets a singular term in an utterance as referring demonstratively to an object will have an unmediated disposition to treat certain present and future informational states, derived

[8] The notion of an information-link, broad though it is, does place certain restrictions on the application of the notion of demonstrative identification, in view of the *belief-independence* of information (see 5.2). This means that we cannot speak of an information-link when there is any process of *inference* on the part of the subject (even though the cognitive state that results in such cases may be causally dependent upon an object, and count as knowledge of it). Gilbert Harman (see *Thought* (Princeton University Press, Princeton, 1973), ch. 11) would say that what I call 'belief-independence' is the consequence of certain inferential processes being automatic and not (or no longer) subject to a person's control. However, it seems to me to be entirely proper to refuse to ascribe such inferences to the *subject*, even if, for whatever reason, one wishes to ascribe them to his brain or nervous system. This distinction is all-important when one wants to give an account of what it is that the *subject* is thinking.

[9] [If we take the condition of being such-and-such a particular object as a limiting case of a condition, this rules out the case where the disposition is mediated by the operation of a recognitional capacity.]

from that object, as germane to the truth or falsity of the utterance.[10]

It is very tempting to suppose that the existence, and discriminatory employment, of such an information-link between subject and object is not merely a necessary condition of demonstrative identification, but a sufficient condition of identification; and given that, it would be natural to adopt the view that being based on such an information-link is constitutive of a theoretically well-motivated conception of *demonstrative* identification. The opposing view would be that the sheer existence of an information-link is not sufficient for identification; that even when there is such a link, the object with which the subject has the link can, in certain cases, be thought of only *as* the object serving as input to the information channel: for instance, as the object of which *this* is a photograph, or the object which is responsible for *these* television images. On this opposing position, these thoughts, although dependent on an information-link, do not have the conceptual simplicity of a genuine demonstrative thought: a conceptual element, requiring an idea of the informational situation, must be present. But why (we might wonder) must it be present? Surely, if a person is selectively disposed, *vis-à-vis* an object, to treat its states and doings as uniquely relevant to the truth-value of a proposition, then he thereby shows himself to know which object is in question, whether or not there are circuits and time-lags in the information channel on which this sensitivity depends?[11]

I do not deny that this conception of demonstrative identification is an attractive one, especially if we remember what it is like to watch the television or to listen to the radio. The situation

---

[10] In fact, in many cases demonstrative interpretation will require the subject to appreciate the relevance, to the truth of a remark, of certain past informational states. A remark may come in the middle of a period of observation of an object. If the subject does not have the capacity to interpret it in the light of past informational states from that object, but takes account of past informational states from another object, then we shall want to deny that he knows which object is in question. (We should realize that we have made a slight alteration to our conception of information-based thoughts. A thought should be seen as information-based, not just when it rests on a certain body of information, but when it rests on a certain information-link. An Idea of an object rests upon, or is associated with, an information-link just in case the subject is so disposed that bits of information delivered by the link will enter the conception that controls thoughts involving the Idea.)

[11] Notice the similarity to the verificationist conception of demonstrative identification sketched in 4.2.

is so like the ordinary one that 'this' and 'that' pop out without the slightest sense of strain. If the nature of our thoughts could be settled by introspection, the present issue would be settled. Furthermore, if we do not accept this conception of demonstrative identification, and do suppose that the thought of the information channel must be in the background in cases like the television and radio case, then we are obviously faced with the question why no such thought need be present in the standard case.[12]

Nevertheless, the sheer existence of an information-link between subject and object does not guarantee the possibility of demonstrative thought about the object. So long as we concentrate upon propositions about the object which can be decided as true or false by information accessible via the information channel, there might seem to be no difficulty: the subject's knowledge of what it is for a proposition to be true can be equated, we might suppose,[13] with his practical capacity to decide its truth. But the Generality Constraint must be remembered, and the consequences that were seen to follow from it (4.3). If the subject has an adequate Idea of an object, it must be capable of sustaining indefinitely many thoughts about that object. Not only thoughts like 'That player has committed a foul', or 'That player is good-looking', as a man watches a game of football on the television, must be accounted for, but also thoughts like 'That player has influenza', 'That player will die of cancer', 'That player weighs 20 stone', 'That player was born in Liverpool'.

---

[12] Russell, as we know, thought it had to be present in all cases in which the object identified was not a private, mind-dependent item. He thought this because in all such cases error, and hence doubt, is possible, and where doubt is possible, the thought 'Does this *G* really exist?' must be intelligible. (See 2.2.) He held that a genuine demonstrative Idea of an object could not exist if there were no object of which it was an Idea; consequently any employment of such an Idea commits the thinker to there being an object of which it is an Idea. It would follow that the Idea involved in the thought 'Does this *G* really exist?' could not be a genuine demonstrative Idea. Russell's diagnosis of the situation seems to me to be entirely correct: the Idea involved in the thought 'Does this *G* really exist?' cannot be a demonstrative Idea. But we do not need to suppose that it must be this Idea (whatever it is) that is employed when there is no question of doubt—when one throws oneself into one's thoughts and one's words. (It is true that one thereby exposes oneself to a grave liability of thinking, which we have seen that Russell did not accept as a possibility. But I have dealt with this: see 2.2.) Throughout this chapter we shall be concerned with ordinary 'committed' thoughts. (I shall discuss existential thoughts in chapter 10.)

[13] But see 6.4.

I argued in chapter 4 that for our thoughts to have this productive quality, an Idea of an object would need either to be a fundamental identification of that object, or to consist in a knowledge of what it is for an identity proposition involving a fundamental identification to be true. In the case of a spatio-temporal particular, this means that an adequate Idea of an object involves either a conception of it as the occupant of such-and-such a position (at such-and-such a time), or a knowledge of what it is for an object so identified to be the relevant object (or, equivalently, what it is for the relevant object to be at a particular position in space and time).

Now the sheer existence of an information channel does not seem to me to guarantee either of these conditions. It certainly does not by itself provide the subject with a fundamental conception, for it may well not enable him to *locate* the object; while its sheer existence cannot provide the subject with a knowledge of what makes it the case that an object, distinguished as the occupant of a position in space, is that object. The truth of an identity-proposition of the form $\ulcorner \delta = $ that man$\urcorner$ (where 'that man' is used of a man seen on television or heard on the radio) can consist in nothing but the fact that δ is a fundamental Idea of a man who is causally responsible for the sounds or images which the subject is perceiving; and so a knowledge of which man is in question can exist only in the presence of the idea of tracing the immediate objects of perception back to their causal source. (I am not suggesting that this idea requires knowledge of the technicalities of wireless transmission.) It is when an information-link *does not provide the subject with an ability to locate the object* that a conceptual element is needed for identification.[14]

It is reported that certain primitive people, when they first heard a radio, were convinced that there was a man inside it whom they could hear. Labouring under this misapprehension, they would naturally attempt to identify the man they thought they could hear, in the standard demonstrative way. Their identification would have no complexity, but nor, in this

[14] [The phrase 'ability to locate' perhaps contains the germ of an answer to the question why a *visual* information-link is not precisely analogous to a *radio* information-link, given the plausibility of the thought that a subject in visual contact with something cannot be wholly without a conception of the perceptual mechanism involved, just because the object is to some extent spatially remote from him. (Evans raised this as a problem for himself.)]

circumstance, would it be adequate. If they were totally mysti-
fied by the apparatus when it was explained to them, and could
not understand the idea that they might be hearing a man very
distant from them in space (and possibly in time), then I should
say that, in this situation, they could form no adequate Idea of
the man they could hear at all. They would simply not know
what it meant to say, of a man identified at another, possibly
distant place, that he was *that* man (the man they heard). To
attribute an Idea of an object to someone in this situation would
involve attributing to him a totally unmanifestable Idea of the
kind against which I railed in 4.6. Of course, we know which
man he *means*, which man he has *in mind*, as he gesticulates at
the radio, but we shall not be misled by these idioms into
thinking that he has the capacity to have particular-thoughts
about him. (See 5.3.)[15]

Given that the existence of an information-link between subject and object is not by itself sufficient for identification, what
makes it possible to have, in the standard cases of demonstrative
identification, a mode of identification that is free of the conceptual element we have been considering? The answer is that in
the standard cases, not only is there an information-link, but
also the subject can, upon the basis of that link, *locate the object in
space*. I shall now turn to the spelling out of this thought, in
order to explain how demonstrative identification in the ordinary case constitutes an adequate Idea of an object. This will
require being much more specific about the fundamental level
of thought about material objects than I have been up to now.

Before doing so, however, I want to clarify what I have said
about thoughts which rely on informational channels involving
circuitousness and time-lags. Although a 'descriptive' component is required in the Idea involved in such a thought, it
would be quite wrong to attempt to assimilate these thoughts
to thoughts involving a wholly descriptive identification of
an object—even to those thoughts of this kind which are

[15] If it is correct that there is an important distinction between the cases of standard
and circuitous information-links, then it constitutes a sort of defence of Russell's Principle that we have been able to bring it out. If it is agreed that a sheer information-link
is not sufficient for demonstrative identification, how is this thesis to be defended without
Russell's Principle? (Notice that the competing position on demonstrative identification,
according to which an information-link is sufficient, is a special application of the
Photograph Model.)

information-based, involving memory and testimony. (See 5.4.) These thoughts constitute a *sui generis* category, which combines features of both kinds of thought—both purely demonstrative thoughts and (information-based) descriptive thoughts. It is thoughts of this *sui generis* kind—requiring the existence and exploitation of an information-link between subject and object—that are required for the understanding of utterances using demonstratives, in the kind of situation we have been considering; such utterances cannot be regarded as just another case of deferred ostension.[16]

6.3 EGOCENTRIC SPATIAL THINKING: 'HERE'

We must first understand what is involved in the identification of places. The places which we think about are differentiated by their spatial relations to the objects which constitute our frame of reference. (We here take note of a well-known interdependence between what differentiates objects from one another and what differentiates places from one another.)[17] Hence a fundamental identification of a place would identify it by simultaneous reference to its relations to each of the objects constituting the frame of reference. A place would be thought about in this way if it was identified on a map which represented, simultaneously, the spatial relations of the objects constituting the frame of reference. This identification has a holistic character: a place is not identified by reference to just one or two objects, and so the identification can be effective even if a few objects move or are destroyed.

Our identification of places has this holistic character whenever we rely, in our thinking about places, upon what has come to be called a 'cognitive map': a representation in which the spatial relations of several distinct things are simultaneously represented.[18] It is essential to the existence of a genuine concept

---

[16] These cases are very similar to what Strawson calls 'story-relative identification' (*Individuals*, p. 18), where one can identify an object with respect to a framework, but cannot locate the framework.

[17] See Strawson, *Individuals*, p. 37.

[18] There is a useful survey of the recent literature on this idea in John O'Keefe and Lynn Nadel, *The Hippocampus as a Cognitive Map* (Clarendon Press, Oxford, 1978). (But for our purposes the psychological literature, which is in general indifferent to the distinction between conceptual and non-conceptual content, needs to be taken with some caution.)

of space, and of objects existing in space independently of perception, that the thinker have the capacity to form and employ representations such as these. As we grow up, and as we are educated, the scope of the representations of this kind that we are able to form greatly increases. Of course, we are not able to form fundamental identifications of all the places in the universe—especially in view of the fact that our conception of the world comprises the idea of vast numbers of microscopic objects simultaneously occupying distinct places. But what matters is that we should have the idea of what a fundamental identification of a place involves.

To say that the fundamental level of thought about the spatio-temporal world—the level of thought to which all our other thinking directs us—is thought which would be sustained by a cognitive map of that world is to stress that our fundamental level of thinking is, in a certain sense, 'objective'. Each place is represented in the same way as every other; we are not forced, in expressing such thinking, to introduce any 'here' or 'there'.[19] (It is often said that in such thinking we are taking the third-person, or God's-eye, point of view, but for a reason I have already explained (4.2), I reject this way of looking at the matter. This formulation expresses ideal verificationism; whereas in fact the thinking is truly objective—it is from no point of view.)

With this background, let us turn to those thoughts about places which we typically express with, and require in the understanding of, utterances containing the word 'here'. One is struck immediately by an important difference between 'here'-thoughts and demonstrative thoughts of the kind we have been considering. While the latter are information-based thoughts *par excellence*, the former do not seem to depend necessarily either upon the subject's actual possession of information from the place, or upon the actual existence of an information-link with the place. Thus one can think 'I wonder what it is like here' when one is blindfolded, anaesthetized, and has one's ears

---

[19] It is true that someone can think in this way only if he has a recognitional capacity for the objects and places constituting the framework. [And that if we are not to fall into a difficulty over the possibility of massive reduplication, this must involve his identification of those objects and places being to some extent 'egocentric'. See the Appendix to chapter 8, and §3 of the Appendix to chapter 7.]

blocked.[20] I think this observation has led some people to think that the special way of gaining knowledge which we have in virtue of occupying a place is irrelevant to our 'here'-thoughts about it, and that in those thoughts we identify the place by description, roughly as *the place I occupy*.

This seems to me to be wrong. Where there is no *possibility* of action and perception, 'here'-thoughts cannot get a grip. Consider the philosophers' fantasy of a brain in a vat: a person's thinking organ kept alive and capable of sustaining thoughts, yet with no avenue of perception or mode of action. We can perhaps imagine being the person whose thoughts are sustained in this way[21]; but in the perpetual darkness and silence of our existence, we could surely have no use for 'here'. If we knew what had become of us, we could certainly think of a place as the place where the brain which sustains our thoughts is located—but this is a mode of identification of a place quite unlike that expressed by 'here'.

The suggestion is wrong, anyway, in giving a primacy to 'I' over 'here'. It is not the case that we *first* have a clear conception of which material object in the world we are (or what it would be to establish that), and *then* go on to form a conception of what it is for us to be located at a particular place. It is true that $\ulcorner p = \text{here}\urcorner$ is the same thought as $\ulcorner$I am at $p\urcorner$; but this does not mean that I identify *here* as *where I am*. This would raise the question 'How do I identify myself, and make sense of my being located somewhere?', but—if we had to keep the capacity to grasp 'here'-thoughts out of the picture—would make it impossible to answer it. (See 6.6, 7.3.)

To understand how 'here'-thoughts work, we must realize that they belong to a system of thoughts about places that also includes such thoughts as 'It's *F over there*', 'It's *F up there to the left*', 'It's *F a bit behind me*'. 'Here'-thoughts are merely the least specific of this series. We may regard this as an *egocentric* mode of thought.

The subject conceives himself to be in the centre of a space

---

[20] We have now what might be regarded as a limiting case of information-based thoughts: the subject's thinking is not necessarily controlled by any conception, but it rests upon an information-link in that the subject is so disposed that his thinking involving the Idea in question will be controlled by information yielded by the link *if any emerges*. (In 5.5 these cases were spoken of as not information-based at all.) For a parallel with 'I', see 7.2.

[21] But see 7.6.

(at its point of origin), with its co-ordinates given by the con-cepts 'up' and 'down', 'left' and 'right', and 'in front' and 'behind'. We may call this 'egocentric space', and we may call thinking about spatial positions in this framework centring on the subject's body 'thinking egocentrically about space'. A sub-ject's 'here'-thoughts belong to this system: 'here' will denote a more or less extensive area which centres on the subject.

Egocentric spatial terms are the terms in which the content of our spatial experiences would be formulated, and those in which our immediate behavioural plans would be expressed. This duality is no coincidence: an egocentric space can exist only for an animal in which a complex network of connections exists between perceptual input and behavioural output. A perceptual input—even if, in some loose sense, it encapsulates spatial information (because it belongs to a range of inputs which vary systematically with some spatial facts)—cannot have a spatial significance for an organism except in so far as it has a place in such a complex network of input–output connections.

Let us begin by considering the spatial element in the non-conceptual content of perceptual information. What is involved in a subject's hearing a sound as coming from such-and-such a position in space? (I assume that the apparent direction of the sound is part of the content of the informational state: part of the way things seem to the subject, to use our most general term for the deliverances of the informational system.)

I have already claimed that it is not sufficient for an organism to perceive the direction of a sound that it should be capable of discriminating—that is, responding differentially to—sounds which have different directions. As T. G. R. Bower writes:

An organism could perfectly well discriminate between values on all the proximal variables that specify position in the third dimension, and yet have no awareness of position in the third dimension *per se*.[22]

When we envisage such an organism, we envisage an organism which can be conditioned to respond differentially to those

[22] 'Infant Perception of the Third Dimension and Object Concept Development', in L. B. Cohen and P. Salapatek, eds., *Infant Perception From Sensation to Cognition*, vol. 2: *Perception of Space Speech and Sound* (Academic Press, New York, 1975), pp. 33–50, at p. 34. Bower credits the point to Irving Rock.

different values of the proximal stimulus which code the direction of sound, for instance by pressing a button, but in which the difference in stimulus is not connected to any difference in spatial *behaviour*. When we hear a sound as coming from a certain direction, we do not have to *think* or *calculate* which way to turn our heads (say) in order to look for the source of the sound. If we did have to do so, then it ought to be possible for two people to hear a sound as coming from the same direction (as 'having the same position in the auditory field'), and yet to be disposed to do quite different things in reacting to the sound, because of differences in their calculations. Since this does not appear to make sense, we must say that having spatially significant perceptual information consists at least partly in being disposed to do various things.[23]

This point also comes out very clearly if we reflect upon how we might specify the spatial information which we imagine the perception to embody. The subject hears the sound as coming from such-and-such a position, but how is the position to be specified? Presumably in *egocentric* terms (he hears the sound as up, or down, to the right or to the left, in front or behind). These terms specify the position of the sound in relation to the observer's own body; and they derive their meaning in part from their complicated connections with the subject's *actions*.

Some people, including, apparently, Freud, are able to understand the word 'right' only via the rule linking it to the hand they write with. (I suppose a similar defect might force someone to rely on the connection between 'down' and the earth's surface—though such a person ought not to travel into space.) But when the terms are understood in this way, they are not suitable for specifying the content of the information embodied in directional perception. No one hears a sound as coming from the side of the hand he writes with, in the sense that in order to locate the sound he has to say to himself 'I write with this hand' (waggling his right hand) 'so the sound is coming from over there' (pointing with his right hand). Rather, having heard the sound directionally, a person can immediately say to

---

[23] The connection of position in the auditory field with dispositions to behaviour is well brought out by George Pitcher, *A Theory of Perception* (Princeton University Press, Princeton, 1971), at p. 189. (Of course the dispositions to behaviour are complex: the behaviour will be conditional also on other beliefs and desires.)

himself 'It's coming from over there' (pointing with what is in fact his right hand), and may then reflect as an afterthought 'and that's the hand I write with.' As Charles Taylor writes:

Our perceptual field has an orientational structure, a foreground and a background, an up and down . . . This orientational structure marks our field as essentially that of an embodied agent. It is not just that the field's perspective centres on where I am bodily—this by itself doesn't show that I am essentially agent. But take the up–down directionality of the field. What is it based on? Up and down are not simply related to my body—up is not just where my head is and down where my feet are. For I can be lying down, or bending over, or upside down; and in all these cases 'up' in my field is not the direction of my head. Nor are up and down defined by certain paradigm objects in the field, such as the earth or sky: the earth can slope for instance . . . Rather, up and down are related to how one would move and act in the field.[24]

We can say, then, that auditory input—or rather that complex property of auditory input which encodes the direction of sound—acquires a (non-conceptual) spatial *content* for an organism by being linked with behavioural output in, presumably, an advantageous way. In the case of adult human beings at least, the connection is very complex, for the appropriate behaviour in response to a sound at such-and-such a position is, when described in muscular terms, indefinitely various. This is not merely because the behaviour may involve the movement of different parts of the body: one can run, walk, crawl, or—as in the case of rats in a famous experiment—swim to a target position. Even if we focus on a particular kind of behaviour, such as reaching out with the hand for a rattle heard in the dark, there is a similar kind of complexity, since an indefinite range of reaching responses (identified in muscular terms) will be appropriate, depending on the starting position of the limb and the route it follows (which need not, and often cannot, be the most direct).

---

[24] 'The Validity of Transcendental Arguments', *Proceedings of the Aristotelian Society* lxxix (1978–9), 151–65, at p. 154. (Notice that spatial positions are not identified, in the egocentric mode of thought we are considering, by descriptions like 'the position three feet in front of my nose'. For something that occupies a position so identified, after one has rotated, is not thought of as occupying the same position as something that was three feet in front of one's nose before one rotated. One would have to think in terms of such descriptions if one were free-floating in space; but it is not our usual mode of egocentric spatial thinking.)

It may well be that the input–output connections can be finitely stated only if the output is described in explicitly spatial terms (e.g. 'extending the arm', 'walking forward two feet', etc.). If this is so, it would rule out the reduction of the egocentric spatial vocabulary to a muscular vocabulary.[25] But such a reduction is certainly not needed for the point being urged here, which is that the spatial information embodied in auditory perception is specifiable only in a vocabulary whose terms derive their meaning partly from being linked with bodily actions. Even given an irreducibility, it would remain the case that possession of such information is directly manifestable in behaviour issuing from no calculation; it is just that there would be indefinitely many ways in which the manifestation can occur.[26]

My use of the term 'egocentric' is close to its literal meaning, but I do not intend to link my views with any others which have been expressed with the use of the term. Notice that when I speak of information 'specifying a position in egocentric space', I am talking not of information about a special kind of space, but of a special kind of information about space—information whose content is specifiable in an egocentric spatial vocabulary. It is perfectly consistent with the *sense* I have assigned to this vocabulary that its terms should *refer* to points in a public three-dimensional space. (Indeed I shall be claiming that that is what they refer to, if they refer to anything at all.)

So far I have been considering the non-conceptual content of perceptual informational states. Such states are not *ipso facto* perceptual *experiences*—that is, states of a conscious subject. However addicted we may be to thinking of the links between auditory input and behavioural output in information-processing terms—in terms of computing the solution to simultaneous equations[27]—it seems abundantly clear that evolution could

[25] For the idea of such a reduction, see Henri Poincaré, *The Value of Science* (Dover, New York, 1958), p. 47.

[26] Egocentric spatial terms and spatial descriptions of bodily movement would, on this view, form a structure familiar to philosophers under the title 'holistic'. For a study of concepts interrelated in this way, see Christopher Peacocke, *Holistic Explanation* (Clarendon Press, Oxford, 1979).

[27] For the mechanism of auditory localization, see, e.g., P. H. Lindsay and D. A. Norman, *Human Information Processing* (Academic Press, New York, 1972), pp. 178–88. For an expression of addiction, see Jerry A. Fodor, *The Language of Thought* (Harvester, Hassocks, 1976), pp. 42–53. One of the disadvantages of the addiction is that it tends to blur the distinction I am trying to explain.

throw up an organism in which such advantageous links were established, long before it had provided us with a conscious subject of experience. If this point is not immediately obvious, it can be brought out by reflection on the following possibility. A conscious adult may display fairly normal responses to stimuli (including directional responses to spatially varying stimuli), and yet have no associated conscious experience (he might sincerely deny that he is perceiving anything at all). A dramatic illustration is provided by the case of the brain-damaged patient, studied by L. Weiskrantz, who was able to point to a source of light despite claiming that he could not see anything at all.[28]

Reflecting upon this kind of case, philosophers and psychologists have thought that what is required for the application of our intuitive concept of conscious experience is that the subject be able to ascribe the experience to himself—to say or think 'I am having such and such an experience'. If one looks at matters in this way, it is understandable that one should find the distinction between (mere) informational state and conscious experience to be of little interest; for surely, one might think, the experience can antedate thoughts about it.

But although it is true that our intuitive concept requires a subject of experience to have *thoughts*, it is not thoughts about the experience that matter, but thoughts about the world. In other words, we arrive at conscious perceptual experience when sensory input is not only connected to behavioural dispositions in the way I have been describing—perhaps in some phylogenetically more ancient part of the brain—but also serves as the input to a *thinking, concept-applying, and reasoning system*; so that the subject's thoughts, plans, and deliberations are also systematically dependent on the informational properties of the input. When there is such a further link, we can say that the person, rather than just some part of his brain, receives and possesses the information.

Of course the thoughts are not epiphenomena; what a con-

---

[28] L. Weiskrantz, E. K. Warrington, M. D. Saunders, and J. Marshall, 'Visual Capacity in the Hemianopic Field following a Restricted Occipital Ablation', *Brain* xcvii (1974), 709-28. 'But always he was at a loss for words to describe any conscious perception, and repeatedly stressed that he saw nothing at all in the sense of "seeing", and that he was merely guessing' (p. 721).

scious subject does depends critically upon his thoughts, and so there must be links between the thinking and concept-applying system, on the one hand, and behaviour, on the other. After all, it is only those links which enable us to ascribe content (conceptual content now) to the thoughts. Further, the intelligibility of the system I have described depends on there being a *harmony* between the thoughts and the behaviour to which a given sensory state gives rise. (This will seem adventitious only to those who forget that the concepts exercised in the thoughts are learned by an organism in which the links between sensory input and behaviour have already been established.)

I do not mean to suggest that only those information-bearing aspects of the sensory input for which the subject has concepts can figure in a report of his experience. It is not necessary, for example, that the subject possess the egocentric *concept* 'to the right' if he is to be able to have the experience of a sound as being to the right. I am not requiring that the content of conscious experience itself be conceptual content. All I am requiring for conscious experience is that the subject exercise some concepts—have some thoughts—and that the content of those thoughts should depend systematically upon the informational properties of the input.[29]

We have not yet built in, or required, in this sketch of the spatial significance of auditory perception, that the subject should be able to hear sounds from different positions simultaneously. But even in the absence of this requirement, we have, in the kind of informational state we have described, a 'simultaneous' spatial representation;[30] for the subject hears a sound as coming from one among indefinitely many, simultaneously existing positions which define egocentric space. Moreover, it is easy to understand what is involved in the subject's having a simultaneous spatial representation in the stronger sense that he simultaneously hears two sounds coming from different positions: this requires him to be in a complex informational state the content of which entails the egocentric location of two distinct sounds.

---

[29] On perception and conscious experience, see also 7.4.

[30] For the distinction between simultaneous and serial spatial concepts, see my 'Things Without the Mind', in Zak van Straaten, ed., *Philosophical Subjects: Essays Presented to P. F. Strawson* (Clarendon Press, Oxford, 1980), pp. 76–116, at p. 109.

Of course, the spatial information embodied in purely auditory perception is very thin (though we have seen that the input–output connections involved are already very complex). We can enrich the content we have to deal with, and approach closer to an appreciation of the complexity of the input–output connections underlying an ordinary conception of egocentric space, by considering tactual-kinaesthetic perception. Although the spatial information which this yields is richer than that available by hearing, and quite different perceptible phenomena are spatially located by it, there is a fundamental point of similarity: the spatial content of tactual-kinaesthetic perception is also specifiable in egocentric terms. Indeed, when he uses his hand, a blind person (or a person in the dark) gains information whose content is partly determined by the disposition which he has thereby exercised— for instance, the information that if he moves his hand forward such-and-such a distance and to the right, he will encounter the top part of a chair. And when we think of a blind person synthesizing the information he received, by a sequence of haptic perceptions of a chair, into a unitary representation (a simultaneous spatial representation), we can think of him ending up in a complex informational state which embodies information concerning the egocentric location of each of the parts of the chair: the top *over there to the right* (connected with an inclination to reach out or to point), the back running from *there* to *there*, and so on. Each bit of this information is directly manifestable in his behaviour, and is equally and immediately influential (since he is a conscious subject) upon his thoughts. (One, but not the only, manifestation of the latter state of affairs would be his judging that there is a chair-shaped object in front of him.)

The spatial content of auditory and tactual-kinaesthetic perceptions must be specified in the same terms—egocentric terms. (Though less of the vocabulary is drawn on in specifying the content of auditory perception.) It is a consequence of this that perceptions from both systems will be used to build up a unitary picture of the world. There is only one egocentric space, because there is only one behavioural space.[31]

[31] See S. J. Freedman and J. H. Rekosh, 'The Functional Integrity of Spatial Behavior', in S. J. Freedman, ed., *The Neuropsychology of Spatially Oriented Behavior* (Dorsey Press, Homewood, Ill. 1968), pp. 153–62.

Now suppose we have a conscious subject with a conception of egocentric space. We have been considering thoughts with egocentric spatial content, directly linked to the subject's perceptual input; but, given the conceptual equipment whose underpinnings we have been discussing, it seems a clear possibility that a subject might entertain a thought about a position or region in egocentric space whether or not he is currently perceiving it. Consider, for instance, a subject who has placed a bottle of whisky by his bed, and who thinks, in the dark, 'There's a bottle of whisky *there.*' We are prepared to suppose that there is a determinate thought here—that the subject has a definite place in mind—because we know that subjects do have the capacity to select one position in egocentric space, and to maintain a stable dispositional connection with it. If the subject does have an Idea of a place (does know which place his thought concerns), this will be manifestable only in manifestations of that stable dispositional connection: thus, in his treating certain perceptions from that place as unmediatedly germane to the evaluation and appreciation of any thought involving the Idea, and in his directing actions towards that place[32] when thoughts involving the Idea, together with other circumstances, indicate that this is a good thing to do. These would be manifestations of a complex dispositional connection with the place, and the subject's capacity to entertain thoughts about the place rests upon this dispositional connection with it.[33]

This holds not only for thoughts about specific places and regions in egocentric space, but also for thoughts about the space itself (vaguely conceived)—thoughts expressible with the use of 'here', on one interpretation. It is difficult to see how we could credit a subject with a thought about *here* if he did not appreciate the relevance of any perceptions he might have to

[32] A place is the object of one's action (one's action is directed towards the place) just in case the success of one's action depends upon some characterization of that place.

[33] The complex dispositional connection involves a sensitivity of thoughts to information from the place, and a disposition to action directed towards the place when one's thoughts make it appropriate. These are two separate prongs of equal status, neither reducible to the other. Both prongs may become, as it were, *merely* dispositional. We have already met the point that the informational connection still obtains even if the subject's senses are not operating; it is a precisely parallel point that the behavioural connection still obtains even if the subject is paralysed. [For more about how these dispositional connections would figure in a fully explicit account of an Idea, see §2 of the Appendix to chapter 7.]

the truth-value and consequences of the thought, and did not realize its implications for action (consider, for instance, a thought like 'There's a fire here').

We now have to enquire what makes such Ideas of places in egocentric space adequate Ideas of positions in *public* space. Such an Idea, p, is adequate provided the subject can be credited with a knowledge of what it would be for $\ulcorner \pi = p \urcorner$ to be true—where π is a stand-in for an arbitrary *fundamental*, and hence holistic, identification of a place. And it seems that we can presume upon such knowledge. For any subject who is able to think 'objectively' about space—any subject who can be credited with a cognitive map of any region—must know what is involved in making precisely such an identification—in imposing his knowledge of the objective spatial relations of things upon an egocentric space. Someone who has a cognitive map of Oxford, for example, must be able to contemplate the imposition of the map in the course of his travels (perhaps in a very dense fog). 'If I am here, midway between Balliol and the Bodleian, then that must be Trinity, and so the High must be down there.' In such a situation, one may have to choose between several ways of effecting a coincidence between egocentric space and one's conception of objective space. Each way of effecting a coincidence would generate hypotheses about what one should be able to observe if oriented in this or that direction, and what one would observe if one moved in this or that direction. At the same time, of course, each way of effecting the coincidence would entail an identification between every discriminable point in egocentric space and some point in objective space.

It is, then, the capacity to find one's way about, and to discover, or to understand how to discover, where in the world one is, in which knowledge of what it is for identity propositions of the form $\ulcorner \pi = p \urcorner$ to be true consists.

The capacity has some important features and presuppositions. The subject must move continously through space (if at all); and the course of that movement must (together with how things are disposed in space) determine, and hence be determinable on the basis of, the course of the subject's perceptions. It must be possible for the subject to engage in the kind of reasoning exemplified by the following: 'If I am between Balliol and

Blackwell's (if here = between Balliol and Blackwell's), then that must be Trinity; and if I went on a bit in this direction, then I would be able to see the High.'[34]

It certainly seems that we must be able to attribute this capacity to anyone who has the ability to think about an objective spatial world at all.

On the one hand, such thought presupposes the ability to represent the spatial world by means of a cognitive map. But nothing that the subject can do, or can imagine, will entitle us to attribute such a representation to him if he cannot make sense of the idea that *he* might be at one of the points representable within his map. We say that the subject thinks of himself as located in space (in an objective world that exists independently of him, and through which he moves); only if this is so can the subject's egocentric space be a *space* at all. But what does this thinking of himself as located mean except that the subject can in general regard his situation 'from the objective point of view'? And this means that in general he has the ability to locate his egocentric space in the framework of a cognitive map.[35]

On the other hand, the network of input–output connections which underlie the idea of an egocentric space could never be regarded as supporting a way of representing space (even egocentric space) if it could not be brought by the subject into coincidence with some such larger spatial representation of the world as is constituted by a cognitive map. For instance, the subject must be able to think of the relation in which he stands to a tree that he can see as an instance of the relation in which (say) the Albert Hall stands to the Albert Memorial. That is, he must have the idea of himself as one object among others; and he must think of the relations between himself and objects he can see and act upon as relations of exactly the same kind as those he can see between pairs of objects he observes. This means that he must be able to impose the objective way of thinking upon egocentric space.[36]

[34] See, further, 7.3.

[35] 'Has the ability' only. Notice that I am not saying that for a subject to be thinking of a particular place as *here*, he must be *exercising* mastery of a cognitive map. (This would rule out an evident possibility of amnesia.) The point is just that the capacity to think of a place as *here* requires the *ability* to apply cognitive maps.

[36] A parallel to the point made here is provided by kinaesthetic perception of a limb, and in fact by the subject's body image in general. We might speak of the body image

In view of this, it seems to me that, provided that the subject does maintain a stable dispositional connection with a place, there is just one proposition of the form $\ulcorner\pi = p\urcorner$ (where p is an egocentric spatial Idea) that is true, and the subject knows what it is for it to be true. The qualification is important: if the subject, unbeknownst to himself, is moving in relation to his frame of reference, then there is no one place which he is disposed to regard as germane to the truth of his p-thoughts, or to direct his actions towards on the basis of those thoughts; and so no thought that he might entertain using Ideas from his egocentric repertoire has an object. In this case, the subject's general knowledge of what it is for propositions of the form $\ulcorner\pi = p\urcorner$ to be true would not determine just one proposition of that form as true. (We shall return to this kind of situation shortly.)

For the subject to have a single place in mind, it is not necessary that he remain immobile. We have the ability to *keep track* of a place as we move around; a stable dispositional connection can be maintained, despite changes in circumstances. (The parallel here is with a thought about an object which is moving around, or relative to which one is oneself moving.)

We are now in a position to see why an information-link with a place does not constitute by itself an adequate basis for a knowledge of which place is in question, and this will bring us most of the way to an answer to our question concerning ordinary demonstratives.

There is a possible position about 'here'-thoughts which parallels the position we considered in 6.2 about demonstrative thoughts. This position would hold that an information-link with a place constitutes an adequate basis for a 'here'-identification of a place. One envisages, for example, a television screen showing pictures sent back from a remotely controlled submarine on the sea bed. Some straggly bits of seaweed appear, and so on. It seems that we can throw ourselves into the exploration: 'What have we here?', we say, or 'Here it's mucky.' (We might

---

as representing a space—the body space. But certainly we have no right to speak of a space here unless the subject can impose upon the data of bodily perception his capacity to think objectively about space, so that we have reason to say that he knows that the state of affairs that he feels, when he feels that his leg is bent, is a state of affairs of the very same kind (in the relevant respect) as the state of affairs he observes when he observes a bent stick.

equally use 'there'.) The attraction and naturalness of the position matches that of its parallel considered in 6.2. But we are now in a position to see the crucial difference between this and the ordinary case of 'here'-thoughts. (This will provide us with the basis of an answer to the question 'What makes demonstrative identification possible?')

We have seen that, in the ordinary case, the subject can be said to know which place is in question because he locates it in egocentric space, and his general capacity to find his way about—to unify egocentric and public space—ensures that his knowledge constitutes an adequate Idea. If the subject, in this non-ordinary case, knows that the information does not concern his immediate environment, he will not locate the place in egocentric space, and so some other mode of identification will be in question. He will think of the place as *where the submarine is*, or *where these pictures are coming from*.[37] If, on the other hand, the information is presented in such a way that the subject is taken in, so that he purports to identify the place in egocentric space, as the natives purported to identify a man in the radio (6.2), then, clearly, he will not know which place is in question. The skills he can bring to bear would certainly not lead to the place on the sea bed; at best they would lead to the room in the psychological laboratory, or the cabin in the surface vessel, in which the experiment is being conducted. (We would not need to say that his thoughts concerned this place: this is a case of a thought which is not well-grounded (5.4, case (2).)

It might be thought that what is missing from this case—which forces the conclusion that either the thoughts are not well-grounded, or else they include a conceptual ingredient that is no part of ordinary 'here'-thoughts—is something corresponding to the *action* element in the underpinnings of an ordinary 'here'-Idea. (With this in mind, one might say: a subject's identification of places in egocentric space depends upon a harmony which exists in the normal case between his perceptions and his actions, but which has been distorted in the experiment, just as it has been in a case in which a subject wears inverting prisms. On this view the conceptual ingredient would

---

[37] Notice that with 'where the submarine is', the place is identified by reference to its occupant. This is certainly not how we identify *here* (which would raise the question—parallel to 'Which submarine?'—'Which person?').

be required because any plan of action *vis-à-vis* the place in question—and, equally, *vis-à-vis* the objects there—would have to incorporate a conception of what it would be to go there—to encounter them.)

But I do not think this is correct. Let us elaborate the story, so that the submarine is equipped with limbs, excavators, etc., and a means of propulsion remotely controllable by the subject. And let us consider a highly trained subject, who can manipulate the limbs thousands of feet below him like the experienced driver of a mechanical excavator. By making this addition, we have certainly added to the strength of the subject's tendency to use 'here' and 'there'. (And equally 'this' and 'that': 'That's a remarkable fish.') The tendency would be especially strong if we insulated the subject from the sounds, smells, sights, and so on around him. Even so, I should want to deny that such a subject is so situated *vis-à-vis* a place that he can think of it with the conceptual simplicity of a 'here'-thought.

The subject can *play at* being where the submarine is ('Here it's mucky'); he can *play at* having that mechanical contrivance for his body ('I'll pick up that rock'). But really *he* is (say) in the bowels of a ship on the surface of the water. This is not just one view he can adopt if he likes; it is the view to which everything in his thinking points. And from this perspective a question arises about the place where the objects that he can perceive and manipulate are: a question he need not permanently pose, but which he must understand how to answer. Somewhere *out there, down there*—somewhere in a space that has him as its origin—there is a place (a rock, a fish) that he is thinking about. What is it for a place to be *that place*? And it is here—in answering a question that cannot even arise for a subject normally located, perceptually and behaviourally, in his egocentric space—that the extra conceptual ingredient is required.

If *that place* is conceived by him to be real—so that what appears to be happening there is really happening somewhere in a unified space which also contains himself and his actual environment—then it must in principle have a designation in his system of egocentric spatial relations: it must be *down there*, or *far away behind me*, or ... (and so on indefinitely).[38] And if

---

[38] The Generality Constraint (4.3) is operative here. We shall not attribute 'here'-

these are possibilities which he can genuinely grasp, then he must know what it is for a place identified in one of these ways to be *that place*—a knowledge which must bring in a conception of the spatially extended causal processes that underlie his afferent and efferent connections with the place.

By contrast, when a place is located in one's egocentric space—within the space of the possibilities of one's action—its position within the world as one conceives it to be is already known. There is no further question, and hence no need for any conceptual ingredient to enable one to understand how a further question might be answered.

Perhaps we can tell the story of the submarine in such a way that the subject's location in the surface vessel becomes less and less important to him. He does not move; he becomes insensitive to the sounds and smells around him. It might be possible (with enough of this sort of thing, and perhaps some surgical changes) for us to think of the submarine as *his body*. Then the centre of his world would be down on the sea bed, and his utterances of 'here' and 'this' could go direct to their objects without the need for conceptual supplementation. The precise details of this case do not matter; nor does its ultimate coherence. Let us grant that it is coherent; it does not affect the point I am trying to make. For now, of course, any information he received from the surface vessel—some sounds breaking through, say—would have to be thinkable from that vantage point (if incorporated into his thoughts at all). He would think '*Somewhere up there* someone is whispering', and his grasp of the thought would have a conceptual ingredient (involving the notion of *where my computing centre is*).[39]

It is not possible for a single subject to think of two (or more) separate places as 'here', with the conceptual simplicity of normal 'here'-thoughts. The point is not that the attempt to do so will lead to *confusion*. (A subject might simply have the *de facto* capacity to keep his 'heres' apart, and to act appropriately,

---

Ideas to a subject who has been trained, e.g., to say 'It's hot here' whenever he feels hot. To be credited with the capacity for 'here'-thinking he would need to be able to make sense of, e.g., 'Was it hot here an hour ago?' (which is not the same question as 'Was I hot an hour ago?'). And this will not be possible unless he has the idea of a persisting spatio-temporal world through which he moves continuously.

[39] For more on this sort of case, see 7.6.

rather as we have a *de facto* capacity to keep our right and left arms apart in thought, and to move them appropriately. We might imagine a switch enabling him to shut out information from one place or the other.) The point is not a practical point but a conceptual point: the subject is supposed to be able to *think*, for instance, 'It's warmer here$_1$ than here$_2$,' (where both 'heres' have the conceptual simplicity of a 'here'-Idea), and I claim that this is not coherent. The subject must conceive himself to *be* somewhere—at a point in the centre of an egocentric space capable of being enlarged so as to encompass all objects. Any position not explicitly conceived in this system of relations must have its location in this system of relations *thinkable*. And this applies to the putative second 'here'. No single subject can simultaneously perceive and think of the world from two points of view. (The world cannot be *centred* on two different points.) We may imagine that we can understand the envisaged scheme of thought by oscillating between taking *this* place as *here* and taking *that* place as *here*; but, as David Wiggins once said (in a different context), wavering between two options does not constitute a third option.[40]

Let us now take stock. A thought about a position in *egocentric* space (including the utterly non-specific *here*) concerns a point or region of *public* space in virtue of the existence of certain indissolubly connected dispositions, on the part of the subject, to direct his actions to that place, and to treat perceptions of that place as germane to the evaluation and appreciation of the consequences of the thought. This dispositional connection with a place rests upon a vastly complex network of links between perception and action which allows us to speak of the existence of a unified egocentric space, and in this context, the subject may be said to have an adequate Idea of a point in public space in virtue of his general capacity to impose a conception of public space upon egocentric space.

I speak of a *dispositional* connection for full generality, but it must be understood that one is employing precisely the same Idea of a place when the links are merely potential, on the one hand, and when one is in fact receiving information from it and this information is controlling one's thinking (in the sense of 5.1), on the other—i.e. when the disposition is actualized.

---

[40] See *Identity and Spatio-Temporal Continuity* (Blackwell, Oxford, 1967), p. 17.

This should put in perspective the apparently consider-able difference between demonstrative thoughts proper and thoughts about points and areas of egocentric space with which we began this section. In the first place, there are dispositional elements in the case of demonstrative thoughts too. Secondly, the crucial idea of thought being controlled by information received from something (an object, a place) has a part to play in both cases. And the basis for the difference between 'this' and 'here' is not difficult to find. Conceivably, one might be so related to a material object that one is disposed to treat infor-mation from it as peculiarly relevant to certain sorts of thought about it, even though one has at present no information from it. One might, in the dark, be struck with the thought that there is something immediately in front of one's nose: if this was correct, then one might be disposed to respond in a certain way to information one would receive from it if the lights went on. But obviously it is not, in general, possible to *know* that one is dispositionally so related to an object—still less to know that one is remaining dispositionally so related to the same object over a period of time—without perceiving the object. Places, however, being—how shall we say?—so much thicker on the ground than objects, a subject cannot fail to have a single place as the target of his 'here'-dispositions at an instant; and, since it is possible for a subject to know whether or not he is moving (relative to the earth's surface, or something compar-able which provides the framework for identifying the place), a subject can know that his 'here'-dispositions over a period have concerned the same place, without needing to have perceived the place during the period.

It seems clear that the way in which a subject identifies a place in egocentric space cannot be regarded as a species of *descriptive* identification. The point is implicit in everything that we have said, and does not need to be laboured. Thoughts of this kind rest upon dispositions to react in certain ways in, and to events in, one's immediate environment, and these dispositions cannot be guaranteed by the apprehension of any thought involving a descriptive mode of identification—not even an information-based thought of that kind (see 5.4). The only possible doubt that might arise is over 'the place where I am', as a candidate formulation of a descriptive mode of identification to be regarded as employed in 'here'-thoughts; but we have dealt with this. In the first place, if this is not just the same Idea dressed up in different words, it wrongly suggests a priority of 'I' over 'here'. Secondly, we have insisted that 'here'-thoughts are part of a general system of thought, which includes thoughts about any position in egocentric space. Once we see that no descriptive reduction is generally available, there will be little point in adopting this contentious descriptive treatment for just one element in the system.

We seem, therefore, to have in these thoughts the first clear examples of thoughts whose content can be regarded as Russellian. If there is no place thought about, there is no thought at all—no intelligible proposition will have been entertained. If, for example, the subject is moving, unbeknownst to himself, so that there is no one place which he is disposed to treat as the object of his thought, then it will be quite impossible to excogitate, out of, for instance, his gestures, any intelligible thought-content for the 'here'-thoughts he essays. To do this would require us to be able to formulate a *condition* for a place to be the object of his thought, even though no place is the object of his thought, and to suppose that his thought is that *the place that meets that condition is F*. But this would be possible only if he identified the place by description, which, as we have seen, he does not do.[41]

6.4 DEMONSTRATIVE IDENTIFICATION OF MATERIAL OBJECTS

We are now in a position to answer the question what makes demonstrative identification of spatially located material objects possible. In the ordinary perceptual situation, not only will there be an information-link between subject and object, but also the subject will know, or will be able to discover, upon the basis of that link, where the object is. Given the subject's general knowledge of what makes propositions of the form $\ulcorner \pi = p \urcorner$ true, for arbitrary π, when p is an Idea of a position in his egocentric space, and given that he has located, or is able to locate, the

---

[41] Notice that there are two parts to this point. It is not enough that we be able to formulate, in a vocabulary that we can understand, what it would have been for his thought to have had an object. (No doubt we shall be able to do this: 'had he been stationary, . . .'.) Not only must there be a formulable condition; it must be a condition which can be regarded as being part of the content of the subject's thought.

object in his egocentric space, he can then be said to know what it is for ⌜This = the object at π now⌝ to be true (for arbitrary π). Hence he can be said to have an adequate Idea of the object.

Now that we can see that an information-link does not suffice, we may give up any pretence that a knowledge of what it is for 'This is F' to be true is—at least in the case of properties assessable on the basis of the information channel—*constituted* by one's ability to decide the proposition's truth-value. Even in these cases one has a clear understanding of the possibility of error. (See, further, 6.5.)

We can also see more clearly now that a *communicative* notion of 'knowing which'—a notion explained in terms of the ability to tell others which (in the sense that they can gain knowledge of which object is in question)—is a superficial notion. Here, and indeed in general, the notion of *understanding* a reference of a certain type is a more fundamental notion than the notion of making a reference of that type, because of the possibility of exploiting an established device of reference in order to manifest the intention to be understood in a certain way, when one is not in a position to understand one's own words in that way (see 3.2, 4.1). Someone may make a demonstrative reference to one of a circle of people surrounding him even when he is blind-folded, simply by pointing in the direction of that person while saying 'That person is F.' If we focused upon the notion of *making* a demonstrative reference, and took account of this case, we should not even be able to discern any essential connection between demonstrative identification and information-links.[42] But if we focus rather on what is involved in *understanding* a demonstrative reference, then that connection—which seems pretty much at the heart of any interesting notion of demonstrative identification—can be preserved. (The description we then give of the blindfolded person's utterance, as one which he is not in a position fully to understand, is neither contrary to reason nor without precedent.)

The importance which being able to locate the object has may encourage the idea that the demonstrative identification of spatially located things can be *reduced* to the identification of positions in egocentric space, so that 'this G' would be equivalent to 'the G (now) at p'. But this does not seem to me to be

[42] See n. 1 above.

generally possible. First of all, in a great many cases a subject may make a demonstrative identification of an object without *actually* knowing where it is. The information-link with the object may *enable* the subject effectively to locate the object without providing very specific information about its location— for example, when one is able to home in upon the beetle eating away in a beam. (The information-link places the subject in a position rather like that of the man who feels something tugging at the end of his fishing line. In such cases we are placed in a position in which we have the *practical ability* to locate the object; it is not necessary to construct some *concept* ('the one at the end of my line') in order to allow the subject's thought to reach out to its object, when he can so effectively do so himself.)[43] Secondly, to define 'this *G*' in terms of 'the *G* now at *p*' would be wrong anyway, because we are certainly able to identify an object upon the basis of perception even when it is moving too rapidly for there to be any question of assigning it a position in egocentric space.

If the suggestion was expressive of the hope that some clear *descriptive* thought can be ascribed to a subject who essays a demonstrative identification but is not in fact perceiving any-thing, then it is misconceived for another reason. For such egocentric spatial descriptions of objects to be adequate, they would have to be pretty precise. A subject can demon-stratively identify and think about one object in an enor-mous array of closely packed and indistinguishable objects— provided, as we say, he keeps his eye upon it. For example, a subject may confront a table-top covered with indistinguishable coloured pills, and have the thought that the one that *X* touched is *that* one. Now, in the absence of an object to anchor our dispositions, we can make only rather gross discriminations of areas or regions in egocentric space. Try to concentrate upon a pill-sized region on a white wall in front of you: even if you keep looking, do you have any confidence, at the end of fifteen seconds, that you are still looking at the same region you began with? The Idea of a point *p* in egocentric space, precise enough

---

[43] Another case of this kind arises when the subject wears prisms which distort his field of vision—either shifting it to one side or inverting it. In such a situation the subject can give no definite location to an object in egocentric space. Nevertheless he can be said to know which object is in question—as long as he keeps his eye on it—because he has an effective method for locating the object.

to be adequate to individuate the pill, exists only because there is something at p—the pill—for the subject's perception to latch on to. Consequently it matters little whether we say that the object is thought about primitively, or that it is thought about by the description 'the pill at p', when we realize that the Idea of p depends upon the perception of the pill, and hence is equivalent to the Idea 'where that pill is'.

I have already anticipated my conclusion: a demonstrative Idea of an object is not reducible to any other sort of Idea, and in particular cannot be regarded as a species of descriptive identification. One has an adequate Idea in virtue of the existence of an information-link between oneself and the object, which enables one to locate that object in egocentric space. (That the Idea is adequate depends on one's ability to relate egocentric space to public space.) Consequently, demonstrative thoughts about objects, like 'here'-thoughts, are Russellian. If there is no one object with which the subject is in fact in informational 'contact'—if he is hallucinating, or if several different objects succeed each other without his noticing—then he has no Idea-of-a-particular-object, and hence no thought. His demonstrative thought about a particular object relies upon the *fact* of an informational connection of a certain kind, not upon the thought or idea of that connection; hence it is unconstruable, if there is no object with which he is thus connected.[44]

[44] Desperate remedies have been adopted to resist this conclusion. For instance, considering a case rather like the one of the pills, Stephen Schiffer (in 'The Basis of Reference', *Erkenntnis* xiii (1978), 171–206, at pp. 195–6) suggests that the object would be identified by means of some such description as 'the one I have my gaze fixed on'. But surely this gets things completely the wrong way round: it is the fact that I have my gaze fixed upon the thing, not the idea that I have my gaze fixed upon something, that determines which object is the object of my thought. And we can drive this point home by a simple dilemma. Either the applicability of the concept 'having one's gaze fixed upon ξ' entails the applicability of the concept 'thinking of ξ' or it does not. If having one's gaze fixed upon something *does* entail thinking of that thing, then, while it is true that I cannot intelligibly raise the question—in the sort of case Schiffer is considering— 'Is this the one I have my gaze fixed on?', the fact is useless; for it cannot be offered as an answer to the question 'What makes my thought concern the object it does?' that something is the object of my thought just in case it satisfies the description 'the one I am thinking of'. If, on the other hand, I can have my gaze fixed upon objects I am not thinking of, then the suggestion falls victim to an Open Question argument; for I can intelligibly raise the question 'Is this *the* one I have my gaze fixed on?' (perhaps I have my gaze fixed upon others as well). After one has lost visual contact with the pill, one must surely think of it, if at all, by means of its one distinguishing property: that one was attending to it, or thinking of it, just before. Here there is no circularity; but surely the contrast between the two cases is obvious enough.

The situation is really very complex, for the information-link on which demonstrative identification proper depends is really serving three functions. In the first place, its previous and present deliverances provide the subject with his governing conception of the object: this is something in common with, for example, thoughts based upon the memory of a perceptual encounter. Second, the subject remains 'in contact' with the object, and is thus (unmediatedly) disposed to alter his governing conception in response to certain future information received from the object: this is something in common with the case where the object is identified via a circuitous channel. But, finally, and crucially, the subject is able, upon the basis of the link, to *locate* the object in egocentric space, and thereby in objective space.

I remarked earlier (6.2) that demonstrative thoughts (about material objects) take place in the context of a *continuing* information-link between subject and object; and this is the second of the three points I have just mentioned. A demonstrative Idea of an object is something essentially spanning some period of information-gathering. At any moment at which someone has a demonstrative Idea of an object, he will already have some information from the object; he will be currently receiving information from it; and he will be suitably sensitive to future information from it. (A demonstrative Idea looks both backwards and forwards in time.) The special informational relationship in which the subject stands to the object can be manifested in the way he responds to some thoughts of the form 'This was F a fraction of a second ago', to some thoughts of the form 'This is F now', and to some thoughts of the form 'This will be F in a fraction of a second'.[45] (In the case of the first of these, the manifestation will consist in the subject's having a view as to the truth or falsity of the thought, on the basis of stimulations received from it a moment before; in the case of the third the manifestation will consist in the subject's being *disposed* to regard certain later stimulations received from the object as germane to the truth or falsity of the thought.)

The fundamental basis, then, of a demonstrative Idea of a

---

[45] The thoughts are those that involve suitable replacements for 'F': namely, predicates decidable (in a broad sense, accommodating defeasibility) on the basis of the sensory modality involved in the information-link.

perceptible thing is a capacity to attend selectively to a single thing *over a period of time*: that is, a capacity to *keep track* of a single thing over a period of time—an ability, having perceived an object, to identify later perceptions involving the same object over a period of continuous observation. In this respect, a demonstrative Idea of a currently presented material object is quite different from the sort of past-oriented demonstrative Idea that might underlie a thought of something as *that flash* or *that bang*. (If one could construct a present-oriented version of the Idea 'that bang', it would constitute a bad model for ordinary demonstrative Ideas.)[46]

The expectations to which the belief 'This will be F' gives rise (where being F is decidable in the sensory modality relevant to the 'this'-Idea involved, and the relevant time is in the immediate future) are expectations (as to the occurrence of F-relevant sensations) which concern a particular object *directly*. A way of explaining what I mean by 'directly' here is as follows: when the expectation is fulfilled, it will not be possible to break down the subject's belief state, manifested now in the judgement 'This is F', into two components: $\ulcorner$This is $F\urcorner$ and $\ulcorner$This $= a\urcorner$, where a is the Idea occurring in the original prediction (or a different Idea suitably related to it). On the contrary, the later judgement manifests the same persisting belief (reinforced by the stimulations in virtue of which the expectation is fulfilled); and it employs the same Idea.

I do not deny that there may be some arbitrariness in arriving at a decision as to when the subsequent verification of a future-tense judgement involving a demonstrative does have such an articulation, and when it does not. Perhaps we should discern this articulation when the gap is a matter of minutes. Similarly, when a past-tense judgement is made after a long enough period of observation: in such a case we might see $\ulcorner$This was $F\urcorner$ as based on $\ulcorner$That was $F\urcorner$ and $\ulcorner$This $=$ that$\urcorner$. But what is important is that we cannot apply this procedure generally, supposing our demonstrative Ideas of objects to cover only momentary slices of the objects' histories. Whenever we discern this sort of articulation in the basis for a judgement, we must be prepared for

---

[46] The difference between keeping track of an object and keeping track of a place underwrites the failure of reducibility between demonstrative Ideas of objects and demonstrative Ideas of places.

the possibility of error in either component of the articulated basis, and in particular for a case where there is misidentification. But if, in an attempted demonstrative identification, the subject has not maintained contact with a single object over a reasonable period, then we have not a case of misidentification but a case where the subject has no thought at all. He has not momentarily identified a series of different objects, but failed to identify any object at all.

It is important to understand that the ability to keep track of an object must allow both subject and object to move during the period of observation. Note also that it would be quite arbitrary to deny that the same ability can be exercised in cases in which the object disappears momentarily behind an obstacle. (It follows that demonstrative Ideas will shade off, without a sharp boundary, into Ideas associated with capacities to recognize objects. These capacities are discussed in chapter 8.)

We have seen that a demonstrative identification of an object is part of a scheme of thought which also allows for a place to be identified as *here*, and that both must be explained in terms of the position of a subject in a spatial world; hence both are connected with the subject's identification of himself. There should be no fear that we are explaining simple Ideas ('here' and 'this') in terms of a less simple one ('I'). Any subject at all capable of thought about an objective spatial world must conceive of his normal experiences as simultaneously due to the way the world is and to his changing position in it (see 6.3, 7.3). The capacity to think of oneself as located in space, and tracing a continuous path through it, is necessarily involved in the capacity to conceive the phenomena one encounters as independent of one's perception of them—to conceive the world as something one 'comes across'. It follows that the capacity for at least some primitive self-ascriptions—self-ascriptions of position, orientation, and change of position and orientation—and, hence, the conception of oneself as one object among others, occupying one place among others, are interdependent with thought about the objective world itself.

6.5 SOME CONSEQUENCES

In the light of this analysis, we can answer certain questions which have been raised about demonstrative identification, and draw out certain consequences.

In the first place, we can understand where to locate demonstrative identification on Moore's continuum (see 6.1). It is certainly not true that we can demonstratively identify only parts of the surfaces of physical things—the remainder having to be identified descriptively, in terms of relations to those parts. We can know, upon the basis of perception, that we are confronting a solid body, and not merely a thin layer (even though we cannot always tell the two situations apart perceptually). Further, and connectedly, we can receive information via perception about the entire solid body: we can come to know that it satisfies predicates like 'rolling', 'wobbling', 'being given to John', 'being pre-Columbian'. We are therefore not in informational contact solely with the part. Finally, we can certainly often locate the *whole* body in egocentric space; it would not be right in all cases to say that we can be said to know which other parts are in question only *conceptually*, as we should if we attempted to identify a family by reference to one of its members.

Nevertheless, Moore was right, it seems to me, to think that there is some connection between demonstrative identification and awareness (if by this we mean information), and hence that there are limits to demonstrative identification, of the kind which he attempted to impose. Sitting in a room in a house, a subject is not in informational contact with a *city*; if he believes there is a city around him, this belief cannot be based solely upon what is available to him in perception, nor can he make judgements about the city on that basis (save, perhaps, judgements which hold good of it in virtue of the condition of its parts).[47] The first two informational elements (6.4) drop out, and only the third—location in egocentric space—applies. So there is no resistance to regarding a thought which might be expressed in the words 'This city is F' as equivalent to a thought which might be expressed in the words 'The city here is F', which of course has a perfectly determinate content, whether the room is in a city or not. (There need not be a sharp line between those cases which may be regarded as genuinely demonstrative, and those which are to be analysed on these lines.)

---

[47] The situation is different when we are aloft in some high building and can survey the city beneath us.

Secondly, it does not appear to be true that demonstrative identification must be accompanied by a *sortal* which sets the boundaries of the thing in space and time. I have allowed (4.3) that a fundamental Idea of an object will involve such a sortal, but a demonstrative identification need not itself constitute a fundamental Idea. It will be adequate, without being fundamental, so long as the subject knows what makes an identity proposition of the form ⌜This = the G at π, t⌝ true, and he can know what makes such propositions true without actually knowing the sort of the thing, provided there is such a thing as *discovering* the sort of a thing, and he knows how to do it.

There is certainly such a thing as discovering the *extent* of a thing—its spatial boundaries. For instance, one sees something half buried in the sand, and wonders 'What is this?' In determining its extent, one will be executing a general routine which reckons a single thing as, roughly, a bounded piece of matter which moves as a piece. Is this the exercise of a sortal concept? Perhaps that of a material body? But if it is, the concept is certainly not one which provides boundaries in time. Moreover, one is not forced to identify such objects as wholes: one can decide to think of a part. And here again, though the boundaries may be delivered by some sortal, they need not be: they can be set quite arbitrarily, as when one focuses upon an area of someone's arm.[48]

The idea of discovering the sort of a thing, identified demonstratively, would not make sense if there was not some ranking of sorts. As Trinculo goes along the beach and espies Caliban for the first time, he asks 'What is this?' It must be presumed that 'This is a living animal' is (at least) a better answer than 'This is a collection of molecules'. Similarly, when the fisherman wonders what he has at the end of his line, the answer 'A statue' is a better answer than 'A piece of clay'. Since we seem to know this ranking, it is not important for us to enquire into its principles: a determinate answer can be given to the question 'What kind of thing is this?' provided a definitely extended object is

[48] A rather similar case arises when one *sees* something as having certain boundaries. (One does not impose them.) This does affect the question what one is thinking of. Consider a case in which one sees what is in fact the corner of a buried trunk as a pyramid lying on the sand. Demonstrative thoughts based on this perceptual link will not be about the trunk but only about the corner. (We shall not say 'He thinks that the trunk is a tiny pyramid'.)

indicated, and such an indication does not by itself presuppose any sortal.[49]

It follows that one can discover oneself to be radically mistaken about the object of one's thought. And—thirdly—this point applies not only to mistakes about the sort of thing it is, but also to mistakes resulting from faulty perception. Our conditions for demonstrative identification do not require that the subject's information-link be functioning well—so long as it provides an effective route to the object. He can misperceive its colour, or its shape, or get altogether quite a wrong view of the thing, while still having a perfectly clear Idea of which thing is in question. A proposition about a material object, $\ulcorner a$ is $F \urcorner$, where a is a demonstrative Idea, is conceived to be rendered true by the truth of a pair of propositions of the form $\ulcorner \delta$ is $F \urcorner$ and $\ulcorner a = \delta \urcorner$, where δ is a fundamental Idea. That is to say that the object of the demonstrative thought must be conceived to be part of the objectively describable, spatially-ordered world (which is not to say that the object of the thought can be specified, in a content-giving account of the thought, other than demonstratively). But anyone who has the conception of the objective spatial world must know that no experience of his own can suffice for the truth of any proposition of the form $\ulcorner \delta$ is $F \urcorner$, where being F is an objective property;[50] and consequently that no experience of his own can suffice for the truth of the corresponding proposition of the form $\ulcorner a$ is $F \urcorner$. This is so even though someone who essays a 'this'-thought must assume that some present experience of his is an experience *of* something, for his 'this' to have a referent: he need not assume that the experience is veridical.

6.6 IMMUNITY TO ERROR THROUGH
MISIDENTIFICATION

The last point, emphasizing the possibility of one kind of error, does not conflict with a second, which stresses the impossibility

[49] There is perhaps another reason here for regarding 'this city' as not expressing a genuine demonstrative identification; for here the sortal concept is essential to the determinacy of the thought.

[50] This is so even if being F is an *observational* property relative to the sensory modality on which the demonstrative Idea in question is based. So it would be a mistake to suppose that the conception of thoughts as being made true by the truth of thoughts at the fundamental level is involved only when the information-link in question does not prompt a view about the ascription of the relevant predicate.

of another kind. I have argued that 'this'-Ideas and 'here'-Ideas are both inextricably linked with ways of gaining knowledge of objects. This has been represented as just a fact about these modes of thinking (though, as we shall see, it is not an accident that there are such Ideas). No one can be regarded as thinking of an object demonstratively, or of a place as 'here', if his thinking is not controlled, or disposed to be controlled, by the deliverances of certain ways of gaining knowledge of the object of his thought. Where a is schematic for an Idea-of-an-object of this kind, there is a way of gaining information of the condition of objects such that for a subject to have information that the property of being F_i is instantiated in this way (for some one of a range of relevant properties, $F_1 \ldots F_n$) just is for the subject to have information that $\ulcorner a$ is $F_i \urcorner$ is true (or, to use our widest term for the deliverances of the information-system, just is for it to seem to the subject that $\ulcorner a$ is $F_i \urcorner$ is true).[51] The Idea tolerates no gap between the deliverances of the relevant information channel and thoughts employing the Idea. Consequently, if a subject judges, upon the basis of the information received, that $\ulcorner a$ is $F_i \urcorner$ is true, it will not be possible to regard the belief that he expresses as the result of two distinguishable beliefs: the belief that $\ulcorner b$ is $F_i \urcorner$ is true, for some distinct Idea b, and the identity belief that $\ulcorner a = b \urcorner$ is true.

When knowledge of the truth of a singular proposition, $\ulcorner a$ is $F \urcorner$, can be seen as the result of knowledge of the truth of a pair of propositions, $\ulcorner b$ is $F \urcorner$ (for some distinct Idea, b) and $\ulcorner a = b \urcorner$, I shall say that the knowledge is *identification-dependent*: it depends (in part) on the second basis proposition, which I shall call the *identification component*. We might say that knowledge of the truth of a singular proposition is *identification-free* if it is not identification-dependent. But we should realize that this will include knowledge of the truth of singular propositions which

---

[51] [The phrases 'have information that $\ulcorner a$ is $F_i \urcorner$ is true' and 'seem ... that $\ulcorner a$ is $F_i \urcorner$ is true' should not be misunderstood as implying that the content of the information in question is in some way metalinguistic, or that a linguistic formulation of its content would involve the use of a truth-predicate. The point of the phraseology is merely to enable us to speak with generality about the content of informational states. (Note that since the content of a seeming—a state of the informational system—is non-conceptual, whereas $\ulcorner a$ is $F_i \urcorner$ is schematic for a conceptual state, a joint exercise of a pair of conceptual abilities, we should not think of $\ulcorner a$ is $F_i \urcorner$ as schematically *giving* the content of a seeming. What it gives is the content of a conceptualization of the seeming. See, further, 7.4.)]

are not information-based (consider, for instance, knowledge that Julius invented something: see 1.7). For our purposes, it will be more useful to define a narrower notion of identification-freedom: knowledge of the truth of a singular proposition is *identification-free in the narrow sense* if (i) it is not identification-dependent and (ii) it is based on a way of gaining information from objects.

Now it is a consequence of what I have said about 'this'-Ideas and 'here'-Ideas that they give rise to the possibility of knowledge which is identification-free in the narrow sense. The way of gaining information from something (an object or a place) with which such an Idea is associated will, in certain circumstances (*normal* circumstances) yield knowledge that some property, say that of being *F*, is instantiated; and, provided that the subject has an adequate Idea of the object (place) concerned, this will *ipso facto* constitute knowledge that *that object* (*place*) *is F*.

Clearly, judgements involving Ideas which give rise to the possibility of identification-free knowledge have an epistemological priority over judgements involving all other Ideas of objects: were there no such judgements or Ideas, no singular knowledge would be possible. (It is for this reason that I said that it is not surprising that there should exist such Ideas as 'this'-Ideas and 'here'-Ideas.) It is a trivial consequence of the definitions that if a singular proposition is to be known, and if knowledge of it is not to rest upon knowledge of an infinite number of distinct singular propositions, then knowledge of it must either be identification-free, or rest upon some singular knowledge which is identification-free.[52] (It must be stressed, however, that it is only one, quite specific pattern of dependence that is denied to identification-free knowledge; it is perfectly consistent with its status as identification-free that it should be inferred from a large set of other propositions.)[53]

[52] ['Identification-free' here means 'identification-free in the wide sense'. But the category of singular knowledge which is identification-free in the wide sense without being identification-free in the narrow sense is not very important; no one could plausibly claim that it constitutes the epistemological anchor-point of all our singular knowledge.]

[53] The notion of identification-freedom marks out a class of singular judgements as basic in an *epistemological* sense which is not to be conflated with the *conceptual* sense involved in the notion of the fundamental level of thought (see 4.4). It does not follow, from the fact that a thought employs a non-fundamental Idea (so that ⌜*a* is *F*⌝ is

The contrast between identification-free and identification-dependent knowledge—and, by extension, judgements—comes out very clearly in the case of propositions involving a 'this'-Idea. If a subject has such an Idea, he will be receiving information from an object in some modality—along some channel. If he knows, or takes himself to know, upon the basis of the operation of the channel, that the property of being red is instantiated, then he may judge 'This one is red', and such a judgement is identification-free. But of course the subject may make judgements of another kind: for instance, he may judge 'This man is a Professor of History', upon the basis of his belief that X is a Professor of History and his belief that this man is X.[54] Clearly, judgements of the first kind are immune to a kind of error to which judgements of the second kind are liable. Since they do not rest upon an identification, they are *immune to error through misidentification*.[55]

Though the point is perhaps less clear in the case of 'here'-Ideas, my argument in 6.3 implies that they too give rise to judgements which are identification-free. Though 'here'-Ideas are not dependent upon the receipt of any actual information from a place, a subject is entertaining 'here'-thoughts about a place only if he is *disposed* to allow his thinking to be controlled by information from the place. Hence when he exercises this disposition, and judges 'It's *F* here' upon the basis of information received from the place, his judgement will be identification-free. It certainly appears that 'here'-Ideas tolerate no gap between information that it is *F somewhere* being received in the relevant ways and information that it is *F here* being so received;

---

conceived to be true, if it is, in virtue of the truth of a pair of propositions, $\ulcorner\delta* \text{ is } F\urcorner$ and $\ulcorner a = \delta*\urcorner$), that the thought is identification-dependent in the sense here being considered; and, conversely, a thought at the fundamental level might be identification-dependent.

[54] Equally, a judgement of the form 'X is now sunburnt', made on the basis of the perception of someone, would be identification-dependent (involving the identification component 'This is X').

[55] The phrase is due to Sydney Shoemaker: see 'Self-Reference and Self-Awareness', *Journal of Philosophy* lxv (1968), 555–67, and 'Persons and Their Pasts', *American Philosophical Quarterly* vii (1970), 269–85. The idea derives from a remarkable passage of Wittgenstein (see 7.2). It has been taken up also by Strawson (*The Bounds of Sense* (Methuen, London, 1966), pp. 164–5), with the suggestion that the idea lay at the basis of Kant's insights about 'I', especially in the exposure of illusions in the Paralogisms. But both these philosophers restrict the point—wrongly, as I shall argue—to 'I'-thoughts (and to a special sub-class of 'I'-thoughts at that).

for example, if it seems to the subject that the property of places, being hot, is instantiated (simply by his feeling it to be hot) then it *ipso facto* seems to the subject that it is hot *here*.

Section 6.3 contains the materials for a functional characterization of 'here'-thoughts, with two components: a component involving the relation between 'here'-thoughts and perceptual intake, and a component involving the relation between 'here'-thoughts and action. We can see the information-link which is a necessary condition for possession of a 'this'-Idea (6.2) as constituting a component in a corresponding functional characterization of 'this'-thoughts. Now there is a general connection between identification-freedom (in the narrow sense), with its corollary of immunity to error through misidentification, and the presence of an informational component of the kind in question in the functional characterization of a range of thoughts.

We have the possibility of knowledge which is identification-free (in the narrow sense) when a subject is in a position, on receipt from an object (place) of information warranting ascription to something of the property of being F, to ascribe that property to that object (place) without relying on an *identification*[56] of the object (place) from which he receives the information. Where knowledge of this kind is not possible, and any judgement made on the basis of the appropriate information from an object must rest upon an identification, a disposition connecting that information to the judgement cannot enter into a functional characterization of the content of the judgement. A failure, on someone's part, to modify his assessment of the truth or falsity of the judgement upon the basis of the appropriate information is perfectly consistent with a grasp of the proposition in question; for the subject may disbelieve the identity. Conversely, if there are ways of gaining knowledge of the truth of singular propositions which are identification-free (in the narrow sense), then it must enter into our conception of what it is to grasp or entertain the propositions in question that they may be established in these ways. (A disagreement over whether a sentence can be established in such a way, if not based on error, must reflect an irreconcilable difference in the meaning attached to the sentence by the disputants.)

---

[56] In the sense of an identification component; *not* in the sense required by Russell's Principle. See 7.2 for the distinction.

It is worth noting that a notion parallel to that of knowledge without identification will be needed in order to give a proper account of the *action* component of a functional characterization. This will generate a parallel distinction between actions which are liable only to one kind of error (namely that they are not instances of the intended action-type) and actions which are also liable to error through misidentification (as when one shoots and kills *someone*, but not, as intended, the President).

The reason why it is less clear, in the case of 'here', that there is immunity to error through misidentification is that there is room, in this case, for an error to appear to be an error of misidentification. It does not make sense for a subject to wonder whether information he is receiving in the relevant channel is information from *this* object: if he has a 'this'-Idea of an object at all, then that information is relevant to judgements made with the use of it. But this is not the case with 'here'. A subject's 'here'-Idea of a place rests upon a disposition to regard as relevant, to thoughts involving that Idea, such information from the place as is available to him in the normal way because he occupies the place. But even when it appears to him that his information is derived in the normal way from the place he occupies, it is a clear possibility, one which the subject may be able to understand, that it is not—that his information is not derived from a place in the normal way. For example, it is possible that the subject is wearing a pair of ultra-lightweight and undetectable earphones, operating in such a way that the sounds he hears are not sounds at the place he occupies at all— they may be sounds occurring in some other place, or sounds produced solely by events internal to the mechanism. There is, therefore, the possibility of the subject's wrongly taking information to be relevant to his 'here'-thoughts. The possibility then arises of a subject wondering whether he is in this situation. Hence, it might appear that when he eventually decides that he is not, and so is prepared to judge 'It's *F* here' upon the basis of the deliverances of the information channel, we can discern the two components characteristic of an identification-dependent judgement: 'That place is *F*', and 'That place is here'.

However, the view I have taken of 'here'-thoughts implies that this conclusion must be resisted. (It is important to do so, not merely for our immediate purposes, but also because this way of looking at matters is an example of a general line of reasoning which is used to produce quite extraordinary conclusions about 'I': see 7.3, 7.5.)

In the first place, if we do try to discern this articulation in our 'here'-thoughts, we shall find it difficult to give an account of the supposed Ideas which would figure in the identification component ('That place is here').

'That place' would have to be understood as reflecting a way of thinking about a place which would leave open the question of where it is in relation to the subject (so that it would be available for use by a subject who does not accept the identification component—a subject who takes himself to be fitted with the earphones). Now, we know that the information-link does not by itself provide an adequate Idea (6.3). How, then, does the subject know what it is for a place to be *that place* in a way which leaves open the question of where it is in relation to his own position? The only possible answer is that he thinks of it explicitly as the causal source of the sounds he is hearing (that is, by description). There is nothing wrong with such an Idea of a place: indeed, this is certainly how we would think of a place when we knew we were fitted with the earphones. But surely such conceptual material cannot be regarded as an essential ingredient in ordinary unreflective 'here'-judgements.

As for the supposed Idea putatively expressed by 'here' in the identification component, we shall find it extremely difficult to give an account of this in such a way as to leave room for the identification component at all.

Notice that what is being represented as decomposable into a predication component and an identification component is a pattern of establishment of propositions which concerns 'I' as much as it does 'here'. The capacity to judge 'It's *F* here' on the basis of one's perceptions is inseparable from the capacity to judge 'I am in a place where it's *F*' on the basis of those same perceptions. (See 6.3, 7.3.)[57]

[57] The equation 'Here is where I am' reflects the interconnections, necessarily involved in one's conception of oneself, between the way the world is, the changing course of one's perceptions, and one's movement through the world. If we exclude from our conception of ourselves what we have (or know how to acquire) on the basis of the pattern of establishment of propositions in question—which is to abstract from our location in space, thinking of ourselves in the first instance as a Cartesian ego—then we make the idea that we might subsequently go on to identify ourselves with some physical thing unintelligible. (See, further, 7.3.)

If this is correct, then it means that it is useless to attempt to provide a wholesale underpinning for this pattern of establishment of propositions, in the case of 'here'-judgements, by appealing to an identification component, 'That place is here', with 'here' understood as *where I am*. For my conception of my location in space has direct and immediate connections with the course and pattern of my perceptions in a way that is manifested by a pattern of establishment of propositions of precisely the kind for which the underpinning was being sought.

I am not saying that the concept of location is different in the case of 'where I am' and 'where John is' (that no univocal expression 'where ξ is' is discernible in both). In particular, I conceive myself, no less than I conceive John, as a physical object located at a place. But when the question 'Which physical object?' is raised, we have to make reference to the way I locate myself on the basis of the course of my perceptions; and that means assuming the legitimacy of precisely the pattern of establishment of propositions that was in question.

Thus if the general legitimacy of this pattern of establishment of propositions were held in question, the subject could no longer be credited with a 'here'-Idea of a place at all; it is no use supposing that in such circumstances a 'where I am'-Idea would serve. What this implies is that it is not intelligible for someone to challenge (to ask for an underpinning for) the relevance to 'here'-thoughts of information from a place which is not taken not to be gained from that place in the *normal* way.[58] It is always intelligible to raise the question whether the current information *is* being gained in the normal way (for instance to speculate about whether one is in the situation of the subject with the earphones). But it is unintelligible to challenge the relevance of the current information to one's 'here'-thoughts without at the same time questioning whether the information is being gained from a place in the normal way.

We must allow, then, that the ordinary judgement 'It's *F* here' (or, equally, 'It's *F* where I am') does rest on an *assumption*: but it is the assumption that the senses are functioning normally, rather than an identity assumption. The subject will be aware that its being *F* where he is is not conclusively established by its seeming to be *F* where he is. But this does not mean that his

---

[58] The point of this roundabout formulation will be explained shortly. See n. 61.

conception of what it is for it to be F where he is is entirely independent of his capacity to establish that that is so on the basis of perception. Quite generally, even with observational states of affairs (consider 'This one is red'), we are aware of the possibility of error; but no one would want to suggest that our conception of what it is for something to be red is wholly independent of our capacity to discriminate red from non-red things. What it is for something to be red is conceived as having implications for *normal* perception, and error is possible because perception need not be normal. (It is frequently said that such an account must be circular: what is normal perception but *accurate* perception? But there need be no circularity if normality is understood statistically.)

Thus a subject who hears the sound of a blackbird singing can indeed say to himself 'It seems to me that a blackbird is singing here, but is there really a blackbird singing here?'; but this does not imply that his conception of what it is for there to be a blackbird singing where he is is a conception of anything other than a state of affairs establishable (defeasibly) by direct observation (without the intermediation of an identification component). He will conceive the possibility that things are not as they seem in terms of the possibility of a malfunctioning, or abnormal functioning, of his perceptual apparatus. And this obviously includes, as a special case, the possibility that he is in the position of the subject equipped with the earphones.

It is worth making explicit something implicit in what I have just said: that we still have, with undiminished force, the fact that in its appearing to the subject via his senses that the property of places, that of being F, is instantiated, what appears to him is precisely that it is instantiated *here*: the earphones produce precisely this illusion. We cannot understand, and we are not required by the example to try to understand, the possibility of its appearing to a subject by the unmediated exercise of his senses that it is F *somewhere* without its appearing to the subject that it is F *in his vicinity*.

The argument we are considering seeks to persuade us to the contrary: that the normal exercise of a subject's perceptual facilities yields knowledge of the condition of *some place or other*, but that this knowledge leaves it quite open whether that place is *here* (where the subject is). But this seems incorrect. Such non-particular knowledge will indeed be gained by the subject in the experiment, if he has been *told* that his auditory perceptions concern, not the place where he is, but another place. In the absence of such information (and obviously we do not normally have such information), there can surely be no question of the subject's *knowing*, via the earphones, that it is F (if that is how it seems) anywhere at all. (The sounds he hears *might* be produced within the mechanism, rather than derived from a place.) Hence it cannot be right to suppose that the basic deliverances of the perceptual process, in so far as they are knowledge-yielding, are neutral with respect to whether or not they concern the place where the subject is. The earphones, as I said, simply produce an *illusion* as to what is going on *where the subject is*.

To sum up: what the example shows is merely the possibility of a certain kind of mistake, one which cannot be regarded as a mistake of identification. Information derived from a place in the normal way is germane to 'here'-thoughts; and it is possible for a subject to mistake information not so derived for information which is so derived—to suppose his senses are functioning normally when they are not. It is correct to see the standard procedure which issues in 'here'-judgements as relying upon an assumption, which can be intelligibly called into question; but it is merely an assumption of the *normal functioning* of the senses, and not an *identity* assumption. The subject's hypothesis that this information does not concern *here* (the place where he is) is the hypothesis that his perceptual system is malfunctioning. (This allows us to register a difference between 'this' and 'here'. In the case of 'this', the assumption of normal functioning of the senses is not, as with 'here', a precondition of the information thus received being germane to the judgements, but a precondition of there being anything at all which is netted by one's intention to think of something—because it is a precondition of one's knowing which thing it is that one intends to think of.)[59]

Earlier in this section I used the phrase 'immune to error through misidentification'. This is a phrase used by Sydney

---

[59] The deluded subject's 'here'-thoughts will be false thoughts about where he is. But his attempts at 'this'-thoughts will net no object at all. (Since he is deluded into thinking that the information-link is normal, there will not be the possibility of a descriptive identification via the circuitous informational channel.)

Shoemaker in connection with some of the knowledge which we have of ourselves.[60] I think my notion of judgements which are identification-free (in the narrow sense) is essentially the idea Shoemaker intends to capture. Certainly Shoemaker argues from the fact that a judgement is not immune to error through misidentification to the conclusion that it is identification-dependent. However, Shoemaker's criterion of immunity to error through misidentification does not quite capture the notion of identification-freedom (in the narrow sense), and as a consequence of this criterion, certain judgements which I wish to regard as identification-free turn out, in Shoemaker's view, not to be immune to error through misidentification. Since the point is closely connected with the one I have just made, and since it will have considerable importance when we come to discuss the first person, I shall briefly explain what I take to be wrong with Shoemaker's criterion.

Shoemaker says that a judgement is immune to error through misidentification if and only if it is based upon a way of knowing about an object such that it does not make sense for the subject to utter 'Something is F, but is it a that is F?', when the first component is expressive of knowledge gained in that way. It is easy to see that our ordinary 'here'-judgements about places do not meet this criterion of immunity. For suppose a subject knows that he is liable to have the undetectable headphones placed on him without notice, and that the headphones always relay the sounds of some other place. And suppose that on a particular occasion there are no headphones, and the subject hears some laughter. Then it will certainly make sense for the subject to think 'There's laughter somewhere, but is it here?', even though the first component expresses knowledge of a place gained in the standard way. I have already given reasons why I think that 'here'-judgements based in the normal way are identification-free, and this explains why I think that Shoemaker's criterion is unsatisfactory.

Shoemaker's criterion can be modified rather simply, to provide a useful test of the phenomenon I am concerned with. What we should say is that a judgement is identification-free if it is based upon a way of knowing about objects such that it does not make sense for the subject to utter 'Something is F, but

[60] See n. 55.

is it *a* that is *F*?', when the first component expresses knowledge which the subject does not think he has, or may have, gained in any other way.[61] A way of capturing the point of this revised criterion is this: the utterance 'Something is *F*, but is it *a* that is *F*?' needs a special background, in the view, of course, of the person who utters it; he has to suppose that the knowledge expressed in the first component was not gained, or may not have been gained, in the way with which the Idea involved in the second component is associated. If the situation is perfectly normal, and the subject does not take it not to be normal, the utterance does not not make sense.

The criterion is circular, of course, if ways of gaining knowledge of objects are individuated by the objects they concern. Its effectiveness depends on our being able to distinguish ways of gaining knowledge of objects not in terms of the objects concerned, but in terms of the sort of causal process involved.

If a judgement that *a* is *F* is based upon a way of gaining knowledge of objects, and it meets this revised criterion, then it will be identification-free (in the narrow sense). For suppose that it is not. It is not identification-free in the wide sense, since it is based on a way of gaining knowledge of objects. So it must be identification-dependent: that is, based upon a way of knowing about objects which yields in the first instance knowledge that $\ulcorner b$ is $F\urcorner$ is true, for some distinct Idea *b*, together with a belief that $\ulcorner a = b\urcorner$ is true. But in that case it ought to be possible for the subject to call the second component of the basis of his belief into question, without challenging the first, and without supposing the knowledge expressed by the first is gained in any way other than the way in which it is in fact gained. So the judgement must be based upon a way of gaining knowledge of objects such that it *does* make sense for the subject to think 'Something is *F*, but is it *a* that is *F*?', when the first component is a result of gaining knowledge of an object in this way, and without the subject's having to suppose that the knowledge which the first component expresses was gained, or may have been gained, in any other way. Consequently, it would appear

---

[61] I use this double-negative formulation in order to avoid saying 'knowledge which the subject takes himself to have gained in that way', and hence to avoid attributing to subjects, in the normal case, views about their ways of gaining knowledge; though whether it would be harmful in this case I do not know.

to be safe to assume that it was *not* based upon a way of gaining knowledge such that it does *not* make sense to think 'Something is *F*, but is it *a* that is *F*?', when the first component is a result of gaining knowledge of an object in that way, and without the subject's having to suppose that the knowledge which the first component expresses was gained, or may have been gained, in any other way. Hence, contrary to hypothesis, it does not meet the revised version of Shoemaker's criterion. And this refutes the supposition that the judgement that *a* is *F* is not identification-free in the narrow sense.

Appendix

1[1]   In understanding the sentence 'Today is fine', said on day d_1, one can be regarded as having a Fregean thought, but is it a thought which one can have on any other day? Frege appears to have thought that it is:

If someone wants to say the same today as he expressed yesterday using the word 'today', he must replace this word with 'yesterday'.[2]

Frege appears to have held that to have on day d_2 just the thought which one has when one thinks 'Today is fine' on day d_1, one must think 'Yesterday was fine'. Presumably this means that it is possible for someone reading yesterday's newspaper to understand sentences like 'The Prime minister is holding a cabinet meeting today' by realizing that it is true if and only if the Prime Minister held a cabinet meeting the day before. Now many philosophers, commenting on this passage, have concluded that Frege intended to abandon a notion of 'what is said', or 'the thought expressed', which was 'psychologically real' in the sense of being the object of propositional attitudes, and was giving expression to the idea that two people would express the same thought provided that they referred to the same object (in whatever way) and said the same thing about it.[3] But such a conception of *what is said*, or *the thought expressed*, is so wholly antagonistic to the theory of language ushered in by the distinction between sense and reference, and is otherwise so wholly absent from Frege's work, that it seems to be doubtful that the passage has been correctly interpreted. Is it clear, for example, that Frege would have been willing to continue the passage:

... he must replace this word with 'yesterday', or 'my birthday', or any other expression designating the same day?

Might Frege not have had in mind an idea of a thought the grasp of which, on a later day, requires just as specific a way of thinking of a day as does its grasp on an earlier day—namely, as the preceding day?

---

[1] Evans intended that this material (from 'Understanding Demonstratives', in Herman Parret and Jacques Bouveresse, eds., *Meaning and Understanding* (De Gruyter, Berlin and New York, 1981), pp. 280–303) should appear in chapter 6; it clearly belongs with the various passages where our ability to keep track of objects and places is mentioned.

[2] 'The Thought', p. 24 in Strawson, ed., *Philosophical Logic*.

[3] See, e.g., Kaplan, 'Demonstratives', p. 43. Dummett comes close to this at *Frege*, p. 384; but there substitutions which preserve the thought expressed are restricted to substitutions of other demonstrative expressions with the same referent.

Pursuing this suggestion, we discover that, far from abandoning the 'psychologically real' notion of a thought in favour of a psychologically quite uninteresting equivalence class of thoughts, Frege may well have glimpsed the results of extending that notion to the sphere of human thinking which depends upon the position human beings have in space and time.

We must agree that, if a subject thinks on d_1, about d_1, to the effect that it is fine by thinking 'Today is fine', and thinks on d_2, about d_1, to the effect that it is fine by thinking 'Yesterday was fine', there is some level of description at which he is thinking of the same day in different ways—the account of what makes his thought about d_1 in the two cases will not be entirely the same. And it is natural to think that this difference in ways of thinking can be exploited to produce the possibility of differing epistemic attitudes to the thoughts, which would then preclude their being the same thought, if thoughts are intended to be the object of propositional attitudes.

However, the natural suggestion is not correct; there is no head-on collision between Frege's suggestion that grasping the same thought on different days may require different things of us, and the fundamental criterion of difference for thoughts which rests upon the principle that it is not possible coherently to take different attitudes towards the same thought. For that principle, properly stated, precludes the possibility of coherently taking different attitudes towards the same thought *at the same time*. Consider a subject S, who accepted the sentence 'Today is fine' when uttered on d_1, and who rejects the sentence 'Yesterday is fine' when uttered on d_2, perhaps because he has misremembered the weather, or because he has 'lost track of time'. Now in order to apply the criterion of difference in this situation, we must first make a decision as to what it would be for S to have exactly the same thought on d_2 as he had when he thought on d_1 'Today is fine'. Because its application requires a prior decision on this question, the criterion of difference cannot, by any means, be the whole story about the identity and distinctness of thoughts, and is powerless to upset Frege's suggestion. For, either we hold that it is possible to think again the thought entertained on d_1 or we do not. If we hold that it *is* possible, no better account than Frege's can be given of the circumstances under which it is possible. (If this is not obvious, some merits of his account will be mentioned below.) Hence, on this alternative, to think 'Yesterday is fine' on d_2 is to think the same thought again, and so no possibility opens up, on d_2, of coherently assenting to the same thought as one accepted when one judged on d_1 'Today is fine', and of dissenting from the thought 'Yesterday was fine'. On the other hand, to hold that it is not possible to have on d_2 the very same thought as one had on d_1, while not a ridiculous proposal, obviously precludes use of the criterion of difference against Frege's contrary view. Some other considerations must be appealed to.

Frege's idea is that being in the same epistemic state may require different things of us at different times; the changing circumstances force us to change in order to keep hold of a constant reference and a constant thought—we must run to keep still. From this point of view, the acceptance on d_2 of 'Yesterday was fine', given an acceptance on d_1 of 'Today is fine', can manifest the *persistence* of a belief, in just the way in which acceptance of different utterances of the same sentence 'The sun sets in the West' can. Are there any considerations which can be advanced in favour of this way of looking at matters?

To answer this question, we must contrast Frege's conception with the opposing one, according to which the thoughts associated with sentences containing temporal indexicals cannot be grasped at later times. On this atomistic conception, what Frege regards as a persistence of a belief is really a succession of different, but related, beliefs concerning the same time. It must of course be acknowledged that these patterns, or sequences, of beliefs are very commonly met with— that human beings do have a general propensity, on forming one belief in this series, later to have the other beliefs in the series. But this fact by itself does not settle the issue. Admittedly, it is not clear what account can be given of this succession of beliefs on the atomistic conception. One belief cannot give rise to another by any *inference*, since the identity belief that would be required to underwrite the inference is not a thinkable one; no sooner does one arrive in a position to grasp the one side of the identity than one has lost the capacity to grasp the other. But one can be suspicious of the atomistic conception for other, deeper, reasons.

On the atomistic conception, whether there are later elements in the series, and whether they concern the same object, are quite irrelevant to the subject's capacity to entertain one of the atoms. The atom must be a perfectly coherent unit of thought by itself, even if it is entertained by someone who has not the least propensity to form the other members of the series. But this, Frege might well have thought, is wrong. No one can be ascribed at t a belief with the content 'It is now ϕ', for example, who does not have the propensity, as time goes on, to form beliefs with the content 'It was ϕ just a moment ago', 'It was ϕ earlier this morning', 'It was ϕ this morning', 'It was ϕ yesterday morning', etc., although, of course, this propensity can be counteracted by new evidence. Frege might be credited with the insight that a capacity to keep track of the passage of time is not an optional addition to, but a precondition of, temporal thought. If this is so, the thought-units of the atomist are not coherent, independent thoughts at all, but, so to speak, cross-sections of a persisting belief state which exploits our ability to keep track of a moment as it recedes in time.

The metaphor of 'keeping track of a moment' originates in connection with another kind of thought about an object, and it provides a useful, if only partial, parallel. Suppose that one is watching a scene in which there are several similar objects moving about fairly rapidly, but not so rapidly as to prevent one keeping track of one of them in particular. In such a situation, one can think about one of these objects rather than any other, but any such thought rests upon a skill we possess of keeping track of an object in a visual array over time. Our eyes and our heads move, perhaps we are also obliged to turn or move our bodies, but these changes are required to maintain contact with the same object over time. So one's thought *at* a time is dependent upon an ability which is necessarily manifested only *over* time. One might begin the period with the belief of an object that it is valuable, and end the period with a belief of the same object that it is valuable. Now a move parallel to the one which Frege made in connection with 'today' and 'yesterday' would be to hold that one belief has persisted over time, despite the local differences which the changing circumstances have imposed upon one. And there is a parallel, opposing, atomistic move which would regard the subject as holding a *sequence* of different beliefs over the relevant period of time, altering as the subject's relation to the object altered. And the objection to the atomistic position here is the same as in the earlier case. If the atomistic position were correct, it ought to be possible to have just one of the members of the sequence no matter which others accompanied it, i.e. in the absence of any capacity to keep track of the object. But if that ability is missing, it is not possible for a subject to have a thought about an object in this kind of situation at all. Now Frege himself did not give this parallel, but he did write, after the passage just quoted: 'The case is the same with "here" and "there".' Indeed it is; our ability to think of a place as 'here' is dependent upon our general ability to keep track of places as we move about (which requires, in general, the ability to know when we are moving); so, once again, there could not be thoughts interpretable as 'It's ϕ here', if they were not entertained by a subject who had the propensity to entertain, as he moves about, thoughts expressible in the words 'It's ϕ there'.

These examples suggest that we have to regard the static notion of 'having hold of an object at *t*' as essentially an abstraction from the dynamic notion of 'keeping track of an object from *t* to *t''*'. And the grasp, at *t*, of a thought of the kind suggested by the passage from Frege, a *dynamic* Fregean thought, requires a subject to possess at *t* a capacity to keep track of a particular object over time. One is not precluded from having only a momentary grasp of a dynamic Fregean thought, for it is not impossible that, after an object has engaged with one's capacity to keep track of objects of that kind, one should lose track of it, and with it, lose track of the thought. Indeed, it is an aspect of this capacity that the subject will, in general, know when this has happened. The capacities upon which certain kinds of thought rest can only be described in dynamic terms; it does not follow that any exercise of those capacities must be extended over time.

Consequently, the *way of thinking of an object* to which the general Fregean conception of sense directs us is, in the case of a dynamic Fregean thought, a *way of keeping track of an object*. This permits us to say, after all, that a subject on d_2 is thinking of d_1 *in the same way* as he did on d_1, despite lower-level differences, because the thought-episodes on the two days both depend upon the same exercise of the capacity to keep track of a time.[4]

2[5]   Section 6.5 fails to broach the following question: is it required, for the demonstrative identification of, say, a woman, that one's information-link with the object provide one with enough properties of the sort characteristic of women for one to be said to see the object as a woman? The suggestion would be that, if one fails to meet that condition, and merely sees something which one is prepared to believe is a woman, then one's identification (perhaps expressed in the words 'that woman') is partly by description ('the woman identical with that'); and there is little difficulty in supposing that 'that' in this spelled-out formulation of the identification nets, e.g., a stone, or a hologram, or a patch of shadow, if that is what one sees and takes to be a woman; so that one's mistake does not mean that one's attempted thought is deprived of content. Whereas if one sees the object as a woman, the identification is genuinely demonstrative; and if what one sees is not a woman (or, at least, a person), then the mistake deprives the attempted thought of content. (There would be a question about

---

[4] Kaplan briefly raises the possibility sketched in this section, under the topic of 'cognitive dynamics', but dismisses it: 'Suppose that yesterday you said, and believed it, "It is a nice day today". What does it mean to say, today, that you have retained *that* belief? ... Is there some obvious standard adjustment to make to the character, for example replacing *today* with *yesterday*? If so, then a person like Rip van Winkle, who loses track of time, can't retain any such beliefs. This seems strange.' ('Demonstratives', p. 70.) But there seems to be no more strangeness in the idea that someone who loses track of time cannot retain such beliefs than there is in the idea that someone who loses track of an object cannot retain the beliefs about it with which he began. If one has in fact lost track of time without knowing it, then one can think one has retained one's beliefs when one has not. But, since in general thoughts associated with Russellian singular terms are such that the subject cannot infallibly know that he has one, we should not jib at denying the subject infallible knowledge of when he has the *same* one.

[5] Here I have attempted to spell out an afterthought interleaved into the typescript of 6.5.

how seriously mistaken one has to be for this to be the consequence. But it seems that we do not attach the same importance to misperceiving a man as a woman, as we should attach to misperceiving, say, a stone as a woman. In the former case, a thought involving a demonstrative identification expressible by 'that woman' is merely incorrect; in the latter case there is some inclination to say that the attempted thought lacks a content.) This suggestion would help to explain why it seems implausible to suppose that a city can be demonstratively identified (see 6.5).

3[6]   The phenomenon of immunity to error through misidentification (see 6.6) is intimately connected with the information-based character of the appropriate thoughts. Section 5.4 argues that a thought can be information-based even if the mode of identification it employs is descriptive; so the phenomenon ought to be found in such cases too. Consider, for example, someone who is in a position to entertain memory-based thoughts about an object, employing a descriptive mode of identification whose descriptive content is captured by 'ϕ'. It will not make sense for such a subject to say 'Someone was F, but was it that ϕ who was F?' when the first component expresses knowledge possessed in virtue of the stored information that constitutes the base of the thoughts in question.

In this sort of case, the explanation of the immunity to error through misidentification is that the thinker's overriding intention is that his thinking be well-grounded; and his thinking is well-grounded only if the mode of identification employed does in fact identify the object from which the information was derived. This secures that the thinking, if it nets an object at all, nets the object which is the source of the information; so that one cannot intelligibly wonder whether it is the object netted by this thinking to which the information relates. (This is secured without our needing to suppose that the thinker thinks of the object of this thought *as* the source of the information—precisely not: he thinks of it as that ϕ. See the Appendix to chapter 5. But we can say, using an attribution of intention of the sort discussed in 5.3, that his overriding intention is to be thinking of the object from which the information derives.)

The case of 'here' is different: we cannot (even in the sense of 5.3) attribute to a 'here'-thinker the overriding intention to think of a place from which a certain body of information derives. For one thing, there need be no such body of information (the case of the subject who is anaesthetized, etc.: 6.3). For another, even where there is an apparently relevant body of information, we have seen that one can

---

[6] This spells out some notes aimed towards a supplementation of 6.6, designed to make its relation to the ideas of chapter 5 clear.

intelligibly raise the question whether the information relates to *here* (6.6). But, as 6.6 argues, the question can be raised only on the basis of the supposition that the information is not being received from a place in the normal way. A 'here'-thinker who is in receipt of an apparently relevant body of information, and who makes no such supposition, has to be credited with the overriding intention to be thinking of the place from which the information derives: and thus, in the absence of the supposition about perceptual abnormality, the structure of the case becomes parallel to the structure of the case considered in the last paragraph. (If one engages in 'here'-thoughts in the absence of relevant information, one must be credited with the overriding intention of referring to the place from which one would be receiving information in the normal way if one were not in fact currently precluded from doing so.)

4 Is there anything corresponding to demonstrative identification in the case of abstract objects?[7] Certainly it would have to be of a quite different character from the demonstrative identification of physical objects, since the fundamental ground of difference of such objects is not spatio-temporal. Nevertheless, there are locutions which are suggestive of such an identification; for instance, 'this colour', 'this song', or 'that point' (said during a philosophical discussion).

These objects are all what we might call type objects; they stand to the physical occurrences which instantiate or realize them as type to token. And the fundamental ground of difference of a type object is given by the set of properties possessed by all tokens which instantiate the type. (It is one of the strengths of the fundamental/non-fundamental dichotomy that we can apply it outside the domain of physical objects.) To be thinking of a shape, for example, via its fundamental ground of difference, is to be thinking of something with such and such geometrical properties (rather than, for example, something much used by Arab draughtsmen, or something much talked about by philosophers).

Demonstrative identification of a type object would require that one have in mind the fundamental ground of difference of that object in virtue of one's perception of it—that one's perception of the object give one the relevant fundamental ground of difference. And why should this not be so? Why should one not be able, by perceiving a token, to be put in mind of the fundamental ground of difference of the object of which it is a token?

We need a distinction between thinking of the object of a thought via a description like 'the type of which this is a token', and thinking

---

[7] Evans seems to have planned a section on this question: this material comes from a set of lecture notes.

of it as *this type*. The latter is a possibility only for someone who perceives the token clearly enough to be able to abstract the properties of the type. And this latter position may be a positive requirement for understanding a remark.

5 There are a number of causes of resistance to the thesis that demonstrative thoughts are Russellian.[8]

One cause has been an inadequate conception of demonstrative identification. If our conception of demonstrative identification is tied in a simple way to the use of demonstrative expressions in English, then we shall include in that category cases like the one in which a man is indicated by means of his footprint. For members of such a category, nothing general may be said about the consequences of there being no identified object. Indeed nothing general may be said about such a rag-bag category at all.

A second cause has been the mistaking of what might be called 'situation-specifying' descriptions of attitudes for content-giving specifications of attitudes. When we say that the hallucinator thinks that the man in front of him is about to charge, we are only sympathetically approximating to his state of mind.

A third cause has been a failure to distinguish cases in which a person demonstratively misidentifies something from cases in which a person identifies nothing at all. When a person takes a pebble to be a fish, there is something which he takes to be a fish. And at least in some cases (see § 2 of this Appendix) he can demonstratively identify that thing: he does not have to be right about the kind of thing he is confronting in order to be able to identify it.

A fourth cause is a failure to see how special is the use of language to 'talk about' things which the speakers know not to exist, as when one discusses the characters in a film one has just seen. This use of language will be discussed in chapter 10.

A fifth cause is an adherence to a conception of the mind as a repository whose contents are unmistakably accessible to us—like a theatre whose actors are incorrigibly known to us. But we must reject this picture. It is already rejected when one acknowledges that if in perception anything is before the mind, it is the public objects themselves, not some internal representative of them. The thesis we have been considering is really no more than a corollary of that realism.

What explains the extraordinary hold this conception of the mind has upon us? It is a consequence of the realism which we have just mentioned that when a person hallucinates, so that it appears to him that he is confronting, say, a bus, then, whether or not he is taken in

---

[8] A note in the latest draft indicates a plan to have a section on causes of resistance. This material is from an earlier draft.

by the appearances, there is literally nothing before his mind. Now why should this seem so counter-intuitive? Why should it seem so right to say that there is something, though not a bus, before his mind?

To answer this question, we have only to ask why it will seem to the hallucinator to be the right thing to say. And we have already answered this question. To hallucinate is precisely to be in a condition in which it seems to one as though one is confronting something. So of course it will seem right to the hallucinator to say that he is actually confronting something; the situation is very like one in which he *is* confronting something. For the same reason it will seem right to a person who sees a stick half immersed in water to say that he is actually confronting something bent.

If after it has been acknowledged on all sides that it seems to the hallucinator that he is confronting something, and to the person who sees a stick in water that he is confronting something bent, one says that it seems reasonable to the generality of mankind to suppose that the hallucinator is actually confronting something, and that the person who sees a stick is confronting something that is actually bent, then one is attempting to double-count the fact that has already been acknowledged.

Now it is essentially the same consideration that underpins the view that if it seems to a person that he is thinking something, then there must be some thought before his mind. Perhaps the same explanation of the attraction this consideration has for us will serve to undermine it in this application as well.

6[9]   Section 1.4 suggests explaining the notion of a way of thinking of something, in terms of which the idea of Fregean sense was glossed, by way of the idea of an account of what makes a subject's thought concern an object. We are to envisage statements of the form

$$S\text{'s thought at } t \text{ concerned } x \text{ because } R(S, x, t).$$

Now it would be easy to understand someone who insisted that two people can be thinking of *different* objects in the same way (though this would not be the right way to interpret 'in the same way' in order to understand Frege). This would be something we might say of two people both thinking 'I'-thoughts, or both thinking 'here'-thoughts. If I am thinking about where I am as *here*, and my Doppelgänger on Twin Earth[10] is thinking about where he is as *here*, then in this sense we are thinking of different places in the same way. I am thinking about place p at t because $R(I, p, t)$; he is thinking about place p' at t because

[9] From a set of lecture notes: the material is sketchy, but some treatment of the 'Doppelgänger' line of thought seems necessary to supplement the material in §5 of this Appendix.

[10] See Hilary Putnam, 'The Meaning of "Meaning"', at pp. 223-7.

$R(\text{he}, p', t)$; and rather than identify the way of thinking at t with the satisfaction of the predicate '$R(\xi, p, t)$', we are identifying it with the satisfaction of the predicate '$R(\xi, \zeta, t)$'.

The methodological solipsist[11] wishes to hold that the content of a subject's mind (in a strict sense), when he thinks a demonstrative thought, is non-Russellian. One route to this thesis is as follows.

When we consider what kind of relation R is in the case of, say, 'here'-thoughts, we realize that S could have had R to p' at t rather than to p; and that S himself would not necessarily have been able to tell the difference. (Imagine S instantaneously transported to Twin Earth. Nothing accessible to his consciousness need change: it would feel exactly the same to be standing in R to p' as it did to be standing in R to p.) This suggests to many philosophers the desirability of breaking up the relation R into two components. The first would be a purely psychological or mental component, $\psi(S, t)$. The satisfaction of the predicate '$\psi(\xi, t)$' is something accessible to consciousness—one cannot change from satisfying it to not satisfying it without being aware of the fact. On plausible assumptions, this means that a specification of the property in question can make no reference to an object that exists outside the mind. The second component is a non-psychological, relational component, $R'(S, p, t)$.

Such philosophers wish, on this basis, to hold that there must be a description of the content of a person's mind, when he entertains a 'here'-thought, which is true simply in virtue of the mental component. Extending the view to the case of demonstrative thoughts about material objects: whenever such a thought is ascribable to someone, this is partly in virtue of a more strictly psychological state (call it an 'M-thought') which (a) he shares with his Doppelgänger, and (b) he could have had even in the absence of the object of the demonstrative thought (this would have been so if the non-psychological, relational component of the analysis had not obtained).

Now §5 of this Appendix argued that there is no reason to accept that thoughts are infallibly ascertainable contents of consciousness. The point was made then in relation to the existence of thoughts, but it goes for their identity as well. A person might lie in bed in hospital thinking repeatedly 'How hot it was here yesterday'—supposing himself to be stationary in the dark. But his bed might be very well oiled, and be pulled by strings, so that every time he has what he takes to be the same thought, he is in fact thinking of a different place, and having a different thought. It is indeed essential, for us to have the ability to

---

[11] See Hilary Putnam, 'The Meaning of "Meaning"', at p. 220; see also J. A. Fodor, 'Methodological Solipsism Considered as a Research Strategy in Cognitive Psychology', *The Behavioural and Brain Sciences* iii (1980), 63-73.

think of places in the demonstrative way that we do, that in fact we do not usually get moved about in this way very often, so that we do in fact fix upon the same place. We have to have the ability to know where we are; but it need not be infallible.

But the conception of M-thinking is independently objectionable. Consider a specification of a thought involving indexical expressions: say 'I am miserable, and it is too hot here with that candle spluttering away ...'. But consider it as a schema, with the indexicals not used to refer to anything. Now the same schema would serve in the specification both of one's Doppelgänger's M-thoughts and of one's own.

The methodological solipsist wants M-thinking to be recognizably *thinking*—which requires at least that it be a representational state—but he wants to think of the object of the state as a *schema*. The content of the state is to be given in schematic terms, so that the criterion for being in the same representational state can be given in terms that are purely inner and accessible to consciousness.

However, it is hard to see how there can be a representational state that meets this condition.

The objection is simple. It is of the essence of a representational state that it be capable of assessment as true or as false. If a state is a representational state, it represents something other than itself as being thus and so, with the consequence that the state is true if and only if the thing concerned is thus and so. This is reflected in the form in which representational states are ascribed: '*S* ϕs that *p*'. But a schema is not assessable as true or false, nor is any state whose 'content' can be given only in schematic terms assessable as true or false. So, since an M-state has a 'content' which is strictly specifiable only in schematic terms, the M-state is not assessable as true or false; hence it is not a representational state.

The intention may have been to follow the model we use in the case of language-uses involving indexical terms; so that M-entertaining a schema is seen as analogous to uttering a sentence containing indexicals (which have meanings, in the sense of roles in the language), and truth comes in consequentially, so to speak. Just as to utter a sentence with a role in the language in a context would be to say something with a truth-value, so M-entertaining a schema in a context would be to think something with a truth-value.

This analogy limps somewhat, when we consider its application to 'I'-thinking, since my being the person that I am cannot be regarded as an aspect of the context or situation I am in; but the whole idea seems to be misguided anyway. The idea is that what matters, from the mental or psychological point of view, is M-entertaining a schema—from the mental point of view, the context of thought is irrelevant, and indeed might not exist. And this means that on the purely mental side of things truth or falsity do not come in. No purely mental state, considered just as such, is a representational state. (Once we remember the importance of truth, we can see the importance of reference; my belief state has a different object from my Doppelgänger's belief state, and this is why they differ in truth-value. And in this perspective, the question of the reference of the state cannot be regarded as an ancillary question, to be left to some mechanism outside the subject's ken.)

It may seem mischievous to suggest that the methodological solipsist argues to the conclusion that my Doppelgänger and I are psychologically indistinguishable from the premiss that things are the same with us from the point of view of what is presumed to be accessible to consciousness. This represents the methodological solipsist as tending towards something like Cartesian dualism, whereas adherents of the position are typically staunch materialists: the basis of the thesis that my Doppelgänger and I are psychologically indistinguishable is that we are *physically* indistinguishable. But there is a point in the mischievous suggestion. Why should it seem so plausible that *internal* physical indistinguishability carries with it psychological indistinguishability? (My Doppelgänger and I are not indistinguishable in our physical relations to what is outside us.) One reason might be adherence, on the part of our thoroughly modern materialists, to a not-so-modern view of the mind—an essentially Cartesian conception of the mental as inner.

However, the methodological solipsist need not merely trade on the picture of the mind as inner. He may also appeal to an argument on the following lines. The brain is the basis of behaviour, in the sense that two people with physically indistinguishable brains will behave in the same way in any given situation. Since mental states are ultimately explanatory of behaviour, and since—the argument goes— my Doppelgänger and I will behave in the same way in the same situation, it follows that we must have the same mental states; if the explicandum is the same in the two cases, the explicans must be the same also.

But this argument is totally unconvincing. If we use singular terms in describing it, the explicandum is *not* the same in the two cases. Suppose S thinks there is a cat where he is, and S' (his Doppelgänger) thinks there is a cat where he is. S may be, for instance, disposed to search p; S' will not be at all disposed to search p, but will be disposed to search p'. S's belief, then, will explain one kind of behaviour, searching p; S''s belief will explain a different kind of behaviour, searching p'. And of course it is not surprising that singular beliefs— beliefs about particular objects—should explain behaviour only in so far as that behaviour is describable with the use of singular terms.

That I am differentially disposed to a particular place in the universe (that I have this place-specific disposition lacked by my Doppelgänger) is due to the fact that I am at that place. This is a fact about me upon which my dispositions, and hence my mental state, depend. Now this place-specific disposition no doubt results from my having a more general disposition, in the spelling out of which one would mention no specific place, and which I share with my Doppelgänger. And this more general disposition I have because of my brain state. But what arguments are there for holding that mental states must be identified with, or individuated in terms of, dispositions of the general sort rather than dispositions of the specific sort?

Chapter 7

Self-Identification

7.1 INTRODUCTORY

I approach the subject-matter of the present chapter with some trepidation. 'I'-thoughts give rise to the most challenging philosophical questions, which have exercised the most considerable philosophers, including Descartes, Kant, and Wittgenstein, and I have no illusion that I am able to answer these questions. (For one thing, there can be no complete understanding of self-identification without an understanding of the self-ascription of mental predicates; and no adequate understanding of the self-ascription of mental predicates without an account of the significance of those predicates—in short, without an account of the mind.)

However, there are reasons why a work on the general theory of reference cannot simply ignore the problems of self-identification, even if it does not purport to give a definitive answer to them. It cannot be assumed that this mode of identification, which is anyway known to give rise to difficult questions, can be fitted into whatever general framework has been constructed for understanding thoughts about particular objects. And while it would be presumptuous to look for much in the way of dividends in the understanding of the general philosophical problems of the self, it is not presumptuous to examine self-identification in the hope that light will be cast upon the modes of identification which we have been considering, and that some of the ideas thrown up in the course of the previous chapter may have application. For, despite considerable differences, 'I'-thoughts are thoughts of the same general character as 'here'-thoughts and 'this'-thoughts.

Let me begin by explaining very generally what I take this similarity to consist in.

When we are interested in 'I'-thoughts, we are interested in thoughts which might typically be expressed with the use of the first-person pronoun.[1] We are not interested in all thoughts which a subject may have 'about himself', for presumably a person may think about someone who is in fact himself without realizing that he is doing so. Oedipus was thinking about Oedipus, that is to say, himself, when he thought that the slayer of Laius should be killed; but Oedipus was not thinking about himself 'self-consciously' (this is just a label for the kind of thinking which interests us), because he did not realize that *he* was the slayer of Laius.[2]

What is it for Oedipus to realize that *he* is the slayer of Laius? One thing seems clear: it is not to realize that the ϕ is the slayer of Laius, for any descriptive concept ϕ. It is not to realize that the son of Jocasta is the slayer of Laius, or that the man who answered the riddle of the Sphinx is the slayer of Laius, because Oedipus might realize these things without realizing that *he* is the slayer of Laius (not knowing that, or having forgotten that, he is the son of Jocasta or the man who answered the Sphinx's riddle); and he might realize that he is the slayer of Laius without realizing these things, for the same reason. (This is too short an argument on a difficult point, but it has been considerably filled out in the literature, and will be substantiated in the course of this chapter.)[3]

There seem to be at least two indispensable consequences which we should expect from such a realization. In the first place, Oedipus must appreciate the relevance, to propositions of the form 'The slayer of Laius is *F*', of the various special ways he has (as every person does) of gaining knowledge about himself. Secondly, Oedipus must realize how to *act upon* propositions

---

[1] Though it seems to me to be completely inessential that there should exist such a device in the subject's language.

[2] However, in order to avoid unnecessary prolixity, I shall use phrases like 'think of oneself' and 'Idea of oneself' in the 'intensional' rather than the 'extensional' sense, so that they are equivalent to 'think of oneself self-consciously' and 'self-conscious Idea of oneself'.

[3] See, e.g., Hector-Neri Castañeda, ' "He": a Study in the Logic of Self-Consciousness', *Ratio* viii (1966), 130–57; and 'Indicators and Quasi-Indicators', *American Philosophical Quarterly* iv (1967), 85–100. The point needs making with some care. Descriptions like 'the person in front of *this*', or 'the person *here now*', might seem to yield counter-examples. But it would be pointless to object on this score. Counting these as counter-examples would require a priority of 'this' and 'here' over 'I', which is indefensible, as will become obvious. (In any case the definition of 'I' in terms of 'here' would be hopeless: one can think of oneself while hurtling through space, and consequently unable to secure a grip on anything for one's 'here'-thoughts: see 6.3.)

of the form 'The slayer of Laius is *F*'. For example, if Oedipus believes that they are looking for the slayer of Laius, and if he does not wish to be apprehended, then he should make himself scarce.[4] That is to say, the Idea which one has of oneself involves the same kinds of elements as we discerned in the case of, say, 'here' (6.3): an element involving sensitivity of thoughts to certain information, and an element involving the way in which thoughts are manifested in action. Such an analysis would certainly explain the widely recognized irreducibility of self-conscious thoughts to thoughts involving definite descriptions: for no descriptive thoughts could guarantee the existence of these special dispositions.

Of course, it must be recognized immediately that there are crucial differences. We clearly do have ways of gaining knowledge of ourselves, and 'I'-thoughts are thoughts which are controlled, or are disposed to be controlled, by information gained in these ways. But the ways in which we are sensitive to the states of ourselves are both more varied and more complex than the sensitivity to places that underlies our 'here'-Ideas. One quite unprecedented feature is the way in which 'I'-thoughts depend upon the knowledge we have in memory of our *past* states (see 7.5). And an even more important difference lies in the fact that the essence of 'I' is *self*-reference. This means that 'I'-thoughts are thoughts in which a subject of thought and action is thinking about him*self*—i.e. about a *subject* of thought and action. It is true that I manifest self-conscious thought, like 'here'-thought, in action; but I manifest it, not in knowing which object to act upon, but in acting. (I do not move myself; I myself move.) Equally, I do not merely have knowledge of myself, as I might have knowledge of a place: I have knowledge of myself *as* someone who has knowledge and who makes judgements, including those judgements I make about myself.

Nevertheless, despite these important differences, the

---

[4] This element in an account of 'I' is stressed in much recent work: e.g. John Perry, 'Frege on Demonstratives', and 'The Problem of the Essential Indexical', *Nous* xiii (1979), 3 21; David Lewis, 'Attitudes *De Dicto* and *De Se*', *Philosophical Review* lxxxviii (1979), 513 43. Neglect, in this work, of the other element produces a strangely one-sided effect—'strangely', because the other element is just as striking, and clearly parallel, and also because the dominant conception of the identification of empirical content concentrates exclusively on the *input* or *evidential* side of things. This chapter will partly redress the balance by rather neglecting the action component.

ingredients are sufficiently familiar for us to believe that we might get to know our way about.

It is worth clearing away, at this early stage, a curious idea, expressed in different ways by Geach and by Strawson, to the effect that the interest of 'I' is exclusively the interest of a *communicative* device—that is, in effect, that there are no Ideas corresponding to the pronoun and available to be exercised in *thinking*. According to Geach,[5] Descartes in his solitary meditations had no need of 'I' in such judgements as 'I'm getting into an awful muddle'; he could have judged 'This is really a dreadful muddle!' Similarly, Strawson[6] suggests that it is right to speak of self-ascription, for instance of pain, only because one *tells others* that one is in pain; otherwise one's judgement can simply be 'There is a pain'. Both these philosophers are preoccupied with the fact that there is no need for me to tell myself who it is who is getting into a muddle, or who is in pain.

But there is a mistake here. Reference, as a communicative phenomenon, involves getting an audience to think of the right object (the intended object). Obviously, *thinking* of an object does not consist in getting oneself to think of the right object (the intended object). But surely this cannot show that there is no such thing as thinking of an object, in a certain way, outside of communicative contexts.

Indispensable though those familiar ingredients (an information component and an action component) are in any account of the Ideas we have of ourselves, our previous reflections (chapter 6) have made it sufficiently clear that they cannot constitute an exhaustive account of our 'I'-Ideas. So long as we focus upon judgements which a person might make about himself upon the basis of the relevant ways of gaining knowledge, the inadequacy may not strike us. A subject's knowledge of what it is for the thought 'I am in pain' to be true may appear to be exhausted by his capacity to decide, simply upon the basis of how he feels, whether or not it is true—and similarly in the case of all the other ways of gaining knowledge about ourselves. However, our view of ourselves is not Idealistic: we are perfectly capable of grasping propositions about ourselves which we are quite incapable of deciding, or even offering grounds for. I can

---

[5] *Mental Acts*, ch. 26.
[6] *Individuals*, pp. 99-100.

grasp the thought that I was breast-fed, for example, or that I was unhappy on my first birthday, or that I tossed and turned in my sleep last night, or that I shall be dragged unconscious through the streets of Chicago, or that I shall die. In other words, our thinking about ourselves conforms to the Generality Constraint.[7] And this means that one's Idea of oneself must also comprise, over and above the information-link and the action-link, a knowledge of what it would be for an identity of the form $\ulcorner I = \delta_t \urcorner$ to be true, where δ_t is a fundamental identification of a person: an identification of a person which—unlike one's 'I'-identification—is of a kind which could be available to someone else. Only if this is so can one's general understanding of what it is for a person to satisfy the predicates 'ξ is dead', 'ξ is breast-fed', 'ξ is unhappy', etc. be coupled with one's Idea of oneself to yield an understanding of what it would be for oneself to satisfy these predicates. (The tenses in the various examples will be taken care of by our knowledge of what it is for $\ulcorner \delta_t = \delta'_{t'} \urcorner$ to be true, when $t \neq t'$; i.e. by our grasp of the identity-conditions of persons over time: cf. 4.3.)

My insistence that 'I'-Ideas be recognized to conform to the Generality Constraint is correlative with Strawson's parallel insistence that the Ideas (or concepts) of properties of consciousness obey a similar constraint: namely (to put it in my terms) that anyone who has a grasp of the concept of being F must be able to understand what it is for an arbitrary proposition of the form $\ulcorner a$ is $F \urcorner$ to be true (where a is an Idea which he possesses of an object).[8] The Generality Constraint requires us to see the thought that a is F as lying at the intersection of two series of thoughts: the thoughts that a is F, that a is G, that a is H, ..., on the one hand, and the thoughts that a is F, that b is F, that c is F, ..., on the other. Strawson has explored the consequences of one kind of generality, and I am exploring the consequences of the other.

It is vital to remember this feature of our thought about

---

[7] This thought is diametrically opposed to a line of thought of Wittgenstein's, in which he encouraged us to look at first-person psychological statements in a way that brought out their similarity to groans of pain—i.e. precisely to think of them as unstructured responses to situations. (He was well aware that this would enable him not to think about certain issues.) See *Philosophical Investigations* (Blackwell, Oxford, 1953), §§404–6.

[8] See *Individuals*, p. 99 (quoted in 4.3).

ourselves. 'I'-thoughts are not, as is sometimes suggested, restricted to thoughts about states of affairs 'from the point of
view of the subject'. Nor can the thoughts I have been discussing
be hived off from genuine self-conscious thought, for example
by suggesting that by 'I will die', I mean that Gareth Evans will
die. Not at all; there is just as much of a gap between the
knowledge that Gareth Evans will die and the self-conscious
realization that I will die as there is between any thought to the
effect that the ϕ is F and the self-conscious thought that I am F.
It is not wholly inaccurate to say that I grasp such an eventuality
by thinking of myself in the way that I think of others; this is
just another way of saying that the fundamental level of thought
about persons is involved. But it is of course essential that I am
aware that the person of whom I am so thinking *is myself*;
certainly I must have in mind what it is for ⌜δ is dead⌝ to be
true, for arbitrary δ, but I must also have in mind what it is for
⌜$\delta = I$⌝ to be true. My thought about myself does satisfy the
Generality Constraint; and this is because I can make sense of
identifying a person, conceived from the standpoint of an objective view of the world, as myself.[9]

It has been suggested that we do not in fact understand what
it is for such an identity to be true. Thomas Nagel has written:

I can conceive impersonally my house burning down, and the individual T. N. standing before it, feeling hot and miserable, and looking
hot and miserable to bystanders . . . If I add to all this the premiss that
I am T. N., I will imagine *feeling* hot and miserable, *seeing* the sympathetic bystanders, etc.; but this is not to imagine anything happening differently.[10]

Earlier he wrote:

The addition of this premiss makes a great difference in *how* [the]
world is conceived, but no difference in what is conceived to be the
case.[11]

---

[9] Even if we consider cases in which the subject is normally in a position to know that
he satisfies a predicate, we do not take an Idealistic view of such judgements. There
remains a gap—the ever-present possibility of error—between evidence and conclusion.
The idea that I can identify myself with a person objectively conceived is often mis-
expressed, e.g. in terms of the idea that I realize that I am an object *to others* (also an
object of outer sense, as Kant says: *Critique of Pure Reason*, B 415). This misleadingly
imports an ideal verificationist construal of the point. (See 4.2, 6.3.)

[10] *The Possibility of Altruism* (Clarendon Press, Oxford, 1970), p. 103.

[11] Ibid.

It is upon this basis that Nagel suggests the existence of an unbridgeable gulf between subjective and objective—between, as I should put it, propositions about persons and objects formulated at the fundamental level of thought, and propositions formulated with such Ideas as 'I', 'here', and 'this'. Nagel envisages the universe considered *sub specie aeternitatis*, and then wonders how to incorporate into that model the fact that such-and-such a person is *me*. Since this identification does not seem to make any difference to the model—nothing is differently conceived—Nagel suggests that we cannot really understand what it is for such an identity-proposition to be true.

But in fact I have already implicitly explained what is involved in grasping such an identity-proposition—in knowing what it is for such an identity-proposition to be true. It seems to me clear that as we conceive of persons, they are distinguished from one another by fundamental grounds of difference of the same kind as those which distinguish other physical things, and that a fundamental identification of a person involves a consideration of him as the person occupying such-and-such a spatio-temporal location.[12] Consequently, to know what it is for $\ulcorner \delta_t = I \urcorner$ to be true, for arbitrary δ_t, is to know what is involved in locating oneself in a spatio-temporal map of the world.[13] (See 6.3.) Such an identity-proposition need not make any difference to how the spatio-temporal map of the world is conceived, but it will make a great difference to how the subject's immediate environment is conceived. (Nagel was looking for the impact in the wrong place.) It is true that we cannot state in non-indexical terms what it is for the identity-proposition to be true; but why should we suppose that everything that is true can be represented in that way? Nagel may conclude that propositions like $\ulcorner I \text{ am } \delta_t \urcorner$ are not *objectively* true—true from the standpoint of eternity. I should not feel obliged to quarrel with this, since it is indeed true that such a proposition is capable of being grasped only by the person who can formulate it; so if 'objective' means 'graspable by anyone', such identifications are indeed not objectively true.

---

[12] I stress that I am speaking of our *ordinary* scheme of thought. There are other conceptions—e.g. conceptions of control systems or information stores—which might serve some of our purposes, and which would involve different fundamental grounds of difference.

[13] [See Appendix, §4.].

Nagel's suggestion—that we do not really understand what it is for us to be identical with objects conceived to be parts of the objective spatio-temporal framework—surely must be wrong. Were it correct, our thinking about ourselves could not conform to the Generality Constraint. We would then have to suppose that we have an Idealist conception of the self.[14] Conversely, just as our thoughts about ourselves require the intelligibility of this link with the world thought of 'objectively', so our 'objective' thought about the world also requires the intelligibility of this link. For no one can be credited with an 'objective' model of the world if he does not grasp that he is modelling the world *he* is in—that he has a location somewhere in the model, as do the things that he can see. Nothing can be a cognitive map unless it can be used as a map—unless the world as perceived, and the world as mapped, can be identified. For this reason, I think that the gulf between the 'subjective' and 'objective' modes of thought which Nagel tries to set up is spurious. Each is indispensably bound up with the other.

Despite the important differences, then, between 'I' and 'this' and 'here', the general structure of our account of these Ideas is the same. In particular, a subject's self-conscious thought about himself must be informed (or must at least be liable to be informed) by information which the subject may gain of himself in each of a range of ways of gaining knowledge of himself; and at the same time the subject must *know which* object it is of which he thus has, or is capable of having, knowledge.

Now even if it is commonly agreed that there is a connection between thinking of oneself self-consciously and thinking in ways that are liable to be informed by certain kinds of evidence or information about oneself which one is capable of acquiring,[15] there is widespread misunderstanding about what kinds of evidence or information they are. For it is widely believed that self-conscious thought is exclusively thought informed by the

---

[14] This would be the same as saying that 'I' does not refer to anything. (This *would* be a reason for the extraordinary conclusion of G. E. M. Anscombe, 'The First Person', in Samuel Guttenplan, ed., *Mind and Language*, pp. 45–65.)

[15] 'Just as I cannot know what form the evidence of a fire will take unless I know whether the fire is past, present, or future, so I cannot know what to expect in the way of evidence that one of the persons in a group has been poisoned unless I know whether it is I or someone else.' Nagel, *The Possibility of Altruism*, p. 103.

knowledge that one may have about one's own *mental* life. I shall show that this is quite incorrect.

It is true, as I said earlier, that the essence of self-consciousness is self-reference, that is to say, thinking, by a subject of judgements, about himself, and hence, necessarily, about a subject of judgements. (This means that we shall not have an adequate model of self-consciousness until our model provides for the thought, by a subject, of his own judgements. Without that, no matter how much it mimicked our own use of 'I', the model would always be open to a sceptical challenge: how can it be guaranteed that the subject is referring to himself?) It follows that in a self-conscious thought, the subject must think of an object in a way that permits it to be characterized as the subject of that very thought. But it certainly does not follow that he must think of himself *as* the author of that very thought—if, indeed, such a thing is intelligible; nor, more generally, that he must think of himself exclusively as an author of judgements, or even as a possessor of a mental life. On the contrary, we shall see that our self-conscious thoughts about ourselves also rest upon various ways we have of gaining knowledge of ourselves as physical things. If there is to be a division between the mental and the physical, it is a division which is spanned by the Ideas we have of ourselves.

Before moving on to an elaboration of the ways of gaining knowledge of ourselves on which our 'I'-thoughts depend, I want to give a warning about a danger inherent in all reflections about self-consciousness.

Up to this point, we have been able to take the subject of thought, and his identity, for granted. We have been able to say such things as 'The subject is disposed to treat this or that state of information as germane to such-and-such a thought'. For instance, we might have said that the subject's knowledge of what it is for such-and-such a future-tense proposition to be true depends on *his* ability to tell, later, whether or not it is true. Now there is no harm in continuing this way of proceeding when we come to consider self-identification: indeed it is unavoidable. But we must realize what we are doing. We are building the subject's identity over time into the description of his situation. This may make it appear that he has an infallible knowledge of what is involved in this identity; but the appearance is nothing but an artefact of our way of describing the situation.[16]

Let me give two connected examples of the kind of mistake I wish to warn against. G. E. M. Anscombe, in her fascinating paper on 'I'-thoughts,[17] observes that it is not possible for the subject to identify *different* things by the various 'I'-identifications he makes over time. It is not possible for there to be an 'unnoticed substitution', so that he thinks that he is identifying the same thing, when in fact he is not doing so. This corresponds to nothing in the case of repeated identifications of objects other than the subject himself, and such a logical guarantee of correctness makes Miss Anscombe suspicious; it is one of the reasons she gives for her extraordinary conclusion that self-conscious thought is not thought *about an object* at all—that the self is not an object. But, of course, the 'logical guarantee' is simply produced by Miss Anscombe's way of describing the situation, in terms of one and the same subject having thoughts at various times. It is a simple tautology that, if it is correct to describe the situation thus, the *self*-identifications are all identifications of the same self, and hence it cannot be a reason for anything.[18]

In the second example, the mistake seems to give a subject an infallible knowledge of what it is for a state of affairs to concern his own future. Pursuing the style of description which served us adequately in the discussion of the subject's grasp of future-tense propositions about other objects, we might say something like this: the subject's knowledge of what is involved in a future state of affairs concerning himself can depend upon his ability, when the time comes, to decide whether or not the state of affairs obtains. We might say: certainly, when time t comes, he will know whether or not the hypothesis that he expressed earlier by 'I'll be in pain at t' was or was not correct, just by whether or not he is in pain at t; so all he has to envisage, when he envisages the future state of affairs of his being in pain, is a future pain. What more could possibly be involved? For this certainly seems to be a foolproof method for verifying the

---

[16] I think Kant may have had this phenomenon in mind, as much as anything which depends specially upon memory, when he spoke, in the Third Paralogism, of the 'logical identity of the "I"' (*Critique of Pure Reason*, A 363).

[17] 'The First Person', op. cit.

[18] There are phenomena (having to do with memory) which are superficially similar to the spurious one that Miss Anscombe describes: see 7.5.

prediction. It is not possible for the subject to have got hold of the wrong person at time *t*.

Now, I do not mean to deny that there is something correct about this, as a description of the subject's envisagings about his own future.[19] But what is suspicious is the complete adequacy we have built into his conception by our way of describing it. Of course it is not possible for the subject to have got hold of the wrong person—as the case is described, there is a logical guarantee of adequacy. But this is, again, an artefact of our way of describing the situation: it certainly does not show that, just by envisaging future situations, a subject has a complete and clear conception of what it is for a future state of affairs to involve himself. The 'method of verification' has a presupposition. Of course we must not say (using the ordinary vocabulary): it presupposes that the subject remains the same over time. But it presupposes that the subject who exists at *t* and 'remembers' the hypothesis expressed earlier is the person who made the hypothesis, and hence is the person whom it concerns. And this is something of which he can have no genuine logical guarantee.

Forewarned against these errors, in what follows I shall continue to use the ordinary vocabulary.

7.2 IMMUNITY TO ERROR THROUGH MISIDENTIFICATION

If an analogy is to be sought between self-identification and one of the modes of identification we considered in the last chapter, it is 'here' rather than 'this' which provides the closer parallel. Just as it is not necessary, if a subject is to be thinking about a place as 'here', that he actually have any information deriving from it, so it seems not to be necessary, if a subject is to think about himself self-consciously, that he actually have any information about himself. A subject may be amnesiac and anaesthetized, and his senses may be prevented from functioning; yet he may still be able to think about himself, wondering, for example, why he is *not* receiving information in the usual ways.[20] But it would be as wrong to conclude from this that

---

[19] My point is not to deny that there is such a thing as criterionless self-ascription of anticipated properties. (I think this is simply the other side of the same coin as criterionless self-ascription of remembered properties, for which see 7.5.) But I do want to deny that this is a matter of a logical guarantee of an identity assumption.

[20] See Anscombe, 'The First Person', pp. 57–8. This is another basis on which she attempts to found her extraordinary conclusion. See n. 21 below.

self-consciousness can be explained without reference to the various ways that subjects have of gaining knowledge about themselves, as we decided it would be to draw the parallel conclusion about 'here' (see 6.3). It is essential, if a subject is to be thinking about himself self-consciously, that he be *disposed* to have such thinking controlled by information which may become available to him in each of the relevant ways. Or, at least, so I shall argue.[21]

So to argue is to claim that each of these ways of gaining knowledge of ourselves gives rise to judgements which exhibit the phenomenon I called in the last chapter 'immunity to error through misidentification' (see 6.6). And certainly there seem to be indications that this phenomenon does arise. To take the stock kind of example, when the first component is expressive of knowledge which the subject has about his own states, available to him in the normal way, and not taken by him to be knowledge which he has gained, or may have gained, in any other way,[22] the utterance 'Someone seems to see something red, but is it I who seem to see something red?' does not appear to make sense. But the phenomenon appears to be more widespread than the stock examples. For example, it seems equally not to make sense for a subject to utter 'Someone's legs are crossed, but is it I whose legs are crossed?', when the first component is expressive of knowledge which the subject has gained about the position of his limbs, available to him in the normal way.

Unfortunately, many philosophers give the quite mistaken impression that it is only our knowledge of our satisfaction of mental properties which gives rise to judgements exhibiting immunity to error through misidentification.[23] This is tanta-

[21] It is not surprising that 'I' follows the model of 'here' rather than 'this'. The explanation is somewhat similar to the explanation for 'here' (see 6.3). A subject does not need to have information actually available to him in any of the relevant ways in order to know that there is just one object to which he is thus *dispositionally* related. (This undermines Miss Anscombe's argument about the anaesthetized man, that since no object is *presented to* him, there is no room for him to use a demonstrative expression referring to himself.)

[22] See 6.6 for an explanation of the need for this qualification (which I shall drop in future).

[23] See Strawson, *The Bounds of Sense*, pp. 164–5: both of his examples relate to mental self-ascription. See also Shoemaker, 'Self-Reference and Self-Awareness'. Shoemaker does note that there are other kinds of statement that exhibit this immunity, e.g. 'I am facing a table' (cf. 7.3 below); but he argues that their possession of the property is only derivative, in virtue of the involvement of the psychological judgement 'There is a table in my field of vision': see p. 557.

mount to the claim that self-conscious thought rests only upon the knowledge we have of ourselves as mental or spiritual beings. And this in turn generates the unfortunate, and quite inaccurate, impression that in thinking of oneself self-consciously, one is paradigmatically thinking about oneself as the bearer of mental properties, or as a mind—so that our 'I'-thoughts leave it open, as a possibility, that we are perhaps *nothing but* a mind. In order to eradicate this impression, we must go back to its source: a remarkable passage of Wittgenstein's, where the phenomenon of immunity to error through misidentification is noticed for the first time.

Now the idea that the real I lives in my body is connected with the peculiar grammar of the word 'I', and the misunderstandings this grammar is liable to give rise to. There are two different cases in the use of the word 'I' (or 'my') which I might call 'the use as object' and 'the use as subject'. Examples of the first kind of use are these: 'My arm is broken', 'I have grown six inches', 'I have a bump on my forehead', 'The wind blows my hair about'. Examples of the second kind are: '*I* see so and so', '*I* hear so and so', '*I* try to lift my arm', '*I* think it will rain', '*I* have a toothache'. One can point to the difference between these two categories by saying: The cases of the first category involve the recognition of a particular person, and there is in these cases the possibility of an error, or as I should rather put it: The possibility of an error has been provided for ... It is possible that, say in an accident, I should feel a pain in my arm, see a broken arm at my side, and think it is mine, when really it is my neighbour's. And I could, looking into a mirror, mistake a bump on his forehead for one on mine. On the other hand there is no question of recognizing a person when I say I have toothache. To ask 'are you sure that it's *you* who have pains?' would be nonsensical ... And now this way of stating our idea suggests itself: that it is impossible that in making the statement 'I have a toothache' I should have mistaken another person for myself, as it is to moan with pain by mistake, having mistaken someone else for me. To say, 'I have pain' is no more a statement *about* a particular person than moaning is. 'But surely the word "I" in the mouth of a man refers to the man who says it; it points to himself ...'. But it was quite superfluous to point to himself.[24]

It is worth briefly observing, first, that where there is immunity to error through misidentification, Wittgenstein draws the conclusion that the word 'I' is not being used to refer to (talk

[24] *The Blue and Brown Books* (Blackwell, Oxford, 1958), pp. 66-7.

about) a particular object (a person). This seems to be just a mistake. For we have seen (6.6) that immunity to error through misidentification is a straightforward consequence of demonstrative identification; it will exist whenever a subject's Idea of an object depends upon his ways of gaining knowledge about it. And demonstrative identification is, precisely, a way in which a thought can concern (be about) an object.[25]

The word 'identify' can do us a disservice here. In one sense, anyone who thinks about an object identifies that object (in thought): this is the sense involved in the use I have just made of the phrase 'demonstrative identification'. It is quite another matter, as we saw, in effect, in 6.6, for the thought to involve an identification component—for the thought to be identification-dependent. There is a danger of moving from the fact that there is no identification in the latter sense (that no criteria of recognition are brought to bear, and so forth) to the conclusion that there is no identification in the former sense. I am not sure that Wittgenstein altogether avoids this danger.

But this conclusion is not our present concern, but rather, Wittgenstein's treatment of examples like 'The wind is blowing my hair'. For it was this treatment which gave rise to the widespread belief that the phenomenon of immunity to error through misidentification, which is so central to the notion of self-consciousness, does not extend to self-ascriptions of physical properties. But of course it does. There is a way of knowing that the property of ζ's hair being blown by the wind is currently instantiated, such that when the first component expresses knowledge gained in this way, the utterance 'The wind is blowing someone's hair, but is it my hair that the wind is blowing?' will not make sense. Wittgenstein's discussion does not take

---

[25] One can perhaps imagine why Wittgenstein drew the conclusion. The information one seems to be presented with is simply that such-and-such a property is instantiated; there does not appear to be anything *in the information* to tell one *which* object instantiates the property (as there might be if the recognizable appearance of an object was also presented). So if one was talking about a particular object (person), one would be going beyond the information given. But we saw that in the case of demonstrative identification this conclusion will not follow if the subject can be credited with a knowledge of which object the information concerns; which he would have, in that case, by virtue of being able to locate it. Now we have not yet enquired into the question in what our knowledge of which person we are consists. But it seems reasonable to suppose that we have such knowledge; and in the context of that supposition, the point about the content of the information by itself goes only a very short distance. (See, further, 7.4 below.)

sufficient account of the fact that the property of being immune to error through misidentification is not one which applies to propositions *simpliciter*, but one which applies only to judgements made upon this or that basis. Once we appreciate this relativity to a basis, which arguably must be taken into account in the case of mental self-ascription as well, the fact that there are cases involving the self-ascription of physical predicates in which 'the possibility of error has been provided for' will be seen not to impugn the fact that there are cases in which it just as clearly has not.

It may be suggested that Wittgenstein is concerned with a different notion: that his question is not whether there is a way of knowing that one instantiates some property which generates immunity to error through misidentification in my sense, but whether there is a way of knowing it which does not. (Only if this last is *not* so will we have immunity to error through mis-identification in the strong sense with which, according to this suggestion, Wittgenstein is concerned.) After all, it may be said, it is the *possibility* of discovering that what is in fact one's own arm is bent, without knowing that it is one's own, to which he appeals.

But, first, the evidence that this is Wittgenstein's concern is uncertain. The relevant direct statement is

The cases of the first category involve the recognition of a particular person, and there is in these cases the possibility of an error, or as I should rather put it: The possibility of an error has been allowed for.

And this statement simply cannot be correctly used to mark off a category of propositions identified solely in terms of the *predicate* involved, independently of the question how one comes to know that the predicate is instantiated.

Secondly, one cannot make this sort of absolute claim of immunity to error through misidentification for *mental* self-ascriptions either—at least not self-ascriptions of the kind Wittgenstein chooses, which includes 'I see so-and-so' and 'I hear so-and-so'. Consider a case in which I have reason to believe that my tactual information may be misleading; it feels as if I am touching a piece of cloth, and my relevant visual information is restricted to seeing, in a mirror, a large number of hands reaching out and touching nothing, and one hand touching a piece of cloth. Here it makes sense for me to say 'Someone is feeling a piece of cloth, but is it I?' (One cannot produce this kind of case for mental predicates whose self-ascription is absolutely incorrigible. But what is the interest of this fact?)

Thirdly, the stronger notion is in any case much less interesting. It is highly important that our 'I'-Ideas are such that judgements controlled by certain ways of gaining knowledge of ourselves *as physical and spatial things* are immune to error through misidentification: that the bearing of the relevant information on 'I'-thoughts rests upon no argument, or identification, but is simply constitutive of our having an 'I'-Idea. (The fact that these ways of gaining knowledge of ourselves must enter into the informational component of a functional characterization of our 'I'-Ideas—of what it is to think of oneself self-consciously— is the most powerful antidote to a Cartesian conception of the self.)

Our task now is to investigate more precisely the ways we have of gaining knowledge of ourselves upon which our 'I'-thoughts depend. In the next two sections, I shall consider the bases of physical and mental self-knowledge; although, as we shall see, they can be separated only artificially.

7.3 BODILY SELF-ASCRIPTION

I shall discuss two ways we have of gaining knowledge of our physical states and properties, both of which give rise to the phenomenon of immunity to error through misidentification.

In the first place, we have what might be described as a general capacity to perceive our own bodies, although this can be broken down into several distinguishable capacities: our proprioceptive sense, our sense of balance, of heat and cold, and of pressure.[26] Each of these modes of perception appears to give rise to judgements which are immune to error through misidentification. None of the following utterances appears to make sense when the first component expresses knowledge gained in the appropriate way: 'Someone's legs are crossed, but is it my legs that are crossed?'; 'Someone is hot and sticky, but is it I

---

[26] I do not include in this list perceptual knowledge of the physical self based upon executing certain characteristic movements, e.g. looking down, or feeling one's body with the sort of motions one uses in washing oneself. But actually I am not at all persuaded that judgements so based ought not to appear on the list, because I am not at all persuaded that they depend upon an identification component.

who am hot and sticky?'; 'Someone is being pushed, but is it I who am being pushed?' There just does not appear to be a gap between the subject's having information (or appearing to have information), in the appropriate way, that the property of being *F* is instantiated, and his having information (or appearing to have information) that *he* is *F*; for him to have, or to appear to have, the information that the property is instantiated just is for it to appear to him that *he* is *F*.

If we attempt to impose some articulation in these cases, seeing ⌜I am *F*⌝ as based on ⌜*b* is *F*⌝ and ⌜I am *b*⌝, then we run into considerable difficulties (of a kind with which we are now familiar: see 6.6). The articulation might be recommended on the basis of the possibility of a deviant causal chain, linking the subject's brain appropriately with someone else's body, in such a way that he is in fact registering information from that other body. As before (6.6), I claim that this possibility merely shows the possibility of an error; it does not show that ordinary judgements of the kind in question are identification-dependent.

In the first place, we cannot think of the kinaesthetic and proprioceptive system as gaining *knowledge* of truths about the condition of a body which leaves the question of the identity of the body open. If the subject does not know that *he* has his legs bent (say) on this basis (because he is in the situation described), then he does not know *anything* on this basis. (To judge that *someone* has his legs bent would be a wild shot in the dark.)[27]

In the second place, there are problems about the Ideas that would be involved in the supposed identification component. The supposed Idea *b* could be adequate only if it involved identification by description, on the lines of 'the body from which I hereby have information'. Such an Idea would certainly be involved in one's thinking if one knew one was in the abnormal situation described; but it is surely too sophisticated to be discerned as an element in the normal case of judgements of the kind we are considering. And, to turn to the other side of the supposed identification component: if our Ideas of ourselves were such as to leave room for such an identification component—that is, if they did not have the legitimacy of this kind of

---

[27] It would not be a wild shot in the dark if the subject had been *told* that he was linked up appropriately with someone else's body. But then he would be in the position of knowing that the information was not being received in the normal way. Cf. 6.6.

physical self-ascription, without need for argument or identification, built in at the foundation—then it is quite unclear how they could ever allow for the identification of the self as a physical thing at all.[28]

The second way of gaining knowledge of our physical properties has an importance in our thought about ourselves which it is difficult to exaggerate.[29] (We have already touched on it at several points: see 6.3, 6.6.) I have in mind the way in which we are able to know our position, orientation, and relation to other objects in the world upon the basis of our perceptions of the world. Included here are such things as: knowing that one is in one's own bedroom by perceiving and recognizing the room and its contents; knowing that one is moving in a train by seeing the world slide by; knowing that there is a tree in front of one, or to the right or left, by seeing it; and so on. Once again, none of the following utterances appears to make sense when the first component expresses knowledge gained in this way: 'Someone is in my bedroom, but is it I?'; 'Someone is moving, but is it I?'; 'Someone is standing in front of a tree, but is it I?'

The explanation of the importance of this way of gaining knowledge is not hard to find. Any thinker who has an idea of an objective spatial world—an idea of a world of objects and phenomena which can be perceived but which are not dependent on being perceived for their existence—must be able to think of his perception of the world as being simultaneously due to his position in the world, and to the condition of the world at that position.[30] The very idea of a perceivable, objective, spatial world brings with it the idea of the subject as being *in* the world, with the course of his perceptions due to his changing position in the world and to the more or less stable way the world is. The idea that there is an objective world and the idea that the subject is *somewhere* cannot be separated, and where he is is given by what he can perceive. For the purposes of an almost entirely

[28] [See Appendix, §4.]

[29] It is a symptom of the importance of this mode of self-knowledge to our conception of ourselves that it, or some shadow of it, is preserved in even the most metaphysical accounts of the self, in which the self is regarded as the origin of the perceptual field, or as a point of view on the world. See Wittgenstein, *Tractatus Logico-Philisophicus* (Routledge and Kegan Paul, London, 1961), 5.6–5.641; and 'Wittgenstein's Notes for Lectures on "Private Experience" and "Sense Data"', *Philosophical Review* lxxvii (1968), 271–320, at p. 299: 'But I *am* in a favoured position. I am the centre of the world.'

[30] See 'Things Without the Mind' for more on this.

arbitrary, though traditional, distinction between the mental and the physical, we are leaving such self-ascriptions as 'I am seeing a tree' until the next section; but in fact they constitute an indispensable part of the little theory which is required for the idea of an objective spatial world. 'I perceive such-and-such, such-and-such holds at p; so (probably) I am at p''; 'I perceive such-and-such, I am at p, so such-and-such holds at p''; 'I am at p, such-and-such does not hold at p, so I can't really be perceiving such-and-such, even though it appears that I am'; 'I was at p a moment ago, so I can only have got as far as p', so I should expect to perceive such-and-such'. These arguments exploit principles connecting the subject's position, the course of his perceptions, and the speed and continuity of his movement through space; and the child must learn to trip round and round those principles, so that he comes to think effortlessly in these ways.[31]

In 7.1 I suggested that our knowledge of what it is for ⌜I am δ_t⌝ to be true, where δ_t is a fundamental identification of a person (conceived of, therefore, as an element of the objective spatial order), consists in our knowledge of what it is for us to be located at a position in space. In 6.3 I argued that this in turn can be regarded as consisting in a practical capacity to locate ourselves in space by means of exactly the kinds of patterns of reasoning that I have just described. It is this capacity which enables us to make sense of the idea that we ourselves are elements in the objective order; and this is what is required for our thoughts about ourselves to conform to the Generality Constraint (4.3, 7.1).

Now if this is right, we can see that the perception-based judgements about our position and our relations to other things which we are discussing must be identification-free.[32] If we try to regard them as identification-dependent, we shall run into the same difficulties as before. First, there is no *knowing* about

---

[31] Do we really have to go any further than this in order to answer Strawson's questions (*Individuals*, p. 93): '(1) Why are one's states of consciousness ascribed to anything at all? and (2) Why are they ascribed to the very same thing as certain corporeal characteristics, a certain physical situation &c?'?

[32] It is difficult enough to make sense of the Cartesian position, in which this is not regarded as a way of gaining knowledge about *oneself* at all (only about something which one 'has'). But I confess to finding myself utterly defeated by the suggestion that while this *is* a way of gaining knowledge of oneself, it is one which exploits an identification.

the position, orientation, etc. of some physical object in the ways in question, in such a way that it is left an open question which object it is. And second, there is the familiar problem about the supposed identification component. The object in question could be identified only by description, as the object about whose position, orientation, etc., information is being obtained in the ways in question; such an Idea would indeed be adequate, and might be used in circumstances which were abnormal or taken to be abnormal, but hardly figures in the normal case. And if we try to give an account of the Idea the subject has of himself, leaving it an open question whether the object whose position and relations can be known about in this way is the subject, it becomes quite problematic how the subject could ever make sense of the thought that he is located somewhere.[33]

The considerations of this section tell against the common idea that our conception of ourselves 'from the first-person perspective' is a conception of a thinking, feeling, and perceiving thing, and not necessarily of a physical thing located in space. The theoretical significance of immunity to error through misidentification is that it shows that evidence of certain kinds bears on thoughts involving 'I'-Ideas *directly* and *immediately*. It is a fact about 'I'-Ideas of objects that evidence of these kinds pertains to thoughts about those objects. (The immediate bearing of such evidence would have to be part of a functional characterization of what it is to have an 'I'-Idea.) Thus the cases of immunity to error through misidentification that we have considered in this section reveal that our conception of ourselves is firmly anti-Cartesian: our 'I'-Ideas are Ideas of bearers of physical no less than mental properties.[34]

7.4 MENTAL SELF-ASCRIPTION

My discussion of the ways in which we have knowledge of our own *mental* states will be extremely incomplete. My purpose is simply to bring to mind some of the main features of this kind

[33] It was precisely for this reason that I argued earlier (6.3) that 'here' should not be regarded as defined in terms of 'I' (as if 'I' had a priority). In fact 'I' and 'here' are exactly correlative: the same capacity underlies understanding of both, namely knowledge of what it is for ⌜I am at p⌝ to be true.

[34] I should argue that the case of our knowledge of our own actions (a subject I have been forced to neglect) similarly compels upon us an identity between the self and a physical thing: the *agent*—the subject of desires, thoughts, and intentions—is identified with the object in the world that moves and changes.

of self-knowledge, so that we can have at least a rough idea of how it can be incorporated into our Idea of ourselves. In fact, I shall concentrate upon the ways we have of knowing what we *believe* and what we *experience*, for I believe that if we get these right, we shall have a good model of self-knowledge (or introspection) to follow in other cases. In particular, I shall quite avoid the idea of this kind of self-knowledge as a form of perception—mysterious in being incapable of delivering inaccurate results.

Wittgenstein is reported to have said in an Oxford discussion:

If a man says to me, *looking at the sky*, 'I think it is going to rain, therefore I exist', I do not understand him.[35]

The contribution is certainly gnomic; but I think Wittgenstein was trying to undermine the temptation to adopt a Cartesian position, by forcing us to look more closely at the nature of our knowledge of our own mental properties, and, in particular, by forcing us to abandon the idea that it always involves an *inward* glance at the states and doings of something to which only the person himself has access. The crucial point is the one I have italicized: in making a self-ascription of belief, one's eyes are, so to speak, or occasionally literally, directed outward—upon the world. If someone asks me 'Do you think there is going to be a third world war?', I must attend, in answering him, to precisely the same outward phenomena as I would attend to if I were answering the question 'Will there be a third world war?' I get myself in a position to answer the question whether I believe that *p* by putting into operation whatever procedure I have for answering the question whether *p*. (There is no question of my applying a procedure for determining beliefs *to something*, and hence no question of my possibly applying the procedure to the wrong thing.) If a judging subject applies this procedure, then necessarily he will gain knowledge of one of his own mental states: even the most determined sceptic cannot find here a gap in which to insert his knife.

We can encapsulate this procedure for answering questions about what one believes in the following simple rule: whenever you are in a position to assert that *p*, you are *ipso facto* in a

---

[35] Christopher Coope, Peter Geach, Timothy Potts, and Roger White, eds., *A Wittgenstein Workbook* (Blackwell, Oxford, 1971), p. 21. (My emphasis.)

position to assert 'I believe that *p*'. But it seems pretty clear that mastery of this procedure cannot constitute a full understanding of the content of the judgement 'I believe that p'.[36] Understanding of the content of the judgement must involve possession of the psychological concept expressed by 'ξ believes that *p*', which the subject must conceive as capable of being instantiated otherwise than by himself.[37] Involvement of this concept in the judgement would be manifested by an appreciation of the fact that the kinds of evidence which he is prepared to recognize as relevant to the ascription of the predicate to others bear also upon the truth of his claim, and a willingness to recognize, as relevant to the ascription of the predicate to others, evidence of their having executed the same procedure—making a judgement as to whether *p*—which underlies his own self-ascription. Without this background, we might say, we secure no genuine 'I think' (' think that *p*') to accompany his thought ('*p*'): the 'I think' which accompanies all his thoughts is purely formal. But adding the background makes no difference to the method of self-ascription: in particular, we continue to have no need for the idea of the inward glance.

The self-ascription of perceptual experiences follows a different model, one we can understand only if we begin by considering the ordinary situation in which a subject is perceiving the world and making judgements about it. In general, we may regard a perceptual experience as an informational state of the subject: it has a certain *content*—the world is represented a certain way—and hence it permits of a non-derivative classification as *true* or *false*. For an internal state to be so regarded, it must have appropriate connections with behaviour—it must have a certain motive force upon the actions of the subject. This

---

[36] 'I believe that *p*' admits of a distinction between internal and external negation. 'It is not the case that I believe that *p*' can be the expression of an open mind. This enables us to express one side of the central notion of objectivity—the idea that truth transcends my knowledge or belief: it may be that *p*, it may be that not-*p*; I do not know, and have no belief on the matter. A connected point is that the prefixing of a sentence '*p*' with 'I believe that' means that my claim does not have to be withdrawn in the circumstance that it is not the case that *p*. Such a state of affairs—expressible in the past tense by 'I believed that *p*, but it was not the case that *p*'—cannot be *believed* to obtain *currently*, but its possibility makes sense. This is the other side of the idea of objectivity: although I believe that *p*, it may be the case that not-*p*. In short, learning the difference between 'I believe that *p*' and '*p*' involves learning the different ways in which the two sentences embed under various operators: crucially negation, modality, and the past tense.

[37] And by himself at other times.

motive force can be countermanded, in the case of more sophisticated organisms (concept-exercising and reasoning organisms), by judgements based upon other considerations. In the
case of such organisms, the internal states which have a content
by virtue of their phylogenetically more ancient connections
with the motor system also serve as input to the concept-exercising and reasoning system. Judgements are then *based upon*
(reliably caused by) these internal states; when this is the case
we can speak of the information being 'accessible' to the subject,
and, indeed, of the existence of conscious experience.

The informational states which a subject acquires through
perception are *non-conceptual*, or *non-conceptualized*. Judgements
based upon such states necessarily involve conceptualization: in
moving from a perceptual experience to a judgement about the
world (usually expressible in some verbal form), one will be
exercising basic conceptual skills.[38] But this formulation (in
terms of moving from an experience to a judgement) must not
be allowed to obscure the general picture. Although the subject's judgements are *based upon* his experience (i.e. upon the
unconceptualized information available to him), his judgements are not *about* the informational state. The process of
conceptualization or judgement takes the subject from his being
in one kind of informational state (with a content of a certain
kind, namely, non-conceptual content) to his being in another
kind of cognitive state (with a content of a different kind,
namely, conceptual content). So when the subject wishes to
make absolutely sure that his judgement is correct, he gazes
again *at the world* (thereby producing, or reproducing, an informational state in himself); he does not in any sense gaze at, or
concentrate upon, his internal state. His internal state cannot
in any sense become an *object* to him. (He is *in* it.)

However, a subject can gain knowledge of his internal informational states in a very simple way: by re-using precisely those
skills of conceptualization that he uses to make judgements
about the world. Here is how he can do it. He goes through
exactly the same procedure as he would go through if he were
trying to make a judgement about how it is at this place now,
but excluding any knowledge he has *of an extraneous kind*. (That
is, he seeks to determine what he would judge if he did not have

---

[38] For the difference between non-conceptual and conceptual states, cf. 5.2, 6.3.

such extraneous information.)[39] The result will necessarily be closely correlated with the content of the informational state which he is in at that time. Now he may prefix this result with the operator 'It seems to me as though ...'. This is a way of producing in himself, and giving expression to, a cognitive state whose content is *systematically* dependent upon the content of the informational state, and the systematic dependence is a basis for him to claim knowledge of the informational state. But in no sense has that state become an object to him: there is nothing that constitutes 'perceiving that state'. What this means is that there is no *informational* state which stands to the internal state as that internal state stands to the state of the world.

Once again, describing this procedure cannot constitute a complete account of what it is to have this capacity for self-knowledge. The subject who genuinely has this capacity for self-knowledge must understand the content of his judgement 'It seems to me as though *p*', and his understanding of it must determine it to have a content different from that of the judgement 'Possibly *p*', or 'Going by appearances, *p*'. This requires a background of a sort analogous to that mentioned above in connection with self-ascription of belief. As my allusion in that context will have suggested, I believe we may have here an interpretation of Kant's remark about the transcendental 'I think' which accompanies all our perceptions.[40] Without the background, we have at most a formal 'I think'; it yields nothing until embedded within a satisfactory theory.[41]

The procedure I have described does not produce infallible knowledge of the informational state, for mistakes of the kind that occur when the subject makes judgements about the world can also produce inaccuracies when the same procedure is re-used for this different purpose. For example, consider a case in which a subject sees ten points of light arranged in a circle, but reports that there are eleven points of light arranged in a circle,

[39] For 'extraneous', see Dummett, 'What is a Theory of Meaning?' (II), p. 95. Obviously the subject can engage in this procedure when he believes his perceptual information is illusory; the rule then obliges him to pretend or suppose that it is not, and ask himself what he would say or judge in that case.

[40] *Critique of Pure Reason*, B 131–2.

[41] The point is that 'I think' (or 'it seems to me') acquires structure ('ξ thinks' or 'it seems to ξ', with 'I' in the argument-place) only when it is related to (at least possible) other exemplifications of the same predicate.

because he has made a mistake in counting, forgetting where he began. Such a mistake can clearly occur again when the subject re-uses the procedure in order to gain knowledge of his internal state: his report 'I seem to see eleven points of light arranged in a circle' is just wrong. However, when the subject conceptualizes his experience in terms of some very elementary concept, such as a simple colour concept like 'red', it is not easy to make sense of his making a mistake. Concentrating upon this kind of case, and feeling extremely suspicious of the idea of a judgement which is about something distinct from itself, yet which cannot be wrong, some philosophers have adopted the contention that the existence of an internal informational state is constituted by the subject's *disposition* to make certain judgements. But this is both extremely implausible in itself and quite unnecessary.

The proposal is implausible, because it is not the case that we simply find ourselves with a yen to apply some concept—a conviction that it has application in the immediate vicinity. Nothing could more falsify the facts of the situation. Further, no account of what it is to be in a non-conceptual informational state can be given in terms of dispositions to exercise concepts unless those concepts are assumed to be endlessly fine-grained; and does this make sense? Do we really understand the proposal that we have as many colour concepts as there are shades of colour that we can sensibly discriminate?

The proposal is unnecessary for the following reason. Logically infallible knowledge does indicate that the state judged about and the judgement are not (as Hume would have said) distinct existences. But there are two ways in which this can be acknowledged. Either the state can be regarded as *constituted by* dispositions to make certain judgements—and this, as we have seen, is not very plausible; or, alternatively, the judgement's being a judgement with a certain content can be regarded as constituted by its being a response to that state. And on reflection, the latter is far the more plausible option: such infallibility as there is arises because we regard it as a necessary condition for the subject to possess these simple observational concepts that he be disposed to apply them when he has certain experiences. This sort of infallibility is rather limited and uninteresting. And it is of a quite different kind from that which arises in the case of the self-ascription of belief.

However, in an important respect these two ways of gaining self-knowledge are similar: namely that neither conforms to the description 'looking within'. In the case we have just been describing, the subject's concentration, as with self-ascription of belief, is on the outside world: how does he, or would he, judge it to be? The cases are different in that in this case there is something (namely an internal, informational state of the subject), distinct from his judgement, to which his judgement aims to be faithful. But it is something necessarily approached in the roundabout way I have described.

We have taken account, then, of the following two facts. First, in a state of information on the basis of which a subject may ascribe to himself an experience as of seeing, say, a tree, what *he* observes (if anything) is only the tree, not his own informational state. (But let me remind you that the procedure I have described, of re-using the conceptual skills which one uses in order to make judgements about the world, is not by itself enough for the capacity to ascribe experiences to oneself.) Second, any informational state in which the subject has information about the world is *ipso facto* a state in which he has information about himself, of the kind we are discussing, available to him. It is of the utmost importance to appreciate that in order to understand the self-ascription of experience we need to postulate no special faculty of inner sense or internal self-scanning.[42]

Not all our reports of experience have the character we have been considering, because not all our characterizations of internal informational states describe them in terms of their content. Although 'It feels to me as though thousands of little pins are lightly touching my skin' and 'It feels to me as though my legs are crossed' are reports of the same kind as those we have been considering, 'I feel a pain in my foot' and 'I feel an itch in my foot' are not. But once we have the general framework of bodily perception and bodily sensations (understood as informational states, which may be illusory, whose content concerns the body and its states and positions), then it is perhaps not too difficult to fit these in. There is no reason why an informational state should have *only* informational properties. Thus we can say that when a subject feels an itch, he perceives (or appears to perceive) a part of his body in a way which makes him very much want

---

[42] There *is* a faculty of internal self-scanning: namely bodily perception (see 7.3).

to scratch, and when he is in pain, he perceives (or appears to perceive) a part of his body in a way which is awful. (One thing that can be said for this approach is that it does explain why pains and itches are necessarily felt in a particular part of the body.)

The features of these modes of self-knowledge have given rise to certain illusions about the self. Hume said:

> For my part, when I enter most intimately into what I call *myself*, I always stumble on some particular perception or other, of heat or cold, light or shade, love or hatred, pain or pleasure. I can never catch *myself* at any time without a perception, and never can observe anything but the perception.[43]

Now in fact we have totally rejected the background of perceptual metaphor in which Hume casts his point, and in particular we have invoked nothing that could be construed as stumbling on perceptions; those inner states of the subject that we spoke of cannot intelligibly be regarded as objects of his internal gaze. However, there is something in Hume's point; indeed, in a manner of speaking, it becomes even stronger when the metaphor is dispensed with. For what we are aware of, when we know that we see a tree, is *nothing but a tree*. In fact, we only have to be aware of some state of the world in order to be in a position to make an assertion about ourselves.

Now this might raise the following perplexity. How can it be that we can have knowledge of a state of affairs which involves a substantial and persisting self, simply by being aware of (still worse, by merely appearing to be aware of) a state of the world?[44]

We must agree that we cannot get something for nothing. So the anxiety will be lessened only by showing how the accounting is done—where the idea of the persisting empirical self comes from. Nothing more than the original state of awareness—awareness, simply, of a tree—is called for *on the side of awareness,*

---

[43] *A Treatise of Human Nature*, Book I, Part IV, chapter VI: p. 239 in the Everyman edition (Dent, London, 1911).

[44] See G. E. Moore, 'Wittgenstein's Lectures in 1930-33' (III), *Mind* lxiv (1955), 1–27, at p. 13: '... and he said of what he called "visual sensations" generally, and in particular of what he called "the visual field", that "the idea of a person doesn't enter into the description of it, just as a [physical] eye doesn't enter into the description of what is seen.' (See n. 25 above.)

for a subject to gain knowledge of himself thereby. But certainly
something more than the *sheer* awareness is called for: the perceptual state must occur in the context of certain kinds of
knowledge and understanding on the part of the subject.
(Otherwise, we might say as before, the 'I think' which accompanies the subject's perceptions is purely formal, or *empty*.) No
judgement will have the content of a psychological self-ascription, unless the judger can be regarded as ascribing to himself a
property which he can conceive as being satisfied by a being not
necessarily himself—a state of affairs which he will have to
conceive as involving a persisting subject of experience. He can
know that a state of affairs of the relevant type obtains simply
by being aware of a tree, but he must conceive the state of affairs
that he then knows to obtain as a state of affairs of precisely that
type. And this means that he must conceive of himself, the
subject to whom the property is ascribed, as a being of the kind
which he envisages when he simply envisages *someone* seeing a
tree—that is to say, a persisting subject of experience, located in
space and time.[45]

We see, then, that the two applications of the Generality
Constraint—one imposing the requirement of generality upon
the concept ξ *sees a tree*, and the other imposing a generality
upon the Idea 'I'—work together, forcing the subject to think
of himself as an element of the objective order.

There is a parallel for this situation. For we want to allow,
equally, that a subject can know that he is *in front of a house*
simply by perceiving a house. Certainly what he perceives comprises no element corresponding to 'I' in the judgement 'I am in
front of a house': he is simply aware of a house. But if we are to
interpret a judgement made upon this basis as having the content 'I am in front of a house', we must have reason to suppose
that the subject regards himself as recognizing the existence of
a state of affairs of precisely the same kind as obtains when, for
instance, a car is in front of a house. So what he envisages, or
judges, certainly comprises two elements spatially related,
although what he sees does not. (This only goes to show that it

---

[45] For the fact that certain judgements about the self can be identification-free,
combined with the claim that links with empirical criteria of personal identity are
nevertheless not severed in the case of such judgements, see Strawson, *The Bounds of
Sense*, p. 165.

is not a good idea, in attempting to determine the content of a person's judgement, to examine nothing but the content of the perceptions which can legitimately give rise to it.)

Presumably it goes without saying that both the ways of gaining knowledge of ourselves that I have discussed in this section give rise to judgements which are immune to error through misidentification. When the first component expresses knowledge gained in one of these ways, it does not make sense for the subject to utter 'Someone believes that p, but is it I who believe that p?', or 'It seems to someone that there's something red in front of him, but does it seem to me that there is something red in front of me?'

We have reached, I hope, a point upon which everyone can agree: someone who understands a term as referring to himself must be disposed to regard, as relevant to the truth or falsity of certain utterances involving that term, the occurrence of certain experiences which he is in a position immediately to recognize. It would appear that nothing is easier than to test for the existence of this disposition: we can stimulate the subject in various ways, and see how his evaluation of the relevant sentences is affected. I have tried to explain why the sheer existence of this disposition does not by itself guarantee that the subject has an adequate Idea of himself, but it is clearly an indispensable element in any such Idea.

However, it needs to be treated with the greatest care, for mis-statements and misunderstandings of this element provide a strong pressure towards solipsism.

A subject's knowledge of what is in question when, for example, he is in pain, or when he sees a tree, can seem to be very similar to his knowledge of what is in question when an observable state of the world obtains. When an eclipse of the sun occurs, he might say, such-and-such experiences are to be expected; and he knows which they are—he can manifest this knowledge by his performance in suitable tests. Equally, he might say, when he is in pain, such-and-such experiences are to be expected; and he knows which ones they are. There is certainly a difference between his being in pain and anyone else's being in pain; and this difference is one which he can detect, just as he can detect the difference between an eclipse of the sun and an eclipse of the moon.

Now we might think of the solipsist as someone who attempts to use this asymmetry in order to state, at least to his own satisfaction, what he means by 'I'. Rather as one might differentiate the sun from the moon by saying that the sun is that object an eclipse of which makes it reasonable to expect such-and-such experiences, whereas the moon is that object an eclipse of which makes it reasonable to expect such-and-such different experiences, the solipsist thinks he can say: I am that object such that when it is in pain something frightful is to be expected.

Consider a pair of different observable possibilities: say a certain armchair being red and it being green. A suitably equipped subject can tell the difference between these states of affairs, because of the difference in the way they appear. And this is how the solipsist construes the asymmetry from which he starts. He supposes that he can adopt the same *impersonal* style of description in characterizing the asymmetry he is concerned with—speaking of what kind of experiences *are to be expected*. Now we can say that a green armchair and a red armchair can be distinguished by a difference in the way they appear (by a difference in the experiences which are to be expected), because we are speaking of what may be expected by *any* observer (or at least any normal observer). But that is exactly not the kind of difference with which the solipsist is concerned. What he can legitimately say is only this: 'I can tell the difference between a state of affairs involving myself and a state of affairs involving someone else by the difference in the ways in which they appear to *me*'; thus he can say 'When I am in pain, something frightful happens to *me*'. Of course, no one in his right mind would want to say that, because it is tautological. And the solipsist's error lies precisely in his desire to extract something informative (non-tautological) about his use of 'I' from the asymmetry.

He is of course right that there is something substantial which must have been learned by someone who uses the first-person pronoun properly, and that it is manifested in his responding differently to the kind of differences from which the solipsist begins. But this knowledge is *practical*: it cannot be transformed into a substantial account of what the subject means by 'I'. It is the solipsist's attempt to transform it into something substantial that yields his desire to say 'By "I" I mean the person such that, when he is in pain, something frightful is to be expected'.[46] And the project of wringing something substantial out of the difference is obviously ruined when the impersonal mode of description is replaced by the appropriate relativized description, yielding a tautology.[47]

7.5 MEMORY

Memory is not a way of gaining knowledge but a faculty of retaining knowledge; so this next section is not parallel to the last two. As I remarked earlier (7.1), the relation of memory to 'I'-thinking introduces quite novel elements, over and above the sort of feature involved in 'here'-Ideas and 'this'-Ideas.

Let me make a preliminary identification of the point I have in mind, to begin fixing ideas, by reference to language. (This formulation will not in fact stand much scrutiny.) We might say: if a subject remembers, at time t', being in a position at time t to assert 'I am F', then he is in a position, without further information, to assert 'I was F (at t)'. (Hence if he is in a position at t' to assert 'I am now G', he is in a position to assert 'Something was F (at t) and is now G'.) There is no such simple rule relating memory to 'here', 'this', or 'now'.

It is better to put the point in terms of how a person's belief system is organized to take account of the passage of time: a subject which David Kaplan has called 'cognitive dynamics'.[48] (This allows us to eliminate any appearance that the subject arrives at the past-tense judgement by some *inference*, the premiss of which is that he *was* in a position to make such-and-such a judgement; which would require us to raise the question of the structure and nature of the premiss.)

It is a precondition of rationality that information acquired at one time should be available to the subject later: hence, given that in a rational creature information (and misinformation) generates beliefs, that beliefs should persist. (And the capacity

[46] Incidentally, although it is *sentience* that the solipsist denies to others, it is not at all essential that his definition of 'I' be restricted to the attempt to extract something substantial from our capacities for *mental* self-ascription. He might just as well have said: I am the person such that, when his legs are bent, *this* is felt: or: I am the person such that, when he moves, changes of such-and-such a kind are to be observed. The solipsist need not be a dualist.

[47] Is this what Wittgenstein meant when he said (*Tractatus* 5.62): '... what the solipsist *means* is quite correct; only it cannot be said, but makes itself manifest'?

[48] In 'Demonstratives'.

to retain information is *memory*.) If we take a belief state, as I think we should, to be a disposition to have certain thoughts or to make certain judgements, then we can say that any rational being must have a cognitive system which brings it about that the dispositions to make judgements he has at one time should be systematically dependent on the dispositions to make judgements he had at earlier times. (There being, presumably, a single persisting structural feature of the nervous system underlying both sets of dispositions.)

Persistence of belief does not always, or indeed even usually, involve persistence of a disposition to make the *same* judgements (if judgements are individuated simply in terms of the forms of words which would express them). For instance, the persistence of a belief that I would have manifested at some time by the judgement 'John is now angry' involves the disposition to judge later not that John is now angry but that John *was then* angry.[49]

There is indeed no general guarantee that a belief will persist. Suppose I perceive an object and judge 'This is *F*', and then lose track of it. There is no guarantee that there will be available to me a past-tense demonstrative Idea (see 5.5), enabling me to judge 'That was *F*'. (If such an Idea *is* available to me, it will need to draw on conceptual material not present in the original demonstrative identification.)

When a subject keeps track of a place as he moves (or does not move), or keeps track of an object as he or it moves (or not), I think we should regard the slightly varying forms of the judgements he is disposed to make as manifestations of a single persisting belief (a continuing acceptance of the same thought). Success here certainly depends upon a *skill* (the ability to keep track). But thinking a thought inevitably takes time, and this kind of skill must be seen as generally underlying demonstrative judgements. I cannot see the later members of a series of judgements 'It's ϕ here', 'It's ϕ there', ..., made while one moves about, keeping track of the place at which one has ascertained that it is ϕ, as based upon an identification. Similarly with times, and series of judgements like 'It is ϕ now', 'It was ϕ a moment ago', 'It was ϕ a while back', ...[50]

---

[49] Why call this persistence of the *same* belief? Because no new evidence is needed to sustain it.

[50] [See §1 of the Appendix to chapter 6.]

Now, if we consider 'I' in this context, we see that the cognitive dynamics of 'I'-Ideas are peculiarly simple. We can isolate the cognitive dynamics of 'I'-Ideas in particular by considering tenseless predicates: if a subject has, at time t, a belief which he might manifest in judging 'I am F' (where 'ξ is F' is tenseless), then the tendency of belief to persist means that there is a non-negligible probability (depending on the gap between t and t') of his still having, at a later time t', the disposition to judge 'I am F'. If we now introduce the consideration of tenses (etc.), we introduce other aspects of cognitive dynamics: combined with the aspect we have hitherto isolated, this yields (for instance): if a subject has at t a belief which he might then manifest in judging 'I am now F', then there is a non-negligible probability of his having, at a later time t', a disposition to judge 'I was previously F'. The later manifestation of the belief still employs 'I' (contrast the need to shift from 'here' to 'there' as one moves but keeps track of a place, or from 'now' to 'then' as one keeps track of a time receding into the past)); and, so far as the 'I'-Idea is concerned, the later dispositions to judge flow out of the earlier dispositions to judge, without the need for any *skill* or *care* (not to lose track of something) on the part of the subject.

We can put this point by using, once again, the terminology of immunity to error through misidentification: a past-tense judgement, 'I was F', is not based upon a pair of propositions, ⌜That person was F⌝ and ⌜I am that person⌝ (where 'that person' captures an identification of an object with respect to a past time).[51]

It would be a mistake to think that this holds only when the disposition to make the past-tense judgement 'I was F' manifests the persistence of a belief originally acquired in one of the special ways of gaining knowledge of ourselves discussed in 7.3 and 7.4. For even when there is an articulation underlying the formation of the original belief, it remains the case that the unthinking operation of cognitive dynamics will yield a subsequent disposition to make a suitable past-tense judgement, without there

---

[51] An identification of an object (an Idea, a) is an identification with respect to the *present* if it follows from the truth of ⌜a is F⌝ that it is now the case that $(\exists x)(x$ is $F)$, *no matter what is substituted for* 'F'. An identification is an identification with respect to the past if there is no such *general* implication. (Of course 'That man is now F' has the implication even if 'That man' is a past-tense demonstrative; but the same identification can figure in judgements that do not have the implication, e.g. 'That man was F'.)

being any need for an identification component in the process whereby the dispositions to make judgements flow into one another. We need, therefore, a more sophisticated notion of immunity to error through misidentification than before: one which can highlight the absence of an identification of a certain kind, or at a certain point in the process that issues in a judgement, rather than the absence of any identification at all.

This feature of 'I'-Ideas means that they span past and present in a novel way.[52] (A 'this'-Idea will typically span a period of time: 6.1, 6.4. But its doing so rests upon the exercise of a skill on the subject's part. Moreover, the time span of an 'I'-Idea may be quite extensive.) An 'I'-Idea gives rise to thoughts dependent upon information received over a period of time. (This opens up a new possibility of ill-groundedness: see 5.4. Whether or not a subject essaying the employment in thought of such an Idea is in fact thinking of anything depends upon whether there is just one thing which is both what the relevant previous beliefs, now retained, were about and what his current self-oriented ways of gaining knowledge concern. See 7.7.)[53]

It is possible to regard this feature of 'I'-Ideas as part of the informational component of a functional characterization. A possessor of an 'I'-Idea has a capacity to ascribe past-tense properties to himself on a special basis: namely the memory of the basis appropriate for an earlier present-tense judgement. This brings out a similarity with the informational components we have already encountered. But we must be careful not to lose sight of the fact that memory is not a way of *gaining* knowledge.

So far in this section we have been exclusively concerned with the retention of *belief*. Thus we might consider a subject who forms the belief that a tree is burning, on the basis of perceptual information he is receiving. We have seen how, by perceiving the world, the subject is *ipso facto* put in a position to gain various

[52] And expectation will bring in the future. (See 7.1.)

[53] If there is really no identification component involved in the past-tense judgements we are considering, then in such a judgement, 'I was *F*', we cannot think of the 'I'-Idea as effecting a purely *present-tense* identification of its object (so that in the event of a serious mismatch of the subject's apparent memories with his own past, we could say that he has, perfectly determinately, a particular object in view, but has a wholly inaccurate conception of its past). The identification is *not* exclusively present-tense: while it is true that 'I was *F*' entails 'There is now something which was *F*', it is no less true that 'I am *F*' entails 'There was something which is now *F*'.

pieces of knowledge about himself: being in a position to assert 'A tree is now burning', he would also be in a position to assert 'I am facing a tree that is burning', 'I see a tree that is burning', more weakly 'I seem to see a tree that is burning', etc.[54] Suppose he forms self-conscious beliefs of this latter kind; then, just as the belief initially expressible by 'A tree is now burning' may persist to a later time, at which it needs to be expressed by, say, 'A tree was burning last night', so the self-conscious beliefs formed on the basis of the same original informational state may persist, needing to be expressed as 'I was facing a tree that was burning', etc.

We should take note, however, of the possibility of cases in which the operation of memory takes place purely at the level of the informational system. In this sort of case, what memory ensures is the subject's possession of a *non-conceptual* informational state, whose content corresponds in a certain respect with that of some earlier informational state of the subject (a perceptual state); although its content differs from that of the antecedent perceptual state in that, if the subject is in the memory state, it seems to him that such-and-such *was* the case. (That is, memory states, even of this kind, are not free-floating images whose reference to the past is read into them by reasoning on the part of the subject.)[55]

Now just as the non-conceptual informational states involved in perception put a subject in a position to acquire present-tense self-knowledge by the exercise of his conceptual capacities, so these non-conceptual informational states put a subject in a position to acquire past-tense self-knowledge by the exercise of his conceptual capacities. A subject can form beliefs which he would express by 'I was facing a tree that was burning last night', etc., in this way, on the basis of a non-conceptual memory state, without needing to have had the disposition to make the corresponding present-tense judgements (without having had the beliefs) at the time of the original perception.

This sort of memory is extremely important. It is frequently

[54] See 7.3, 7.4.

[55] How there can be such informational states, with a content which concerns the past, and frequently more or less specific past times, and how the behaviour of the subject must be dependent upon such states for such a content to be ascribed to them— these are difficult questions, which it is fortunately not necessary, for my current purposes, to answer.

said that memory provides us, in the first instance, with information about our past experiences; but this is certainly quite wrong about the kind of operation of memory that I have just described: we no more have, in memory, information which is primarily about our past experiences than we have, in perception, information which is primarily about our present experiences. Just as perception must be regarded as a capacity for gaining information about the world, so memory must be regarded as a capacity for retaining information about the world. The truism about perception is not upset by the fact that there are occasions on which we are in a perceptual state without gaining information about the world—for example, when we hallucinate. In the same way, the parallel truism about memory should not be upset by the fact that there are occasions on which we use our memories without being in a position to make any knowledgeable past-tense judgements about the world—as when we remember a hallucination. In the first case we gain misinformation about the world; in the second case we retain misinformation about the world. (Of course, when the information we retain was originally derived from our own bodies, then the memory state can be said to be primarily about ourselves: for example, I may remember in this way that I was pushed and pulled last night. But obviously this is a special case.)[56]

This kind of operation of memory—in which a self-conscious past-tense judgement is based upon a non-conceptual memory state involving information about some past state of the world, in a way analogous to that in which a self-conscious present-tense judgement might have been based on the non-conceptual perceptual state whose informational content has been retained by the memory (even though no self-conscious present-tense judgement was so based)—seems to exemplify the phenomenon of immunity to error through misidentification. When the first component expresses knowledge which the subject has gained (and does not suppose he has not gained, or may not have

[56] Remembering an episode in this way is frequently described as remembering it 'from the inside'. One remembers an episode involving oneself 'from the inside' if one retains information of a character such that if one were to possess its 'present-tense' counterpart now, one would thereby be enabled to make the various first-person judgements one's capacity to make which at the time was constitutive of one's involvement in the episode.

gained) in this way, it does not appear to make sense for him to say 'Someone saw a tree burning last night, but was it I?', or 'Someone was in front of a tree last night, but was it I?', or 'Someone was pushed and pulled last night, but was it I?'

Shoemaker, however, has recently argued that this is not so: the appearance that judgements about oneself based on memory are identification-free is claimed to arise from the trivial linguistic fact that we would not describe a person whose information about the past was not originally acquired by himself as *remembering*.[57]

But it is not true that the apparent identification-freedom in question is a mere appearance, wholly due to this linguistic phenomenon. It is true that Strawson rather lays himself open to the accusation of trading on the linguistic phenomenon, when he tries to illustrate the identification-freedom in question by considering the deviance of the utterance 'I distinctly remember that inner experience occurring, but did it occur to me?'[58] But the claim can be made, as I made it above, without explicitly using the notion of remembering in the first component ('Someone was F', not 'I remember that someone was F'), and hence without any necessary reliance on linguistic restrictions imposed by the concept of remembering.

Shoemaker's argument that memory judgements about oneself are identification-dependent, and hence not immune to error through misidentification, is this. We can imagine a case in which a subject's apparent memories are causally derived, not from past informational states of his own, but from someone else's past informational states. In such a situation the subject would have information about past states of the world, and, carried upon the back of that information, information about past states of some observer of the world; but he would not have information about past states of his own, but rather information about the past states of the person from whom his apparent memories causally derive.[59] Such a situation would arise if a perfect duplicate of a person (including his brain) were made: in this case the new person would appear to remember all the

---

[57] See 'Persons and Their Pasts'.

[58] *The Bounds of Sense*, p. 165.

[59] Similarly for the 'retention' of beliefs (the operation of memory considered at the beginning of this section).

events which the original could remember—and appear, more-over, to remember them 'from the inside'.

We could not legitimately speak of the subject's remembering a tree burning, or of his remembering seeing a tree burning, or of his remembering being pummelled; this is because of the restriction built into the term 'remember', on which we have just been commenting. So Shoemaker introduces the term 'quasi-remembering', explained in such a way that we can say that the subject quasi-remembers the tree burning and quasi-remembers seeing the tree burn.

Given that quasi-remembering (q-remembering) is a possible situation, it would appear that a subject might grasp that it is a possible situation, and even believe, perhaps for good reason, that he is in it. Such a subject would seem to be able to utter, perfectly significantly, 'Someone stood in front of a burning tree, but it was not I'—even when the first component expresses information which he has in his memory.[60] And a second subject might genuinely have reason to doubt whether this was his situation, so that he might say 'Someone watched a tree burn-ing, but was it I?'—being unsure, for example, how long ago the event occurred, and so whether it occurred after the time at which he started his independent existence.

This argument is of a kind with which we are already familiar, and we have seen that it fails to establish its conclusion. (See 6.6 on places, and 7.3 on physical self-ascription.) The argument presents us with a case in which information apparently pos-sessed about an object in a certain way—the normal way—can underlie a judgement about an object which is based upon an identification. But it certainly does not follow from this that judgements about an object, based upon this way of possessing information about it, *must* be based upon an identification. And it seems to me that we cannot regard the ordinary memory judgements which we make about ourselves as articulable into the two components, 'That man was in front of a burning tree' and 'I am that man'. The argument against the present sugges-tion parallels the argument I offered against a similar suggestion in the case of 'here' (6.6).

In that case, I argued that it is not intelligible to challenge the direct relevance to 'here'-judgements of perceptual information

[60] Here 'memory' includes q-remembering.

acquired in the normal way—on pain of not having an adequate 'here'-Idea of a place, or at least not one which is recognizably like the one we have, to sustain the challenge. For I argued that what enables us to credit a thinker with an adequate knowledge of which place is in question in his 'here'-judgements is his capacity to identify his whereabouts in the spatial framework. This depends upon his capacity to use his perceptions, and the changing course of his perceptions, to determine his position; and this in turn depends upon a willingness to allow current (normal) perceptions to bear upon the question how things stand *here* (where he is).

There is a similar difficulty in the present case about the nature of the 'I'-Idea that would figure in the supposed identification component. I have suggested (see 7.3) that in general a subject's possession of an adequate Idea of himself depends upon the same capacity that underlies his ability to use 'here'-Ideas—the capacity to determine his position in the objective order. But this capacity depends no more upon current perception than upon a subject's willingness to use his memory, in order to bring information about the course of his past (though usually recent) perceptions to bear upon the question of his past position, and thereby upon the question of his current position. Self-location cannot in general be a momentary thing. For one thing, places are not always immediately recognizable. For another, self-location crucially depends upon the axiom that the subject moves continuously through space; and that axiom can be brought to bear upon particular questions of location only if the subject has the capacity to retain information about his previous perceptions, and to use that information in making judgements about his past, and thereby his present, position. If we imagine a subject who cannot retain information for more than a few seconds, or, equally, a subject who refuses to argue from such retained information as he possesses to propositions about *his* past position, then we have imagined a subject who just does not have the practical capacity to locate himself in space.

Furthermore, there is an equal difficulty with the other term of the identity. We are supposed to be able to regard the normal situation in which a subject judges that he was *F* as being the result of two judgements, one of them being that he is the same person as ... —but as who? We must see the judgement 'I was seeing a tree burn' as resting on the judgements 'That man was seeing a tree burn' and 'I am that man'—but now what Idea of a man is represented by 'that man'? We know that the sheer existence of an information-link does not suffice for an adequate Idea. As before, we might consider an Idea that is adequate by virtue of involving a description: *that man* is identified as the man whose past informational states are causally responsible for these apparent memories. Now it is perfectly all right to ascribe such an adequate Idea to a person who has been apprised of his situation (or who has anyway been brought, perhaps falsely, to think of his situation) as being that of a duplicate. But it is surely far-fetched in the extreme to suppose that such an Idea is generally involved in our past-tense self-ascriptions.

There is another reason for being dissatisfied with the picture which emerges when we think of judgements about one's past, based upon memory, as identification-dependent. The picture requires us to be able to think of memory as a way of having knowledge of an object which leaves its identity (in particular, its identity with the subject) an open question. It will be agreed that the normal subject will have *knowledge* of his own past, but this will be seen as the result of two pieces of knowledge, expressible as 'That man was F' and 'I am that man'; and it must be the case that the subject could have knowledge of the truth of the first component, independently of the truth of the second component. But it does not appear to me to be possible to think of memory as an 'identity-neutral' way of having knowledge of the past states of a person. (And this is not the result of some trivial linguistic truth about what we would *call* 'memory'.)

Suppose we surgically 'transfer the memories' from the brain of subject S' to the brain of a subject S, and suppose S does not know that this has happened. S will, of course, make judgements about his past in the normal way. But suppose that he discovers that he was not F, and he was not G, ... —that in general his memory cannot be relied upon as an accurate record of his past. Suppose that, fantastically, he then retreats to making *general* past-tense judgements: 'Someone was F, and was G ...'. *These judgements could not possibly constitute knowledge.* Even to be intelligible in putting them forward, S would have to offer what had actually happened, or something very like it, as a hypothesis;

but he could not possibly be said to know that it was true. It would be a sheer guess. Consequently he could not be said to know anything based on it. (We must remember that it is not sufficient for knowledge that a true belief be causally dependent on the facts which render it true.) And if S cannot know the truth of these general judgements, he certainly cannot be said to know the truth of the supposed judgements 'That man was F', etc., which are stronger than they.[61]

So the theory does not fit the facts. Memory is not a way of possessing knowledge about an object of a kind which leaves open the question of the identity of that object. If a subject has, in virtue of the operations of his memory, knowledge of the past states of a subject, then that subject is himself.

Of course, it is possible for memory to *serve as the basis* for a different way of having knowledge about the past; if a subject knows that his apparent memories are systematically correlated with the past states of some other object (via being systematically correlated with its memories), then he can *infer* from the existence of a present apparent memory to the past state of that object. But it surely cannot be suggested that this is the normal operation of memory—that we infer, via a general belief about the correlation between our present apparent memories and our past states, from the present apparent memories to those past states. There is here a fundamental asymmetry between two ways of gaining knowledge of the past: the one depends upon a general belief, but the other, being underwritten by evolution, does not. Indeed, I should be prepared to argue that if one attempted to arrive at past-tense judgements *only* in the inferential way (in the absence, that is, of a capacity for direct memory), one would not be equipped to *understand* the conclusions of the supposed inferences.

We have found, therefore, no compelling reason for giving up the view that our Ideas of ourselves do not permit a gap to open up between knowing, in virtue of the operation of memory, that *someone* saw a tree burning, and knowing that it was *oneself* who saw a tree burning. For a subject to have information (or misinformation) in this way, to the effect that *someone* saw a tree, just is for the subject to have information (or misinformation)

---

[61] This argument should be capable of being recast in terms of the subject's having knowledge of states of the world, e.g. that a tree was burning.

to the effect that *he* saw a tree. For a subject to have an apparent memory of a tree burning is for it to seem to him that a tree burned, and by the same token, for it to seem to him that *he* saw a tree burn. As Shoemaker said in an earlier work:

I do not express my memory of eating eggs for breakfast by saying 'I had eggs for breakfast' because I think that it is convenient, or advisable, that such memories be expressed in this way; I do so because my memory is, precisely, a memory that *I* had eggs for breakfast.[62]

Shoemaker's later work has made it seem to some philosophers that this must be wrong. Derek Parfit, for instance, has written:

When I seem to remember an experience, I do indeed seem to remember *having* it. But it cannot be a part of what I seem to remember about this experience that I, the person who now seems to remember it, am the person who had this experience. That I am is something I automatically assume. (My apparent memories sometimes come to me simply as the belief that *I* had a certain experience.) But it is something that I am justified in assuming only because I do not in fact have *q*-memories of other people's experiences.[63]

But our earlier reflections enable us to see what is wrong with this passage: namely that it assumes that the identification which 'I' effects (for me now) is an exclusively present-tense identification. (Notice the gloss on 'I': 'the person who now seems to remember [the experience]'.) Whereas we saw at the beginning of this section that it is of the essence of an 'I'-Idea that it effects an identification which spans past and present.[64]

Since I think many philosophers would dispute the conclusion I have reached, it may be worth saying a word about why they might do so.

Some of them have been influenced by an observation by Bernard Williams about the imagination.[65] To imagine *being in*

---

[62] *Self-Knowledge and Self-Identity* (Cornell University Press, Ithaca, 1963), pp. 33-4.

[63] 'Personal Identity', *Philosophical Review* lxxx (1971), 3-27, at p. 15.

[64] This has a connection with the idea that memory suffices for personal identity. My judgement (or seeming judgement) 'I was *F*', made on the basis of apparent memory, can go wrong only in certain ways. Either there is no past state of affairs of which the apparent memory constitutes information (no one was—relevantly—*F*); or the object involved in the state of affairs was indeed myself; or, finally, *I* do not exist. (This last possibility will seem paradoxical; but see 7.6.)

[65] 'Imagination and the Self', in *Problems of the Self* (CUP, Cambridge, 1973), pp. 26-45.

the West Indies (as opposed to imagining someone being in the West Indies) presumably involves producing in oneself informational states of roughly the kind which might underlie the first-person judgement 'I am in the West Indies': visual impressions of palm trees and steel bands; auditory impressions of the band's music intermingling with the breaking of the waves; perhaps suitable kinaesthetic impressions of lying on a beach with the hot sand under one's body. Now Williams argues that imagining being in the West Indies, in this way, is not necessarily to imagine that *one* is in the West Indies, or to imagine *oneself* being in the West Indies. I think this is correct: it does not follow, from the fact that a certain piece of imagining involves certain states of information which would, if they actually occurred, warrant the judgement that p, that the piece of imagining can be described as imagining that p. (I think this can be seen from the fact that it may be just as wrong to describe the subject as imagining that the place he occupies—*here*—is in the West Indies, even though the same imagined states of information would, if actual, warrant the judgement that *here* is in the West Indies.) So there is a difference between what might be described as imagining being in the West Indies (from the inside), and imagining *one's* being in the West Indies; and I think this has encouraged some philosophers to think there is a similar gap between remembering, or seeming to remember, being in the West Indies (from the inside) and remembering, or seeming to remember, *one's* being in the West Indies.

Williams's observation does preclude anyone from mounting a purely grammatical argument for the *identity* of these informational states; but it cannot show their *distinctness*. After all, imagining a tree is not necessarily imagining a tree *here*, even though seeming to see a tree *is*, necessarily, seeming to see a tree *here*. Williams's point tells us something important about the imagination, but I do not see that it shows us anything about memory.

An equivocation on the term 'quasi-memory' ('q-memory') provides another reason why philosophers have not accepted the equation I have suggested. The notion of q-memory was originally introduced in this way (making it perfectly intelligible): a subject q-remembers an event e if and only if (i) he has an apparent memory of such an event, and (ii) that apparent memory in fact embodies information deriving from the perception of that event by a person who is not necessarily himself. Given the notion thus introduced, we are able to say that a subject q-remembers an event that he did not witness, and in consequence that he q-remembers witnessing an event, being in front of a tree, etc., when he did not witness the event, was not in front of a tree, etc. (Of course introducing such a definition leaves the question of the *content* of memory states quite untouched; it can still be right to say, as I have, that an apparent memory of ϕ-ing is necessarily an apparent memory of oneself ϕ-ing.) But now it is somehow supposed that the intelligibility of the notion of q-memory, thus introduced, demonstrates the possibility of a faculty which is both like our memory in giving subjects knowledge of the past, and unlike it in that the content of the memory states in no way encroaches upon the question of *whose* past is concerned. The informational states of a q-memory faculty announce themselves, so to speak, as *merely* q-memories, so that it seems to the subject that someone or other ϕ-ed without its in any way seeming to him that *he* ϕ-ed.

Obviously this is a fallacy. I can introduce the term 'q-perceive', in such a way that a subject can be said to q-perceive a tree provided that he seems to see a tree as a causal result of a process which takes that tree as input, whether or not that tree is where the subject is disposed to locate it either in space or in time. But, by this purely linguistic manoeuvre, I have not shown the intelligibility of a faculty of q-perception: one which involves informational states whose content is simply of the existence, *somewhere* in space and time, of such-and-such a kind of thing. The manoeuvre does not show the possibility of its perceptually seeming to the subject that there is a tree without its seeming to him that there is a tree where he is.[66]

---

[66] I think similar fallacies are evident in the use that has been made of the analogous notion of q-intending.

A rather different kind of memory must be postulated to account for a subject's knowledge of certain others of his own past mental states; e.g. his knowledge of what he was thinking five minutes before, or of what he was then about to do, i.e. intending to do. This kind of memory is neither a matter of the persistence of belief, nor the shadow cast by memory of the past states of the world. There is little we can say about it, save that it is a primitive capacity, and one upon which all intelligent reflective life depends. Any thinking needs to be able to keep track of what has gone before (what question was being addressed, what subsidiary conclusions have been reached, and so on). An organized process of thought will therefore inevitably include thoughts which—without

7.6 THE POSSIBILITY OF REFERENCE-FAILURE

It seems to me to be a corollary of the reflections in this chapter that our ordinary thoughts about ourselves are liable to many different kinds of failings, and that the Cartesian assumption that such thoughts are always guaranteed to have an object cannot be sustained.

I have emphasized that a subject's Idea of himself does not require him to have a current conception of himself; what is required, in the exceptional circumstances in which the various avenues of self-knowledge are blocked, is that the subject be disposed to accept any information accessible in those ways as germane to the thoughts we regard as manifesting self-consciousness. But in the normal situation, of course, these dispositions are exercised, and he has an evolving conception of himself, embodying information derived in the various ways, and partly retained in memory, which informs his thoughts about himself. As with other thoughts which are information-based, there is a presupposition that there is just one thing from which the various elements of the conception derive.

Now it appears relatively easy to elaborate examples in which this presupposition is not true. The 'memory-transfer' case we discussed in 7.5 provides a simple example of this kind: provided that the subject was ignorant of the situation, he would bring both present-tense physical and psychological information and past-tense physical and psychological information to bear upon his self-conscious reflections, and there would be no one thing from which both kinds of information derived. The subject

---

being prompted by any specific query—enable us to say that the subject remembered what the question was, remembered this or that conclusion, and so on. Now it is important for this facility to come under a subject's control, so that, e.g., when he is interrupted or distracted he can take up again where he left off, or when the train of thought simply peters out he can set it up again. We might think of the subject having a 'rewind' button, which enables him to reproduce thoughts identified by their location in a chain of thought. As I say, this is a primitive capacity—one which there is no explaining philosophically or mentalistically. But it is clear that we do have such a capacity. And this provides us with another, rather different way in which a current state of a subject is reliably dependent upon, and hence provides a way of knowing about, an earlier state. For there is the possibility of this primitive capacity being put to the service of self-ascription: one can press the 'rewind' button not merely when one needs to go on, but also when one's interest is in one's own past. And of course these self-ascriptions also show immunity to error through misidentification: it does not make sense to say, when the first component expresses information possessed in this way, 'Someone recently thought that p, but was it I who recently thought that p?'

would be in a muddle, rather as can happen when a subject uses a demonstrative in connection with two information-links (via different sense-modalities).[67] Of course the subject could be apprised of the situation and draw in his horns, inhibiting the temptation to make past-tense self-ascriptions upon the basis of his apparent memories. But the fact that a more guarded mode of thought can have an object in this situation certainly does not establish that his original thought did.[68]

A similar kind of situation would arise if the subject received kinaesthetic information from a body other than that at the origin of his egocentric space; or if the subject's actions were in fact manifested in a body distinct from the body which he perceives and from which he perceives.

A more alarming kind of situation would arise if there were in fact no body which could be regarded as the subject's body. Consider, for example, the perennial nightmare: the idea that a human brain might exist, from birth, in a vat, subjected by clever scientists to a complex series of hallucinations (including kinaesthetic hallucinations), of a kind which would enable the brain to develop normal cognitive faculties. (I shall pretend that I am convinced that this speculation is fully intelligible.) Here we have a case where a considerable element of the subject's conception of himself, both present and past, derives from nothing. In all his physical self-ascriptions, there is simply nothing from which his information derives. When he thinks he is moving, or that his legs are bent, there is nothing of whose physical condition he is, even inaccurately, informed.

In this case, unlike the others, there does not appear to me to be anything to which the subject can intelligibly retreat. For if the subject were apprised of the facts, he would have to abandon the Idea of himself as the occupant of a position in space, determinable upon the basis of the course of his perceptions. He would have to attempt to think of himself as nowhere. And this means that he has lost the essential basis of his knowing which element in the objective order he is. He would not, therefore, have an adequate Idea of himself.

[67] Suppose one uses the expression 'this cup' when one is seeing a cup and feeling a cup (in fact, though one does not know it, *two* cups).

[68] In considering this case, we must guard against being tugged in the direction of a purely linguistic or communicative interpretation of the subject's 'I', correlative with someone else's 'you' addressed to him. See below.

It may be conceded that, if a subject is to have an adequate Idea of himself, he must be able to make sense of his identity with an element of the objective order; but objected that in this case there is a perfectly good such element, namely a brain, with which the subject, in this nightmarish situation, can identify himself. But can we make sense of a self-conscious conception of himself, on the part of the subject, which makes such an identification possible—which permits him to understand, and possibly accept, 'I am a brain'? The subject is to think 'Somewhere in the world there is a small parcel of grey matter, wrinkled, moist, and soft, about three inches high, and that is me.' I think that we can feel a resistance to this identification, of the same kind which Nagel, and others, wrongly supposed to arise upon the contemplation of our identity with a particular living animal in the world (see 7.1). For this is unlike the ordinary case. There is nothing in this subject's self-conception which speaks for this identity. In the ordinary case, a subject will be able to make such judgements as 'I am sitting on a bench in a park facing a round pond, with my legs slightly bent'; and it is these elements of one's self-conception—as intimate as any others—that allow the identification of oneself with a human being, located at such-and-such a position in space and time, to get a grip. But obviously the physical side of the conception of himself which our unfortunate subject possesses does not encourage any identification of himself with a brain; and anyway, we are now considering a case in which such elements are extruded from the subject's conception of himself, being, as he now realizes, without any foundation in fact. So the identification is, so to speak, wholly theoretical, and it remains quite obscure what mode of thinking about himself renders it even thinkable.

Many people will regard the remarks I have made about this case as quite unintelligible. For I have spoken of *the subject* thinking ... and wondering ..., while at the same time I have denied that his 'I'-thoughts—whether revised or unrevised—have an object. Surely (people will object) this is unintelligible, for if there is a subject, thinking 'I'-thoughts, then his 'I'-thoughts will concern himself. But why is it thought that self-identification, or thoughts about oneself, are as simple as this—so that, whenever there is a subject, then there is at least one thing he can unproblematically think about, namely himself?

This idea comes, I think, from a false analogy with the functioning of 'I' as a *communicative* device.[69] For it seems perfectly true that provided there is a speaker, he can *refer to* himself, using the device of self-reference 'I'. (If such a device does not exist in the language, it can be introduced unproblematically.) But what this means is that it is always possible for an audience to think of the referent of a token of such a device as the person who uttered that token. That is, the audience identifies the referent, in the first instance, *by description*, as the utterer of certain sounds (or the producer of a certain inscription)—even if the notion of 'uttering' is sufficiently sophisticated to allow the utterer to be regarded as possibly distinct from the person from whose lips the words issue.[70]

To attempt to apply the analogy, we should have to suppose that self-reference in *thought* is achieved because we think of ourselves (at any time) as *the thinker of this thought*, or possibly, as *the subject of these experiences*. In fact, we already have a considerable amount of evidence that we do not actually think of ourselves in this way: the suggestion neglects the way in which our Ideas of ourselves rest upon various avenues of self-knowledge whose bearing upon 'I'-thoughts cannot be regarded as underwritten by any identification. But nor is it clear that the suggestion describes a possible way in which anyone *could* think of himself. We have proceeded too far for us to allow such demonstratives as are here invoked—*this* thought, *these* experiences—to pass without scrutiny. For this is the point at which the analogy with the interpretation of 'I' in speech must break down. It is perfectly intelligible for someone to identify certain *words* demonstratively—to have a perfectly clear understanding

---

[69] Encouraged, perhaps, by the following train of thought: having allowed 'I'-thoughts to the anaesthetized amnesiac, we suppose that *all* self-conscious thoughts involve no more than his 'I'-thoughts do—that we may exclude from the basis of our own self-conscious thoughts all the actual information that we take ourselves to have of ourselves, thereby excluding the multiplicity of information-links that gives rise to the possibility of ill-groundedness. But it is really not obvious that the supposition is correct. Is it supposed that the Idea I associate with the name 'Gareth Evans' is one which would genuinely permit it to be a *discovery* that *I* am Gareth Evans? (In the terminology of 8.6, one might say: ordinary 'I'-Ideas are *mixed*, and not *decomposable* except as it were by violence—by inducing, e.g., amnesia.)

[70] See Anscombe, 'The First Person', p. 60.

of which words are in question—without having any idea of their author, or even of whether any such person, or just one such person, exists. Hence he can know which person is in question in his interpretation of 'I', for, knowing which sounds are in question, he knows what it is to identify a person as their author. But the analogy does not work, precisely because it is not possible to have an adequate Idea of certain pains or thoughts independently of an adequate conception of the person whose thoughts or pains they are. Mental events are distinguished from one another, and from all other things, by reference to the distinctness of the person to, or in, whom they occur. So the sheer demonstrative element—what we might attempt to regard as an information-link—cannot by itself constitute an adequate Idea of such things. A subject can gaze inwardly with all the intensity he can muster, and repeat to himself 'this pain', 'this pain', as he concentrates upon his pain, but he will not thereby be able to know which pain is in question unless this provides him with a basis for identifying the pain with a pain conceived as an element in the objective order—which means a pain conceived as the pain of this or that person in the objective order. Consequently, he cannot have an adequate Idea of these mental events unless he knows to which person they are happening. So he cannot identify himself by reference to them.[71]

I do not see, then, that it is absurd to suppose that there might be a subject of thought who is not in a position to identify himself, and whose attempts at self-identification fail to net any object at all.

I have used an extreme case to make this point, rather than the more familiar kind of fantasy, in which a brain which was once the controlling organ of a human being is extracted from the body and kept alive *in vitro*, because I am less clear about whether the subject in the more familiar case should be said to have no adequate Idea of himself. In order to see why this is open to question, we must reflect a moment about the situation of a man who is paralysed, and who has lost the use of his senses.

[71] His situation is rather like that of someone who can perceive certain things but has no idea of where they are. But notice that the let-out available for that subject is not available for this one: he cannot think of the thoughts or pains as 'the pains of which *I* currently have information' or 'the pains which are causally responsible for *these* informational states' (which informational states?).

Now, terrible though this situation must be, we need not automatically think that the subject has lost the capacity to make sense of an identification of himself with an element in the objective order; we might want to say that he retains knowledge of how to make such an identification, even though *practically* it is now beyond him. We might be willing to make such a statement because we are willing to accept the conditional judgement that, if the normal use of his body and of his senses were restored to him, he could locate himself. (Similarly, even though his knowledge of the *right-hand side* rests upon dispositions which he cannot now manifest, we might be prepared to allow that he has a perfectly determinate side of himself in mind.) It is certainly less clear, but it is at least arguable, that the same kind of thing should be said of a disembodied brain. Being one of us, the victim would of course think of himself as *somewhere*; he would think 'I could find out where I am, if only this damned darkness would lift'. And perhaps the dispositions remaining to the subject—dispositions which could be exercised only if he were re-embodied—might be thought to allow us to say that he had a quite definite place in mind as the one he occupied: a place which would in fact be the position (or close to the position) of his brain; and it might be thought that this provides a basis, if only a slender basis, for an identification of himself with his brain.

If this is so, it rests upon a contingent fact about our construction, namely that the control centre of the human animal is located within it. It seems possible to envisage organisms whose control centre is outside the body, and connected to it by communication links capable of spanning a considerable distance.[72] An organism of this kind could have an Idea of itself like our own, but if it did, it would be unable to cope with the situation that would arise when the control centre survived the destruction of the body it controlled. Thinking like us, the subject would of course have to regard itself as somewhere, but in this case it would not make any sense to identify a particular place in the world as the place it thought of as *here*. The place occupied by the control centre is certainly not the subject's *here*; and even if we counterfactually suppose the control centre re-equipped

---

[72] I have to confess that it is difficult to understand how such beings could have evolved naturally. But perhaps we can think entirely of artificially produced specimens.

with a body, there is no particular place where that body would have to be. Because its 'here' picks out no place, there is no bit of matter, no persisting thing, which the subject's Idea of itself permits us to regard as what it identifies as itself. Here, then, we have a very clear situation in which a subject of thought could not think of itself as 'I'; its 'I'—its habitual mode of thought about itself—is simply inadequate for this situation. (It forces the subject to think in ways which are no longer appropriate.)[73] This case helps us to see that the reason we do not find the '*dis*embodied brain in a vat' case very disturbing, conceptually, is that the brain is also the last remaining part of the subject's body. (The case is often presented as a limiting case of amputation.) A tiny foothold is thus provided for the idea that the subject is where the brain is, and hence for the idea that the brain is what the subject is.[74]

7.7 CONCLUSIONS

The preceding reflections constitute only the most preliminary approach to this difficult subject, but I shall try to draw the threads together by stating some tentative conclusions.

(1) Our self-conscious thoughts about ourselves are irreducible to any other mode of thought; in particular, they cannot be regarded as involving the identification of an object by any description. Self-conscious thought about oneself is thought informed, or at least liable to be informed, by information which the subject has (or can normally acquire) about himself in a variety of different ways. There is always a gap between grasping that the ϕ is F, and grasping that I am F—there is always

---

[73] If *we* can think of this subject, it is with the aid of newer and more sophisticated machinery; not by thinking ourselves into his situation.

[74] Other cases where the empirical presuppositions on which our Ideas of ourselves rest would be false are easy to describe. We can imagine cases in which two control centres are linked to a single body, though perhaps with a 'gate' which blocks off control to one while the other is executing a plan. (See Daniel C. Dennett, 'Where am I?', in *Brainstorms* (Harvester, Hassocks, 1978), pp. 310–23.) Alternatively, we can think of a situation in which one control centre controls and receives information from two distinct bodies, perhaps alternating between them in a regular fashion. (This is akin to a fantasy imagined by A. M. Quinton, 'Spaces and Times', *Philosophy* xxxvii (1962), 130–47.) We can describe these cases perfectly easily, but I do not think we can fully think ourselves into them as subject, with our customary Ideas of ourselves. I believe this is one of the morals of Thomas Nagel's paper 'Brain Bisection and the Unity of Consciousness' (in *Mortal Questions* (CUP, Cambridge, 1979), pp. 147–64); it is also very well illustrated by Dennett's 'Where am I?' For a parallel and related claim about 'here', see 6.3.

room for the realization that I am the ϕ—because there is no description ϕ such that grasping that the ϕ is F guarantees the subject's realization of the bearing of the information which he has, or is in a position to acquire, in these various ways, upon the proposition that the ϕ is F. (There is just as much of a gap between the subject's grasp of 'The ϕ is F' and of 'I am F' when he is amnesiac, anaesthetized, and without the use of his senses as there is when he currently has a conception of himself acquired in these various ways.) Furthermore, the way in which the subject knows which object is in question—his grasp of what it is for an identity-proposition of the form $\ulcorner$I am $\delta_t\urcorner$ to be true—cannot be reduced to knowledge of what it is for $\ulcorner \delta_t =$ the $\phi \urcorner$ to be true. The only plausible candidate for an instance of 'the ϕ' that would falsify these claims is 'the person here'. But this produces the quite misleading impression that there is some priority of 'here' over 'I', whereas one's 'I'-Idea and one's 'here'-Ideas are really two sides of a single capacity, each wholly dependent upon the other. Both 'I'-thoughts and 'here'-thoughts are ways in which the subject's capacity to locate himself in the objective spatial order is exploited. (See 6.3.)

(2) Despite recent philosophical claims to the contrary, our thoughts about ourselves are about *objects*—elements of reality. We are, and can make sense of ourselves as, elements of the objective order of things. Our thinking about ourselves conforms to the Generality Constraint—we are able to conceive of endless states of affairs involving ourselves, and what we conceive is not necessarily what it is like for us, or what it will be like for us, to be aware of, or be in a position to know the existence of, such a state of affairs. Therefore we are not Idealists about ourselves, and this means that we can and must think of ourselves as elements of the objective order. All the peculiarities we have noticed about 'I'-thoughts are consistent with, and, indeed, at points encourage, the idea that there is a living human being which those thoughts concern.

(3) Our thoughts about ourselves are in no way hospitable to Cartesianism. Our customary use of 'I' simply spans the gap between the mental and the physical, and is no more intimately connected with one aspect of our self-conception than the other.

(4) The Ideas we have of ourselves, like almost all Ideas we have, rest upon certain empirical presuppositions, and are simply inappropriate to certain describable situations in which these presuppositions are false.

Appendix

1 G. E. M. Anscombe, in her project (slightly different from, but connected to, that of this chapter) of understanding the semantics of first-person pronouns,[1] begins by considering the idea that all one needs to say about 'I' is that it is a device which each of us uses to refer to himself. She argues that either 'John refers to himself' is simply equivalent to 'John refers to John', in which case the observation is wrong (Oedipus can refer to himself, in this sense, using the words 'the slayer of Laius': see 7.1); or else it means something which can be elucidated only by reference to the first-person pronoun, in which case the observation is useless. The axiom that in using 'I' a subject is referring to himself (or—to relate the point more immediately to the project of this chapter—that 'I'-thoughts are thoughts that a thinker has about himself) thus rather disappears from Miss Anscombe's treatment. (This helps to make room for her conclusion that in using 'I' a subject is not referring to anything at all.)

Miss Anscombe does consider the suggestion that we should say that 'I' is a device which each of us uses knowingly and intentionally to refer to himself. (Oedipus may have referred to himself by the words 'the slayer of Laius', but not knowingly and intentionally.) Her reply is, essentially, that the suggestion cannot satisfactorily explain what the relevant intention is supposed to be. The idea seems to be as before: either 'x intends to refer to himself' simply amounts to 'x intends to refer to x' (which yields 'The slayer of Laius intends to refer to the slayer of Laius'—so that what is special about 'I' has not been captured); or else, once again, it can be explained only in terms of the first-person pronoun.

But this does not seem to be correct. It is perfectly possible to ascribe to a subject the intention to refer to himself, in the sense of the intention of bringing it about that he satisfies the one-place concept-expression 'ξ refers to ξ'. Of course intending to satisfy the one-place concept-expression 'ξ refers to ξ' is the same as intending to satisfy the one-place concept-expression 'ξ refers to me' (since 'I satisfy $\lambda x(x$ refers to $x)$' is logically equivalent to 'I refer to me'). But it does not follow that in order to elucidate the intention of satisfying 'ξ refers to ξ', we need a grasp of the self-conscious Idea-type that we have of ourselves. Indeed, it seems plausible that the explanatory direction goes the other way: the fully self-conscious use of 'I' can be partly explained,

---

[1] 'The First Person'.

precisely, as a use in which the subject knowingly and intentionally refers to himself (satisfies $\lambda x(x$ refers to $x)$). Miss Anscombe is right to say that the requirement that a self-conscious thought be self-consciously about the subject is not by itself an adequate basis for an account of self-consciousness; but it is nonetheless a principle which must be respected.[2]

Let us try to bring this out by considering what happens when the principle is neglected. Consider a hypothetical subject who makes judgements, which he would express with 'I', on the basis of special ways, like ours (7.3), of gaining knowledge of his physical condition, location, etc., and who also manifests the action component of an ordinary 'I'-Idea (cf. 7.1)—for instance, he reacts in the appropriate way to the thought that he is about to be attacked by a bear. We have enough here to attribute to the subject thoughts in which he is not just thinking of a particular creature (the creature which is in fact the subject), but thinking of it in a very special way, which at least bears a close resemblance to our self-conscious modes of thought. But if this is all we have, then this subject's thought 'about himself' falls short of full self-conscious thinking; for the subject's thinking does not in any way register the fact that the object he is thinking of is himself—that is, that in these thoughts he is satisfying the concept-expression 'ξ is thinking of ξ': that there is an identity between the subject of thought and the object of thought. (There is such an identity, but the subject's thinking does not embody or reflect it.)

What is required for a subject genuinely to be aware that he is a self-thinker is a difficult and obscure question. Some would say that this is missing, in the present case, simply because we have not allowed for mental or psychological self-ascription. Clearly it follows, from the fact that someone is thinking about himself, that the object of that thought is a thinker: specifically, the thinker of that thought. So it must follow, from the fact that someone realizes that he is thinking about himself, that he realizes that the object he is thinking about in that thought is the thinker of that thought. Hence, it is not implausible to hold that there is an essential connection between self-consciousness and the conception of oneself as the subject of certain psychological properties: specifically, thinking, and any properties that are necessarily possessed by a thinker. According to this view, what we need to add to the description of the present case, to secure full self-consciousness, is more of the same sort of thing: a disposition on the part of the subject to ascribe thoughts to himself (of course, still on the basis of the special ways we have of gaining knowledge of ourselves). In particular, it might be suggested that the full force of a subject's

[2] It is useful to reflect on the etymology of 'the self'. The self is presumably whatever it is about which a thinker thinks when he thinks about *himself*.

realization that, in thinking 'I am hot', he is both subject and object of the thought might come out in his willingness, later, to judge 'I was hot, and I thought that I was hot' (understanding the judgement, of course, in such a way as to imply that there is something which both was hot and thought that it was hot).

Some philosophers would argue, however, that full realization that in self-conscious thought one is both subject and object would require something much more demanding and vertiginous. Some would even argue that it is not an intelligible realization: that although it is of course possible to conceive in general of an instantiation of 'ξ is thinking of ξ', it is not possible to realize that this concept-expression is satisfied in the case of any particular thought of one's own. (One reason for this idea is, perhaps, the difficulty a subject has in doing anything with the idea: the subject of *this very thought*.) This thesis could be expressed by saying: it is not really possible for a subject to have the thought, in some particular case, that the object of this thought is the subject. And if full self-consciousness is strictly impossible, then of course it cannot suffice for self-consciousness that one have the capacity to 'self-ascribe' earlier thoughts.

Without getting into this controversy, it is worth making two comments on reflections that have been prompted by the view that a fully self-conscious thinker will be aware that he satisfies the concept-expression 'ξ is thinking of ξ' (which we may call 'the self-reference principle').

First, we have here an explanation for something which seems, on the face of it, to need some explaining: why there has been such a persistent tendency to equate the Idea 'I' with the Idea 'the thinker'. A philosopher, engaged in philosophical reflection, asks himself 'What am I?' The question answers itself, says Heidegger: I am the author of that question.[3] Similarly, later, Gabriel Marcel: 'Who am I indeed—I who interrogate myself about my own being?'[4] It seems plausible that such answers—the propensity to think of the self primarily as a thinker—come about from the application of the self-reference principle. We enquire about ourselves as the objects of 'I'-thoughts. (Our question is 'What is the object of an "I"-thought?') And the self-reference principle tells us that the object of an 'I'-thought is its subject. So the identity of the self and the thinker becomes established as indubitable, simply because we enquired into the nature of the self by asking about the object of certain thoughts. (The identity

[3] See Arthur C. Danto, *Sartre* (Fontana/Collins, Glasgow, 1975), pp. 65-6; cf. *Being and Time* (Blackwell, Oxford, 1962), p. 150: 'The question of the "who" answers itself in terms of the "I" itself, the "subject", the "Self".'
[4] *The Mystery of Being*, vol. 1 (Gateway Editions, South Bend, Indiana, 1978), p. 148. (Originally published by Harvill Press, London, 1950.)

of the self and the *speaker* might have assumed an equally—and equally misleading—central position in an enquiry which focused on the reference of the pronoun 'I'.)

According to the view of persons taken in this chapter, a person is no more a thinking thing than a bodily thing, located in the physical world as one of its physical constituents, and capable of acting on and reacting to other physical things. (See 7.3.) Many philosophers have been prepared, contrary to this, to find an asymmetry here: to recon-strue the grammar of their self-ascriptions of bodily predicates in such a way as to yield the form '$F(b)$ and $R(I,b)$' ('b weighs 11 stone and b is my body') instead of '$F(I)$'. But no one seems to have had the idea of a similar reconstrual of the grammar of self-ascriptions of thoughts, to derive 'b has the thought that P and b is my thinking organ'. We now have an explanation of this fact: the project would be self-defeat-ing, for, in the reconstrued thought-ascription, the 'I' (or 'my') must refer to what has the thought that is ascribed, on pain of conflicting with the self-reference principle.

That I am a thing which thinks, then, is certified as true by the self-reference principle. That I am a bodily thing cannot be so certi-fied: the incoherence of the idea that I am distinct from my body, and somehow owner of it, cannot be shown simply by appeal to the self-reference principle.

This brings us to the second comment. The self-reference principle cannot by itself be regarded as an adequate general account of self-conscious thought.[5] Perhaps it can enable us to generate the idea that I am the subject of my thoughts; but this is not an adequate answer to the question 'What am I?'—an adequate account of the Idea that a subject has of himself. For the notion of the subject of thought is a merely formal notion. It is a device for avoiding the circumlocution involved in this sort of formulation: in any thought on x's part which he could express by 'I ...', the object of the thought is x. And such a principle cannot be used to determine what, in any instantiation, x is: for example whether x is bodily or not.[6]

[5] The idea that the self-reference principle suffices to give an account of self-conscious thought is one reason for the idea that 'I'-thinking is guaranteed an object. (To reinforce the thesis that the self-reference principle is not enough, consider the analogous principle for 'you', namely that it refers to the person being addressed. Knowledge of this principle does not suffice for *understanding* a 'you'-remark addressed to oneself, since one may not know *that one is the person being addressed*. We need an account of the thought involved in this realization.)

[6] In an unfinished lecture-course, Evans planned to begin with an artificially intro-duced demonstrative pronoun ('je*'—roughly glossed as 'this body', or, better 'the body', though not to be taken as functioning like a definite description). This would figure in the expression of versions of the thoughts discussed in 7.3 and (most interest-ingly) 7.5. (The cognitive dynamics of 'je*' would have the simplicity described in that section. This is another, and a particularly striking, way of bringing out how wrong it

2 At a number of points in chapters 6 and 7, there appears the idea of a 'functional characterization' of one of the Idea-types there dealt with—a characterization of the Idea-type in terms of the special relations of thoughts involving it to certain sorts of evidence and to behaviour. It must not be supposed that such a functional characterization would constitute a complete account of the Idea-type in question. In fact, the correct picture of the structure of an account of one of these Idea-types is quite complicated. Such an account would involve two components. First, the functional characterization: an account of the relation of certain thoughts involving an Idea of the type in question to certain special ways of gaining knowledge of its object, and of the way in which certain thoughts involving such an Idea would be non-mediately manifested in action. Notice that this component of the account would relate only to *some* of the possible employments of such an Idea: for example, the evidential component of the functional characterization of a demonstrative Idea of a material object based on a visual information-link with it would deal only with judgements involving concepts whose application can be determined on a visual basis. But the Idea characterized will be susceptible also to employment in other connections (recall the Generality Constraint: 4.3). The second component of the account would be an account of the way in which the subject having such an Idea knows which object is in question: this would be needed not only to secure conformity to the Generality Constraint, but also to allow for the possibility of error, even in the special employments of the Idea that figure in the functional characterization (cf. 6.5). In order to show the adequacy of an Idea, it would always be necessary to show that this second, background component harmonizes with, and makes sense of, the special behaviour of the Idea which is characterized by the first component.

One might be tempted by the view that the background account could be given in such a way that it constituted a single general account, adequate to the occurrence of the Idea in all thoughts, from which the special behaviour described in the functional characterization could be deduced as a consequence, when the background account was taken together with the facts about the concepts involved in those special cases. But this seems an impossible dream. Human thought is anarchic and irregular. Our acquisition of one of the

---

is to associate the immunity to error through misidentification of 'I'-thoughts exclusively with *mental* self-ascription.) The plan seems to have been to work up from there to a picture of fully self-conscious thought, perhaps partly by a consideration of self-ascription of psychological properties (7.4), but certainly partly by a consideration of the 'vertiginous' thought that the object of *this* thought is its subject. There are some notes towards this latter project, but the above passage, adapted from a preliminary lecture, seems to be the only worked-out material on the subject.

Idea-types in question takes the form of, first, being trained on the lines of the functional characterization, and then approximating, partly on the basis of what the training has yielded, to a more general grasp of how the thoughts we have learned to deploy relate to the world. The general conception is not something prior to the behaviour characterized by the functional characterization—something from which that behaviour could be deduced. Rather, it is something built up partly on the basis of that special behaviour. There need be no single grand conception from which the legitimacy of (e.g.) the battery of evidential procedures involved in a functional characterization of our 'I'-Ideas may be deduced.

It will be clear that the relation between the two components is complex. It is not that the 'background' component, the 'way of identifying' the object, is simply extra to the matters dealt with in the functional characterization. For the subject's possession of an appropriate sensitivity to evidence, and an appropriate propensity to act on certain thoughts, are among the considerations that we may appeal to in arguing that the subject does indeed know which object is in question. Generalizing this thought: although the subject's Idea of an object cannot be simply *equated* with his conception of it (the information which controls his thinking about it), on pain of obliterating the possibility of his being simply in error about the object (cf. 6.5), nevertheless the Idea and the conception cannot be straightforwardly separated. For any element in the conception may in principle be appealed to (if it serves the purpose) in the course of justifying the claim that the subject does indeed have an adequate Idea (does indeed know which object is in question).

It is essential to see that the material of the functional characterization—which connects the subject, via a complex battery of dispositions, to a specific object in the world which is disposed to affect his thinking and to be affected by his actions—can enter into the account of how the subject satisfies the requirement that he know which object is at issue. Otherwise we would be liable to an unnecessary worry over whether our singular thoughts are adequately pinned down to a particular set of objects, when we contemplate the possibility of Twin Earth cases. If we suppose, not merely that the special dispositional connections are insufficient for an adequate Idea (as is argued in chapters 6 and 7), but that the special dispositional connections are quite *separate* from the subject's possession of an adequate Idea, we shall disqualify ourselves from what seems the only possible answer to the question what makes it the case that a subject's 'I'-thoughts (say) concern himself rather than his Doppelgänger on Twin Earth (and so on).[7]

---

[7] See, further, §3 below; §6 of the Appendix to chapter 6; and §3 of the Appendix to chapter 8.

3 There is a difficulty about the shape of the 'background' component (the account of the subject's knowledge of which object is in question). In the book as it stands, this is a matter of knowledge of what it is for an arbitrary identity-proposition of the form $\ulcorner\delta = a\urcorner$ or $\ulcorner\pi = p\urcorner$ to be true, where δ is a fundamental identification of an object and π is a fundamental identification of a place.

Now, one worry is whether this position (involving as it does the notion of the fundamental level of thought) is not needlessly elaborate. Perhaps all that is needed to make sense of a subject's capacity to entertain the thought that a is F is (i) a knowledge of what it is for an arbitrary object to be F and (ii) a knowledge of what it is for an arbitrary object to be a. The second would be a piece of knowledge of exactly the same kind as the first; so perhaps there is no need to suppose that there are singular thoughts which somehow more closely involve the exercise of this knowledge (thoughts of the form $\ulcorner\delta = a\urcorner$), and hence no need for the concept of a fundamental identification.

However, just as a knowledge of what it is for something to be F would be a knowledge of what it is for an arbitrary element *of the objective order* to be F, so a knowledge of what it is for something to be a would be a knowledge of what it is for an arbitrary element *of the objective order* to be a; and this means that even if the idea of fundamental identifications had been dropped, the overall picture of 'this'-thinking, 'I'-thinking, and 'here'-thinking would have been similar in an important respect: the role played, in the book as it stands, by the notion of the fundamental level of thought would have been played instead by the notion of the objective or impersonal conception of the world, with mastery of such thinking dependent on an understanding of how it relates to the world as objectively conceived. One must conceive the states of affairs one represents in one's 'egocentric' thoughts—thoughts expressible with 'this', 'here', or 'I'—as states of affairs which could be described impersonally, from no particular standpoint.

But there is a problem about what exactly this requirement comes to—what exactly it is to know what it is for an arbitrary element of the objective order to be this, or here, or me. In the text as it stands, knowledge of what it is for this to be F is a matter of knowing what it is for arbitrary propositions of the form $\ulcorner\delta = a\urcorner$ and $\ulcorner\delta$ is $F\urcorner$ to be true, and knowing that it is true that this is F, if it is, in virtue of the truth of a pair of propositions of those forms. But it is not clear what we should make of the requirement if we do not suppose that the subject can formulate, and in favourable circumstances decide the truth of, propositions of these kinds. And it seems that we are not entitled to that supposition. Section 6.3, for instance, gives the impression that the objective or impersonal mode of thought about space can be understood as a mode of spatial thinking organized around a framework of known objects and places—the 'frame of reference'. But such a mode of thinking will not be capable of achieving a higher degree of impersonality than that achieved by the subject's thought about the objects and places which constitute the frame; and (especially if we think here about Twin Earth cases), it seems plausible that a subject's right to be counted as thinking about these familiar objects and places turns partly on his conception of the role they have played in *his* past life—being visited by him, seen by him, etc. (See the Appendix to chapter 8.) In that case, the seemingly objective mode of thinking about space is, after all, contaminated by egocentricity. (It still seems that there is something right about 6.3, considered as an account of how a subject's egocentrically expressed spatial thoughts can be conceived by him as representing objectively spatial states of affairs; but the matter is not straightforward.)[8]

4 It would be wrong to assume, on the strength of the brief remarks in 7.1, that Evans thought of the capacity to locate oneself (discussed in 6.3 and 7.3) as a self-contained skill, sufficient on its own to settle worries, like Nagel's, about the possibility of identifying oneself with a physical thing—with an element of the objective order. In a fuller treatment, it would be necessary to mention, in addition, bodily perception, and also the knowledge of one's own body that one has in action.

On the latter of these, consider the following passage from Schopenhauer:

The meaning for which we seek of that world which is present to us only as our idea ... would never be found if the investigator himself were nothing more than the pure knowing subject (a winged cherub without a body). But he is himself rooted in that world; he finds himself in it as an *individual* ... his knowledge, which is the necessary supporter of the whole world as idea, is yet always given through the medium of a body ... His body is for the pure knowing subject, an idea like every other idea, an object among objects. Its movements and actions are so far known to him in precisely the same way as the changes of all other perceived objects, and would be just as strange and incomprehensible to him if their meaning were not explained for him in an entirely different way ... the answer to the riddle is given to the subject of knowledge who appears as an individual, and the answer is *will*.[9]

On the former, consider the following from G. F. Stout:

Each of us has experience of his own body in a way essentially different from the way in which anyone else can have experience of it. This is especially

---

[8] I hope I have here captured the gist of a worry that exercised Evans.

[9] *The World as Will and Idea* (1818) vol. i, Book 2; cited from p. 129 of G. N. A. Vesey, ed., *Body and Mind* (George Allen and Unwin, London, 1964).

obvious in organic sensations such as thirst, hunger, fatigue, sexual excitement, and, in general, the bodily excitement inseparable from emotion; also in motor sensations such as are involved in the actions of looking, listening, handling, lifting a weight, eating, walking, strenuous thinking. For each of us his body as thus privately experienced forms an integral part of what he means by himself when he uses the word 'I' ...

What self-consciousness reveals is not mere mind or 'mental phenomena', but mind and body together in the inseparable unity of the embodied self. Thus the supposed contrast between merely bodily processes and merely mental is in fact always, in part, a contrast between the body as external object and the same body as internal object ...

What we are thus immediately cognizant of in primary self-consciousness is our own body and bodily processes.[10]

A worry like Nagel's is expressed in this passage from Sartre:

Actually if after grasping 'my' consciousness in its absolute interiority and by a series of reflective acts, I then seek to unite it with a certain living object composed of a nervous system, a brain, glands, digestive, respiratory, and circulatory organs whose very matter is capable of being analyzed chemically into atoms of hydrogen, carbon, nitrogen, phosphorus, etc., then I am going to encounter insurmountable difficulties. But these difficulties all stem from the fact that I try to unite my consciousness not with *my* body but with the body *of others*. In fact the body which I have just described is not *my* body such as it is *for me* ... So far as the physicians have had any experience with my body, it was with my body *in the midst of the world* and as it is for others. My body as it is *for me* does not appear to me in the midst of the world.[11]

Evans remarked about this that in one way it is correct: I can identify myself with a bit of matter only if I know that bit of matter 'from the inside'—so that a groundwork for the identification is laid in the ordinary self-ascriptive statements I learn to make. But what this constitutes a groundwork for is an ability to identify myself with an element of the objective order—a body of others, if you like— unreservedly.

[10] *Mind and Matter* (CUP, Cambridge, 1931); cited from pp. 258, 261, 262 of Vesey, *Body and Mind*.

[11] *Being and Nothingness*, translated by Hazel E. Barnes (Methuen, London, 1969), p. 303.

Chapter 8

Recognition-Based Identification

8.1 INTRODUCTORY

Suppose a subject perceived an object at one time, and later brings to mind information which he acquired at that time and has retained. I am thinking of the kind of case in which one can be described as remembering the object—that is, cases in which one retains non-conceptual information from the original encounter.[1] Given my adherence to Russell's Principle, I must hold that to retain the information upon which a demonstrative identification might have been based is not necessarily to retain an adequate Idea of an object. Having once been in a position to make the judgement 'This ϕ is F', one is not automatically placed in a position to make a judgement 'That ϕ was F' simply by the passage of time and the retention of the information upon which the former judgement was based. For one's original capacity to make a judgement about the object rested on more than one's possession of information from that object; one's Idea was adequate because one was able, upon the basis of one's perceptions, to locate that object in space (6.4). And this is clearly not a capacity which one can retain when one ceases to perceive the object. If a thought based upon memory is to have an object, then, a quite different mechanism of identification must come into play. Earlier, we saw how a subject could make a judgement about one out of an enormous array of small and indistinguishable objects by keeping his eye upon it; this might be the basis upon which we could ascribe to him the belief, about one of the objects, that, for example, it had been touched by X. (See 6.4.) But now let the subject cease to perceive the array. Clearly this mechanism ceases to be operative, and no

[1] We colloquially draw a distinction between remembering that there was such-and-such a thing and remembering the thing, and between remembering that there was such-and-such an incident or episode and remembering the episode. I believe that this distinction turns on the kind of information retained.

matter how vividly he can recall the array—even if his powers of recall are total—his utterance '*X* touched *that*' will be just so much mouthing, unless he now has some other way of identifying which object he means.[2]

Very often, the subject will identify, or attempt to identify, the object in question by exploiting some individuating fact, such as the fact that it was the unique object observed on such-and-such an occasion, or the object occupying such-and-such a position then, or the object that distinguished itself then by such-and-such a piece of behaviour. This is a mode of identification with which we are very familiar. (I have tried to explain that it does not follow, from the fact that the subject relies upon such a mode of identification, that his thought can be regarded as a descriptive thought in the style of Russell. In the subject's choice of description, he can be regarded as aiming at something, namely the object from which he acquired, and of which he retains, information, and so there is room to speak of error here—with its consequence of ill-grounded thoughts—in a way which is completely absent in the case of descriptive thoughts as construed by Russell. See 5.4.)

In the present chapter, however, I want to concentrate upon another way in which a subject can be said to know which object is in question when he makes a judgement about an object he can be said to remember, namely, when he can *recognize* the object concerned. Many philosophers have been prepared to allow that being able to recognize an object does constitute an adequate way of discharging the requirement that one know which object one is judging about; but one gains the impression that they regard it as something of a limiting case.[3] Now it is indeed rare, though possible, for a subject who can be said to remember an object to be able to draw *only* upon his capacity to recognize it in identifying the object in question; for usually some additional information will have been derived

[2] It follows from this that *images* (whether of memory or imagination) cannot represent particular objects in the way that perceptual states can. A perception necessarily has a reference to the here and now built into it; the reference of images must be quite different. Indeed they cannot represent particulars by themselves, but only in the context of surrounding thoughts and beliefs.

[3] See, e.g., Searle, *Speech Acts*, p. 90; Dummett, *Frege*, p. 488 (see also pp. 97–8); Ayer, 'Names and Descriptions', at p. 145; Strawson, *Subject and Predicate in Logic and Grammar*, at p. 47.

from the original perceptual encounter or encounters. The subject will very likely have some more or less rough conception of the original encounter, including a rough idea of the time and the place of its occurrence, and, possibly, who was with him at the encounter, what preceded and followed it, together with some information about what the object was doing, or how it was disposed in relation to other things.[4] So, even without exercising his recognitional capacity, he will usually be able to offer some descriptive identification of the object in question. However, the importance of recognition-based identification does not depend upon those rare cases in which it is all that exists, for it has a quite dominant role even in those cases in which it is not. For, if a subject is disposed to identify a particular object as the object of his thought, and in so doing is exercising a genuine recognitional capacity stemming from the encounter or encounters from which the memory-information that saturates his thought[5] derives, then, it seems to me, that object is the object of his thought, irrespective of whether or not it can be identified by means of any descriptions which the subject might otherwise use. The subject may have a perfectly erroneous view of the place and time of the encounter, and quite misremember what took place in it, without this preventing him from having a perfectly clear Idea of the object he means. We would certainly not obtain this result if we thought of a recognitional capacity as merely amounting to the knowledge of one description (presumably a description of the thing's appearance), to be thrown with the other descriptions into a composite descriptive identification; for if the subject was radically mistaken in his other beliefs, such a composite description would identify nothing.

For the time being I shall have to rest this point upon intuition; later (8.2) I shall try to explain why recognitional capacities have this dominant position in identification. But the nature of the claim should not be mystifying, for although I did not comment upon it at the time, it was implicit in my discussion of demonstrative identification (chapter 6) that a similar kind of dominance was being attached to perceptual location over

---

[4] I am adhering to my policy of considering pure cases of the various modes of identification (see 5.2); so I do not include here information which may have been derived from the testimony of others.

[5] See 5.1.

the other ways in which the subject might attempt to identify the object of his thought. Even in a pure case of demonstrative identification, where the subject has not identified the object as one he had antecedent knowledge of, it is likely that the subject will be prepared to offer various kinds of description of the object—descriptions of its appearance, and of its situation in relation to other things. Yet it seems to me that these are trumped by the mechanism of identification which I laboured to explain in chapter 6.

We are in fact accustomed to assigning just this kind of dominance to the recognitional element of a person's concept or Idea, when we consider the question which *property*, or *general characteristic*, an Idea comprising such an element is an Idea of. Someone who has learned a colour word in the standard way will have a capacity to recognize the colour when presented with it, but will also have many other ways of identifying it; he will know or believe that it is the colour of this or that object, and very possibly he will know or believe such things as that it is the colour favoured by radical political parties, and the colour said to enrage bulls. But it is to the colour he is disposed to identify on sight that we attach dominant weight in considering which colour he has in mind; if there is a particular colour he is consistently disposed to recognize, then that is the colour he has in mind, no matter how erroneous these other beliefs might be. Philosophers have been prepared to attach considerable theoretical importance to recognitional capacities in their accounts of what it is for a subject to have an Idea of a property, or kind, of particulars, while relegating recognitional capacities for particulars to a theoretically insignificant position in their account of what it is for a subject to have an Idea of a particular; it is the aim of the present chapter to redress the balance.

In the sections that follow, I shall attempt to explain what is involved in a subject's having a capacity to recognize an object. It is not enough for one to recognize an object that it strike one as familiar; one must identify it *as* something—usually, though not exclusively, as the object encountered upon such-and-such a previous occasion. In those exercises of recognitional capacities which interest us, the subject will identify the object as the object he was thinking about. For we are considering a subject who is thinking about an object which he can remember (of which he has retained information): his thought $\ulcorner a$ is $F\urcorner$, or perhaps $\ulcorner$That G is $F\urcorner$, must rest upon a knowledge of what it is for an arbitrary proposition of the form $\ulcorner \delta_t = a\urcorner$ or $\ulcorner \delta_t = $ that $G\urcorner$ to be true, and in the case we are concerned with, this knowledge depends upon a capacity to pick out an object *as* the object of his thought upon being presented with it, as a consequence of having been presented with it in the past. This knowledge of what it is for $\ulcorner \delta_t = a\urcorner$ to be true is of the same *general* kind as the knowledge of what it is for $\ulcorner \delta_t$ is red$\urcorner$ to be true, though it is essential for him to have an adequate Idea of a particular object that there be one, and only one, object which he is disposed to pick out in this way. (The subject may be disposed to pick out an object he has not even encountered before, or from which the information he retains, which controls his thought, is not derived; in these cases, the subject's thought will not be well-grounded: see 5.4.)

We do not wish to assimilate cases in which a person's Idea of an object depends upon a recognitional capacity to cases in which his knowledge of which object is in question simply exploits a description which happens to be decidable upon the basis of a presentation of the object. The inclusion of the clause 'as a consequence of having been presented with it in the past' is a gesture in this direction. I shall be discussing the question whether a capacity to recognize an object can be reduced to a knowledge that it satisfies some description (8.4 and 8.5 below), and I shall try to show that it cannot. Given this, the gesture is inadequate, since it fails to distinguish between a case where a subject has acquired a genuine recognitional capacity from an encounter, and a case where he retains nothing but the knowledge that the object satisfies a description like 'the one with a white spot on it'. Nevertheless, no great harm is done if we work with a preliminary conception which lumps these two cases together.

There seem to be two obvious difficulties in the way of supposing that a recognitional capacity, as we ordinarily envisage it, can underlie an Idea of an object adequate by the lights of Russell's Principle. The first arises because it is doubtful that someone who has the capacity to recognize his cat, or even his mother, has the capacity to distinguish that object (on being presented with it) from all other things; it seems fanciful, or

even possibly sentimental, to suppose that an ordinary recognitional capacity is proof against all that science may contrive,
or nature provide, in the way of duplicates. I shall discuss this
difficulty in 8.3.

The second difficulty arises because individuals may change
beyond recognition. Such a change would annihilate my
capacity to recognize a thing, and, to the extent to which my
Idea of an object rests upon a recognitional capacity, it might
appear that it must annihilate that Idea as well. But it is difficult
to believe that any way we have of thinking about objects is so
sensitive to the mutability of their appearance. I shall try to say
a word about this difficulty now. Before doing so, it is as well to
recall that the difficulty, if it exists, is a difficulty for everyone
who has been prepared to allow a place, however insignificant,
to the possibility that identification may depend upon a
capacity to recognize an object.

In fact, the difficulty is not one particularly concerned with
recognition: it is an aspect of a more general problem which
arises from combining our realistic attitude towards the past
tense with the idea that a knowledge of what it is for certain
very fundamental classes of proposition to be true consists,
wholly or partly, in a practical capacity to effect certain discriminations relevant to their truth by the use of our senses. Thus
we allow, and seem obliged to allow, that a knowledge of what
it is for something to be red consists in, or at least requires, the
capacity to tell, by looking at it, whether or not it is red.[6] And
we suppose that this, together with our general understanding
of the past tense, will yield knowledge of what it is for the
proposition ⌜This object *was* red⌝ to be true. This can be only
because we suppose that a capacity to recognize the colour red
enables us to know quite generally what it is for ⌜δ_t is red$_t$⌝ to be
true, irrespective of the time indication. Given this, we can
know what it is for ⌜This was red⌝ to be true in virtue of knowing
what it is for ⌜This $= \delta_{now}$⌝ to be true, what it is for ⌜$\delta'_t = \delta_{now}$⌝ to
be true (where t is earlier than now), and what it is for ⌜δ'_t is
red$_t$⌝ to be true (where t is earlier than now).[7]

Given these views of ours, which I record without defence,

[6] The precise statement of this capacity would have to take account of the possibility
of blindness. (Cf. 7.6 on the paralysed subject who still knows which is the right-hand
side.)

[7] See 4.4 for the apparatus used here.

we do not have to suppose that a change in an object's appearance 'beyond recognition', or its ceasing to exist, need deprive the subject of a knowledge of what it is for propositions of the form $\ulcorner a$ is $F\urcorner$ to be true, when a is an Idea of an object which rests upon a capacity to recognize it. (I shall suppose that the subject *did* have an effective capacity to recognize the object in question—even though we do not yet know quite what this means.) We think of the subject as possessing, in the first instance, a grasp of the concept of an object's being $\ulcorner$recognizably $a\urcorner$; it is mastery of this concept (which entails, but is not entailed by, the simple being $\ulcorner$identical with $a\urcorner$ which he displayed, before the object changed, in effecting a discrimination between objects upon the basis of their appearance; and it is this element of his Idea a which resembles his concept of a colour. Treating this element in the same way, we must allow it to enable the subject to know what it is for an arbitrary proposition of the form $\ulcorner \delta_t$ is recognizably $a\urcorner$ to be true, irrespective of the time indication δ has, and in particular, irrespective of whether t is earlier than now. Thus the subject's knowledge of what it is for $\ulcorner a$ is $F_{t'}\urcorner$ to be true can be represented, in general, as the result of his knowledge that it is true in virtue of the truth of some triple of propositions, $\ulcorner \delta_t$ is recognizably $a\urcorner$, $\ulcorner \delta_t = \delta'_{t'}\urcorner$ and $\ulcorner \delta'_{t'}$ is $F_{t'}\urcorner$ (where *possibly* $t = t'$), and his knowledge of what it is for each of these propositions to be true. In other words, if a capacity to discriminate colours, together with a general knowledge of the identity-conditions of objects of the relevant kind, enables a subject to know what it is for $\ulcorner$This was red$\urcorner$ to be true, then a recognitional capacity, together with the same general knowledge, must be allowed to enable a subject to know what it is for $\ulcorner$This was recognizably $a\urcorner$ to be true, even if the capacity is no longer operative. Provided the subject has retained the ability to make the discrimination in which his possession of the concept $\ulcorner$recognizably $a\urcorner$ consists, and is debarred from manifesting it only by the change in, or disappearance of, the relevant object, then he must be allowed to know what it is for an arbitrary proposition of the form $\ulcorner \delta_t = a\urcorner$ to be true, even though he cannot *decide* whether or not it is true.[8]

---

[8] We may have every reason to believe that a subject is such that, had he been presented with x before x's change in appearance, he *would* have identified x as the object of his thought.

8.2   RECOGNITION AND THE INFORMATIONAL SYSTEM

In order to understand why we attach so much weight to the deliverances of a recognitional capacity, we must understand the importance of the capacity to recognize individuals in the informational system which we possess.[9] It is easy to underestimate its importance. We are all too well aware of the vast tracts of historical and geographical information which we have acquired from others, about individuals we have never encountered, let alone have the capacity to recognize; so we can readily understand the position of the scholar who was said to know more about, and feel more intimate with, the people and streets of Ancient Rome than the people and places around him. When we are in this mood, the fact that some among the individuals about which we have information are individuals we are capable of recognizing can seem like an incidental detail, of no theoretical importance. But that there must be something seriously wrong with this perspective can be seen when we reflect that the bodies of information about particular individuals which we acquire from others, especially the rich bodies of information which are of most interest to us, almost certainly derive from subjects who did have a capacity to recognize the individuals concerned.[10]

There is one line of thought which attempts to reverse this erroneous perspective, which I want to mention but leave on one side. It has been argued that a precondition of our operating with a conception of a spatial world is that we have the ability to *re*-identify places, and hence physical bodies; and it has been suggested that a necessary condition of our being able to *re*-identify bodies is that we have the capacity to recognize them — to make at least *prima facie re*-identifications upon the basis of their appearance.[11] This argument appears to me to be very plausible, but I think the importance of our capacity to recognize individuals can be brought out in another, perhaps less abstract, way.

We are beings who not only store information, but store

---

[9] On the informational system in general, see 5.2.

[10] This point is developed extensively, in connection with the use of proper names, in chapter 11.

[11] See, e.g., Richard Swinburne, *Space and Time* (Macmillan, London, 1968), pp. 24-5.

information about particular objects; and our thoughts about particular individuals which are not present to our senses depend upon this. It is a very fundamental aspect of our cognitive functioning, but not a necessary one. We can envisage beings who retain, from an information-yielding encounter with a particular object, only information of a general kind. After being bitten by a dog, a subject comes to believe that dogs are, with a certain degree of probability, likely to bite, and after being bitten by several dogs, he comes to believe that dogs are very likely to bite.[12] Information for these beings would always be about kinds, and not about individual members of those kinds. Now, presumably, a capacity for retaining information about particulars has evolved in us because possession of that kind of information was advantageous. Overwhelmingly the most natural place to look for advantageous deployment of retained information concerning *x* alone, rather than information concerning the general kind to which *x* belongs, is in subsequent dealings with *x*: that is, in behaviour directed towards *x*. Consequently, if such cognitive mechanisms are to evolve, the objects with which the organism deals must differ, within their kinds, in ways which affect the appropriateness of behaviour directed towards them; and those objects must possess the characteristics to which these differences are due with a degree of stability proportional to the likely interval between encounters. And secondly, not only must there be a reasonably high degree of probability that a good number of individuals will be encountered more than once; there must also be a way, and a moderately expeditious way, in which the organism can tell when an individual previously encountered is re-encountered. And this means that the organism must possess something like a capacity to recognize individual members of the kinds with which it has to deal. (Information that an individual which satisfies the description 'the sheep I met at *t*' or 'the sheep that ate the daffodils yesterday', is thus and so is a perfectly good piece of particular information from the theoretical point of

[12] It is not important for my purposes to think of these beings as not having *any* particular-beliefs (other than those about objects currently being perceived, places currently occupied, and themselves)—e.g. to think of them as not having particular-beliefs, in their absence, about their brothers, or their homes. All that is necessary is to suppose that something characteristic of our scheme of thought is present in theirs to a very much less marked degree.

view. But it is as good as useless from the practical point of view, because of the difficulty of knowing, of a currently confronted sheep, that it satisfies these past-tense descriptions.) In fact, the organism must have more than the simple capacity to find previously encountered objects familiar; a recognitional capacity must be associated with (i.e. enable the subject to recall) the appropriate dossier of information.[13] Under these circumstances, selection pressures would strongly favour organisms which possessed, or were capable of developing, this capacity.

Most organisms have at least a rudimentary[14] capacity to recognize at least some among the other members of their own species, if only their parents and offspring; and since so much of an organism's welfare (especially among the social animals) is dependent upon successful interrelation with other members of its species, we should expect to find an informational system, of the kind I have outlined, developing out of this primitive capacity as early as any other.[15] Certainly, nowhere does our extraordinary capacity to recognize previously encountered objects reach more extraordinary heights than in our ability to recognize the faces of other human beings.[16]

Consequently, we should expect that, in any system in which information is stored about particular objects, there will be a central core of cases in which the subject has associated information with a capacity to recognize a particular individual. In this core, we should expect to find some cases in which a rich and detailed picture of an individual has been built up over an extended period of time. This is because occasions on which an individual is *re*-identified are not only opportunities for the apt deployment of information already acquired; they are also opportunities for acquiring additional information, whether consequential on, or in the absence of, behaviour directed towards

---

[13] The word 'dossier' is borrowed from H. P. Grice, 'Vacuous Names'.

[14] Rudimentary, because not obviously informed by spatio-temporal considerations: see 8.3.

[15] For an example of the kind of advantage which can accrue to an organism which has the capacity to recognize other members of its own species, see Richard Dawkins, *The Selfish Gene* (OUP, Oxford, 1976), pp. 199–200.

[16] There is still controversy over whether this can be regarded as a capacity specially selected for. (The question whether there is a disease of prosopagnosia is the same question.)

that individual. These are the paradigm cases: evolving clusters of information generated in a pattern of encounters in which the recognitional capacity was triggered, and still linked with that capacity, which serves as the means to identify opportunities for using old, and gaining new, information. But we find every sort of deviation from this paradigm. There are cases in which the dossier of information survives the loss of the recognitional capacity. Then there are cases in which the presentation of the object elicits nothing but a feeling of familiarity—cases in which the dossier of information has decayed to nothing, or else the recognitional capacity has become detached from it, perhaps only temporarily. Again, two objects may have been confused, while an object whose appearance frequently changes, or has changed, may be the target of two distinct recognitional capacities not known to concern the same object.

I do not claim that an informational system capable of dealing with information about particular individuals could definitely not emerge in the absence of the capacity to recognize individuals, but only that, by so vastly increasing the effectiveness of such information, it vastly increases the probability that systems for dealing with it will emerge. This explains why I do not think that we can regard it as an accident that our store of information includes many cases in which we have information about individuals we are capable of recognizing. And it is the superior *effectiveness* of a recognitional capacity in bringing information to bear upon an organism's dealings with the world that explains why we allow it to trump other, possibly conflicting, pointers to identification which might be present at the same time. (The fact that we give a dominant weight to perceptual location in situations of demonstrative identification is open to a similar explanation.)[17]

---

[17] I do not at all want to revive the mistakes which have arisen from an excessive concentration upon imagery in the theory of meaning—mistakes so effectively criticized by Wittgenstein in his later philosophy. Nevertheless, we can surely see, in the importance we are unreflectively inclined to attach to imagery in an account of what it is to be thinking of something (having something in mind), a dim appreciation of the importance of recognitional capacities in the functioning of the informational system. In fact imagery has a rather uncertain connection with recognition (see 8.5); but it is not surprising that in a system designed to retrieve information upon the subject's perceiving an object, the internal reproduction of the perceptual information-state should have an important role to play when the subject draws upon his information store in thinking and reasoning.

8.3 RECOGNITIONAL CAPACITIES AND SPACE

If a recognitional capacity is to provide the basis of an Idea of an object that is adequate by the lights of Russell's Principle, it would appear that it must enable the subject to distinguish the object concerned, upon the basis of its appearance, from all other things. But it is by no means certain that someone who possesses a capacity to recognize another person, for example, can in fact distinguish that person, upon the basis of his appearance, from all other persons in the universe. And, what is more worrying, it is difficult to see that whether the subject has a determinate thought or not can depend upon whether or not there is, tucked away somewhere in the universe, a person he would confuse with the person he has met. Surely, it might be said, we can imagine that somewhere in the universe there is an exact duplicate of the solar system and all of its contents, containing doubles of each of us.[18] If such a hypothesis were true, none of us would have a capacity to distinguish the objects of our thought from all other objects by their appearance; yet surely our thoughts would continue to have objects, and the very objects that they would have had, if the hypothesis had not been true. This is the first of the two difficulties I mentioned in 8.1, and I want to try to deal with it now. Some people have drawn from this speculation the conclusion that recognitional abilities are irrelevant to identification, and others have drawn conclusions hostile to Russell's Principle. I shall try to show that neither kind of conclusion follows.

To see a way out of the difficulty, we must realize that while a recognitional capacity, as we ordinarily understand it, does require the ability to distinguish an object from all other things, such a discrimination is made not only on the basis of the object's *appearance*, but also on the basis of its *location*. Indeed, it is precisely what distinguishes individual-recognition from kind-recognition that the former is sensitive to considerations bearing upon the identity of a single object from time to time, and this means sensitive to spatio-temporal considerations. No one can be regarded as recognizing an individual unless he

---

[18] This speculation is essentially the same as that suggested by Putnam in his Twin Earth example. (See *Mind, Language and Reality*, pp. 223 ff.) It is easy to see how it can be used to support the Photograph Model (see 3.4); for that does distinguish the objects in home territory, rather than those in alien territory, as the objects of our thoughts.

understands that the current appearance of an object can be only a *defeasible* basis for its *re*-identification as something previously encountered. However good a child is at responding differentially to presentations of his mother's face, he cannot be credited with recognizing a particular person, rather than a comforting type of person, unless he has the resources for rebutting, on spatio-temporal grounds, provisional *re*-identifications of other objects rendered plausible by their appearance.

The role of these spatial considerations in recognition shows up very clearly in cases in which the subject has a short-term capacity to recognize something. Suppose, for example, that a subject is watching a group of sheep on the side of a mountain, and sees one of them cough. It is possible for the subject to retain, at least for a short time, information about one of the sheep (that it coughed) without keeping his eye on the sheep; he can have a belief or thought about one of these sheep without its being a demonstrative thought. For he may be able to recognize the relevant sheep. Despite the fact that the sheep may look pretty much alike to him, the appearance of the relevant sheep may be sufficiently distinctive for him to be able to distinguish it from all the other sheep *in this restricted spatio-temporal setting*. The fact that he could not tell it apart from a sheep across the valley does not prevent him from having a capacity to *re*-identify it—i.e. to know when he is confronted with it again. He would not be considering sheep on the other side of the valley.

In this case, there is an area—the area of search—such that the subject is disposed to identify an object as the relevant sheep, provided it presents a suitable appearance within this area. The extent of this area is a function of the subject's estimate of the probability and speed of movement, and the time that has elapsed since the last sighting, and it will centre upon the estimated position of the last sighting. And the subject's location of the relevant area is *egocentric*; the origin of the relevant area is given by the position the animal occupied at the last sighting, and the subject can know his location in relation to the area by his knowledge of his movements since that time. He can know that he has not moved, or has not moved much in relation to the diameter of the area, since that time. In these circumstances, we can say that the subject does have a capacity to recognize a particular sheep x, provided that (i) he is disposed to identify x

as the relevant sheep upon the basis of its appearance, (ii) there is no other sheep within the area of search which he is disposed to identify as the relevant sheep upon the basis of its appearance, and (iii) x is the *right* sheep, i.e. is the sheep from which the information saturating his thought was derived. As you can see, if the subject is able, in this sense, to recognize a particular sheep, then there is just one sheep in the entire universe which he is disposed to pick out—there is just one sheep in the entire universe on which his dispositions, and hence his thought, are targeted. For any disposition he has to pick out something outside the area of search does not count, and he is disposed to identify just one thing within it.[19]

In a case like this, where the subject's identification of the relevant area is egocentric, his retention of a recognitional capacity, and hence his retention of this Idea of an object, depends both upon his not moving (or not moving much) in the interim and upon his capacity to know that he has not moved (or not moved much) in the interim. If he were to move right away from the area, then *this* connection with a particular sheep would be broken.[20] But the subject might have known where he was when the original sighting took place, and this would give rise to a rather different, and more stable, kind of recognitional capacity—one which could survive his change in position. The capacity most of us have to recognize bits of furniture and domestic equipment is of this kind. I can distinguish my radio, upon the basis of its appearance, from all other objects in the restricted spatial setting of my home, despite the existence of thousands, perhaps millions, like it, and although I would be hard put to it to claim knowledge of my radio outside my home—in a police display of stolen goods, for example. The relevant area is identified non-egocentrically, as my home, with the consequence that I can have this capacity, and thoughts about my radio resting upon it, no matter where I am. However, Ideas of objects of this kind will usually require the subject to have a capacity to recognize other things and places which is not of this kind.[21]

---

[19] The importance of spatial considerations in recognition is acknowledged by Shoemaker in 'Persons and Their Pasts'.

[20] Though there will inevitably be others: see below.

[21] Given the distinction between egocentric and non-egocentric recognitional capacities, we should count with the egocentric capacities those which depend upon the

It is more difficult to see the egocentric element in our ordinary, settled, capacity to recognize people, places, and things, but the speculation of massive reduplication brings it out. The time intervals, and distances, are much greater, but the structure we discovered in the example of the sheep on the mountainside also exists in, say, an ordinary capacity to recognize a person. If I have not seen a man for many years, the area of search may be very wide, possibly taking in all of the Earth's surface, but it still will not take in the entire universe. And I shall know where the relevant area of search is *egocentrically*: we can think of it as being indicated by a very extensive 'around here'. I can know that I have not moved the tremendous distances which I would need to have covered if I were to have got outside such an area of search.

The existence, therefore, of a Twin Earth, somewhere else in our galaxy, no more undermines our possession of uniquely targeted recognitional capacities for objects on this Earth than the existence of an indistinguishable sheep across the valley undermined our subject's capacity to recognize one sheep in particular. But it is essential, for our possession of these absolutely discriminating capacities, that we move through space in regular and predictable ways, and that we are generally able to tell when we move—as, indeed, we are, because movement, when we are conscious, has characteristic concomitants, and it does not generally take place (unless we have specifically arranged for it) during sleep.

Philosophers often find it helpful to consider computer models of human capacities, but the consideration of excessively simple models can lead them astray, as it has when the Twin Earth fantasy has been discussed. We must realize that if a computer is to model our individual-recognizing capacities, it must not only contain a pattern-recognizing device of great sensitivity; it must also contain an interconnected device which is devoted to keeping track of its movements through space. Such a computer would not be disposed to 'recognize' candidates on Twin Earth. Of course, you could tamper with it, and move it to the other planet without its movement-sensitive device registering the

---

subject's identifying the area of search as one which he can regain by doing such-and-such (e.g. retracing his steps).

move. This would destroy its capacities to recognize individuals on Earth; but it would hardly show that before the computer was tampered with, it did not have those capacities—that its dispositions were not uniquely targeted upon individuals on Earth.

I hold, then, that a subject's Idea of an object, adequate by the standards of Russell's Principle, can be grounded upon an ordinary capacity to recognize an object, irrespective of whether there are indistinguishable objects, so long as they are sufficiently far away. Such capacities are undermined only when the duplicates are introduced into the relevant area.

But now we come to the second part of the question, which is to explain how it is possible for an Idea of an object to rest upon a recognitional capacity. For, if a person's recognitional capacity for an object is destroyed by the introduction of a duplicate into the relevant area, his capacity to *think about* that particular object surely is not.

Now it is perfectly true that no one who was in a position to be credited with a recognitional capacity in the first place would be totally flummoxed by the appearance of two objects which he seemed to recognize. He encountered at most one of them previously, and *that* is the one he means or has in mind. So, of course, he is able to discriminate the object of his thought from all other things, and to go on thinking about it. Nevertheless, I think we ought to acknowledge that there is a difference between a purely recognition-based Idea and a complex Idea having a recognitional component and, also, such descriptive elements as 'which I met', etc.

In the normal case, when a recognitional capacity is effective, such a descriptive component is redundant: the content of any *re*-identification will of course include 'I've met this before', but that is not a *basis* of the *re*-identification.[22] This is precisely what makes a recognitional capacity so effective. Now it is always a possibility that the discrimination that a subject can make on the basis of an object's appearance needs to be supplemented

[22] Thus my objection to including such an element in an account of the Idea in the normal case is quite different from my objection to the element 'from which these memories causally derive' (which I have also steadfastly refused to countenance). The objection in the latter case is not that the element is present, but not a basis of the identification; it is that (on pain of falsifying the content of the thoughts in the normal case) the element is not present at all.

with material of another kind. If I meet two twins whom I know I cannot tell apart, my Idea of one might have to involve some such element as 'the one who plays chess', or 'the one who speaks louder', even if it also comprises a 'recognitional' component—one capable of narrowing the field down to the two twins. The Idea I would have after the disturbing discovery of the duplicate would be a mixed Idea of this kind.[23]

It is not merely the dictates of theoretical purity which make me insist that the Idea has changed; there is surely a rather important practical difference between someone whose thoughts about an object rest solely upon a recognitional capacity and someone whose Idea is only individuating because of some such element as 'which I met' or 'which I observed'. Our subject on the mountainside could be said to have an opinion as to which sheep had coughed, and, possibly, to know which sheep had coughed. But suppose the look-alike sheep does come into the relevant area, thereby rendering his recognitional capacity ineffective. We should then deny that he knows which sheep coughed. I do not advance this fact about the colloquial use of the term 'know which' in order to claim that the subject no longer has an adequate Idea *at all*. I have already warned (in 4.1) against taking the colloquial use of 'know which' seriously in connection with Russell's Principle; and we know quite well that the subject in this case does have an adequate Idea of some kind. (He continues to be able to believe, concerning some particular sheep, that it coughed.) But what the colloquial distinction indicates is that, upon the demise of his recognitional capacity, he no longer knows *in the same way* which object it is concerning which he has the belief that it coughed.[24]

So while I accept that the introduction of the look-alike object

---

[23] Recognitional capacities involving non-egocentrically identified areas of search are also mixed cases of this kind.

[24] This point bears some resemblance to one I made in 6.4 (n. 44) in criticism of the treatment of demonstrative identification by certain 'description theorists', who take it to involve such descriptions as 'the one I am (or have been) attending to'. That theory also made light of a considerable difference—the difference between the case where individuation is effective because I have kept my eye on the thing and the case where I can no longer identify it in that way. (This difference also could be registered by the colloquial use of the 'know which' idiom.) The cases are not exactly parallel, because after I have lost visual contact with the object my Idea of it does not even partly depend upon that capacity.

(or other ways of undermining the recognitional capacity)[25] do not prevent the subject from thinking of the object, I do maintain that they destroy one particular Idea; one particular way of thinking about an object is no longer available to him. But I acknowledge that there is (necessarily) a fall-back way of identifying the object available to him.

8.4 RECOGNITION AND RECALL

As I said in 8.1, several philosophers have been prepared to allow that a recognitional capacity can be the basis of an adequate Idea of an object. But, typically, these philosophers have not been sympathetic to a broadly Russellian conception of reference. They seem to think that Ideas of this kind can be treated just like those involving descriptive identification—at least in that someone can possess an Idea of this kind whether or not there is anything of which it is an Idea. For example, Searle writes:

It needs to be re-emphasized that in a limiting case the only 'identifying description' that a speaker could provide would be to indicate recognition of the object on sight.[26]

This indicates at least a tendency (if a hesitant one) to regard a recognitional capacity as involving possession of an identifying description. Dummett explicitly says that Frege's theory of sense and Meaning can accommodate itself perfectly well to the admission that a capacity to recognize an object can be one way of satisfying the requirement that the subject know which object he is referring to:[27] and Dummett says this on the assumption that Frege's theory involves the claim that a singular term's sense is always independent of the question whether or not it has a referent.[28]

But it is not by any means obvious that this is correct. It is difficult to see what could be the content of a thought which purported to rest upon a recognitional capacity, if there was no unique object which the subject was (or at least had been)

---

[25] For instance (if the universe is symmetrical about a point) taking the subject and his Doppelgänger to the midpoint and spinning them around.

[26] *Speech Acts*, p. 90.

[27] *Frege*, p. 488; cf. also pp. 97–8.

[28] See especially pp. 403–4: 'Frege never lapsed so far from plausibility as to maintain that to utter a sentence containing a name lacking a bearer is to fail to say anything in the sense of failing even to express a thought. That would be absurd ...'

disposed, in the exercise of the purported capacity, to identify.[29] It would appear that in the cases in which the capacity is (or was) effective, what gives the thought its object is simply the fact that the thinker is disposed to identify that object as the relevant object. It is difficult to see how we could extract from this some *condition* whose satisfaction by an object renders it the object of the thought, in such a way that the condition is capable of being grasped whether or not there is an object that satisfies it.

Let me begin the discussion of this question by drawing attention to a distinction between two different ways in which we may exercise a memory ability: a distinction which is confirmed both in psychological studies of memory and in the experience of ordinary life. It is the distinction between what has been called 'recognition' and what has been called 'recall'. The difference is difficult to make precise, but easy to illustrate. Suppose that, as part of a psychological experiment, I am given a list of forty words, and after an interval, I am asked to name as many words on the list as I can remember. In answering this question, I am obliged to *recall* words on the list. My *recognition*-memory for the list, however, is tested in a different way. The forty words will be mixed with a set of 'distractor items', and I shall be presented with each of the members of the extended set, and asked to say whether or not it was on the original list. If I correctly answer 'Yes' to one of these questions, I shall be said to recognize the word. (Notice that this is a different sense of 'recognition' from that with which we are currently concerned—it is type recognition, rather than token or individual recognition.) Now it is a fact confirmed by common experience, as well as by psychological experiment, that words which could not be recalled will be recognized, and that, in this sense, recognition memory can be 'better' than recall memory. Typical differences in test scores would be these: up to forty per cent of the words on the list can be recalled some hours later, while recognition scores can be up to ninety per cent.[30]

[29] The case in which the subject is disposed to 'recognize' an object other than the one from which the relevant information derives is to be treated rather differently—as yielding thought-episodes which are ill-grounded, in the sense of 5.4.

[30] I am aware that it is difficult to make sense of a direct comparison between these scores, since the recognition-memory is highly sensitive to the set of items chosen as distractors. 'It is in fact possible, by increasing the similarity between old items and new

If asked to describe a route on which I frequently travel, I may be able to recall only a certain number of features or properties, but when I actually travel the route, many things will strike me as familiar which I was unable, even after extended reflection, to recall. For example, there may be a derelict house at one point, and upon coming across it I may say 'Yes, I had forgotten that'. By this I mean that I now remember it— I am quite sure that it was there when I last travelled the route, and has not become derelict only recently; but it was not something I was able to recall. The presence of the house itself has prompted me to remember it (though frequently a less specific prompt may serve, as when I am asked 'Are there any unusual houses on the route?'). Now the recognition of a route as the right one is plainly an exercise of recognition memory. The facts about it which I can *recall* might be quite inadequate to individuate it; yet, confronted with a route of which everything I can recall is true, I might confidently reject it, because of the large number of things which strike me as unfamiliar, while I may be able to recognize the correct route, because of the large number of features which it prompts me to recall. In driving along a road, intending to retrace my steps to an objective I have previously reached, I may get uneasy—'I don't remember that'—and reject the route, even though, ahead of time, I would have been able to recall almost nothing about it.

I do not want to raise the somewhat unprofitable question whether, in a situation in which a person will recognize something as familiar which he could not recall, he may properly be said, before being prompted, to remember it (for example, whether or not, in the case I have just described, the subject can be said to remember, and to know, that the route passes by a derelict house). We certainly do use the verb 'to remember' in a dispositional sense, and this question becomes a question about the appropriate conditions for activating the memory. If we are to say that the subject does remember, such a statement must be consistent with the statement that he has forgotten; and other connections, between the concept of remembering and

---

fillers, to reverse the usual relationship and produce poorer recognition than recall scores': Alan D. Baddeley, *The Psychology of Memory* (Harper and Row, New York, 1976), p. 286.

those of belief and knowledge, are also likely to be disturbed. Obviously, in some sense the information has been retained; but it is not accessible to the subject, and will not influence his thoughts and actions in the way which is customary with things one knows or believes. What does seem to me to be clear, however, is that no fact which the subject 'remembers' only in this sense—no fact which is, without prompting, beyond his recall—can enter into a specification of what the subject is thinking. If the subject in the previous example is thinking about the route, it would be quite incorrect to attempt a no-tional—content-giving—report of what he is thinking along the lines of 'he is thinking that the route upon which there is a derelict house is thus and so'. That he is thinking about a route in this way is simply not consistent with his having forgotten that there is such a route.

Now let me bring these considerations to bear on our question whether recognition-based identification is appropriately un-derstood on the model of descriptive identification. Consider a subject who entertains a thought of the relevant kind, which he might express in the words 'That Russian was drunk'. Certainly he must *remember* the relevant man (8.1); and we shall expect him to be able to recall something about how things were with him on the occasion of the encounter to which the past-tense demonstrative adverts. But he can know perfectly well which object he has in mind, even if what he is able to *recall* of that object is both extremely sketchy and somewhat inaccurate, so long as he does genuinely have the capacity to *recognize* the referent when confronted with it. As we have just seen, we are not restricted, in recognizing something, to observing whether or not it possesses features we are able to recall; and the gap between the features we can recall and those we are able to recognize can be quite wide.

It seems to me to be a consequence of these reflections that the content of these thoughts cannot in general be adequately reported in descriptive terms—i.e. terms mentioning the appearance of the thing. Nothing that has been forgotten, or that is beyond the subject's recall, can figure in a specification of what he is thinking; and if we attempt to fashion a description from the properties of the object's appearance which the subject can recall, it is extremely unlikely that the description will *uniquely* apply to the object which the subject can recognize, if it applies to it at all.

Opposition to this point is likely to rest upon a mistaken view of the phenomenon of recognition. As Wittgenstein wrote:

It is easy to have a false picture of the process called 'recognizing'; as if recognizing always consisted in comparing two impressions with one another. It is as if I carried a picture of an object with me and used it to perform an identification of an object as the one represented by the picture.[31]

Only the conviction that it must be so, that the process of recognition would be incomprehensible unless it were so, could blind one to the fact that it is not so. Perhaps, in some sense or other, information about the object's appearance is stored in the nervous system, but this is not information which the *subject* has, or in any sense *uses* to effect an identification.

Although the distinction between recognition memory and recall memory is sufficient to call this model of identification into question, Wittgenstein's point goes deeper. For, even when we can recall the object quite well, we do not in the normal course of events *use* the information which we can recall in making an identification; even when we can vividly recall the object, we do not summon up an image of it and compare the image with what we see. *We* need not *use* anything to make an identification. The capacity to recall the appearance of something, perhaps in the form of an image, and the capacity to recognize it should be regarded as joint effects of a common cause, and since the recognition does not work via what we can recall, the possibility is open that, even when we can 'recall' the object, what we 'recall' is a fairly poor guide to which object we shall recognize.

Both the philosophical temptation to try to 'explain' our use of language, our repeated use of general terms or of proper names, by the postulation of mental mechanisms, of which 'comparing what we see with a memory image' is a paradigm example, and the philosophical resistance to the idea that there are certain things which we just do, for which a neural, but not mental, explanation should be provided, are brilliantly analysed by Wittgenstein, both in the *Blue and Brown Books* and in the

---

[31] *Philosophical Investigations*, § 604. (Cf. *The Blue and Brown Books*, at pp. 88, 165.)

Philosophical Investigations. This is not the place to discuss or to develop his analysis. I mention these wider considerations because I think it illuminating to see the 'description theory' of singular reference as a product of the same philosophical ideas and tendencies underlying various influential, and traditional, conceptions of the way in which general terms function. For of course what I say about the process of recognition applies no less to the recognizing of something as a dog (the recognition of a type) than to the recognition of particular instances of that type.

This is the first respect in which I believe the model of identification by description is defective as an account of recognition-based identification. For the purposes of this first objection, I have not challenged the claim that a recognitional capacity can be 'captured' in descriptive terms, in the sense that one can formulate some description of the appearance of an object which all and only those objects which trigger the recognitional capacity will satisfy; I have simply pointed out that if there is such a description, it will not, in the general case, be accessible to a person who possesses the recognitional capacity.

8.5 RECOGNITION BY DESCRIPTION

However, it does seem that the claim that a recognitional capacity can be 'captured' in descriptive terms can be called into question. So let us abstract from the difficulties with which we have been concerned in 8.4, supposing that the subject with whom we are concerned can recall the appearance of the relevant object vividly; let us even suppose that he will *use* this information in making an identification, in the way in which someone in possession of a picture can identify a criminal from it. The question still remains: even under these circumstances, can an account of his thought about this object be stated in descriptive terms?

Let us begin by asking what kind of description of the appearance of the object we are entitled to expect. Consider the case of something we are rather good at recognizing—the faces of other human beings (at least of one's own racial group). X, we shall suppose, can vividly recall the face of his good friend Y, and it is this capacity which is involved in his ability to entertain thoughts about his friend employing recognition-based identification.

We are to consider the idea that these thoughts are appropriately understood on the model of descriptive identification. So what kind of description are we to expect to figure in a descriptive specification of the content of the thoughts in question?[32]

The appearance of a human face can be broken down into a variety of distinctive features. Some of these features are familiar to us; for example, the feature of having a receding hair line, or a long nose, or widely spaced eyes. But if we wish to approach a description which has any chance of being uniquely satisfied by Y, even among persons met by X, we must go beyond these familiar concepts. If we were programming a computer to recognize faces, we should programme it to be sensitive to the ratios of the distances between various facial landmarks, and it is to these features that our nervous system is sensitive.[33] However, I take it that concepts such as these have no place in a specification of X's thought; they are likely to be concepts with which he is quite unfamiliar, and the information that in Y's face the ratio of the distance between the eyes and the distance between the chin and the mouth is greater than average may come as a complete surprise to him, even if he is in a position to understand it.

When we say that X can recall Y's face very well, we do not have it in mind that there is a list of such descriptions which he remembers; rather, we suppose that he can form a vivid mental image of Y's face. When we take account of this, it may appear that we can fashion a description of Y's face, while at the same time doing justice to the way in which X remembers Y's face, by supposing that the relevant description comprises an element of the form 'looks like this', where 'this' refers to his image-representation of the face. It would appear that 'ξ looks like this' is a perfectly good concept-expression, which many different things might satisfy; and it is intelligible whether or not there is anything which does in fact satisfy it. Why should we not suppose that X's thought can be specified by using such a description as

---

[32] I assume that any appearance description which we find must be supplemented with, at the very least, a description along the lines of 'which I have met'; otherwise the account will be open to the most obvious kinds of counter-examples. I shall assume this point taken care of in what follows.

[33] See Susan Carey and Rhea Diamond, 'From Piecemeal to Configurational Representation of Faces', *Science* 195 (1977), 312–14.

this, or, more strictly, the description 'looks more like this than anyone else I have met'?

It is slightly unfortunate to have a reference specifically to the subject's image in the appearance description, since ultimately it is intended that just such a description might figure in a specification of what is said or communicated between two speakers of the language. It is therefore better to think of the relevant property as one that would correspond to an unstructured predicate 'ϕ', which can figure in a specification of the content of the mental picture (in the sense that we can say 'X's image of Y's face represents it as being ϕ'), and which is also to apply to anything which looks similar.

In either case, crucial reliance is being placed upon the concept 'looks like', so we must briefly examine this concept. However, before we do so, it is as well to take Wittgenstein's advice, and replace the private image with a public representation. So let us suppose that X has the benefit of an excellent police artist, or photo-fit expert, with whose assistance X is able to arrive at a publicly perceivable picture which exactly captures the appearance of Y as remembered by X.[34] Externalizing the picture can only help the case of the description theorist, by making it easier to accept that there is such a commonly graspable predicate as the unstructured 'ϕ'. One can imagine such a predicate actually being introduced into the language, with training in its use involving the use of the publicly perceivable picture. Someone instructed to find a person who is ϕ would act in exactly the same way as someone who is given the picture and told to find a person it looks like, but the predicate 'ϕ' would not *mean* 'looking like this picture', and we would not be precluded from translating a predicate of another language by 'ϕ', if it were introduced in connection with a similar looking picture (or person).

The case for recognizing this form of identification by description can look extremely strong. After all, we do give people pictures and photographs of objects to assist them in arriving at an identification, and the procedure bears a striking resemblance to more obvious forms of identification by description—

---

[34] In fact subjects are almost always dissatisfied with the efforts of police artists, but for purposes of argument I shall suppose what I do not believe, namely that this is a merely technical difficulty.

as when we tell someone to meet, off an aeroplane flight, the man wearing a red carnation. Indeed, since we are waiving the points I made in 8.4 about the process of recognition, this is exactly how we are now to suppose that X does recognize Y. However, if there is a description, it either explicitly or implicitly relies upon the concept of similarity, or 'looks like', and we must ask what this amounts to.

I do not think that what is intended here is a use of an *absolute* notion of similarity, according to which one thing can be similar (in appearance) to another *sub specie aeternitatis*. There are doubts as to whether any such absolute notion of similarity makes sense, but there is an even greater uncertainty as to whether, supposing it did make sense, things which strike human beings as similar could always be regarded as similar in such an absolute sense. If they could be so regarded, then we should have to hold that any perceiving being, no matter how different his conceptual scheme, the circumstances under which his species had evolved, and his interests, must find similar what we find similar, or be charged with being blind to something. It seems generally better, and certainly adequate for the purposes at hand, to think of the relation 'looks like' as what we might call a *secondary relation*—on analogy with the secondary qualities of traditional philosophy, which hold of objects in virtue of the effects they have upon human beings. According to this view, something will *objectively* look like something else if it strikes people as like that other thing; or, rather more usefully, b is objectively more like a than is c if and only if b strikes people as more like a than c does.[35]

It is essential to this way of looking at similarity, and a general feature of a conception of a quality as a secondary one, that the reaction which the object occasions in human beings can be regarded as something other than a judgement. (I do not believe that there is much promise in an account of what it is for something to *be* ϕ which appeals to the disposition it has to cause people to *judge* that it is ϕ.) But it seems possible to give a characterization of what it is for two things to strike a person as similar which does not appeal to his *judging* (in some possibly incoherent sense) that they are similar.

[35] See W. V. Quine, *Word and Object* (M. I. T. Press, Cambridge, Mass., 1960), pp. 83 ff.; and 'Natural Kinds', in *Ontological Relativity and Other Essays*, pp. 114–38.

The model we can follow, to a certain extent, is that provided by stimulus-generalization experiments with the rat. Psychologists probe the similarity space of the rat by conditioning some response to the presentation of a stimulus *a*, and then by seeing which of *b* and *c* has a greater tendency to elicit this response; the greater the tendency, the more similar the rat finds it to the original stimulus *a*.[36]

The similarity space of human beings is certainly susceptible to probing by similar experiments, but it is perhaps doubtful whether the method is sufficiently fine-grained. A baby can strike me as like his father, but I may have no tendency to respond to him as I do to his father: even on a brief presentation on a dark night, I will have no tendency to confuse them. But the baby will *remind me* of his father, *even without my knowing the relationship*; I take this to mean that he has a tendency to get me to think of his father, and this is certainly a similarity in the effect the baby and the father have upon me. In effect, I am taking a point from the traditional doctrine of the association of ideas and turning it the other way around. The traditional theory of the association of ideas held that there was an absolute sense in which mental contents could be said to be similar, and advanced it as a hypothesis that the mind will be led from one of a set of similar things to another. I hold that things between which our minds move, *without prior association or semantic connection*, are things we find similar, and that things which we all find similar are objectively similar.[37]

Now, as I have stressed, for one thing to strike me as like another is simply a *reaction* which those things occasion in me; it is not a judgement, to which the question of truth or falsity can significantly be applied. This would remain true even if we were to train people to express the reaction in a verbal way, by uttering something like 'How like his father he is!' Utterances issued in this way can be regarded as judgements only when the issue of truth or falsehood arises, which can be only when the

---

[36] In these experiments, we presume that neither *b* nor *c* has antecedently been regularly associated with *a*, and that neither has previously had any tendency to elicit the response.

[37] Cf. Wittgenstein, *The Blue and Brown Books*, p. 130. [Evans became uncertain whether the proviso 'without prior association or semantic connection' was enough to exclude cases in which people's minds are led from one thing to another without the fact being any guide to what they find similar.]

possibility of error has been provided for. In the case of the other secondary qualities, this arises in a variety of ways, but the most important of them exploits the control provided by the reactions of other people. 'How like his father he is!' constitutes a judgement about the world when it is issued subject to the control of human agreement—when the speaker is prepared to acknowledge that he is wrong by withdrawing his remark in the face of an incapacity to get others to agree with him, to see things his way. The baby may remind me of his mother, but if I am not disposed to withdraw my utterance 'How like his mother he is!' in the face of divergent reactions on the part of all who know both mother and baby, then it is not a judgement about the world—about the baby and his mother—but merely a verbal expression of my reaction.

Let us bring all of this to bear upon X and the picture of his friend Y. There *is* a perfectly good property of *looking like*—an objective property of pairs of objects, anchored in the reactions they occasion in people. Hence there is nothing wrong with the description 'looks more like this than anyone else I have met'. But we have to ask: is it certain that the intended object, Y, will meet this objective description? The picture we have elicited from X with the aid of the police artist certainly strikes him as like Y; it certainly reminds him of Y more than of anyone else, so that we can safely assume that, had X never known Y, and had he been given this picture, and confronted by the relevant set of men with the instruction 'Pick out the man who strikes you as more like this than any other in this set', X would have picked out Y. So much we are vouchsafed by the assumptions we have made for purposes of argument.[38] But is there any necessity that what would remind X of Y will remind people in general of Y? Might not X be rather insensitive to certain properties of faces to which other humans are very sensitive, but sensitive to other features which other humans ignore, so that the picture which the police artist produces is a good likeness for X but not for others? Why should X not have an idiosyncratic similarity space in this area? Yet it would surely be absurd to be driven to the conclusion that X was really thinking of Y's brother (whom he has also met), and not Y, on the ground that most

[38] Remember that this is all relative to our waiving the points made about the process of recognition in 8.4.

people find the police artist's representation more like Y's brother than Y.[39]

It might be tempting at this point to retreat to the claim that the relevant appearance-property is that of looking like this *to* X, or rather, such a property of appearance as corresponds to a predicate 'ϕ' which applies to the man in the picture and to anything which strikes X as similar. This would be a genuinely private concept, since no one other than X can be master of it, and therefore it is useless for the description theorist to appeal to it. It certainly can play no part in a specification of what is said or communicated by X to some person W. And although this is sufficient to make one's interest in the suggestion evaporate, one's objections can in fact go much deeper. Anyone influenced by Wittgenstein will argue that there *is* no such concept, no such property. A concept is something abstracted from the practice of judging—a capacity exercised by someone in the course of making a judgement; which is a performance assessable as being correct or incorrect. But this pseudo-concept cannot be exercised in any such performance. Whatever seems right to the subject is right, which only means that we cannot speak of 'right' here.[40]

Obviously this is not the place to enquire whether or not Wittgenstein's argument, briefly recalled here, against the possibility of such private concepts is effective. But, whether or not this charge of incoherence can be made out, notice how far away we are from the kind of explanation which at one time it might have appeared that the description theorist was offering us. We were encouraged to regard X's identification of his friend Y as a form of identification by description; with X having, ahead of the identification, a property or criterion in hand by which he can determine whether or not a given object is Y. If this were the model, X would have a *reason* for identifying Y as

[39] It is no doubt important that our judgements of similarity do generally agree, but they are not required to agree at every point.

[40] Cf. Wittgenstein, *Philosophical Investigations*, § 258. (A complete treatment of this conception of recognition would require some discussion of the phenomenon of being *guided* by a picture. This is certainly possible even when there is no systematic possibility of being corrected in what one does: though of course one cannot do just anything and still count as being guided by the picture. But being guided by a picture and applying a concept are different. And a similar distinction applies in the case of recognition: where, rather than saying one is guided by an inner picture, we might say one is guided by one's memory of how things were with Y.)

his friend—for recognizing him as Y; namely, his belief or know-ledge that Y satisfies this property. But by invoking a property of which X possesses a private concept, we have thrown away any semblance of applying this model. We cannot say that X recognizes Y because Y satisfies the property ϕ; rather, we can say, at most, that Y satisfies property ϕ in virtue of X's recog-nizing him.

8.6 MIXED IDEAS

In this chapter, as in chapter 6, I have deliberately concentrated upon what might be described as *atomic* thoughts about parti-cular objects: thoughts which do not involve more than one way of thinking about an object. Very often, however, a subject makes a *re*-identification (that is, a judgement of the form $\ulcorner a = b \urcorner$, when both a and b are Ideas connected with ways of gaining information),[41] and goes on to think in ways which depend on it. (On '*re*-identification', see 5.2.) To give a simple example, suppose a person met someone on the previous day, and retains information which permits him to have thoughts involving an Idea expressed by 'that man'; then he meets some-one today, and, exercising the recognitional capacity which that Idea involves, he judges, using in addition a demonstrative Idea proper, 'This man = that man'. This is a *re*-identification. Subsequent thinking about the man in question will be con-trolled both by information from the previous encounter and by information acquired in the present encounter. This subsequent thinking will therefore be of a new kind: it will involve a new Idea.[42]

In a simple case like this, the new Idea is a very simple product of the two Ideas we could discern in the *re*-identifica-tion. The condition for an object to be the object thought about is simply for it to be both *this man* and *that man*. If the subject has made a mistake, and has misidentified someone as *that man*, then I think his thoughts involving the new Idea have perfectly clear truth-conditions (although they are impossible to satisfy). So this would be a case in which the non-existence of the object

---

[41] See 5.2.

[42] Although any linguistic expression of the subsequent thoughts will favour one rather than another of the amalgamated Ideas, in a way which will be explained (9.3), there is no reason whatever to read this fact back into the thoughts, desires, or intentions.

does not deprive a thought of content. We might say, in such a case, that the new thoughts are not only *mixed*, but also *decomposable*. For the latter to be the case, the subject must still possess both the original Ideas; and a criterion of this is whether the subject can understand the negation of the *re*-identification.

It would be possible for a subject who has met a man on each of the two previous days to be credited with two distinguishable Ideas, which we might represent by 'that man$_1$' and 'that man$_2$'. His subsequent thinking about the man should be regarded as not only mixed, but also decomposable. Such a subject would be able to entertain the hypothesis 'That man$_1 \neq$ that man$_2$'; in order to do this (in order to be credited with two distinguishable Ideas), he would have to be able to segregate the information acquired in each encounter. (I must stress that the content of the hypothesis is not reducible to something of the form 'The man I met on $d_1 \neq$ the man I met on d_2': see 8.3.) This segregation of information may be possible, especially if the two episodes were both very different and very memorable.

But it is equally possible, and in very many situations altogether more likely, that the information is combined in an undecomposable way, so that although the new Idea results from a *re*-identification, this is not a *re*-identification which the subject is now capable of grasping. In such a case, the subject cannot be credited with the capacity for distinguishable kinds of information-based thought about the object. The resulting Idea may be very similar to an Idea he has lost: for example, it may rest upon recognition-based identification. But, as with all mixed Ideas, there is now a new possibility of error—the possibility that there should not be just one object which the Idea identifies. And in this kind of case (unlike the case of decomposable mixed Ideas), where this possibility obtains, no coherent thought-content can be found.

Repeated *re*-identification, usually by means of a recognitional capacity, leads, as I remarked in 8.2, to rich and detailed bodies of information. Thoughts involving an Idea resulting from this process may not be decomposable into thoughts involving as many Ideas as the identifications and *re*-identifications upon which the mixed Idea rests. But some limited decomposition may be possible. For example, in suitable circumstances most people could grasp a hypothesis expressed in such words as 'That man was not (after all) your friend X', where the demonstrative adverts to an encounter on the previous day, and perhaps even to a holiday spent together.[43]

Mixture also results, of course, when a subject *re*-identifies the object being spoken of with an object which he heard being spoken of earlier, or with an object known about in other ways. (These *re*-identifications are what referential discourse is all about: see 9.1.) Once again, the resultant Ideas may or may not be decomposable.

[43] A subject may make a *re*-identification $\ulcorner a = b \urcorner$ when both a and b are rich and complex Ideas of an object.

Appendix

There is a broad analogy between memory-based singular thoughts in general, on the one hand, and demonstrative singular thoughts, on the other. An account of memory-based singular thinking would have two components: first, an 'information-link' between the subject and the object (the subject's possession of retained information derived from an encounter with the object); and, second, an account of how the subject knows which object is in question. The first component can be present when the second is missing, if the subject retains information derived from an object but (a) cannot place the object in his own past and (b) would not recognize the object if confronted with it.

The chapter as it stands concentrates on (b), and suggests that recognition-based thinking about an object constitutes an autonomous mode of identification, which is supplanted by a different mode of identification, comprising a recognitional element and also elements from (a)—a more or less vague placing of an encounter with the object in one's past—only when one's recognitional capacity for the object of one's thought proves vulnerable to duplicates (8.3).

But Evans seems to have wondered whether this did not give the wrong weight to the fact (8.2) that recognitional capacities are dominant in determining the object of thoughts in which they are involved. A self-conscious subject necessarily has the idea of himself as having traced some definite path through the world; and he will have some conception—more or less indefinite at different points—of his own past history (organized around a framework of landmark events), which is equally, of course, a conception of the history of a part of the world (the world as he knew it). It follows that events remembered, and participants in them, can always be identified by reference to oneself—though not necessarily uniquely. (This does not yield a generalized identification-dependence, because, as we know, the identification of oneself partly depends on one's propensity to rely on one's memory.) In the light of this, it seems undeniably the case that at least part of the conception that one has of an individual one can think of, in the way that is the concern of this chapter, is that it is a conception of an individual which one has met. (Very often the conception includes more: that it is an individual that one met at such-and-such a period of one's life, perhaps regularly over that period.) When one takes oneself to be recognizing someone, it seems to be an undeniable part of the way we think that, when one is wrong (e.g. because of the existence of an indistinguishable twin), it is because were one to trace one's life back, one would not—at least not at the appropriate period—reach an encounter with *this* individual. On this view, the only partly recognition-based mode of identification considered in 8.3 as a fall-back position, when recognitional capacities prove unequal to distinguishing their objects from duplicates, would be the general rule after all.

This suggests a different line from that taken in 8.3, with respect to the apparent threat posed to Russell's Principle by the apparent fact that our recognitional capacities for individuals are not absolutely discriminating. The argument in 8.3, exploiting spatial considerations, is that—properly understood—our recognitional capacities *are* uniquely targeted. The different line would be to deny that the Ideas in question are exhausted by our possession of recognitional capacities. As before, one's way of identifying the individual in question involves a more or less definite location of an encounter with it in one's own past; the recognitional capacity is merely an effective—though defeasible—way of knowing when one has encountered the same individual again. (Compare a 'recognition-based' competence with a natural-kind concept. The capacity to recognize instances need not be uniquely targeted on members of the kind. For there may be superficially indistinguishable duplicates. As long as the superficially indistinguishable non-members are present, in the subject's environment, in sufficiently small numbers, their presence will not undermine his claim to be able to recognize members of the kind—to know them when he sees them. We shall simply say that his recognitional capacity—which we shall surely continue to count as an important component in his competence with the concept—is defeasible. In this case, since we envisage the non-members and the members present together in the same environment from the start, there is no room for a strategy involving the exploitation of spatial considerations in a way analogous to that of 8.3.)

The modification makes it easier to dispose of a worry that arises about the argument of 8.4 and 8.5. The thesis which that argument aims to protect is that recognition-based singular thinking is Russellian. But what 8.4 and 8.5 argue is that recognition-based identification does not reduce to descriptive identification. Now, one might wonder whether that is the *only* way in which a mode of identification can fail to be Russellian (can be available to be employed in singular thoughts whether or not there is an object which it identifies): might there not be a position according to which recognition-based identification is agreed not to be reducible to *descriptive* identification, but according to which, nevertheless, it figures in non-Russellian thoughts? Indeed, the suggestion has a certain plausibility. One might say: a recognitional capacity is a disposition to respond in certain ways to an object on the basis of its appearance (the basis being agreed not to be capturable in a description); and surely someone could have such a disposition even if no object capable of presenting the triggering appearance had ever existed—it could still be true that *if* an object were to present the requisite appearance it *would* activate the disposition. But if we adopt the composite conception of the mode of identification we are concerned with, we can see that simply being such that it would activate such a disposition would not suffice to make an object count as the object identified by such a mode of identification. (We can now see that when we say that a recognitional capacity is a disposition to respond in certain ways to an object on the basis of its appearance, we have to give the phrase 'an object' wider scope than the specification of the content of the disposition.)

Part Three

Language

Chapter 9

Communication and Information

9.1 INTRODUCTORY

In section 2.3 I argued that the concept of a descriptive name is a coherent one; a proper name, or any other syntactical singular term, may have its reference (as used on a particular occasion) fixed by a description, with the consequence that (as used on that occasion) it is not functioning as a Russellian singular term. But I said at the time that such uses of referring expressions are an oddity: most referring expressions are used in a quite different way. In fact, the uses of referring expressions which do not follow the model of descriptive names are themselves quite diverse, with the differences between them traceable to the different modes of identification with which they are connected. Nevertheless there is a characteristic almost all of them share, and upon which I want to focus in the present chapter.

The characteristic is this: in order to understand an utterance containing a referring expression used in this way, the hearer must link up the utterance with some information in his possession. Thus, if a speaker utters the sentence 'This man is F', making a demonstrative reference to a man in the environment he shares with the hearer, the hearer can understand the remark only if he perceives the man concerned, and, bringing his perceptual information to bear upon his interpretation of the remark, judges 'This man is F: that's what the speaker is saying'.[1] Or a speaker may advert to information which he presumes the hearer retains from a previous encounter with an object, saying, perhaps, 'That man we met last night is F'; and here again, I do

---

[1] See G. E. Moore, *Commonplace Book 1919–1953*, edited by Casimir Lewy (George Allen and Unwin, London, 1962), p. 158: 'Can we say "that thing" = "the thing at which I am pointing" or "the thing to which this finger points" or "the nearest thing to which this finger points"? No, because the prop[osition] is not understood unless the thing in question is *seen*.'

not think that the hearer can have understood the remark unless he actually remembers the man, and thinks 'That man is F: that's what the speaker is saying.' (I call such uses of the demonstrative form 'that ϕ', 'past-tense demonstratives'.) Or again, the speaker might advert to information he presumes the hearer has from the testimony of others, perhaps from a newspaper article, or a rumour, or a conversation, saying something like 'That mountaineer is F'; here I do not think that the hearer can be said to have understood what the speaker is saying unless he possesses this information and thinks, in a way which is informed by it, 'That mountaineer is F: that's what the speaker is saying.' (I call these uses of demonstratives, 'testimony demonstratives'.) These are clear cases, and I shall concentrate upon them in the discussion that follows; but the phenomenon is much more widespread, including most normal uses of proper names. (I shall discuss the use of proper names in chapter 11.)

It was Strawson who first noticed this tremendously important feature of referring expressions. He wrote:

Very often a speaker knows or assumes that a thing of which he has [identifying] knowledge is also a thing of which his audience has [identifying] knowledge. Knowing or assuming this, he may wish to state some particular fact regarding such a thing, for example, that it is thus-and-so; and he will then normally include in this utterance an expression which he regards as adequate, in the circumstances of utterance, to indicate to the audience *which* thing it is, of all the things in the scope of the audience's identifying knowledge, that he is declaring to be thus-and-so ... When an expression ... *is* used in this way, I shall say that it is used to *invoke* identifying knowledge ...[2]

However, it is unfortunate that Strawson attempted to harness this insight to defend the position on definite descriptions which he had adopted in opposition to Russell's. That position, as we saw (2.1), involved treating all uses of definite descriptions as Russellian singular terms; for Strawson held that, if one utters a sentence of the form 'The ϕ is F', when the description is empty, one says nothing. I shared Russell's surprise at this contention, for when we have someone making a *pure* use of a definite description, as in 'The inventor of the zip is an English-

[2] 'Identifying Reference and Truth-Values', *Logico-Linguistic Papers*, pp. 75–95, at pp. 77–8. Compare also Grice's use of the notion of a *dossier* in 'Vacuous Names' (but notice that Grice makes no use of the notion of information).

man', it does appear that he will have put forward a perfectly clear proposition, with perfectly determinate truth-conditions, irrespective of there being anything which uniquely satisfies the description. In any case, whether or not Strawson's view that these pure uses of definite descriptions are Russellian can be maintained, it is clear that the notion of 'invoking identificatory knowledge' has to be considerably diluted if it is to apply to them. It can no longer be understood in terms of a presumption of the possession of *information* from a particular object, for, clearly, no such presumption is made in the pure cases. So it must rather be interpreted in terms of a presumption of *belief,* or, at least, a presumption of willingness to believe something. It probably *is* a feature of the pure use of definite descriptions that one does not appropriately utter a sentence of the form 'The ϕ is F' if one expects it to be controversial, or even interesting news to one's audience, that there is something which is uniquely ϕ. (In Strawson's terminology, this comes out as the claim that in uttering such a sentence one *presupposes* but does not assert that there is something which is uniquely ϕ.) If this is all that the notion of invoking identificatory knowledge or belief amounts to, then nothing very much can be deduced from it. (Recognition of the applicability of this notion, in cases of the pure use of definite descriptions, is even consistent with treating descriptions as quantifiers: see 2.4.)[3] As we shall see, the same cannot be said of the quite different property of presuming upon the audience's possession of information from an object.

It is important to realize that the difference between a pure use of a definite description, or a use of a name like 'Julius' (1.7, 1.8), on the one hand, and a use of an ordinary referring expression, on the other, is not a matter of the *richness* or *detail* of the belief which the speaker presumes his audience to possess. Understanding the kind of use of a referring expression I am considering is not a matter of having beliefs with the right sort of content, but a matter of having, and using, information from the right source. To see this, consider the following case. S and A were in the habit of going hunting together in their youth.

---

[3] As 2.4 showed, there is no need for Russell's recasting of the form of 'The ϕ is F', which leaves an assertion of it looking like, in part, an assertion of the existence of something ϕ; this is what Strawson's use of the notion of presupposition is meant to reject.

On one of their hunting trips, they saw a dazzlingly beautiful bird perched in a pine tree. Years later, *S* (the speaker) may advert to this incident, and say something like: 'Do you remember that bird we saw years ago? I wonder whether it was shot.' *A* (the audience) may not remember the episode. In order to jog his memory, *S* may say 'Surely you remember; a hunting trip years ago; we saw, on a pine tree, a magnificent bird'; and *S* may be able to indicate a very similar bird, perhaps in a photograph, or in the wild. *A*, knowing *S* to be trustworthy, will believe all that he says, and will of course be prepared to bring his belief (which may become quite rich and detailed) to bear upon *S*'s original remark. But I do not think that he can be said to have understood the remark, as it was intended to be understood, until he *remembers* the bird—until the *right* information is retrieved. This may happen quite suddenly: 'Oh yes! Now I remember. You mean *that* bird.' And there need be no difference in the *content* of what *A* believes before and after the flash of recollection. After the flash of recollection, the subject is in a different *informational* state, with a different causal history, but its content, and the beliefs based upon it, need not change. Understanding information-invoking uses of referring expressions requires, upon the part of the audience, an information-based thought, and, as we know (5.4), this is not just a matter of having a thought of the form 'The ϕ is F', no matter how rich and detailed 'ϕ' may be.[4]

This is merely one example of a general phenomenon noted in 5.4: information-based thoughts are distinct from descriptive thoughts, simply in virtue of being information-based. There can be no description 'ϕ'—no matter how rich and detailed— such that entertaining the thought that the ϕ is F is *ipso facto* entertaining an information-based thought. For an information-based thought requires the use of the subject's informational system, and no description 'ϕ'—no matter how rich and detailed—can guarantee an appropriate link with the subject's informational system. For instance, in order to have a demonstrative thought (one that rests upon perceptual information), the subject must be able to make the object out in

---

[4] The phenomenon of recall mentioned here has been discussed in A. J. Ayer, *The Problem of Knowledge* (Penguin, Harmondsworth, 1956), p. 146; and in Strawson's review of *The Problem of Knowledge*, *Philosophy* xxxii (1957), 302-14, at pp. 309-310.

what he perceives; and there is necessarily a gap between grasping 'The blonde girl who looks thus and so is *F*' and 'That blonde girl is *F*', because there is always room for an intelligible realization: 'Ah! So *that's* the blonde girl you mean!'[5]

It is possible to regard Strawson's insight as having suffered from the general neglect of the concept of *information*, of which I spoke in 5.2. Strawson no doubt started from the central cases, in which a link-up with information from an object is intended; but he would have described them in terms of the traditional concept of *knowledge* (a species of belief).[6] When he realized that the presumed information is very often incorrect, this became 'knowledge *or belief*'; and so the interesting idea that certain uses of referring expressions invoke information was exchanged for the rather less interesting idea that certain uses of referring expressions presuppose existential propositions.

But before extracting the consequences of the phenomenon which Strawson so perceptively noticed (even though he mistook its precise nature), we had better get a little clearer about the actual mechanics of referential communication.

9.2 HOW COMMUNICATION IS EFFECTED

There is no infallible linguistic guide to when the understanding of a remark requires the invocation of information, since most expressions which are conventionally apt for such a use also have other uses. For example, *pronouns* have a clearly recognized information-invoking use: they can be used like ordinary demonstratives (to refer to items in the shared perceptual environment); like past-tense demonstratives (as when one says 'He was in a hurry' after the departure of a man from a room); and like testimony demonstratives. But they are also used as bound variables. *Demonstrative expressions* like 'this man', 'that girl', etc., *almost* always indicate that an information-invoking use is being

[5] A similar gap exists when the thought rests not so much upon some information in the subject's possession as upon his *disposition* to acquire information in a certain way (our rather *recherché* cases of 'I' and 'here'). Here again, no grasp of a descriptive proposition can guarantee the required link-up with the subject's informational system (can guarantee the required dispositions).

[6] Indeed, most of Strawson's article is written in terms of the notion of invoking identifying *knowledge* of a thing. See, e.g., p. 76: '. . . we might often say that it could not be true of a speaker that he intended to inform the audience of just *that* particular point unless he presumed in his audience certain empirical knowledge.'

made, and the implication of an expected identification by the audience is very strong, as can be seen by comparing utterances of these two sentences: 'I am having dinner with the waitress of the village tea shop tonight', and 'I am having dinner with that waitress of the village tea shop tonight.' Nevertheless, I observed in 6.1 that such expressions can be used (in connection with 'deferred ostension') like descriptive singular terms; and recently, in dialects other than my own, the form 'this ϕ' has acquired the use of indicating that the speaker himself is giving expression to an information-based thought, in the absence of any expectation that his hearer will grasp an information-based thought ('Then I met this beautiful girl . . .').[7] *Proper names* are perhaps the most reliable indicators that an information-invoking interpretation is intended. I do not mean that proper names (as a syntactic category) are always used in this way, for we know that there can be such things as descriptive names (1.7, 1.8, 2.3). I mean that anyone who knows the sense of a proper name will know whether it is governed by a descriptive reference-fixing convention, or is an ordinary proper name; and the use of an ordinary proper name is always information-invoking. (It is considered impolite to use the name of something right off if one does not expect one's audience to be able to identify the referent. In such a situation, politeness demands that one say, not 'I had dinner with NN', but 'I had dinner with someone called "NN".')

Let us suppose that a speaker utters a sentence containing an expression which has a conventionally recognized information-invoking role, and that it is clear that such a use is intended— perhaps from the boringness of the remark if taken as complete in itself. The audience must proceed beyond this, to the *right* (i.e. intended) interpretation. And if he is to be credited with understanding, he must *know* that it is the right interpretation. For it is a fundamental, though insufficiently recognized, point that communication is *essentially* a mode of the transmission of knowledge. In application to the case we are particularly interested in, this means that, if the speaker S has knowledge of x to the effect that it is F, and in consequence utters a sentence in

<hr />

[7] Whether ordinary definite descriptions have a conventionally recognized information-invoking use is a controversial question which I shall consider briefly below (9.3).

which he refers to *x*, and says of it that it is *F*, and if his audience *A* hears and understands the utterance, and accepts it as true (and there are no defeating conditions), *then A himself thereby comes to know of x that it is F*. If we are prepared to take for granted our grasp of the semantical concepts which this principle employs, we can use it to yield epistemological dividends. But it is possible to use the principle the other way round, bringing our intuitions about *knowledge* to bear upon the explicitly semantical concepts—the concepts of reference, saying, and understanding—in the middle. We shall then be thinking of communication as a relation between speaker and hearer which can constitute a link in a chain of knowledge-transmission. We already show tacit appreciation of this point when, looking at the link from the hearer's point of view, we typically gloss understanding as knowing what the speaker is saying; but when we look at the relation from the other side, we might equally say that in order to say something, one must enable an audience to know what it is that one is saying.[8] A speaker who is to say something by uttering a sentence containing a referring expression must make it *manifest* which object it is that he intends to be speaking about—which object an audience must think of in understanding his remark.

I shall not even begin to offer a full account of the ways in which such intentions can be made manifest, for the cues are often very complex and remote from consciousness. (Giving such an account is a task for psycholinguistics.)

A very important factor, but by no means the only one, is the choice of referring expression. The conventions governing referring expressions are such that, as uttered in a context of utterance, they are associated with a property which an object must satisfy if it is to be the referent of the fully conventional use of that expression in that context; I call such a property '*the referential feature* which the expression conventionally has in that context'. For instance, the utterance of the expression 'I' on a particular occasion is associated with the property of *being the person making that utterance*; and the utterance of the expression 'you' on a particular occasion is associated with the property of *being the person addressed in that utterance*. Very often the property

[8] Only so can we make it intelligible that by hearing and understanding one he might come to know *that it is so*.

is much less discriminating.[9] All that the conventions governing
the referring expression 'he' insist upon, in any given context, is
that the object referred to should be male. 'This' and 'that' are
even less specific, contributing merely the vaguest suggestion of
a contrast between nearer and further (in some generalized
sense); but this exiguous contribution can be supplemented with
an associated description: 'this ϕ' and 'that ϕ' are clearly
associated with the referential feature *being ϕ*. When an expression in a context of utterance has the property of being ϕ as its
referential feature, it will generally be at least partly in virtue of
the audience's knowing, of an object, that it is ϕ that the
audience will be able to know, of that object, that it is the object
to which the speaker intends to refer.[10]

A common way in which audiences are enabled to know
which object is the referent of an expression in a particular
context is by virtue of the speaker's exploitation of the object's
salience. The salience can be brought about by the speaker
himself, as when he accompanies the utterance of a demonstrative expression by a pointing gesture, or by rendering an object
salient in some other way, for example, by shaking it, wobbling
it, or causing a searchlight beam to fall upon it. Alternatively,
a speaker can exploit some extreme or heightened salience
which an object has anyway (without his bringing it about); for
instance, a speaker might say 'He's had enough', as one in a line
of soldiers renders himself salient by collapsing. In either sort of
case, if an object is salient, it will be so only to those who have
a certain sort of information from the object (perceptual information, in the examples we have considered), and hence only
to those who are in a position to think of the object in a certain

[9] This fact precludes any simple functional definition of the notion of 'a referring
expression in an utterance' as the expression which indicates which object the speaker
is talking about. Often the *predicate* does more to narrow down the range of possible
interpretations of the referring expression than does the referring expression itself.
(Perhaps such a functional definition could be made to work at the level of classes of
expression rather than individual members.)

[10] Given that it is the function of the referential feature conventionally associated with
the expression 'that ϕ' to invoke antecedently existing information—which it can do
only if the audience believes, or is prepared to believe, that the object concerned is ϕ—
we have a cast-iron guarantee that the form of words 'That ϕ is F' will not be used to
inform the audience that something is ϕ. This may well be the explanation of the
phenomenon of presupposition, which has become attached to that grammatical form.

Proper names can perhaps be regarded as associated with the referential feature *being
named or commonly called 'NN'*.

information-invoking way (demonstratively, in our examples). For an audience to *know*, of an object, that it is the referent of an expression, when this is the communicative mechanism exploited by the speaker, it must be in virtue of the effect of the object's salience on the audience's informational system that the audience thinks of the object in understanding the remark.

In 9.1, I suggested that certain referential remarks require for their understanding not merely *some* information-based thought about an object—not merely some connection or other with the audience's store of information—but an information-based thought *of a particular kind*. Thus I said that, in order to understand an utterance, 'This man is *F*', said of some man in the shared perceptual environment, the hearer would need not merely to make *some* connection with information about the man, but to make a connection with the information he is currently receiving from the man in *perception*, thereby thinking 'The speaker is saying that *this* man is *F*.' It might be thought that this puts an additional burden upon the speaker, requiring him to indicate not only which object he wishes the hearer to think of, but, in addition, *how* he wishes him to think of it. But this is quite the wrong way to look at matters, for the speaker manifests the *kind* of thought he expects of his audience by the way in which he manifests which object the thought is to concern.

To see this, consider a case in which salience is exploited: a speaker says 'He's had enough' as someone makes himself salient by fainting. An audience will understand the remark only if he knows, of some object, that it is the object in question; and someone possessed of ordinary epistemic powers, and without anyone else's help, will be able to *know* this only if he can identify the object in question demonstratively. Of course, if someone trustworthy were to whisper in his ear that Prince Charles has just fainted, he could thereby come to know of someone (Prince Charles) that he had just fainted, and so, possibly, that he was the referent of the speaker's remark, without thinking of him demonstratively; but this is obviously not a mechanism upon which the speaker linguistically manifests an intended reliance. So, in this context, the demonstrative identification is the minimal identification of the referent which is consistent with the requirement that there should be an identification of the referent, that it should be known, and that it should not rely upon extraneous or abnormal ways of gaining knowledge. As such, I think we can say that it is the kind of identification which the speaker linguistically manifests the intention to secure. Of course, a hearer who correctly identifies the object of the remark demonstratively may believe that the man who has just fainted is Prince Charles, and thereby go on to make further *re*-identifications. But this is strictly optional from the point of view of understanding what the speaker says; so that even if the hearer has *mis*identified the man concerned as Prince Charles (and is thus thinking of the wrong man), it does not follow that communication has not been successfully effected.

Let me take another example: the expression 'you'. If a speaker addresses a remark to someone, saying 'You are a crook', it is surely clear that an identification is called for on the part of the audience; in order to understand the remark, it is not enough that one know that there is one, and only one, person whom the speaker is addressing, and that the speaker is saying of that person that he is a crook. But it is also clear that a quite specific *kind* of identification is called for; the person addressed has not understood the remark unless he realizes that the speaker is saying that *he* is a crook. The fact that a quite specific way of thinking of the referent is required can be seen, in this case, to be a consequence of the referential feature which the expression 'you' has in a context: namely, *being the person addressed*. It follows immediately that understanding the remark requires the hearer to know *of* an individual that he is being addressed—that some identification is required. And in the normal conversational context, a subject will *know*, of an individual, that he is being addressed, when that individual is himself, *only by having the self-conscious knowledge that the speaker is addressing him*. (Think, in this connection, of coming to know, of an individual who is in fact oneself, that the speaker is gazing at him.)

Similarly, the identification of the referent which the speaker linguistically manifests the intention to secure, when he refers to it as 'I', seems to be a demonstrative identification (the hearer's thought would be naturally expressible as 'This man is *F*: that's what this man is saying'); for one will know, of an individual, that he is speaking by knowing *in the first instance* something expressible in the words 'This man is speaking.' This we may call the lowest-level identification. Of course, in this as in every other case, one may make a further identification; but this would depend upon information on which the speaker did not linguistically manifest intended reliance, and would be, from the point of view of understanding the remark, an optional extra.

One very fundamental way in which an object may be salient for purposes of reference is through having been referred to previously in the conversation (or in a previous conversation).[11] What mode of identification does the speaker linguistically manifest the intention to secure by exploiting this kind of salience? Well, if the audience is to *know*, of an object, that it was mentioned in a previous remark, without assistance from anyone else, this will be because he remembers the remark; hence he will identify the object as he identified it in understanding that remark.[12] Thus our principles would explain why someone who refers to an object in this way makes a reference with the same semantical properties as the original reference to which he was alluding, for exactly the same things would be required of an audience in order to understand it.

If this argument is correct, then we can recognize at least a limited applicability of the Fregean notion of sense to expressions of the kind we are concerned with; but without in any way gainsaying the idea that what is primary, for purposes of communication, is the referent. The limited recognition of sense comes in with our claim that understanding the remarks we are concerned with requires not just that the hearer think of the referent, but that he think of it in the *right way*. But we recognize the primacy of the referent by recognizing that the hearer always confronts just one question, 'Which object does the speaker mean?'—not two questions, 'Which object does the speaker mean?' and 'How am I intended to think of it?' The second question is answered in passing; for if he understands the remark, he will *know* which object is meant; and in the normal

[11] This kind of reference ('co-reference') is typically effected by the use of pronouns or demonstratives. In 'Pronouns' I argue that we must recognize a category of *rule-governed* co-reference.

[12] [This seems questionable: the earlier identification may have been demonstrative, and the object need no longer be present to the subject's senses.]

course of events (i.e. without assistance from others, etc.), he will *know* which object is meant only if he thinks of it in the particular way intended by the speaker.[13]

But this is a very limited vindication of Frege. We do not have Frege's full model of the role of sense in communication (see 1.5); for we do not have the thesis that communication between speaker and hearer requires them to think of the referent *in the same way* (in any plausible or natural sense of that phrase). The nearest we come to the full Fregean model is with expressions like 'here' and 'now'; the furthest we move away from the full model is with expressions like 'I' and 'you'. As we shall see, although understanding the various kinds of demonstratives normally requires thoughts which are pretty similar on the part of speaker and hearer, divergences in ways of identifying can exist. (See 9.5.)

We are now in a position to say something about the notion of *the speaker's intended referent*, and the role it plays in communication. As I mentioned earlier (6.1), it is possible for a speaker to make a fully conventional information-invoking use of a singular term to secure identification of an object of which he himself has no information—when, for example, a blindfolded speaker in a game infers that there is someone in front of him, and, pointing in that direction, says 'This person is *F*.' In this case, the speaker's intention is to be referring to *whoever is in front of him* (that is, to whatever object satisfies the referential feature); so, provided there is someone in front of him, that person is the intended referent. However, in the normal case, the speaker will make information-invoking uses of referring expressions in order to give expression to his own information-based thoughts, and his intention could itself be expressed in one such thought: 'By *t* I mean that one.' Now, it would be natural to take the intended referent of this kind of use of a singular term to be the object which these thoughts concern; but this natural position cannot be accepted as it stands.

The difficulty is this. A speaker's thoughts may rest upon a *re*-identification he has made, and so involve a complex but

---

[13] Saying 'I'm only interested in finding out which object to think of; I'm not interested in finding out how to think of it' would be just as foolish (and for parallel reasons) as saying 'I'm only interested in finding out which things are true; I'm not interested in finding out which things I know.' See Bernard Williams, *Descartes: The Project of Pure Enquiry* (Penguin, Harmondsworth, 1978), ch. 1.

decomposable Idea of an object (8.6). For example, a speaker may have misidentified a man he can see (*a*) as the man he met on a previous occasion (*b*); in this case, his thoughts and intentions (e.g. 'I mean him') are complex, and concern *a* and *b* equally. If the suggestion we are considering were correct, then we would have to say that there is no one intended referent of his use of singular terms in this situation. Now, although there is nothing intrinsically absurd about such a description of the case, it just does not seem to be correct. There seem to be some remarks that the subject might make in this situation of which *a* is clearly the intended referent, and other remarks of which *b* is equally clearly the intended referent. For example, if the speaker uttered the words 'That man over there is *F*' the intended referent would surely be *a*, whereas if he uttered the sentence 'That man we met yesterday is *F*' the intended referent would surely be *b*.

The difference between the cases lies in the way in which the audience is expected to identify the referent. In the first case, the speaker intends a demonstrative identification, and, in thinking in accordance with the speaker's intentions, the hearer will think of *a*, not of *b*; whereas if he thinks in accordance with the speaker's intentions in the second case, he will be thinking of *b* and not *a*.

Thus the notion of the intended referent is rather like the notion of a *target*. Suppose the subject, in the case we have been considering, had aimed a gun at the man he could see. Even if his general plan was to shoot *b*—for example, because the offence he wished to avenge occurred in the previous encounter—it is undeniable that *a* was his target, and that he intended to shoot *a*. His *lowest-level* action plan concerned *a*; success in it would involve the shooting of *a*. Similarly, *a* is the speaker's *linguistic* target when he utters the sentence 'That man over there is *F*'; this time he is directing, not a gun, but his audience's attention. It is *a* whom his audience must think of if the speaker's lowest-level linguistic action plan is to be carried out. This is so even if he might be credited with the higher-level intention to be referring to *b*—because, in using the predicate *F*, he is giving expression to information gained in the previous encounter. (Suppose, for example, that he says 'That man over there behaved badly last night.') Now it is in the nature of shooting that it is not possible for a shooting plan other than one of the demonstrative kind we have discussed to be the lowest-level plan governing some action; 'Shoot that man we met last night' must always be broken down into lower-level plans in order to be carried out. But the same is not true with referring, for one can direct one's audience's thoughts to things other than the here and now, and this is why *b* can be the linguistic target (of the remark 'That man we met last night is *F*'), even though it cannot be the person's literal target.

Thus the intention-expressing thoughts whose object is the speaker's intended referent are the thoughts which involve the Idea-of-an-object which figures in the *lowest-level* linguistic plan. So, just as any further identifications of the referent which the hearer might make are irrelevant to the question whether he has understood the speaker's remark (cf. the Prince Charles example above), so some *re*-identifications of the intended referent made by the speaker can be irrelevant to the communicative process. In the ordinary case of referential communication it is true that both speaker and hearer will have information-based thoughts, and that communication will require that they are thinking of the same object, but this coincidence concerns the thought which involves the lowest-level identification of the referent on the hearer's part, and the thought involved in the lowest-level linguistic plan on the speaker's part. Divergences beyond this are consistent with successful communication.

I have given expression at several places to the view that for a hearer to understand a speaker making a reference, he must know which object the speaker intends to refer to (in the sense I have just been explaining). Since understanding involves knowing which object a speaker refers to, I am maintaining that a *necessary* condition for a speaker to have referred to an object by the use of an expression is that it be the intended referent of that use of the expression.[14] This position has aroused opposition, and it is probably a good idea to say a word about it.

First of all, I should stress some qualifications inherent in my

---

[14] I am thus agreeing with Michael Dummett when he wrote (in 1973): '... if I use the name "Harold Wilson", and intend thereby not to refer to the leader of the Labour Party but to some other man of that name, then I have not referred to the leader of the Labour Party, although I may be taken as having done so and held accountable for having been so taken' (*Frege*, p. 149). I take it that Dummett meant: my intentions do not concern the man who is in fact the leader of the Labour Party.

understanding of the thesis. First, and most emphatically, I am not maintaining that possession of the requisite intentions is *sufficient* for referring to something. For one thing, I insisted earlier that in order to say something, the speaker must make his intentions adequately manifest (adequately, that is, for the transmission of knowledge); and, anyway, the speaker must use a referring expression conventionally suitable for reference to the intended object. I mentioned earlier an epistemological principle governing such notions as saying and understanding; another, equally important principle is that, if a speaker refers to something, and says of it that it is *F*, when it *is F*, then he will have said something true, and his utterance will have been *correct* (even if lacking grounds or ill-judged). Thus if a speaker intends to refer to a boy in saying 'That girl is *F*', he cannot have succeeded in doing so, even if his intentions are perfectly plain; for his utterance cannot be judged to be *correct*, even if the boy is *F*.

Secondly, I am not saying that the speaker must always have available a *rich characterization* of the intended referent. (In a salience-exploiting case, he may think of it only, for example, demonstratively.)

Thirdly, when I say that a speaker cannot correctly be judged to have referred to something other than the intended referent, the term 'intended referent' is to be understood in the sense I have just explained, so that much of what the speaker thinks about the referent may be irrelevant to what he says.

It is clearly absurd to restrict reference to just those cases where referring expressions are used which are conventionally associated, in a context of utterance, with a uniquely identifying referential feature. Those who oppose the position I have expressed must hold that it is possible to be *correct* in identifying, as the referent of an expression whose referent is conventionally underdetermined, an object other than the object the speaker intended to refer to. Yet it must be acknowledged that the only question the hearer can intelligibly ask himself in attempting to disambiguate the reference is 'Which one does the speaker intend?' So the only possible view allowing the referent of an expression to be distinct from the speaker's intended referent is a view according to which something is the referent of an expression if and only if in the social and physical context of the speaker's utterance it would be reasonable and natural to take it that a speaker, speaking conventionally in that context, would mean to refer to that object.[15]

I find it difficult to see the point of pressing this position—which itself accords a central theoretical place to the concept of the speaker's intention, but, so to speak, at one remove—against the one I have outlined. And I see one major disadvantage. For it seems to me that the epistemological principle which I formulated earlier, as constraining the notions of saying, referring, and communicating, should debar us from certifying anything as constituting successful communication which is *intrinsically* incapable of conveying knowledge. And any link which allows the hearer to fasten upon an object other than that intended by the speaker is intrinsically incapable of being a link by which knowledge can be conveyed.

Clarity in the theory of reference will be served if the following concepts are clearly distinguished: that of the referent of an expression as used by a particular speaker on a particular occasion; that of the intended referent of an expression; and that of the object which the speaker means.[16]

9.3 THE INFORMATION-INVOKING USE OF DEFINITE DESCRIPTIONS

This is a convenient place to say something about an issue which has aroused a good deal of controversy: is there another use of definite descriptions, in addition to their use as quantifiers (2.4)? I have emphasized the adequacy of the quantificational treatment of descriptions in what I have called *pure uses*—where no link-up with antecedently existing information from an object is intended (9.1). For the understanding of such a use of a

[15] This is a slight adaptation of a lucid formulation of the position given in Strawson's *Subject and Predicate in Logic and Grammar*, p. 62. (The position must take this form, since the only realistic general way of gathering together the information which bears on the interpretation of utterances is as bearing on what speakers intend by them.)

[16] Being the intended referent is necessary, but not sufficient, for being the referent. The notion of the object which the speaker *means* is the one distinguished earlier in this section in connection with indecomposable Ideas: where a speaker's Idea is an indecomposable result of amalgamating Ideas of two different objects, there may be nothing which he *means*, even though an object may be the intended referent, and the referent, of some utterance of his.

A fourth notion to be distinguished from all these is the notion of what the speaker is *talking about*. This belongs with the psychological idioms discussed in 5.3, and is really only peripherally connected with our subject.

definite description, as in 'The inventor of the zip is an English-man', nothing other than a grasp of the satisfaction-conditions of the embedded concept-expression ('ξ is the inventor of the zip') is required. But are there uses of definite descriptions for the understanding of which it is necessary that one have, and invoke, information from some object? The question is often phrased as 'Is there a *referential* use of definite descriptions?', and the phraseology is in harmony with my own, in that a conventionally-certified information-invoking use of definite descriptions would certainly be a referring use; although we should bear in mind that, as I use the notion of reference, *being intended to invoke information* is only a sufficient, and not a necessary, condition for a referring use of a singular term. (See the remarks on 'Julius' in 2.3.)

It must be conceded on all sides that speakers very often do use definite descriptions with the intention and expectation that their audience will identify the satisfier of the description as an object of which he has information: speakers frequently use 'the ϕ' where they might just as easily have used 'that ϕ'. A speaker can utter the sentence 'The man standing underneath that oak tree is honest' with exactly the same communicative intentions with which he might have uttered the sentence 'That man standing underneath that oak tree is honest.' But the question we have to ask is whether an identification on the part of the audience is strictly required for *understanding* the remark—that is, knowing what is said by it. An alternative position would be to maintain that descriptions are unambiguous (always quantifiers), and to explain the fact that speakers often intend information-invoking identification on the part of the audience as the result of the operation of standard conversational factors.[17] (After all, one might intend information-invoking identification with a sentence like 'Under that tree stands an honest man', but this would not lead one to postulate an ambiguity in the expression 'a man', claiming that it has a referential, as well as a quantificational use.)[18]

---

[17] This is essentially the position advanced by Kripke: see 'Naming and Necessity', p. 343, n. 3, and 'Speaker's Reference and Semantic Reference', in French, Uehling, and Wettstein, eds., *Contemporary Perspectives in the Philosophy of Language*, pp. 6–27.

[18] It can easily be seen that much more is required in this discussion than showing that there are two 'uses' of definite descriptions. In that easy sense, there are two uses of 'a man . . .'.

There are in fact two kinds of case in which one might want to speak of definite descriptions as referring expressions. In one, which I have already mentioned, descriptions are used like the various sorts of demonstrative expressions (ordinary, past-tense, and testimony demonstratives). In the other, descriptions approximate more to proper names, for the identification is intended to exploit the common knowledge of a *practice* of using the definite description to talk about a particular object. I shall defer discussion of the second kind of case until 11.2.

Those who wish to argue that definite descriptions are ambiguous, and have a fully conventional information-invoking use, must support their position by producing cases in which (a) the truth-conditions of the purely quantificational interpretation and those of the proposed referential interpretation diverge, and (b) our intuitive judgements of the correctness or incorrectness of utterances support the ascription to the description-containing utterance of the referential, rather than the quantificational, truth-conditions. Such evidence for an ambiguity would not be conclusive, but it would be a start.

Now previous discussion of this issue has proceeded upon the assumption that there would be the following divergence in truth-conditions: when the description in 'The ϕ is F' is being used quantificationally, the statement's truth would require the existence of something that is both ϕ and F (this is certainly true); but when it is being used referentially, the statement can be true without there being anything that is both ϕ and F. For it was thought that when a speaker manifests the intention, with respect to an object, of securing identification of it, by uttering a sentence containing a definite description 'the ϕ', then that object is the referent of the description, whether or not it is ϕ— whether or not it satisfies the referential feature. Thus it was held that when the description is being used referentially, I can say something true by uttering the sentence 'The man drinking champagne is F', so long as the man I mean (and manifest the intention to speak of) is F, even if he is not in fact drinking champagne.[19]

But this kind of argument is intrinsically incapable of serving its purpose—that of showing that there is a fully conventional use of descriptions to refer. For, if we formulate the truth-conditions of sentences containing the non-quantificational use of

[19] See Donnellan, 'Reference and Definite Descriptions'.

descriptions so as to have this result, we shall not be able to complete the second part of the argument ((b) above). We would not judge an utterance of 'The man drinking champagne is *F*' to be *correct* in the circumstances envisaged above. Undeniably, a mistake has been made, and the sentence should not have been uttered.

I think a more promising way to try to establish the ambiguity is to concentrate upon a different divergence in truth-conditions.

When a speaker makes an information-invoking use of a referring expression, he presumes upon a background of information which is, at least to some extent, shared. For example, suppose there is a widely disseminated story in the community that the Pope has been assassinated by a mad bearded anarchist, and a speaker, adverting to this story, says 'That assassin of the Pope is an Italian.' Now it is surely clear that it is not sufficient, for something to be the referent of this demonstrative (a testimony demonstrative), that it satisfy the referential feature 'being the assassin of the Pope'; no one can be the referent of the expression unless it is he whom the background story is about— unless it is he from whom the information embodied in the story derives. If the rumour in the community is the result of a malicious fabrication by the agents of a foreign power, then the demonstrative has no referent; the correct thing to say is '*That* assassin of the Pope does not exist—is an invention of our enemies.' And this is true, even if by chance, and unbeknownst to anyone other than his immediate entourage, the Pope has in fact been assassinated. In general, I have argued, nothing can be the referent of a use of a singular term unless it is the speaker's intended referent (9.2); and when, as in this case, the intention is to direct the hearer's thoughts to something from which the speaker also takes himself to have information, nothing but the object from which that information derives can be the referent of that use of the term. Thus, if the speaker is hallucinating, and utters a sentence containing a demonstrative, 'This man is about to attack us', in the belief that his audience can perceive the same person, the demonstrative is without a referent: the right thing to say is 'Calm down: *that* man does not exist'—even if, by chance, there happens to be some man in the general direction indicated by the speaker.

So another possible way of establishing that definite descriptions have a fully conventional information-invoking use would be to show that there are utterances of the form 'The ϕ is F' which we would *not* judge to be correct, even though the quantificational statement '$(\mathrm{I}x)(\phi x; Fx)$'[20] is true, because the satisfier of the description 'ϕ' is not the source of the information on which the utterance is based. Suppose the speaker, in our example, had uttered the sentence 'The assassin of the Pope is an Italian': would it be *wrong* to judge his utterance to be correct, when the facts about the hushed-up assassination came out? Here again, however, it is very difficult to make out a case, because the quantificational sentence is undeniably *correct* in that situation—the quantificational sentence could undeniably be asserted by anyone who knew the facts. (If someone were to say 'The assassin of the Pope does not exist', obviously he would not be speaking the truth.)

The best line of argument for those who maintain the ambiguity of definite descriptions stems from the fact that in information-invoking uses of expressions of the form 'the ϕ', it is very often clearly not the speaker's intention to maintain that 'ϕ' is uniquely exemplified. Confronting a group of people, I might say 'The man is married to the girl', and it is clearly not my intention to be taken to be maintaining that there is one, and only one, man in the world. Let us call these 'incomplete descriptions'. Now the existence of incomplete descriptions is not by itself conclusive evidence against a quantificational treatment of all uses of descriptions, for there are uses of incomplete descriptions which can perfectly well be given a quantificational treatment: it is just intended that the incomplete description be supplemented and completed. For instance, travelling in a car through the United States, I might pass through a town whose roads are particularly bumpy, and in consequence say 'They ought to impeach the mayor'. I do not intend my audience to identify the object spoken about as one of which he has information; I intend merely that he take me to be saying that the mayor of this town, through which we are passing, ought to be impeached, and this statement is adequately represented quantificationally. However, to generalize this solution to all cases in which an incomplete description is used commits one to the implausibility of maintaining that in each such case there is a

---

[20] See 2.4.

uniquely correct and intended supplementation. When an information-invoking use of a description is made, the task of the audience is surely to fasten upon the right *object*, rather than upon the right complete description; there will be several equally good candidates ('the man over there', 'the man under the tree', 'the man beside the woman'), between which it will be quite pointless to choose.[21]

Whether or not we agree that there is an ambiguity in the English word 'the', between the quantifier of 2.4 and something akin to 'that', is not really very important. It is more important that we should realize what exactly we are, or are not, agreeing to; and being clear about this is being clear about the very idea of an information-invoking use of any singular term. The characterizations which have been offered of the 'referential use' of descriptions in the literature simply will not do. Using a description referentially is *not* just a matter of having some particular individual in mind; that is, having and giving expression to an information-based thought. One schoolmistress may say to another 'The youngest child in my class is the most mature', and it is certain that, in saying it, she will be giving expression to an information-based thought; there will be a quite definite individual from whom she has received information, perhaps over an extended period of time, and whom she aims to be speaking about.[22] (Aiming a thought in this way introduces the possibility of missing the target: the individual concerned may not in fact be the youngest in the class. See 5.4.) But it seems to me that when we are classifying *uses* of expressions—uses on which we want to see the logico-semantical properties of utterances as depending—we must appeal to facts which concern what it is to *understand* those utterances; and the fact that a speaker has a particular individual in mind when uttering a sentence containing a definite description is, by itself, irrelevant to the question of what it is to understand that utterance. If it

---

[21] Cf. Searle, *Speech Acts*, p. 92: '... in an utterance of "the man" the only descriptive content carried by the *expression* is given by the simple term "man", but if the reference is consummated the speaker must have communicated a uniquely existential proposition (or fact), e.g., "There is one and only one man on the speaker's left by the window in the field of vision of the speaker and the hearer."' The argument against this is set out by Strawson in discussion with Karl Popper and Geoffrey Warnock, in Bryan Magee, ed., *Modern British Philosophy* (Secker and Warburg, London, 1971), pp. 131–49.

[22] In a quite loose and general sense of the term.

is not manifest, in a conventionally appropriate way, that the audience is intended to think, in an information-based way, of a particular object, then all that someone who understands the schoolmistress's remark need grasp is precisely the thought that the youngest child in the class is the maturest—a content to which the quantificational treatment is perfectly adequate. Even if we had a device for indicating that the speaker was using the sentence containing the description to give expression to an information-based thought, it would not affect the logical properties or the content of his utterance. I observed in 9.2 that the demonstrative 'this' appears to be gaining a use of this kind; but there is no difference in *content* between the statement 'Then I met this beautiful girl' and the statement 'Then I met a beautiful girl'. Equally there would be no difference in content between 'The* youngest child in the class is the most mature'— where 'the*' is the hypothesized conventional indicator that the speaker is giving expression to an information-based thought— and the corresponding quantificational statement employing the 'Ix' quantifier of 2.4.[23]

9.4 INFORMATION-INVOKING SINGULAR TERMS ARE RUSSELLIAN

I come now to the first of the arguments designed to show that singular terms which are intended to 'invoke identifying information' are Russellian. This argument proceeds by establishing the lemma that, in order to understand such a term, one must onself believe that there is something to which the term refers. (This thesis is in fact implicit in my claim that such singular terms require information-based thoughts for their understanding, since, according to my explanation of the notion of information-based thoughts, such thoughts commit the subject

---

[23] These remarks are directed against Donnellan's original characterization of the referential use of definite descriptions (in 'Reference and Definite Descriptions'), which has not been subsequently improved upon. A brief survey will show that most of his tests or criteria for the referential use are satisfied so long as the speaker 'has someone (or something) in mind'. It is true that his explicit characterization of the referential use mentions audience-directed intentions: '... to enable [the] audience to pick out whom or what he is talking about ... we express and intend our audience to realize whom we have in mind' (p. 285). This is the characterization of referring with which we began this investigation (see the Introduction): we followed Russell in finding it wanting, because it is just not clear why it does not apply in the 'pure' cases of definite descriptions. (On Donnellan, see also n. 14 to chapter 2.)

to the existence of something as their object (5.1). But it is now time to defend and elaborate that claim.)

One way of defending the thesis that understanding requires belief is clearly not open to me. I certainly cannot argue that in order to *possess* the information which is to be invoked, the subject must believe that there is such-and-such a thing. For I maintained earlier that it is a distinguishing feature of *informational states*—states produced by the operation of the informational system—that they are 'belief-independent' (5.2). It is precisely this fact which casts such a shadow over the theory of reference, for it makes possible operations which are highly similar to understanding, in the absence of the commitments which understanding involves. Even if a person believes that he is hallucinating, it seems to be possible for him to make a link between his perceptual state and another person's remark—a link of apparently just the same kind as he would have made had he not believed that he was hallucinating. Certainly there is a very sharp difference between hearing the words without making such a link, and hearing the words and making a link. However, when we examine more closely what it means to speak of 'invoking information' and 'making a link', we shall see that it is a procedure which does not make sense in the absence of belief. (The subject who engages in apparently similar procedures in the absence of belief is engaged in a sophisticated form of *pretence*. This idea will be developed in the next chapter, which must be regarded as integrally related to the present one, for no defence of the Russellian status of information-invoking singular terms will be fully convincing until an explanation is offered of our apparent capacity to make a meaningful use of such terms in the known absence of a referent.)

If a hearer is to understand an information-invoking singular term, information already in his possession must be invoked. But what exactly does this mean? It is not simply a matter of calling the information to mind; it must be brought to bear upon the interpretation of the remark. This must mean that the hearer *evaluates* and *appreciates* the remark according to the content of the relevant information; this is the way in which intelligent use can be made of information when listening to the remarks of others. By 'evaluating the remark', I mean arriving at least at a provisional assessment of its truth or falsity. This is a complicated process, which involves balancing the antecedent improbability of the truth of the remark (in the light of the other information one possesses) with the kind of authority one is prepared to assign to the speaker, when the remark is put forward as an assertion. If one already possesses information to the contrary, then the balancing will also have to take into account what, if anything, one can remember of the authority of the source of the contrary information. By 'appreciating the remark', I mean thinking out what would be the consequences if it were true, thereby coming to appreciate its interest or importance.[24]

I shall concentrate upon the use of information in the appreciation of a remark. Now it might seem that we can follow the model of 'Julius' here. Someone who understands the utterance 'Julius is F' will come to believe that if what the speaker says is true, then there is someone who invented the zip and who is F. Equally, where '$\phi_1, \ldots, \phi_n$' represents the content of the information being invoked, someone who understands an information-invoking utterance, 't is F', will come to believe that if what the speaker said is true, then there is something which is $\phi_1, \ldots, \phi_n$ and F. We might suppose that coming to have this latter belief (as a consequence of possession of the information invoked) is, so far as appreciation of the remark is concerned, what is meant by 'bringing the information to bear'. The first belief does not commit the hearer to the existence of someone who invented the zip; nor does the second commit the hearer to the existence of something which is $\phi_1, \ldots, \phi_n$. So the bringing to bear of information, in appreciating an information-invoking remark, does not support the lemma; or so it might seem.

But we must go deeper, and ask not merely about the form of the belief, but about its justification.

The property which figures in the belief arrived at by the hearer in the course of understanding sentences containing 'Julius' owes its place in that belief to the speaker's manifest

---

[24] These sketchy remarks are designed only to warn against the excessively simple-minded views of the procedure of bringing information to bear on the interpretation of a remark which one can derive from the literature. See, e.g., George A. Miller and Phillip N. Johnson-Laird, *Language and Perception* (CUP, Cambridge, 1976).

and overriding intention to refer to something satisfying that property. In this kind of case, we may say, the hearer's belief results from an attempt to be faithful to the speaker's *conception* of the object, if any, to which he is referring. Such a conception may be conveyed, and such a belief arrived at, in the absence of any object it concerns.

But no such justification can be offered for the inclusion of the properties of being $\phi_1, \ldots, \phi_n$ in the belief arrived at by the hearer in the course of understanding the utterance '*t* is *F*'. It cannot even be assumed that these properties figure in the content of a belief of the speaker's about the referent, still less that the speaker can be credited with an overriding intention to refer to something with these properties. (We must remember here that a speaker need have no such detailed beliefs about the referent: recall the case (6.1) in which a speaker refers demonstratively to an object he cannot himself perceive. Even when it is clear that the speaker's informational position is similar to the hearer's—for instance, the speaker manifestly sees the object— it still cannot be assumed that the content of his informational state coincides with that of the bearer. There may be special cases in which the informational states coincide, and can be known to coincide; but this is not the general rule. This point will be further elaborated in 9.5.)

The inclusion of this or that property in such an appreciation of a remark is not an attempt to be faithful to the speaker's conception of the referent, but represents the hearer's view as to how things stand with a particular object. The only possible justification of the belief that, if what the speaker said is true, there is something which is $\phi_1, \ldots, \phi_n$ and *F* is that it follows from some belief of the form 'The speaker is referring to *a*', together with a view as to how things stand with *a*. So, unlike the belief that one might form on hearing an utterance of 'Julius is *F*', the appreciation-constituting belief in the case of an information-invoking remark is expressive of the hearer's belief about the world—about how things stand with one particular object in it. (This is why the hearer's view about the consequences of the remark must evolve, and be revised, as his view of the object evolves and is revised. There would be no possible justification for retaining some property, being ϕ_i, as an element which contributes to the hearer's appreciation of the remark, if he no longer believed of some particular object that it is ϕ_i.)[25]

So, even though it is possible to possess information in the absence of belief, it does not appear to be possible to bring this information to bear, coherently, upon the interpretation of a referential remark, unless one believes that there is a particular object to which the speaker is referring, and to which the information concerned is faithful. (One can go through the motions of bringing information to bear if one *pretends* that there is a relevant particular object: see chapter 10. But we can leave 'conniving' uses of singular terms on one side for the moment.)

Now this lemma might be readily conceded, even by those who wish to resist the conclusion that information-invoking singular terms are Russellian, on the ground that it shows only that a certain belief is required on the part of those who understand the remark, not that the belief must be *true*. But I do not think this represents a coherent stopping point on the way to a fully Russellian position.

When it is denied that a singular term is Russellian, it is being maintained that a speaker will have said something by uttering a sentence containing the term, whether or not there is anything to which it refers. If this is true, then there is some true proposition such that knowledge of its truth constitutes understanding the utterance. But when the singular term is information-invoking, it seems to me that if there is nothing to which it refers, then we must deny that there is any such true proposition.[26] For we have established, by establishing the lemma, that if there is a proposition such that knowledge of its truth constitutes understanding the remark, it is a proposition which commits someone who accepts it as true to the existence of a referent; and *ex hypothesi* there is no such proposition.

Someone who accepts the lemma but wishes to deny the conclusion might hope to defend his view that someone who utters a sentence containing an empty, but information-invoking, singular term says something, by holding that at least those

---

[25] The lemma should not be thought of as expressing a very revolutionary doctrine. The doctrine is in fact encapsulated in this thought: understanding the speaker's remark involves knowing which thing it is that he is referring to.

[26] This is why it is so important that we are able to identify the referents of the theoretical terms in false theories which nevertheless approximate to the truth; otherwise we should have to say that those who expressed such theories were not saying anything.

who are under the *illusion* that the term has a referent are able to understand—i.e. grasp what is said by—an utterance of that sentence. But, surely, if there really *is* something said, then it cannot possibly require a false belief for one to *know* what is said. Truth is seamless; there can be no truth which it requires acceptance of a falsehood to appreciate. (It is surely an axiom of any theory of truth that any true proposition is compatible with any other true proposition.) So the purported 'understanding' is not the knowledge of any truth about what is said; and hence it cannot be genuine understanding at all.[27]

I should stress that this argument rests upon the view (defended in 9.1) that the actual *use* of the information in question is required for understanding the sorts of utterance we are concerned with[28]—that it is not enough to know, e.g., that the speaker intends to refer to an object he sees in front of him, or to an object which formed the subject-matter of such-and-such a conversation. (If the latter sort of knowledge did suffice for understanding, the argument, of course, would not go through.)

The argument which establishes the lemma constitutes the defence of my claim, in 5.1, that an information-based thought manifests a belief about the world on the part of the subject. As I explained there, information-based thinking about an object is governed or controlled by a conception of the object which embodies information derived (mediately or immediately) from it. When I say that thoughts are governed by a conception of an object, I mean that the way the thoughts are entertained as true, false, probably true, or probably false, and the consequences which are supposed to follow from their truth depend upon the content of this conception. To say this is to do no more than advert to the obvious fact that thinking about the world, even if it consists in entertaining thoughts rather than judging them to be true, requires us to make intelligent use of the information that we possess. What we must realize is that using information in this way is not a neutral activity. One can intelligibly use information in this way only if one takes it to be

---

[27] The defect is not just a formal failing; it would not be correct to say that although one does not know what the speaker is *saying*, one can perfectly well know what he *means* (to say).

[28] This argument, then, does not apply to cases where the relevant cognitive state is dispositional (a possibility, as we have seen, with 'here' and 'I' or 'you').

veridical; on learning that a certain element in one's conception of an object is erroneous, one no longer has any business using that piece of information (misinformation) in controlling one's thoughts.

9.5 SUPPLEMENTARY ARGUMENTS

To understand a remark made with the use of an information-invoking singular term, it is obviously not sufficient merely that one make some judgement of the general kind we have indicated; understanding, as we would naturally put it, requires that one make a judgement of this kind *about the right object*—i.e. about the object which the speaker refers to with his use of the term. Now, if this is the only way in which we can state the requirements upon the understanding of an utterance involving an information-invoking use of a singular term, then terms used in this way are, necessarily, Russellian. For clearly, if the conditions of understanding require the audience to be thinking of an object which is also the object the speaker refers to, then, if there is no object the speaker refers to, those conditions cannot be satisfied, and his remark cannot be understood. The two subsidiary arguments I want to consider now are attempts to show that there is no other general way of stating the requirements for understanding these utterances.

I argued earlier that a speaker may make an information-invoking use of a singular term when he himself has no information of the kind he intends to invoke (6.1: the point is appealed to in 9.2 and 9.4). For example, a blindfolded man may infer that he is in front of a man, and, pointing ahead of him, say 'This man is F'. But if he is pointing in mid-air, it really does seem very hard to specify what information-based thinking would count as understanding the remark.[29]

When philosophers suppose that information-based communication and understanding can take place in the absence of an object, their idea is that there can be cases where, even though there is no object, both speaker and hearer have information-based thoughts, and that communication and understanding can be seen to take place in virtue of a certain

---

[29] Recall that I claim that, when the speaker has the intention, concerning a particular object, to be speaking of it, understanding his utterance requires knowing, of that object, that he intends to be speaking of it. See 9.2.

correspondence between the thoughts of the speaker and the hearer, depending on a correspondence in the ways in which they are based upon information.[30] These philosophers believe that the required correspondence can be explained without appealing to the idea that there is an object of which both speaker and hearer are thinking—so that it makes sense to say that two people are focusing on the same place (to adapt Geach's phrase),[31] even though there is nothing there. In examining whether or not this is so, I want to try to abstract from the considerations of Part Two, which seemed to show that subjects simply do not have coherent thoughts involving demonstrative or recognition-based identification when no object is identified. I shall do this partly by concentrating on cases where identification is 'by description', and partly by pretending that the considerations of Part Two are incorrect.

The arguments I want to consider start from two different points at which it might appear that an appeal would have to be made to the existence of an object, in determining whether or not a suitable correspondence exists between the thoughts of speaker and hearer.

The first argument takes note of the fact that, even when a quite specific kind of information-based thought is manifestly intended, it cannot generally be required that speaker and hearer identify, or purport to identify, the referent in exactly the same way.

Demonstrative communication can clearly take place between a speaker and a hearer who are sufficiently far away from one another to observe different parts of the same rather large object. What makes it communication, rather than misunderstanding, is simply the fact that there is a single inclusive object encompassing both the part perceived by the speaker and the part perceived by the hearer. In other words, if we pretend that demonstrative identification involves identification by

---

[30] The discussion of *intended referent* in 9.2 induces a complication which this formulation does not leave room for: a speaker may be credited with the intention to refer to an object, and thus take part in communication about it, even though (because of indecomposability) he cannot be credited with thoughts about that object.

[31] See 'Intentional Identity', in *Logic Matters*, pp. 146–53, at p. 147: 'We have intentional identity when a number of people, or one person on different occasions, have attitudes with a common focus, whether or not there actually is something at that focus'.

means of a description like 'The *G* which is at least partly at *p*', the descriptions provided by speaker and hearer will not always involve reference to the same position in space. The only thing that can bring unity out of this diversity is the fact that there exists an object of which both spatial descriptions are true.[32]

Similarly, communication can surely take place between two people whose identification of a person rests upon their capacity to recognize him, where one recognizes the person by his face, and the other depends rather more upon the voice.[33] But what, apart from the fact that there is a single person they are disposed to identify, could possibly unify these capacities, and show that a communication-allowing 'correspondence' existed between thoughts depending upon them?

Even when descriptive identification is admittedly at issue, it cannot be generally required for communication that speaker and hearer identify the object by reference to exactly the same descriptions. While communication depends upon a certain *overlap* between the information possessed by the speaker and the information possessed by the hearer—an overlap which the referential feature must exploit if the hearer is to *know* which object is meant—a considerable difference can exist in their information, and this would seem to be bound to lead to the possibility of their appealing to different facts in attempting to distinguish the object concerned from all other things.

Those who find no difficulty in the idea that speaker and hearer might be focusing on the same empty place concentrate upon what appears to be a sufficient condition of communication: where speaker and hearer purport to identify the referent in exactly the same way. But if the argument above is correct, and referential remarks are of a character which allows them to be understood by those who identify the referent in different ways, then that apparently sufficient condition of understanding is not a sufficient condition of understanding at all.[34]

---

[32] This is an acute problem for description theories which rely on descriptions on the lines of 'the object causing this sense-datum'; this is necessarily not a description that can be common between speaker and hearer. (A similar point to that in the text can be made by considering communication involving perceptions in different sensory modalities.)

[33] Similarly if one person recognizes a piece of music by its first movement and the other person recognizes it by its second.

[34] [The argument is somewhat elliptical, and it may well be tempting to object that what has been shown is only that the condition in question is not a *necessary* condition—

Let me give a parallel to this situation, which might initially appear surprising. Quantities admit of measurement on different kinds of scale. Perhaps the simplest scale is an *ordinal scale*, which allows us to rank objects as being higher or lower upon this scale, but does not allow us to attach any significance to a ranking of the *distances* between objects on the scale. A quantity which allows us to make sense of this kind of ranking of distances between objects is called an *interval* scale. Now suppose we are considering the ranking of objects in respect of a quantity which in fact permits of measurement only upon an ordinal scale, but we happen first to consider the case of three objects *a*, *b*, and *c*, ranked in that order. Thinking only about this case, we might be very sure that the quantity allows us to rank distances, since we know—or so it might appear—that the distance between *a* and *c* is greater than the distance between *a* and *b*. But, when we try and fail to rank distances between arbitrarily placed objects, we shall have to revise the judgement that the distance between *a* and *c* is greater than the distance between *a* and *b*. If intervals are not generally rankable, they are not rankable in this special case. It looked like an aspect of a general phenomenon, and that was why we described it in the way that we did, but now we see that it is not.

Similarly, when we focus upon the special case of *identity* between the ways in which speaker and hearer purport to identify the referent, it seems that communication can take place in the absence of a referent. But when we take a more extensive view of the matter, we realize that referential communication depends upon the existence of an object, so that our initial view of this special case has to be revised. It looked like an aspect of a general phenomenon, and that was why we described it in the way that we did, but now we see that it is not.

This argument, then, which we might call the argument from diversity, attempts to show that the only candidate

---

which leaves it open that it may be sufficient. A less elliptical formulation, not vulnerable to that merely formal objection, might be on these lines: *given* that the condition is not necessary, the only thing that can unify the quite diverse informational relations this allows us to recognize as possibly obtaining between the information of a speaker and a hearer who communicate in the way we are considering is the existence of an object; so we see that *that* is a necessary condition for the occurrence of such communication.]

communication-allowing relation, between the thoughts of speaker and hearer, which is discoverable in the absence of an object—that they both involve exactly the same way of identifying, or purporting to identify, an object—is far too strong a requirement to impose upon referential communication in general. The second argument has the same structure, but the starting-point is quite different. To bring this out, let us ignore the first argument, and pretend that it is a necessary condition of communication that speaker and hearer should purport to identify the referent in exactly the same way. Let us assume, for purposes of argument, that both speaker and hearer are prepared to identify the referent as the ϕ.

We know that, for a hearer to have understood a speaker, it is not sufficient that he have an information-based thought whose object he is prepared to identify in the same way as the speaker. For consider the case where there is an object, x, which the speaker has in mind, and refers to. The hearer cannot be said to have understood the speaker's utterance unless he is also thinking of x. And if the hearer's information is from an object other than x, or from no object at all, his thought will not be of x. (Assuming x is the ϕ, the hearer's thought will be ill-grounded, in the terminology of 5.4.) For example, let there be a widely disseminated true story about the doings of someone, x. The speaker, taking the audience to have heard this story, utters the sentence 'That ϕ is F', adverting to the story. The audience has not heard that story, but has heard another with the same content, wholly fabricated by someone attempting to deceive him. In having a thought based upon this information, he will not be thinking of x, or of anyone; '*That ϕ*', we might say, 'is just a figment of so-and-so's imagination.' It follows that the statement of the conditions for communication must make some reference to the origin or pedigree of the information upon which speaker and hearer respectively base their thoughts.

The natural suggestion, in filling this gap, is once again Russellian in its implications. This is to say that the information of the speaker and hearer must derive (in ways which typically produce knowledge) *from the same object*. Once again, it is not hard to think of certain apparently sufficient conditions for a communication-producing correspondence which can be satisfied in the absence of an object.[35] When the relevant information derives from the testimony of others, for example, it might appear to be sufficient, for speaker and hearer to be focusing upon the same empty place, that their information derive from the same source, in the journalistic sense of that word. But once again, it is far too strong to impose this as a necessary condition for communication involving the use of a 'testimony demonstrative', which can surely take place between a speaker and a hearer whose information derives from the same object via independent original observers.[36] Equally, when a speaker adverts to information he presumes to be in the audience's possession as a consequence of an earlier encounter with an object, what links the speaker's retained information with the hearer's retained information is generally nothing but the fact that they derive from the same object. For example, a speaker and a hearer may attend a party at which they circulate independently of one another. On the next day, the speaker may say 'Did you meet that Russian? He was extraordinarily drunk', and the hearer may understand him in virtue of retaining and invoking information acquired in quite separate episodes from those which gave rise to the speaker's information. This constitutes communication because, and only because, the same object was involved in both sets of episodes.

So the challenge, to those who wish to argue that information-invoking referential communication can take place in the absence of an object, is to state a communication-inducing relation between the origin of the speaker's information and the origin of the hearer's information which does not presuppose that the information originates in episodes involving the same object, but which, when the information *is* from an object, holds in just those cases when it is from the same object. I do not say that it cannot be done, but I myself do not see how to do it.[37]

---

[35] We can think of parallel apparently sufficient conditions in the case of demonstrative identification.

[36] [See n. 34.]

[37] It is fair to point out a limitation on the scope of this argument. There are many different ways in which a thought-episode can lack an object, and some of them may be relatively immune to the difficulty in the text. For example, I should argue that a subject's demonstrative thought which he would express with the words 'that woman' would be without an object if he had taken a patch of shadow for a woman. [See § 2 of the Appendix to chapter 6.] Here there *is* an object (the patch of shadow) which can provide a common point of focus for speaker and hearer even if both are deluded.

9.6 UNDERSTANDING WITHOUT AN OBJECT?

I have presented several arguments for the view that information-invoking uses of singular terms are Russellian. I have tried to show that nothing is said by the serious use of these terms when there is nothing to which they refer, by trying to show that nothing of the kind that normally counts as understanding such a use of these terms can take place when there is no referent. (These general arguments are intended to be reinforced, in certain cases, by the considerations of Part Two, which seemed to show, along different lines, that no coherent thought-content can be ascribed to a subject when he purports, but fails, to identify an object in one of the ways there discussed.)

I do not expect that opposition to my conclusion will be total. If we consider a subject who, hallucinating, points into empty space and says 'He's coming to get me', I expect everyone to agree that he has failed to *say* anything (for he has clearly failed to make manifest the sort of intentions he would need to have made manifest in order to have said something). Nor do I expect total opposition to the view that there was not anything that he *meant* to say. I expect people to agree, in other words, that this case is quite different from the case of someone who points into empty space because he is wearing inverting prisms. For it is extremely difficult to see what belief available to the hearer could count as knowledge of what the hallucinating subject even meant to say. And a similar difficulty attaches to any case in which the supposed information on which the speaker intends to rely simply does not exist: for example, when the speaker adverts to a past episode he takes himself to have experienced with the hearer, but which in fact took place in a dream; or when he adverts to information he presumes to be widely disseminated, but which in fact stems from a wholly imaginary conversation. I do not expect opposition in these cases, because it is a quite widely recognized fact that referential communication depends upon the hearer's possession of certain information; when the required information is, so to speak, simply not there to be possessed, communication will not only not take place, it will not even be possible.[38]

---

[38] I do not mean to deny that one can arrive at some kind of understanding of what is going on, if one realizes that the speaker is hallucinating and intends to be speaking of a man he sees. (One could even say: if there were a man he was seeing in having this

Opposition to my general claim will arise from the consideration of cases in which a background of shared information does
exist—the sort of case which I described in 9.5 as satisfying
apparently sufficient conditions for communication. Perhaps
speaker and hearer take the same stone object in the shadows to
be a woman, or perhaps they have both heard a story from the
same source. When there is this common information, or common misinformation, it seems very tempting to suppose that we
can draw just the same distinction between understanding and
misunderstanding as we do in the case where there is a referent.
We cannot say that the hearer who understands has got hold of
the right object; but he can, so to speak, attach the remark to *the
right information*.

But I have tried to weaken this temptation. I have tried to
explain why the information really cannot be described as the
right information (9.5). And even if we waive this point, I have
argued (9.4) that the distinction which we undeniably can draw
cannot be regarded as a distinction between those who understand and those who do not; for how can understanding a
remark require a false belief?

The argument will now shift to those who have the required
information (the shared perceptual illusion or whatever) but do
not take it at its face value (they know it is an illusion). I claimed
(9.4) that their disbelief debars them from making the link
which understanding requires. But however convincing the
theoretical argument on this point may have been, there certainly appears to be *something* that a disbelieving subject can do
to bring (what he takes to be) misinformation to bear upon the
interpretation of the remarks of (what he takes to be) a deluded
friend.

And indeed there is. For he can *pretend* that there is an object
from which he has information, and think accordingly. Seeming
to see a woman in the shadows, although he knows there is no
one there, he can pretend that he is seeing a woman, and
interpret his companion's remark ('That woman is beautiful')
within the scope of this pretence. Pretence of this kind—that

---

hallucination, then that man would be the referent of his utterance.) But this kind of
understanding does not count as *understanding the remark*: it is not the kind of
information-based response the speaker was intending to produce.

there are objects of which we have knowledge, when we know that there are not—comes so naturally to us, and can be engaged in so effortlessly when the informational props[39] are provided, that we frequently slip into it without realizing that that is what we have done. (Indeed almost all our representational art—whether in the form of plays, novels, films, or paintings—depends upon our capacity to engage in this form of pretence.)

Now, it seems to me that a proper appreciation of the nature and extent of linguistic pretence holds the key to an adequate theory of reference. For it, and it alone, enables us to hold on to the insight that singular terms are (generally speaking) Russellian, while taking a realistic and credible view of phenomena apparently inconsistent with that insight. I mean, in the first place, the phenomenon to which I have just alluded—that not all uses of empty singular terms need be utterly *opaque* to an undeluded and suitably informed observer. But, far more importantly, we can exploit this notion of pretence to give an account of the conniving[40] *use* of empty singular terms—the use of an empty singular term knowing it to be such. Even though such uses involve pretence, they can be made for a serious purpose, as notoriously they are in such remarks as '*a* does not exist'. It is to the understanding of these conniving uses of empty singular terms, and thus to the completion of our Russellian conception of reference, that the next chapter is devoted.

[39] That is, states of the informational system, e.g. perceptual states. (On the belief-independence of the informational system, see 5.2.)

[40] The term is Quine's: see *Word and Object*, p. 50.

Appendix

1 Section 9.3 was to be supplemented with an account of a distinction between two different ways in which information-invoking communication can take place, both involving the use of definite descriptions: *truth*-based communication and *information*-based communication (to give them labels). In the first, the speaker expects to achieve communication by saying 'The ϕ is F' (or 'That ϕ is F'), because he expects the audience to have information, concerning the object in question, that it is ϕ; he expects this because the object *is* ϕ, as the speaker knows, and the speaker takes it (as will often be reasonable) that the audience has, and has exercised in connection with the object, accurate and reliable methods of gathering information. In the second kind of case, the basis of the speaker's expectation that he will achieve communication is, again, that he expects the audience to have information, concerning the object in question, that it is ϕ; but his expectation is based not on the fact that the object is ϕ and has itself directly affected the audience's information-gathering capacities, but rather, on the fact that people who acquire information about the object from others, in the community in question, acquire the information that it is ϕ (the information is widely disseminated among those who have information about the object). In this case it is inessential to the speaker's putting the audience in mind of the right object that the information be true of the object—although if it is not true, the speaker's utterance will not be correct; and if he does not believe it to be true, he ought to register this by saying 'The person (object) supposed to be ϕ is F'.

2 It seems, from 1.9, that Evans planned a more elaborate discussion of the Fregean model of communication (according to which communication requires the speaker and hearer to associate the same thought with the words used) than the brief remarks in 9.2. It is well known that Frege himself placed the case of 'I' (and by implication 'you') in a special position.[1] In some lectures of his, Evans once drew a connection between the thought that we come close to the full Fregean model with 'here' and 'now', and the idea of dynamic Fregean

---

[1] See 'The Thought', at pp. 25–6 in Strawson, ed., *Philosophical Logic*. Strictly, what Frege does is to insist on a construal of the thought conveyed by uttering an 'I'-sentence that conforms to the model, at the price of opening a gap between what is expressed by the words and the fully self-conscious thought which the speaker can entertain.

thoughts (see the Appendix to chapter 6, § 1). As one moves about while keeping track of a place, one may need—in order to continue to express the same thought—to alter one's designation of the place from 'here' to 'there'; similarly, as time passes while one keeps track of a time, one needs—in order to express the same thought—to alter one's designation of the time from 'now' to 'a little while ago'; and so on. If a 'there'-sentence on my lips can express the same thought as a 'here'-sentence uttered before I moved, then the 'there'-sentence with which you might express the thought you associate with a 'here'-sentence of mine that you hear and understand can express the same thought likewise, perhaps; and if so, communication can be conceived on the Fregean model.

Chapter 10

Existential Statements

In chapter 9, I argued for the thesis that nothing is said by someone who makes a normal, information-invoking use of a singular term that has no referent. Anyone who presents such a thesis must come to terms with the fact that there are apparently intelligible uses of such terms, made in the full knowledge that they have no referent. Such utterances are intelligible only because they can be interpreted in such a way that there is the possibility that they are *true* when the term has no referent.

Utterances of this kind fall into two sorts. Most notorious are *negative existential statements*, in which empty singular terms are apparently used to register the fact that they are empty. Secondly, there are cases in which empty singular terms are knowingly used, not in the first instance to state how things stand in the world, but to convey the content of some *representation* of the world. Stated generally, this no doubt sounds mysterious, but we are all familiar with remarks such as 'David Copperfield was born in penury', which concern what is said or implied in a story, and similarly, empty singular terms are used to convey the content of a painting, an illusion, a film, or a myth.

These two uses cannot be given exactly the same treatment, for if we interpret the existential statements as conveying the content of a representation, then 'David Copperfield exists' should be true, not false. Nevertheless, I believe that they are very closely connected, and that one can understand the existential statements only as a further elaboration of the 'language-game' in which singular terms are used to convey the content of a representation. (See 10.4 below.)

The challenge presented by these cases to the thesis that *normal* information-invoking uses of singular terms are Russellian is not direct, for it is clear that such cases are abnormal. At least in the case of statements that convey the content of a representation, there is the sharpest possible proof of this, since, on anyone's view, it is not possible for a normal statement-making use of an atomic sentence, '*t* is *F*', to be *true* unless '$(\exists x)(x=t)$' is true. There is a challenge, nevertheless. For we must explain how communication and understanding can take place in the absence of an object when the use of the term is conniving, if it cannot take place when the use is normal.

I take it to be obvious that in these cases the singular term is *used* (albeit connivingly) and is not merely mentioned. That is to say that no less of a gap exists in these cases, between grasping any proposition *about the term* (as uttered on that occasion) and grasping what is said, than in the case of a normal use of a singular term. This means that we cannot contemplate the kind of *metalinguistic* analyses of singular existential statements which have been so popular among those who subscribe to the Russellian status of singular terms.[1] No one would be attracted by a metalinguistic analysis of the conniving use of empty singular terms to convey the content of representations, but such analyses of singular existential statements seem to fall equally dramatically short of the mark. If a speaker says something like 'That woman does not (really) exist', in the context of a shared perceptual illusion, a remembered film, or a story, he surely cannot simply be represented as saying something like 'This use of the demonstrative "That woman" does not refer'; no one who merely grasped *that* could be said to have understood what the speaker said. Understanding these uses of singular terms requires from the hearer something *of the same general kind* as is required to understand ordinary information-invoking uses of singular terms: the hearer must possess some information or misinformation, and somehow bring it to bear upon his interpretation of the remark. How this is so much as possible is, as I said earlier, precisely the challenge presented to those who subscribe to the Russellian status of such singular terms as normally used, but no service is done to that position by turning away at the first hurdle.

So, one constraint upon our analysis of a negative existential statement involving a conniving, but apparently informa-

---

[1] See, for example, Donnellan, 'Speaking of Nothing', in which 'α does not exist' is analysed as 'The historical chain underlying the name "α" ends in a block'.

tion-invoking, use of a singular term is that it should not be metalinguistic. Some other constraints upon the analysis can be derived from consideration of the way the word 'exists' is used.

There seems to be very strong evidence that the English word 'exists' is used, at least on some occasions, to signify a first-level concept, true of everything. Coupling this concept-expression (which I shall represent as '$E(\xi)$') with a singular term denoting any object in a simple function and argument construction yields a truth.

The evidence for the use of 'exists' as a predicate is *not* provided by singular negative existential statements, of the kind we are considering, because the recognition of 'exists' as a first-level concept-expression does not help us to understand those statements. It is true that when we have a non-Russellian singular term, like 'Julius' (1.7, 1.8, 2.3), the statement 'Julius does not exist' can be regarded as having the form

$$\neg\,[a]E(a),$$

involving a wide-scope negation. But a wide-scope negation cannot be regarded as building a truth out of something which fails to express a proposition at all, so we cannot suggest that 'That woman does not exist' be analysed as

$$\neg\,[\text{That woman}]\,E(\text{That woman}).$$

(This is just to repeat the problem provided for us by negative existential statements.)

Nevertheless, there are other sentences involving the expression 'exists' which seem to force us to recognize that it functions as a first-level concept-expression.

Moore first drew attention to the need to give an analysis of such modal sentences as 'This might not have existed',[2] which is naturally construed as

$$\Diamond\,\neg\,E(\text{this}),$$

that is, as making a statement which is true if and only if there is a possible world with respect to which the embedded sentence, '$\neg\,E(\text{this})$', is true—if and only if there is a possible world in

---

[2] 'Is Existence a Predicate?', *Aristotelian Society Supplementary Volume* xv (1936), 175–88, at p. 186.

which the object referred to by 'this' does not exist.[3] J. L. Mackie[4] noticed another kind of sentence best construed as involving an operator upon the basic existential statement 'E(this)', namely sentences like 'John does not know that this beach exists', which is naturally interpreted as having the form

$$\neg \, K_j \, (\, E(\text{this beach})).$$

As a final example of the same kind, there are many tensed statements of existence, such as 'Once upon a time, this did not exist', which are best analysed as involving a past-tense operator, **P**, applied to the negation of the basic existential statement 'E(this)', thus:

$$P(\neg \, E(\text{this})).$$

(Construing the statement in this way does not involve the idea that 'E' is a 'change-predicate', like 'is red', which an object can satisfy at some times in its life and not others.[5] Obviously, an object satisfies 'E' as long as it exists. Nevertheless, a tense logic will assign to the 'E'-predicate a different set of objects at different times—precisely the objects which exist at those times—and this is all that is necessary for 'E' to enter into statements which admit of significant tensing.)[6]

Quantified existential statements, like 'Some tame tigers exist', 'No tame tigers exist', etc., also provide strong evidence that 'exists' is used as a first-level concept-expression true of everything; for if we assume that it is, and mechanically apply to the sentences exactly the same treatment as is applied to any other quantified sentence involving a concept-expression, we get exactly the right truth-conditions. Thus, just as we analyse

---

[3] A modal logic adequate to formulate these claims must be a Free Logic, employing *some* restriction upon the rule of Existential Generalization. Otherwise we should have

$$\vdash A(t) \rightarrow \exists x A(x),$$

which by necessitation yields

$$\vdash \Box \, (A(t) \rightarrow \exists x A(x)).$$

Given '$\Diamond \, \neg \, E(t)$' and the principle '$\Box \, (P \rightarrow Q)$, $\Diamond \, P \vdash \Diamond \, Q$', we could then derive '$\Diamond \, (\exists x) \neg \, E(x)$', which is false.

[4] 'The Riddle of Existence', *Aristotelian Society Supplementary Volume* l (1976), 247–67, at p. 249.

[5] This is intended to deal with Dummett's objection, at *Frege*, pp. 386–7.

[6] The case of tensing requires a restriction upon Existential Generalization similar to that required in the modal case (see n. 3 above).

'Some tame tigers are brown' and 'No tame tigers are brown' as

$$\text{Some } x \text{ [Tame tiger}(x); \text{ Brown}(x)]$$

and

$$\text{No } x \text{ [Tame tiger}(x); \text{ Brown}(x)]$$

respectively,[7] so we analyse the two existential statements as

$$\text{Some } x \text{ [Tame tiger}(x); \text{ E}(x)]$$

and

$$\text{No } x \text{ [Tame tiger}(x); \text{ E}(x)],$$

and a quick calculation will show that these sentences have exactly the intended truth-conditions. If we extend the treatment to existential sentences involving the quantifier 'the', we provide a natural rendering of the sentences 'The smallest prime exists' and 'The largest prime does not exist', namely

$$\text{The } x \text{ [Smallest prime}(x); \text{ E}(x)]$$

and

$$\neg \text{ The } x \text{ [Largest prime}(x); \text{ E}(x)].[8]$$

The scope ambiguity of the second sentence is difficult to perceive, because a reading on which the negation sign has narrow scope is obviously unintended. But the sentence 'The first man in space might not have existed' is easily heard as ambiguous, and it is a desirable consequence of recognizing the 'E'-predicate that we can give the same explanation for this ambiguity as we can for the ambiguity of 'The first man in space might not have been a Russian', namely that the sentence can have either of these forms:

$$\text{The } x \text{ [First man in space}(x); \diamondsuit \neg \text{ E}(x)]$$

and

$$\diamondsuit \neg \text{ The } x \text{ [First man in space}(x); \text{ E}(x)].[9]$$

---

[7] See 2.4 for these binary quantifiers.

[8] 'The $x[\ldots x \ldots]$' is the 'I' quantifier of 2.4.

[9] I owe this point to Saul Kripke's unpublished John Locke Lectures, given in Oxford in 1973. (In general those lectures did much to develop my own understanding of the problem of singular negative existential statements.)

There is absolutely no objection to recognizing the existence of a concept-expression true of everything. Philosophical perplexity arises when an attempt is made to think of such a concept-expression as being just like other concept-expressions. We might then think we know its *Meaning* (a function which maps every object on to the True), but have no notion what its *sense* is. We search for some filling for the dots in the formula

$$(x)(x \text{ satisfies 'E' iff} \ldots x \ldots),$$

and we have no idea of what it could be. But this is to misunderstand the kind of sense which 'E' has. Its sense is precisely fixed by saying that it is true of everything. Thus its sense is *shown* by the formula

$$(x)(x \text{ satisfies 'E'}).$$

We might say that this makes 'E' a formal, or logical, predicate.[10]

An analogy may make this clearer. There are various logical systems which have a constant symbol denoting the False; with such a symbol, e.g. †, we can define the negation of a proposition P as $P \rightarrow \dagger$. Now there is no objection to recognizing such a symbol (a sentence which is false no matter what; or equally a sentence which is true no matter what). But we would be obviously muddled if, wondering what its sense could be, we expected a sense for it of the kind possessed by ordinary sentences. We should not expect a clause of the form

$$\dagger \text{ is true iff} \ldots,$$

but simply one of the form

$$\dagger \text{ is false.}$$

It may be a good idea to say a word at this point about a solution to the conundrum of negative existential statements

---

[10] This may make it easier to accept the very close relation which exists between 'E' and the quantifiers. (Cf. Dummett, *Frege*, p. 386: '... what difference of sense could be greater than one involving a difference of logical type, that between a quantifier and a first-level predicate?') I would suggest a similar way of looking at the identity predicate: we are not to look for some filling in the formula

$$(x)(y)(\langle x,y \rangle \text{ satisfies '='} \text{ iff} \ldots x,y \ldots),$$

but simply to regard its sense as given by the stipulation

$$(x)(\langle x,x \rangle \text{ satisfies '='}).$$

containing Russellian singular terms which recently has been proposed (rather tentatively) by Saul Kripke.[11]

Kripke emphasizes the requirement that (in the cases we are interested in) singular terms must be seen as *used*, in both negative and affirmative existential statements. As I have said, I think this is absolutely correct; indeed, it is partly constitutive of the problem.

Kripke suggests that, although the sentence '*Fa*' fails to express any proposition if the singular term is empty, one may nevertheless form an intelligible description, 'a proposition which says of *a* that it is *F*', *using* the singular term '*a*' in what Kripke calls 'a special sort of quasi-intentional use'. Using this description, we can form the intelligible proposition 'There is a proposition which says of *a* that it is *F*, and that proposition is true'; this proposition is false, since there is no proposition conforming to the embedded description.

This apparatus is applied by Kripke to existential statements in two slightly different versions (differing in the analysis of the affirmative statement '*a* exists'). According to the first version, someone who says '*a* exists', where '*a*' is empty, purports to put forward a proposition of the form '$E(a)$', and so says nothing. Now the sentence formed by applying the ordinary negation operator to his words would itself not be available for saying anything; but we can understand a different negation operator, which, when applied to a sentence '*Fa*', yields a sentence which is true if and only if there is no true proposition which says of *a* that it is *F*. And the negative existential statement uses this different negation operator. According to the second version, someone who says '*a* exists', where '*a*' is empty, does not purport to put forward a proposition of the form '$E(a)$', but puts forward the intelligible, and false, proposition 'There is a true proposition which says of *a* that it exists'; and the negative existential statement is the negation of this.

Now, we are told that there is a special use of a singular term (a 'quasi-intentional' use) available to those who believe the term is empty. But we are not told what this use amounts to. We are not told how—given that there cannot in general be an intelligible description, 'standing in such and such a relation to *a*', in which the name is used—there can nevertheless be an

[11] In his John Locke Lectures.

intelligible description, 'saying of *a* that it is *F*', in which the name is used. And since we are given no account of this use, it remains intensely problematic how it can be that, although there is no proposition expressed by '*Fa*', there can nevertheless be a proposition expressed by 'There is a proposition which says of *a* that it is *F*'. If the significance of '*a*' is contaminated by its having no referent, why is the significance of 'proposition which says of *a* that . . .' not equally subject to doubt?

There are two incompatible replies which might be made to this.

First, it might be said that I have misunderstood Kripke. His idea (according to this objection) is that the description 'proposition about *a*' is just as unintelligible as '*Fa*', if '*a*' is empty. All that matters is that there should be, in English, a negation sign yielding a true sentence when applied to a sentence which does not express a proposition: then the logical form of '*a* does not exist' can be 'N(E(*a*))', where 'N' represents this negation sign.

However, this interpretation of Kripke's solution is incompatible with Kripke's insistence that the singular term must be seen to be *used*. If it is being used, then we are entitled to ask for an account of what is required for understanding it. If the form 'N(E(*a*))' is to be distinguished from 'The sentence "E(*a*)" expresses no true proposition'—which is an inadequate analysis of the negative existential statement, because it is metalinguistic—then it must be possible to explain exactly how the singular term '*a*' is used in the context 'N . . .'.

The second reply is to claim that it is one thing to say that '*Fa*' expresses no proposition if '*a*' is empty (as Kripke does), but quite another thing to say that it is unintelligible. Suppose, for example, that '*a*' has its referent fixed by the description 'the ϕ', which is, as it happens, empty. In that case '*Fa*' would (so the objection goes) express no proposition; but it would be intelligible because it would be clear under what circumstances it *would* express a proposition.[12] Hence the description 'a proposition which says of *a* that it is *F*' would be a perfectly intelligible description, which, however, applies to no proposition, since there is no such item as the ϕ.

[12] This reply involves taking a Russellian line about names like 'Julius' (1.7, 1.8, 2.3). Kripke does indeed take such a line.

I have two objections to this reply. First, the reply attempts to distinguish what proposition a sentence can be used to express from a condition which must obtain if the sentence is to be capable of being used to express a proposition at all. But why is one not permitted to include the condition simply as part of the proposition which the sentence can be used to express? Suppose it is said that a sentence *S*, of the kind in question, expresses a proposition only if *A* obtains, and that if both *A* and *B* obtain, then *S* expresses a true proposition. Why are we not permitted to say instead that *S* expresses the proposition that *A* and *B* obtain? (This is surely what would be grasped by someone who heard and understood an utterance of *S*.)[13] Second, the reply appears to work only for names which are associated with descriptions; indeed that is its point.[14] But the puzzle about negative existential statements applies to singular terms of sorts which are associated with quite different modes of identification.

Kripke's attempted solution to our problem aims to respect not only our first constraint, that the singular terms should be seen to be used and not mentioned, but also a second, which emerges from our reflections on the use of 'exists': given the evidence in favour of recognizing that 'exists' is used as a first-level concept-expression, it seems reasonable to require that an adequate solution to the problem of singular negative existential statements represent such statements as involving that concept-expression. Now a plausible third constraint emerges when we raise the question how exactly that concept-expression is involved.

We know that a statement of the problematic kind cannot be regarded as the negation of a simple existential statement, say 'E(that woman)'; for where 'that woman' has no referent, there is no such statement to negate. And there is another reason for not regarding the problematic statements in this way, which applies even in a case where the first reason does not.

---

[13] See Dummett, *Truth and Other Enigmas*, pp. xiv ff. (But note that Dummett thinks these considerations constitute an argument against the very possibility of a sentence's being correctly said to express no proposition on the ground that it contains an empty singular term; whereas the argument in the text is restricted to singular terms whose reference is fixed by descriptions.)

[14] 'Appears' only; it does not work if it is correct to resist a Russellian view about such names.

Consider a case in which a speaker *wrongly* supposes that his information is deceptive, so that, for example, although he takes himself to be under a perceptual illusion, there really is a little green man (namely *x*) sitting on a wall in front of him. The speaker utters the sentence 'That little green man does not exist', intending to alert his companion to the trick of the light. Even though the use of the term is conniving, I think we must accept that he refers to *x*. But should we regard this speaker as having denied the very statement someone might make by referring to *x* in a perfectly ordinary way, and saying of him that he exists? (I have been calling this 'the basic existential statement'.) Does this speaker deny the very same statement which we declare might have been false (would have been false, had *x*'s parents never met)? The question is a delicate one, but I think the answer to it should be 'No'. One indication that the speaker's statement is not just the denial of a basic existential statement is the very close connection his statement has with such statements as 'That little green man does not *really* exist', 'That little green man is not *real*', and then 'That little green man is a trick of the light', etc. Now, the concept 'is real' is very different from the concept 'exists'. When we say that, if *x*'s parents had never met, he would not have existed, we are not saying that if his parents had never met, he would not have been *real*.[15] So far, this is only a hint, and an obscure one at that, since the concept 'real' is a tremendously complicated one. But I think it does suggest that we should look for an account of singular negative existential statements which employs not only the concept 'exists', but also the concept 'real'.[16]

---

[15] Equally, when we say 'John does not know that this beach exists', we do not intend to assert that what John does not know is that this beach really exists, or is real. And so on.

[16] If this is correct, the standard situation (when there is an object) provides the opportunity for a subject to make *two* positive existential statements: one is a basic existential statement, and the other is the statement which the negative existential statement negates. (See 10.4.)

It needs to be stressed that the content of 'That little green man does not exist' cannot be represented descriptively. 'There is no little green man there' does not capture the force of '*That* little green man does not exist'. And a specification of the content does not involve *reference* to the information ('The little green man of whom *this* purports to be information ...'); although someone who has understood and accepted the statement will know not to trust the information.

10.2 GAMES OF MAKE-BELIEVE

The fundamental idea is to regard utterances containing empty singular terms used connivingly as moves in a linguistic game of *make-believe*. We make believe that there is an object of such-and-such a kind, from which we have received, or are receiving, information, and we act within the scope of that pretence. It is fairly easy to see that a story-teller is pretending to have knowledge of things and episodes. But we must recognize that audiences of novels, plays, films, etc. are also drawn into a pretence. This, it seems to me, is the only way in which we can make sense of the thoughts and emotions which constitute their aesthetic response.[17] More importantly for our purpose, it is the only way in which we can make sense of their discourse 'about the characters in the novel' (or 'film', 'painting', 'play', etc.). And just as a deliberate initial pretence on the part of a story-teller or film-maker can provide people with the informational props which encourage them to continue the make-believe, so those props can be provided by shared illusions (current or remembered), or mistaken testimony, not originally the product of any artistic or imaginative process.

In order to develop this idea, we must become clearer about the general structure of a game of make-believe.

I shall take as my starting-point a very useful analysis of games of make-believe provided by Kendall L. Walton.[18] Walton regards make-believe truths—truths created by a game of make-believe—as a species of the genus of fictional truths. According to Walton, what is distinctive about make-believe truth is that it rests upon a foundation of actual fact, other than someone's having expressly imagined or stipulated that it is to be so. Thus it is a characteristic of games of make-believe that one can discover such-and-such to be make-believedly the case.

Walton's main example of a game of make-believe is that of a children's mud pie game. This is a game in which children pretend that globs of mud of a certain shape and size are pies. Within the scope of this initial pretence, they make-believedly make and cut pies, give pies to one another, take pies from one

---

[17] This point has been developed well by Kendall L. Walton in a series of papers: see especially 'Pictures and Make-Believe', *Philosophical Review* lxxxii (1973), 283-319, and 'Fearing Fictions', *Journal of Philosophy* lxxv (1978), 5-27.

[18] In 'Pictures and Make-Believe'.

another, and so on. In discussing games of make-believe, I shall follow Walton, and write 'It is make-believedly the case that P' as '$*P*$'.[19] The expression '$*(\ )*$' is therefore a sentential operator in the language we have for talking about the game. This language will not itself involve any pretence, so that the sentences upon which '$*(\ )*$' operates must be perfectly literal, and intelligible, sentences of English.[20]

Any game of make-believe can be thought of as governed by principles of three different kinds.[21] The basic principles stipulate outright a (possibly infinite) set of make-believe truths. In the mud pie game, the basic principles are something like

(x)(Glob of mud(x) & Fashioned into pie-
  shape$(x) \rightarrow *$Pie$(x)*$);
(x)(Small black pebble$(x) \rightarrow *$Raisin$(x)*$);
$*$This metal object is a hot oven$*$.

Secondly, there is a general *incorporation principle*, which permits the incorporation into the game of any truth not ruled out by the initial pretence.[22] Using counterfactuals, we might formulate this as:

If B is true, and there is no set $A_1 \ldots A_n$ of make-believe truths such that the counterfactual 'If $A_1 \ldots A_n$ were true, B would not be true' is true, then B is make-believedly true.[23]

Finally, there is a *recursive principle*, which we might formulate in similar terms:

If $A_1 \ldots A_n$ is a set of make-believe truths, and the counterfactual 'If $A_1 \ldots A_n$ were true, then B would be true' is true, and there is no set of make-believe truths $A'_1 \ldots A'_n$ such that the counterfactual 'If $A'_1 \ldots A'_n$ were true, then B would not be true' is true, then B is make-believedly true.

[19] I shall omit Walton's qualification 'MB' (Walton uses the asterisk notation for fictional truths generally), because all the fictional truths I shall discuss are make-believe truths.

[20] There will in fact be certain things about some games which we cannot report without playing them: see 10.2, end.

[21] Here I go beyond Walton.

[22] The existence of an incorporation principle means that we must not think of '$*P*$' as entailing, or even rendering probable, '$\neg P$'.

[23] Perhaps it should be required that the counterfactuals be *believed* true by participants. (Similarly in the recursive principle, below.)

These principles allow for the discovery, for example, that *the pies are burnt*. By the incorporation principle we may have it that *Harry placed these objects in this metal object twenty minutes ago*, by the basic principles we may know that *these objects are pies* and *this metal object is a hot oven*; in that case we can establish, by the recursive principle, that *these pies are burnt*, since if these objects had been pies and this object had been a hot oven and these objects had been in this object for twenty minutes, these objects would be burnt pies.[24]

By formulating the rules of the game of make-believe explicitly in terms of counterfactuals, I do not intend to suggest that the capacity to understand the counterfactual idiom is a more primitive capacity than the capacity to engage in games of make-believe. In fact I think that they are the *same* capacity. (Using counterfactuals is engaging in a purely cognitive pretence; though it might sometimes be better to speak of cognitive acts within the scope of a supposition rather than a pretence.)[25] This is obviously not the place to attempt the analysis of this capacity. However, I should say that it is important for my purposes that counterfactuals such as the one I formulated at the end of the last paragraph can be *true*, and this probably means a rejection of the popular 'possible-worlds' analysis of counterfactuals.[26] For almost all of these counterfactuals have *impossible* antecedents; there simply are no possible worlds in which these mud pats are pies. Equally, and more relevantly to our proper concerns, there is no possible world in which the illusory information which we receive is not illusory. The initial supposition generating the game of make-believe within which we make conniving use of empty singular terms is that certain information, which is in fact deceptive, is information from actual objects and events. And I would argue that there are no possible worlds in which just that information is veridical; as we observed in 5.2, information is individuated by causal origin,

---

[24] The principles governing fictional truth are more complex than this, and there are different approaches which might be taken. See David K. Lewis, 'Truth in Fiction', *American Philosophical Quarterly* xv (1978), 37–46, for some of the details.

[25] See, e.g., J. L. Mackie, *Truth, Probability, and Paradox* (Clarendon Press, Oxford, 1973), ch. 3 (especially section 9).

[26] See, e.g., David K. Lewis, *Counterfactuals* (Blackwell, Oxford, 1973).

which makes it impossible to understand how the same bit of information might have had a different origin.[27]

The principles I have laid down generate an extensive network of make-believe truths. However, some additional principles are probably required to capture the structure of the game as it is played by children. We cannot yet provide for *eating a pie*, save by actually swallowing a bit of mud, so that it must be separately laid down that a series of hand-to-mouth gestures constitutes *eating a pie*. More importantly, the children are themselves crucial participants in the game, and their world of make-believe will not be coherent unless some provision is made for the ascription of propositional attitudes to them within the game. For example, many of the make-believe actions which the children perform are, make-believedly, actions which can be performed only by someone who has appropriate beliefs and intentions. For instance, if we are to provide for *stealing a pie from Mary*, we must provide for '*He knew it wasn't his*' and '*He meant to take it*'. And these are not provided for at present.

(If they were already provided for, this could be only via the incorporation principle or the recursive principle. The *incorporation* principle would serve only if the children had non-make-believe beliefs and intentions concerning pies and the like, which they presumably do not. The *recursive* principle would provide for these attitudes only if the children were such that, were the initial pretence about mud pies and ovens true, they would have beliefs and intentions about pies and the like; this might be the case in this example, but the analogue will not hold generally. One can see this by shifting to an example in which the initial pretence might actually be discovered to be true. Thus, suppose a person, John, is in the audience at a play of a kind in which the audience is very explicitly brought into the world of make-believe created by the actors on the stage—the audience is, perhaps, make-believedly a crowd of people in a revolutionary epoch, alternately harangued, threatened, and courted by various actors, some of whom are actually positioned in the gallery. Suppose the man next to John gets up and starts brandishing a pistol. We want to be able to attribute to John the make-believe

[27] Lewis half-perceives this as a problem for his possible-worlds analysis of truth in fiction: see 'Truth in Fiction', p. 40.

belief that the man next to him is threatening him with his life; it is to this make-believe belief that certain make-believe emotions such as fear and the like can naturally be traced. But John, being a relatively sophisticated theatre-goer, does not really believe that the man next to him is threatening him with his life. And this remains true of him even if this part of his pretence turns out to be true—so that there is in fact a member of the audience, quite unconnected with the play, standing next to John, brandishing a pistol in his direction. So evidently the counterfactual 'Were the man next to him really to be a political activist brandishing a pistol, he would believe that there was someone threatening his life' is not true, and no other counterfactual with a more extensive collection of make-believe truths as antecedent and the same consequent is going to be true either.)

Two natural principles which seem to provide the required make-believe propositional attitudes are

$$(x)(\text{If } x \text{ believes that } *P* \text{ then } *x \text{ believes that } P*)$$

and

$$(x)(\text{If } x \text{ intends that } *P* \text{ then } *x \text{ intends that } P*).$$

Other propositional attitudes cannot be introduced in this way; although it is certainly the case that certain films bring it about that the film-goer *fears that he will be attacked*, this is not because of a real fear that *he will be attacked*, for such a fear is not one that we can attribute to him. I think these additional attitudes and emotions can be dealt with by the recursive principle, but this is not a point immediately germane to our present concern.[28]

Once we have introduced these propositional attitudes within the game, we can also introduce linguistic actions. A subject can utter a sentence *intending to get his audience to realize that his utterance is true if and only if P*. This will be because he *really* intends that *his audience realize that his utterance is true if and only if P*. And this state of affairs which he aims to produce is the audience *really* realizing (believing) that *his utterance is true if and only if P*, i.e. realizing that *his utterance is true* if and only if *P*.[29]

---

[28] For more on this subject, see Walton, 'Fearing Fictions'.

[29] Notice that I am here making a sharp distinction between the *belief*, which is a real belief (about the game), and the *saying*, which is not genuine.

I think Walton makes a mistake here, for he introduces the make-believe truth '*S says that P*' by the rule

If S says that *P* then *S says that P*.

But this is to miss an important distinction. When, in the course of the game, I make pretended assertions, I am not to be taken to be making real assertions about the game. My utterances are not up for assessment as really true or false (not even as really true or false in virtue of certain facts about the game); they are only up for assessment within the game. We do not want to end up with

S's utterance is true if and only if *P*,

but only with

S's utterance is true if and only if *P*.

The fact that an utterance is determined as *true* by facts about the game does not mean that it is a real assertion about the game. Of course, in a very natural exploitation of the game, we shall make utterances within it which are understood as being up for evaluation as true rather than *true*, and hence understood as *real* assertions about the game. But this is a development of the game, not something which is necessarily present at the beginning.

The mud pie game differs radically from the kind of game which interests us, in that it is an *existentially conservative* game. That is to say, whenever we have

$$*(\exists x)(A(x))*,$$

we also have

$$(\exists x)*A(x)*$$

—that is, a true sentence can be constructed of the form '*A(b)*', where 'b' is a perfectly ordinary referring expression, referring (say) to a glob of mud, or an old tin can. The kind of pretence which is involved in the conniving use of empty singular terms is *existentially creative*; the pretence is not that something which there is is other than it is, but that there is something which in fact there isn't.

An example of an existentially creative game of make-believe is shadow-boxing, in which a boxer pretends that there is an opponent he is fighting. Two boys may play a similar game in pretending that they are being attacked by an Indian. But these games are still rather different from those we are interested in. We are interested in those that are existentially creative in virtue of an initial pretence that things are as they *seem*—that things are as the information we share presents them as being.[30] Playing, at least cognitively, within the scope of this kind of pretence is generally very much easier and more natural than playing within the scope of the shadow-boxing kind of pretence, because one can let the automatic and habitual responses of one's cognitive system take over and produce the make-believe thoughts, emotions, and reactions which playing the game normally requires. One can throw oneself into the pretence by suppressing the impact of disbelief. Here we should remember the rich and complex backdrop of information provided for us by so much of our art and entertainment, and the way in which this engages us effortlessly in a world of make-believe. Perhaps one thinks first, in this connection, of film and theatre; but a skilfully told story can provide a backdrop of equal richness and complexity, which can capture our thoughts and emotions to the same extent, if not in exactly the same way, as a play or a film. (This is an important point; for it is one of the first to which I would turn if I were called upon to defend the view, assumed throughout this book without argument, that information from the testimony of others is properly so called, and genuinely belongs with the other elements of our belief-independent informational system: see 5.2.)[31]

I do not want to exaggerate the importance of a rich informational backdrop, since in some cases in which we are encouraged by a speaker to engage in make-believe (by his knowingly using an empty singular term, for example), the informational props are pretty exiguous—perhaps nothing more than a brief but vainglorious account by an unreliable mutual colleague of

[30] All such games, of course, exploit the fundamental characteristic of the informational system, that informational states are belief-independent.

[31] A story-teller pretends to tell (inform) us about things. He pretends to be informed about these things. (That is, he pretends to be informationally related in some way or other to the events he relates; although the precise relation need not enter into the pretence.) We, hearing him, are prone to carry on the pretence (see, further, 10.3): we pretend to have been told of these things (to know them by testimony).

a heroic and unlikely episode. (When the informational back-drop is as bare as this, we would not expect a very interesting game of make-believe.) Nevertheless, to make the points that follow more vivid, I shall illustrate them by considering a case in which the shared informational background is a common perceptual illusion. Two men, let us suppose, both seem to see a little green man on a wall, and are persuaded, with reason, that there is no such thing; they are, they think, victims of a trick, perhaps involving the use of holograms. There will be two different ways of telling the story; one in which they are right in thinking this, and one in which they are wrong. For the time being, let us suppose they are right. This shared perceptual information provides an ideal backdrop for an existentially creative game of make-believe. The basic stipulation—that things are as they seem—immediately generates a whole mass of make-believe truths (e.g. that *the little man on the wall has a beard*, etc.).

An existentially creative game of make-believe can give rise to the possibility of someone make-believedly thinking of, or referring to, something without actually thinking of, or referring to, anything. This is in sharp contrast to the mud pie game, in which all referential thoughts and linguistic actions within the game involve reference to things existing outside it. '*The speaker is referring to a pie*', '*The audience is thinking of a pie*', and '*The audience is thinking of the same pie as the speaker is referring to*' all come in by the use of the incorpor-ation principle: the speaker is actually referring to a piece of mud, and it is the same piece of mud as the audience is thinking of.

In the existentially creative game in which two boys pretend they are being attacked by an Indian, it may be true, without the speaker's actually referring to anything, that *the speaker refers to an Indian*. (Suppose one of the boys says 'He's gone'.) Make-believe communication can take place because *the audience knows which person the speaker is referring to*. But in this case, this is because *the audience knows that the speaker is referring to *the Indian attacking them**. In other words, what makes make-believe communication possible in this case is the fact that it is part of the initial pretence that just one Indian is attacking them. So their thoughts can focus on the same (empty) place *in virtue of containing the same description.* Referential communication within games of this kind must always depend upon a common description; consequently it would become very much more difficult if the pretence were to include several different Indians.

But make-believe games which take place against a backdrop of shared information permit the make-believe occurrence of the kind of referential communication which is secured by the normal information-invoking use of singular terms.

In the first place, the possibility is open of *a subject's thinking of something* without *his thinking of something by description*. For example, in the game surrounding the illusion of the little green man, there is the possibility that *a subject demonstratively identifies a little green man*, not as something which has to be stipulated in the basic principles, but as something brought in under the recursive principle. It may be, for example, that *the subject thinks, of a little green man, that he has a sad face*. The subject, acting under the stimulus of the information received, can allow his thinking to be controlled by that information—accepting certain thoughts and rejecting others according to the content of the information—in just the way he would if he did not mistrust the information. Of course, these thoughts occur within the scope of the pretence, and are no more expressive of the subject's real beliefs than the remarks they might prompt are, though they will often be expressive of real beliefs about what is make-believedly the case. Nevertheless, it is clearly possible for the subject to suppress the impact of his disbelief upon his thinking, in the same way as he can suppress its impact upon his speaking, and to incorporate into his thinking the information he receives as if from a little green man.[32]

This is why I say that make-believe demonstrative identification can be brought into the game via the recursive principle. For it seems to me that the counterfactual conditional 'Were the perceptual information to be really from a little green man, the

---

[32] It is not possible to make sense of any activity of thinking, and certainly not of thinking controlled by information, which does not take place in a situation in which what is true can be distinguished from what is false. But here the division is made by reference to the *content* of the information. (This is why thinking within the scope of the pretence requires the subject to take the information at face value, and why I say that the judgements made within the scope of the pretence are expressive of belief about what is make-believedly the case.)

subject would have demonstratively identified him, and would be thinking of him' can be true. In order to see this, let us switch to the other version of the story, in which the subject and his companion are *mistaken* in believing that their senses deceive them—there *is* a little green man on the wall. It seems clear that a subject in this situation, thinking within the scope of the pretence in the way I have outlined, would actually be thinking of that little green man—entertaining various thoughts concerning him.[33] In allowing his thoughts to be controlled by the information, he is in fact responding to the properties of the little green man. (I call this phenomenon 'the game-to-reality shift'.)

Secondly, the fact that *the speaker and the audience are thinking of the same object* (and hence, ultimately, the fact that *the speaker communicates referentially with the audience*) is a derived make-believe truth which does not depend upon their thoughts involving a common description. For without that being the case, their thoughts can be such that, were the pretence actual, they would be thinking of the same object. This will be the case provided that the information incorporated in their thoughts has a common origin, so that the hypothesis that the information of the speaker is veridical entails the hypothesis that the information of the audience is veridical, and that it concerns the same object. (This condition is satisfied in those cases we described, in 9.5, as satisfying 'apparently sufficient conditions' for communication; for example, when speaker and audience derive their information from the same story-teller, or the same film, or when they radically misperceive the same object. These merely apparent sufficient conditions for genuine referential communication are genuinely sufficient—and necessary—conditions for make-believe referential communication, at least within the game of make-believe resting upon a shared informational backdrop.)

Let us take stock. We have outlined the structure of a game of make-believe in which use may be made of empty singular terms in make-believedly referring to things. Something is pro-

---

[33] Notice that this requires that in doing something (*A*) within the scope of a pretence one can be actually doing *A*. (One might mistake a baby for a doll: then in stroking a baby within the scope of a pretence, one would be actually stroking a baby.) This is why '*φ*-ing within the scope of a pretence' is a better phrase for our purposes than 'pretending to *φ*' (which more strongly suggests that one is not *φ*-ing).

vided that counts as make-believedly understanding such reference, and this requires, as its basis in actual fact, that a hearer
possess, and call upon, certain information. An audience's
make-believedly understanding such a reference (I shall here-
after call it 'quasi-understanding') requires him to have certain
thoughts which he can have only by suppressing the impact of
his disbelief and engaging in the pretence. For instance, he must
think 'He means that little green man over there—the one with
a beard'; and this only makes sense as a move within a pretence.

Notice that we have, in this kind of case, *thoughts about an
object* which we can report only by engaging in the game
ourselves. In the case of the boys and the Indian, we can say,
for example, that a boy *believes that the Indian who was
attacking them has gone*, without ourselves engaging in the
pretence. But the *demonstrative thoughts about that little
man* can be attributed to their subjects only if in doing so we
ourselves engage in the pretence. Not every make-believe truth
can be expressed without engaging in the relevant pretence
oneself.

So far, none of the games of make-believe we have been
considering has been endowed with any serious point; they are
just games. In particular, there is no real assertion, no real
understanding, no real truth. But at the next stage these are
provided for.

10.3 DISCOURSE 'ABOUT THE NOVEL' (ETC)

The fact that an action is a move within a game of make-believe
does not mean that it does not have a serious point. (After all,
although the shadow-boxer is pretending, he is not *only* pretending. Metaphors and non-literal uses of language quite generally
involve make-believe, but this does not prevent them from being
used in the making of serious assertions.) Now any of the games
of make-believe we have been discussing can be exploited in the
making of serious statements *about* the game, and about what is
make-believedly the case within it. One makes such a statement
by *making a statement* (i.e. making a move within the game),
but in such a way as to manifest the intention that what one does
should be up for assessment as correct or incorrect (i.e. *really*
correct or *really* incorrect) according to whether or not *the
statement one makes is correct or incorrect*. Thus the speaker

says something absolutely true or false by *saying something true* or *saying something false*.

One can imagine such a development in the mud pie game. Perhaps two fathers are prevailed upon to play, and a dispute breaks out involving their children; one child accuses another of having stolen some pies. The fathers are drawn in, taking the sides of their offspring, of course; tempers are high, voices are raised, jackets removed and sleeves rolled. There is not much doubt that the issue is serious. But they may still exploit the pretence. 'Listen! Your boy started out with three pies, right out of the oven. Then he gave one to Mary, and ate one—he should only have one left.' People are engaged in exactly this kind of serious exploitation of pretence when they 'discuss what went on in the novel' (or 'film', or 'play', etc.) by knowingly using empty singular terms.

Now it is commonly agreed that story-tellers, actors, etc., engage in pretence when they create the informational backdrop which this sort of discussion concerns; but it is not so generally recognized that serious discussion of 'what went on in the novel' or 'what went on in the play' also involves pretence.[34] This is partly because it is not realized that pretence can be exploited for serious purposes, and partly because of an illusion that this serious discourse can be adequately represented as involving an intensional operator such as 'It is fictionally the case that . . .'.[35] But the recognition of such an operator cannot provide a general solution to the problem posed by the conniving use of empty but Russellian singular terms. For if a sentence fails to be properly intelligible when used on its own, the same will hold of any more complex sentence in which it is embedded. If one's theory has the result that a sentence containing the singular term 'that man', used in such a way as to secure a demonstrative identification, fails to be properly intelligible when there is nothing to which the term refers, one cannot then proceed as though the sentence 'It is fictionally the case that

---

[34] '[The actor] on a stage plays at being another before a gathering of people who play at taking him for that other person': Jorge Luis Borges, *Labyrinths* (New Directions, New York, 1962), p. 248. (Cited by Walton at p. 12 of 'Fearing Fictions'.)

[35] See, e.g., Lewis, 'Truth in Fiction'. (Although I do not believe that an operator treatment of 'discourse about what goes in in fiction' can solve our problems, Lewis's paper is valuable for its careful treatment of several delicate points relating to fiction, and for bringing out the connection between fictional truth and counterfactuals.)

that man is bald' were intelligible; for if it is constructed according to the same pattern as other complex sentences, it is a necessary condition for understanding it that one understand the embedded sentence.[36]

The idea that discourse 'about what went on in the novel' (or 'in the film' or 'in the play') involves a continuation of the pretence in which these creations originated enables us to reconcile the serious use of singular terms in such discourse with the Russellian status of such singular terms in their normal employment. We can acknowledge that there is something that constitutes *understanding* remarks of this kind, such as 'That blonde girl was after his money'; and we can acknowledge that it requires something of the hearer very similar to what is required for the understanding of terms of this kind as normally used.

What is required is, first, that the hearer quasi-understand the utterance, and, second, that he realize that the utterance is absolutely true if and only if it is make-believedly the case that he has, in quasi-understanding it, thought something true. Since quasi-understanding requires the hearer to possess information and (within the scope of a pretence) to bring it to bear upon the interpretation of the remark, there is a clear justification for claiming that the term is used, rather than mentioned; and we have been able to specify in what this intelligible, if indirect, use of the terms consists.

I have spoken of the speaker and the hearer *continuing* someone else's antecedent pretence, but this is not always the case. The pretence may exist only in their serious exploitation of it. The speaker and hearer who seem to see a little green man but doubt their eyes may find themselves expressing a serious disagreement about the nature of the illusion by uttering such sentences as 'He's a hunchback' and 'No! He's carrying something.'[37]

The recognition of these serious uses of empty singular terms is consistent with the Russellian position of chapter 9 only because I am distinguishing uses. I am saying that the use of the

---

[36] See Geach, *Mental Acts*, pp. 85–6.

[37] Discourse 'about mythical objects' is somewhat like this. We can seriously exploit a make-believe game involving, e.g., the names of Greek gods. Here there is a story that purports to tell of such-and-such events (not involving any pretence on the part of the original tellers); we, knowing the story is false, treat it rather as the speaker and the hearer, in the case described in the text, treat their misleading perceptions.

singular term 'that thief', in the sentence 'That thief was a fool', uttered by someone who reads a novel as a report of historical fact, and purports to be restating one of those purported facts, is to be distinguished from the use of the singular term in the same sentence, uttered by someone who reads the novel as a novel, and is intending to make a remark about the novel. (The latter is a conniving use.) Now, no doubt in general one should avoid distinguishing uses, but in this case one cannot. For there is no getting around the fact that the person who utters the sentence with the intention of giving expression to a historical fact *cannot* be judged to have spoken truly, while the same is not true of the person who uses the name connivingly. (To repeat something I said in 10.1, even the most anti-Russellian of philosophers could not want to say that an atomic sentence, '*t* is *F*', can be *true* when the singular term is empty.)

It should be mentioned that this account of the serious (conniving) use of empty singular terms yields a straightforward treatment of sentences like 'Harry admires that thief' and 'John is attracted by that blonde' (used to attribute *propositional attitudes* to knowing participants in the pretence). The initial pretence is that the novel (story, play, . . .) gives us information about things; but we know that further make-believe truths are generated by the initial pretence, and can be reported in the same way.[38] This is another great advantage of my account over the treatment in terms of the operator 'It is fictionally the case that . . .', which does not extend to these sentences.[39]

There is another kind of analysis of 'discourse about fictional objects', quite different from the one I have proposed, and I want to end this section by contrasting them. This alternative analysis explicitly introduces an ontology of *fictional* (or apparent, or filmic) *objects*. I do not have in mind a Meinongian

---

[38] These cases bring out that it is better to say that the hearer does what he does within the scope of the pretence rather than that he pretends to do it. (See n. 33 above.) He pretends *that* there are such-and-such people, and within the scope of the pretence he admires or loathes them. (One does *actually* laugh, feel depressed, and so on.)

[39] What cannot be understood in this way is the attempt to report the attitudes of non-participants in the pretence—people who take a novel as history or a myth as true. Consider, e.g., 'The Greeks admired Zeus', or 'The Greeks believed that Zeus was powerful'. I am not sure how these are to be understood. Perhaps they should be understood as assertions within the game *with the Greeks as part of the story*; or perhaps as attempts to approximate to the state of mind of the Greeks. But they are not to be taken as *literally true*.

account, which invokes an ontology of *unreal objects*—that is to say, objects which have such properties as 'being a man', 'being six feet tall', but also which do not exist. I don't want to bother with that. I mean an ontology of *abstract* objects—the kind of ontology we explicitly invoke when we say such things as 'There are only three characters in the whole of English literature who kill their mothers', or 'The character of Falstaff has a long history in comic drama.' Such an ontology is certainly intelligible,[40] and we *could* take the singular terms in 'discourse about fiction' to refer to these entities.[41] We would have to reconstrue the predicates slightly; when we say 'That sister of his was after his money', we are not ascribing the property of *being after his money* to an abstract object. But the reconstrual is perfectly general.

My objection to this kind of treatment is threefold. In the first place, it fails to make it a requirement for understanding these remarks that the hearer possess and invoke information (or misinformation) in a way which mimics the understanding of remarks involving ordinary singular terms. Secondly, it fails to recognize the undeniable element of pretence present in this kind of discourse. Thirdly, such an ontology is excessively sophisticated for the needs of this discourse, in which a general conception of the identity-conditions of these abstract objects, *characters*, is not presupposed. Someone can engage in a conversation 'about what went on in the novel' perfectly competently, without in any way needing to know how one might count characters, whether two authors can use the same character, and the like.[42]

When successful communication can take place involving this use of singular terms, we do not have to invent an object for both speaker and hearer to be thinking of. I agree that it is central to any account of 'discourse about fiction' that it explain what it is for two people to be thinking of the same fictional object (i.e.

---

[40] The identity-questions have sufficiently clear answers. (We could say the same about what might be called 'anthropologists' gods'.)

[41] Kripke, in his John Locke Lectures, suggests invoking this ontology to deal with statements like 'John admired Sherlock Holmes'.

[42] I am appealing here to a principle I explain and defend in 'Identity and Predication': not to recognize discourse as involving reference to and predication concerning objects of a given kind unless the mastery of that discourse requires mastery of the identity-conditions of objects of that kind.

for them to be *thinking of the same object*). But this does not involve the application of a new criterion of identity for a new kind of entity (the abstract objects); it involves the application, *within a pretence*, of perfectly familiar criteria of identity for perfectly familiar kinds of objects. Identity between games is a quite separate matter.[43]

G. E. Moore asks, in one of his most penetrating lectures, the question 'What is required for two people to be thinking of the same imaginary object?'[44] His answer (which is given within the framework of a generally descriptive view of reference) is that their conceptions (descriptions) 'of the object' must be similar, *and must also be causally related*—one person's conception must cause the other's, or else both must be causally derived from some third person's similar conception. We can now see that (abstracting from the general descriptive framework) Moore gives the right answer, but to the wrong question. The requirement of a causal relation between 'conceptions' (*Ideas*) simply flows out of the requirement that parties to this sort of communication must be *thinking of the same thing*: that is, that they must be so related that, had the pretence been real, they would actually have been thinking of the same thing. It is not part of a new criterion of identity for a special sort of thing (imaginary objects).

---

[43] Geach's several discussions of this issue (under his own term 'intentional identity') seem to me to suffer from a failure to distinguish these two issues. He sees the main problem posed by discourse about fiction, myth, etc., as the question of the conditions for what I have called 'identity between games': 'Suppose X and Y both worshipped the deity of the Sun. Do they or do they not worship the same God? ... What criterion are we to apply? ... This is a grave and inescapable problem. A lot of what we take to be our understanding of other men's discourse consists in understanding when they are referring over and over again to one and the same object—without ourselves needing either to identify the object or to know that their intended reference succeeds.' ('The Perils of Pauline', in *Logic Matters*, pp. 153–65, at pp. 164–5.) Some indication that this is on the wrong track comes when we observe that 'criterion of identity for a non-existent object' makes no sense. If what the Egyptians worshipped is literally *the same as* (or different from) what the Japanese worshipped, then it makes no sense to go on and say 'Yet there was no thing that the Egyptians worshipped'. We have brought the Egyptians to worship something real—albeit an abstract anthropologist's god, not a real live god. Nevertheless, Geach's papers on this subject (especially 'Intentional Identity' and 'The Perils of Pauline') are very rewarding reading.

[44] ' "Real" and "Imaginary" ', in *Lectures in Philosophy*, edited by Casimir Lewy (George Allen and Unwin, London, 1966), pp. 20–43. (I owe this reference to Simon Blackburn.)

10.4 SINGULAR NEGATIVE EXISTENTIAL STATEMENTS

I propose that we regard singular negative existential sentences as another serious exploitation of a game of make-believe. The general idea is that someone who utters such a sentence should be likened to someone who makes a move within a pretence in order to express the fact that it is a pretence. He is not like someone who tries to prevent a theatre audience from being too carried away by jumping up on the stage and saying: 'Look, these men are only actors, and there is no scaffold or buildings here—there are only props.' Rather, he is like someone who jumps up on the stage and says: 'Look, Suzanne and the thief over there are only characters in a play, and this scaffold and these buildings are just props.' The audience must be engaged, or be prepared to engage, in the make-believe, in order to understand what he is saying.

As I mentioned in 10.1, it is clear that the rules which govern these negative existential statements are different from the rules which govern those serious exploitations of the game of make-believe we have been considering in 10.3; for, construed as a statement of the latter kind, 'That little green man does not exist' is false, not true. Nevertheless, there is a very close connection between the remarks considered in 10.3 and these negative existential statements. A singular negative existential statement involves a make-believe reference, which must bring with it the possibility of make-believedly having, or soliciting, an answer to the question 'Which one are you referring to?' 'Which one is it', we might say, 'that you are saying does not really exist?' And giving an answer, or even being prepared with an answer, to this question inevitably draws one into the pretence. 'That little green man on the top of the wall—that is the man I am saying does not exist.' Answers like this make sense only in a context in which a distinction is provided between 'truth and falsity about the little green man'—and this is the context of the language-game discussed in 10.3.

In order to explain the truth-conditions of these statements, I want to introduce the concept 'really' into the picture. (Although the term is explicitly used only on some of the occasions on which singular negative existential statements are made, I take it to be understood on the occasions on which it is not explicitly used.) 'Really' is a word which, when prefixed to a sentence, produces a sentence such that an utterance of it is true (absolutely) if and only if the sentence preceded by 'really' is itself such that there is a proposition expressed by it when it is uttered as a move in the relevant game of make-believe, and this proposition is true (absolutely)—not merely *true*. Now, this elaborate formulation would not be necessary for the introduction of the operator 'really' into an existentially conservative game of make-believe; for in such a context, 'really' could simply be taken as indicating that the utterance to which it is prefixed is not to be taken as a move in the game at all, but as a straightforward assertion, to be evaluated normally. But if this were all we could say about 'really', then 'Really (That little green man exists)' would fail to be significant when 'that little green man' fails to refer, as would its negation 'It is not the case that (Really (That little green man exists))'; so we would have made no progress towards understanding singular negative existential statements. If 'This does not (really) exist' is to be intelligible when 'this' is empty, it must somehow involve the exploitation of a pretence; and if it is also to be regarded as the ordinary *negation* of 'This does (really) exist', the latter must also be regarded as a move in the game of make-believe, even though someone who *sincerely* utters it would also be prepared to attempt to make a reference in the normal way. This is why I have given 'really' the complicated explanation above. If someone is to understand 'Really' ⌒ S, he must quasi-understand S — that is, it must be true that he make-believedly understands S; and further, he must realize that the whole utterance is (absolutely) true if and only if, in quasi-understanding S (i.e. in *entertaining a thought as expressed by S*), he is in fact entertaining a thought which is true.

At this point, it is crucial to remember the phenomenon I labelled 'the game-to-reality shift' (10.2). I argued that if someone wrongly took himself to be deceived by the appearances, and on the basis of this false belief entered into a pretence comprising such utterances as 'This little green man is F', then, although he would take himself to be merely quasi-understanding some reference, he would in fact be demonstratively identifying a little green man whom he could see, and entertaining various thoughts about him. This is precisely the situation in which 'Really (That little green man is F)' would be true (if the little green man *is* F); in quasi-understanding the embedded sentence, one would have grasped a proposition which is true. But the claim 'Really (That little green man is F)' is one that can be understood even when it is not true. For understanding it requires quasi-understanding the embedded sentence (as a move in the pretence), in the context of knowledge that the whole thing is true if and only if one has thereby entertained (as *expressed by the embedded sentence*) a true proposition, and this is something that has been provided for when the term 'that little green man' is without a referent.

'Really (That little green man exists)' is therefore true if and only if the information is not hallucinatory, and in receiving it, the subjects are seeing a little green man; for, under those circumstances, quasi-understanding the embedded sentence would involve entertaining the proposition normally expressed by 'E(That little green man)', which is true. So, finally, 'Not (Really (That little green man exists))'—or 'That little green man does not (really) exist'—is the denial of such a claim.

Let us look at this analysis from the point of view of the constraints upon analyses with which we began (10.1). First, and most importantly, we have an account of the utterance according to which the referring expression is *used*. It is not used in the normal way; it is used in the normal way within the scope of a pretence (i.e. *used in the normal way*). Still within the scope of that pretence, there is a gap between understanding it and not understanding it. There is a real difference in which that make-believe difference consists, and in which the difference between really understanding the utterance (as a serious exploitation of the game) and not really understanding the utterance consists.

Secondly, the utterance is seen to employ the first-level predicate 'E(ξ)'. And, thirdly, someone who asserts 'Not (Really (This exists))' does not simply deny the basic existential statement, even when he is mistaken and there is in fact something to which he is referring. This is because in those circumstances, the two claims 'This exists' and 'This really exists' are not equivalent. One cannot understand 'really' in the latter sentence without knowing what game of make-believe or pretence one would have to play in order to quasi-understand the embedded sentence. In the case of a demonstrative quasi-reference (and possibly reference), it is clear that the background is some shared perceptual information, in whose veridicality the truth of the claim 'Really (This exists)' ultimately consists. But it cannot be said that the truth of the basic existential statement 'E(this)' consists in the veridicality of some shared perceptual information. This is why the two utterances embed differently in counterfactuals: contrast 'Had this man's parents not met, this man would not have existed' with 'Had this man's parents not met, this man would not have really existed.'

Chapter 11

Proper Names

Although proper names share many characteristics with the referential devices we have so far considered, I have reserved them for separate treatment in the present chapter because they introduce quite novel elements. Hitherto we have considered what might be called 'one-off' referential devices: the functioning of such a device does not depend upon the existence of any practice, within the community, of using that device to refer to a given thing. The 'social dimension' of language is not wholly absent from these referential performances, since the speaker relies upon the existence of a practice, within the community, of using this or that expression (e.g. 'he') to refer to a certain sort of thing (e.g. a male thing). But the fact that an utterance involving a 'one-off' referential device represents a particular individual is clearly to be explained in terms of the thoughts and attitudes of those immediately involved with that particular utterance; whereas with proper names, it appears, we have linguistic symbols which represent particular individuals in something like the way in which concept-expressions represent concepts or functions; and so the fact that an utterance containing a proper name represents a particular individual is far less dependent upon the thoughts and attitudes of those immediately involved with that particular utterance. The contrast I am trying to draw in the case of singular terms can be discerned in the case of concept-expressions, if we compare the use of such utterances as 'It was red' and 'He had a limp' with the use of 'It had *that* colour' and 'He walked like *this*'.[1]

The fact that linguistic symbols are ambiguous means that

---

[1] There are difficulties in assimilating proper names to symbols belonging to a language (like 'red' or 'limp'), just because the groups of people who know these expressions are often so small. (There is clearly *some* useful notion of the English language according to which proper names are not parts of it, but at best parts of particular idiolects.)

the representational properties of particular utterances cannot be explained in complete independence of the thoughts and intentions of those involved with them. If a speaker is to say something using a proper name, he must make it clear which individual's name he is using. This has led some philosophers to assimilate the use of proper names to the various kinds of demonstrative reference we have previously been studying. 'Jack Jones is *F*' is interpreted as 'That Jack Jones is *F*', which itself amounts to something like 'That man called "Jack Jones" is *F*'. The demonstrative element is presumably intended to suggest that the speaker is adverting to some information in common possession; the demonstrative may be a 'testimony demonstrative' or a 'memory demonstrative'.[2]

I do not have a knock-down argument against this view, but it does seem to me to fail to bring out the way in which utterances containing proper names are dependent upon the existence and coherence of a general practice of reference. Suppose, for example, that the speaker and the audience inhabit a community in which the name 'Jack Jones' was bestowed upon two individuals who happened to look alike, with the consequence that they were regularly confused. Instead of there being two separate name-using practices, it may be that information from both men has become merged, so that there is a single name-using practice with no one referent. In this community, I would maintain that the name 'Jack Jones' does not have a referent. Utterances involving the name are flawed because of a widespread confusion. And, it seems to me, this is the right thing to say about *any* utterance involving the name in this community, even when it so happens that the speaker and the audience both have in mind just one (the same one) of the men whom the community has confused. If we construed an utterance of 'Jack Jones is *F*' as involving a 'one-off' reference, we might have to suppose that the speaker had successfully let the audience know which person he had in mind (a person, who, by hypothesis, 'is a Jack Jones'). But when we place the utterance in its social setting, we can see how the flaws in the practice are necessarily inherited by the utterance. The hearer may acquire a true thought about the person the speaker has in mind, but he has

---

[2] For this account of proper names, see Tyler Burge, 'Reference and Proper Names', *Journal of Philosophy* lxx (1973), 425-39.

not been *told* something true: he has not been given some information, linguistically represented, which he can take away from the utterance and put to use in further conversations.

Hilary Putnam once wrote:

... there are two sorts of tools in the world: there are tools like a hammer or a screwdriver which can be used by one person; and there are tools like a steamship which require the cooperative activity of a number of persons to use. Words have been thought of too much on the model of the first sort of tool.[3]

I do not think Putnam has identified quite the right parallel, since the traditional position has always been to regard words as instruments for communication, and hence as tools which two people 'use'; a better contrast would be one between a steamship or a factory on the one hand and a double-handed saw on the other. Nevertheless, I think Putnam's contrast is clear; and while a viewpoint which takes the two-person communicative situation as basic seems appropriate for 'one-off' referential discourse, it seems to me absolutely correct to regard interpersonal communication involving a name as essentially a fragment of a larger picture: something which can be understood only when the other elements of that picture—other speakers, hearers, and communicative episodes—are taken into account.

The change in viewpoint I am recommending forces us to think about two interconnected things. We have to ask: what makes it the case that a symbol has the property of representing, or referring to, a particular individual? Is the connection with the thoughts and attitudes of users of the expression wholly severed? And if, as seems likely, it is not, then we have to ask two related questions. First, how are the social facts (e.g. the fact that such-and-such an expression is a name of such-and-such an object) dependent upon facts about the psychology of individuals? Secondly, and conversely, what is the role of linguistic symbols, whose semantic properties are a social matter, in the psychology of the individuals who use them? These are instances of general problems in the theory of language, but we cannot assume that the answers are going to be the same in all cases.

[3] *Mind, Language and Reality*, p. 229.

11.2 PROPER-NAME-USING PRACTICES

Let us consider an ordinary proper-name-using practice, in which the name 'NN' is used to refer to the person x.[4] The distinctive mark of any such practice is the existence of a core group of speakers who have been introduced to the practice via their acquaintance with x. They have on some occasion been told, or anyway have come to learn, a truth which they could then express as 'This is NN', where 'This' makes a demonstrative reference to x. Once a speaker has learned such a truth, the capacity to re-identify persons over time enables him to recognize later occasions on which the judgement 'This is NN' may be made, and hence in connection with which the name 'NN' may be used. To have an effective capacity to 'go on' in this way would normally require a recognitional capacity for x, in the sense of chapter 8, and an association of the name 'NN' with that capacity (i.e. the subject can recognize x as NN); though we must remember that x himself may have a capacity to use his own name from time to time. Members of this core group, whom I shall call 'producers' (for a reason that will become apparent), do more than merely use the name to refer to x; they have dealings with x from time to time, and use the name in those dealings—they know x, and further, they know x as NN. They use the name in speaking to x, in giving each other commands and instructions in connection with situations in which x has been encountered, and in transmitting information gained from their encounters with x.

The practice of using the name may originate in a baptism, or in a situation where a speaker manifestly uses an expression which is not x's given name as if it were x's name, whether knowingly (a nickname) or unknowingly (a mistake). But the expression does not become a name for x unless it has a certain currency among those who know x—only then can we say that x is *known as NN*.

Any producer can introduce another person into the name-using practice as a producer by an introduction ('This is NN'),

---

[4] Since writing this chapter, I have found the terminology of 'proper-name-using practices' used, with a different meaning, by Michael McKinsey, 'Names and Intentionality', *Philosophical Review* lxxxvii (1978), 171–200. (He takes as basic the notion of an *individual's* practice with a name.) The model I shall generally follow is that of personal proper names; but it seems to apply fairly well to proper names for animals, places, buildings, pieces of music, . . . —cases in which, although 'recognition' is perhaps not always the right word, there is *presentation* of an object.

and *x* may introduce himself. But a formal introduction is not necessary; the name may be picked up by observing the practice of other speakers ('Now NN has got the ball; let's see if he can do anything with it'). And there is no special importance in the first encounter an individual has with a name. A practice of using the name will normally be continually reinforced by the manifestly harmonious practice of others, and subsequent acquaintance with the practice of others can override an erroneous introduction to the use of the name.

Perhaps in the early stages of its existence all the participants in the name-using practice will be producers, but this is unlikely to remain so for long. Others, who are *not* acquainted with *x*, can be introduced into the practice, either by helpful explanations of the form 'NN is the ϕ', or just by hearing sentences in which the name is used. I shall call these members 'consumers', since on the whole they are not able to inject new information into the practice, but must rely upon the information-gathering transactions of the producers. What counts as an adequate introduction of a consumer into the practice is something I shall discuss below (see 11.3); all that matters for the general outline I am presenting is that it be acknowledged that there are non-producing participants. A speaker may be introduced into a name-using practice as a consumer by either a producer or a consumer, and once again there is no particular weight to be attached to the *first* introduction.

Although it is inexact in some respects, I have chosen the 'producer/consumer' analogy, rather than Putnam's related analogy of 'the division of linguistic labour', because his analogy suggests a mutual dependence between the two groups of name users which does not seem to me to exist. Producers stand in no need of consumers; while the dependence of consumers on producers is absolutely plain.[5] A consumer who hears and accepts a sentence of the form 'NN is the ϕ' knows, if he takes 'NN' to be an ordinary proper name, that the statement amounts to a substantial hypothesis about a particular person, a person known as NN, and that, if it can be known to be true, this will be either because an individual observed to be the ϕ is recognized or identified as NN, or because it can be warranted by

[5] 'Consumers' is here used to mean 'non-producing consumers': in a wider use of the term, producers of information are themselves consumers.

propositions known in this way. Knowing 'NN' to be an ordinary proper name, no one would dream of responding to a challenge to the statement 'NN is the ϕ' by saying 'Oh! I was under the impression that "NN" is just our name for whoever is the ϕ.'[6] When someone hears the claim 'NN is the ϕ', and takes 'NN' to be an ordinary proper name, he supposes that there is (or was) a person going about the world known as NN; and that the claim embodies not only information that there is something that is uniquely ϕ, but also an identification of that object as the object *known as NN*. It follows that a consumer who takes 'NN' to be an ordinary proper name knows that simply by being led to accept various sentences employing the name, he cannot have been given a *complete* introduction to the use of the name. He has been given certain propositions which require defence, without the means, on his own, of providing that defence. (Only a producer can provide the defence.)

Thus I am claiming that there is a difference *in kind* between the introduction to a name-using practice which a producer receives and the introduction which a consumer receives. One might say that an ordinary proper name is used subject to a convention, but that it is only the producers who can be credited with knowledge of this convention. Contrast a descriptive proper name: the convention is to use 'NN' to refer to whatever is the ϕ, and this leaves no work to be done by a distinction between producers and consumers. This convention might (though it need not) have been explicitly expressed in a stipulation which initiated the practice: 'Let us use "NN" to refer to the ϕ.' Analogously, we might envisage the convention which governs an ordinary proper name as explicitly expressed in a practice-initiating stipulation: 'Let us use "NN" to refer to this man.' Knowledge of *this* convention could be manifested only in judging, from time to time, 'This man is NN'; this is something only a producer is in a position to do. If someone is introduced to the use of an ordinary name by means of an 'introduction', 'This is NN', he comes to know the convention,

---

[6] Throughout this book (but see especially 1.7, 1.8, 2.3), I have emphasized that there is nothing incoherent in the idea of a proper name for which this kind of response would be appropriate, and examples actually occur: 'Jack the Ripper' is the name bestowed on whoever performed certain gruesome murders, and 'Deutero-Isaiah' is the name scholars use to refer to whoever it was who wrote the second part of the Book of Isaiah. But these are definitely not ordinary proper names.

and thereby comes to have a knowledge of the use of the name which *does* admit of a semantical defence: he can sensibly respond to a challenge to his later utterances of 'This is NN' by saying 'Oh! I was under the impression that "NN" is just our name for this man.'

A name-using practice is sustained by two mutually reinforcing general propensities on the part of members of a speech community. First, people make an effort to learn and remember the names of persons in whom they have, or feel they might have, any interest. Second, people generally use the name of a person (if they know it) when they are speaking of him. There are exceptions, for instance when it is taken to be common knowledge between speaker and hearer that the person spoken of bears the name he does: if a person well known to both of them is plainly visible, the speaker need not say 'NN is up early'; he may simply say 'He is up early'. Again, there are little communities in which the practice is to refer to a person (whose name is known) by some salient description (e.g. 'Father', 'Mother'). But, such situations apart, when there is common knowledge that a speaker does know the name, 'NN', of an individual, the failure to use that name will generate a strong implication, either that there is some special point being made by the chosen mode of reference (as in 'I'm not going to dine with the person who insults my wife'), or that the speaker does not believe that the individual referred to *is* NN.

The second of these tendencies is *self*-reinforcing, for the more people conform to it, the sharper will be the sense of unwanted associations attendant on failure to use the name, and hence the stronger the motive to use the name. But it is clear that the two tendencies are mutually reinforcing. The more it is the practice of speakers to refer to persons by name, the more important it will be, for those wishing to gain information about, or enter into discussions of, a person, to know his name. Conversely, the more people can be relied upon to know the names of individuals, the more speakers will be provided with a motive to use those names, rather than cast about for other ways of identifying the referent of their remarks for their audience.

Underlying these tendencies is the fact that generally speaking there will not be a naturally arising overlap between the information possessed by different people, adequate to ensure that any pair of people who possess information from an individual, and who can profitably engage in discussion and exchange of information, will be able to do so using a description. Think, for example, of a fairly large factory. Two people who both have information from a certain worker may not *eo ipso* have any clear way of achieving communication about him. Even if they both have met him, most people are bad at describing someone's appearance (even when they have an effective recognitional capacity for the person in question); so unless the person has a highly distinctive appearance, no such description will serve. And it is easy to construct (and find) cases in which no other description will serve either. The institution of bestowing a name on someone—thereby producing an arbitrary distinguishing feature which everyone learns—certainly lessens the difficulty of achieving referential communication. (It is true that people share names, but the supplementation of a name by some other piece of information, which by itself would have been virtually useless, is often adequate.)

Theoretically, names as we know them might be eliminated in favour of, say, dates of birth. We can imagine a community who make it a convention to learn some particular piece of antecedent information about people, for instance their dates of birth, and to use the dates in referring to people. But these linguistic devices would simply *become* names. The practice of referring to a person by a date of birth would not rely upon each participant's independently established information that the person in question was born on the day in question, with communication depending upon the likelihood that the person concerning whom X has received the information that he was born on that day is the same as the person concerning whom Y has received the information that he was born on that day. Communication would depend, rather, upon the probability that each participant has been properly initiated into the practice of using the expression to refer to a given person.[7]

---

[7] This case brings out the fact that what matters is not that the name has been *assigned* to the thing but that it is used for the thing. (Cf. G. E. M. Anscombe, *An Introduction to Wittgenstein's Tractatus* (Hutchinson, London, 1959), p. 41.) [The linguistic devices in question might have the syntactic form of definite descriptions: 'the man born on ...'. On that supposition, the case is an example of the use of definite descriptions in a way that makes them approximate to proper names, a discussion of which is promised in 9.3.]

An ordinary proper-name-using practice can be thought of as having a natural life-cycle. We have traced it from infancy to maturity. In its maturity, producers will gather information, which will then circulate more or less widely among both producers and consumers, being linked up with information previously acquired and circulated, so that some information which almost everyone associates with the name is the result of the information-gathering transactions of others. In its final phase, which may last for a very long time, the name-using practice has only consumers as participants, with the stock of information existing from the time of its maturity usually diminishing as time passes. I shall say something about the last phase of the life-cycle in 11.4; for the present, I shall concentrate upon ordinary proper-name-using practices in their maturity.

It is easy enough to understand what is meant by saying that a name-using practice *survives* over time; the practice survives through the introduction of new members by those who are already members. But something should be said about what is meant by 'a *single* name-using practice'. What differentiates practices is not the individuals named; intuitively, we can have a single practice which concerns two individuals, and two practices which concern the same individual. The first kind of case can come about in two rather different ways. A good number of the producers may regularly confuse two individuals; or, alternatively, the producers may divide into two groups, each regularly and consistently recognizing one of the two individuals, without this being known, so that information from two different individuals is pooled as information 'about NN'. (It would be extremely unlikely, though not impossible, for this fact to remain undiscovered.) A most vivid example of the second kind of case is found in R. L. Stevenson's *Dr. Jeckyll and Mr. Hyde*, in which two names, believed to refer to different persons, are in fact used of the same person. But the distinctness of the names is not essential for the distinctness of the practices: Stevenson could easily have told the story with the same name used in two distinct practices, with no one having the least idea that the nice Mr Hyde and the terrible Mr Hyde are one and the same person. So what is it for there to be one rather than two 'Hyde'-using practices? Intuitively, there exist two distinct practices involving the use of the name 'NN' if uses of the name can be associated with two distinct networks of communication in the community, such that information circulates through each network, but does not pass between the networks.

11.3 THE DETERMINATION OF THE REFERENCE OF A PROPER NAME

It seems reasonable to suggest that what makes it the case that an ordinary proper-name-using practice involving the name 'NN' concerns a particular individual is that that individual should be *known to the producers in the practice as NN*. It is the actual pattern of dealings the producers have had with an individual—identified from time to time by the exercise of their recognitional capacities in regard to that individual—which ties the name to the individual. The information circulating in the practice will normally provide good evidence for which individual it is that has been recognized from time to time as NN by the producers in the practice, for much of it will be a trace of some encounter between a producer and an individual, although countless equally relevant identifications of an individual as NN will leave no permanent trace upon the practice.

To see the actual pattern of recognition and identification by the *producing* members of the practice as the fundamental mechanism whereby ordinary proper names are endowed with a reference is to see a parallel between those names and the ordinary words we have for *natural kinds* of things and stuffs. It is an essential feature of the practices associated with terms like 'elm', 'diamond', 'leopard', and the like that there exist members—producers—who have a *de facto* capacity to recognize instances of the kind when presented with them. I mean by this an effective capacity to distinguish occasions when they are presented with members of that kind, from occasions when they are presented with members of any other kinds which are represented in any strength in the environment they inhabit. This recognitional capacity is all that is required for there to be a consistent pattern among the objects which are *in fact* identified as elms, or whatever, by members of the speech community— for all the objects *called* 'elms' to fall into a single natural kind— and no more is required for a natural-kind-term practice to concern a particular natural kind.[8] Although many utterances

---

[8] I have not attempted to give a full account of what a capacity to recognize members of a kind consists in. A capacity to recognize elms *does* require a capacity to distinguish

of producers, and all utterances of consumers, in the kind-term practice have other functions, there will be a subset of utterances involving the term in which some particular tree or trees may be said to have been (authoritatively) *called* by that term. It is these utterances involving the term—which may be regarded as the point of contact between the practice and the world—that determine which kind the term, as used throughout the practices, refers to. If the predicate 'called "an elm"' is understood in such a way that trees which have never been perceived cannot satisfy the predicate, then it is correct and illuminating to say that something falls into the kind referred to by 'elm' if and only if it is of the same kind as the trees called 'elms'.[9]

I am suggesting that we attribute just as much importance to the analogous point of contact between a name-using practice and the world—that we regard a name-using practice as concerned with the object (if any) which is regularly *called* 'NN' by *producing* members of the practice. Provided that some one individual is consistently and regularly identified by producers as NN (known as NN), that individual is the referent of the name as used by participants in the practice. And it is in terms of this notion of a name's having a reference that we should seek to understand particular utterances involving the name, *whether uttered by producers or by consumers*. For when a speaker refers to an object by using a name, this will be because he intentionally utters a name which in fact has that object as its referent.

---

elms from all other trees growing in appreciable numbers in the community's environment, but it does not require a capacity to distinguish elms from every other kind of tree in the universe. I believe that the concept of knowledge holds the key to the principle at the bottom of this intuition (cf. 8.3). Someone who has acquired the capacity to recognize members of a kind from his encounters with some of them must be able to be regarded as expressing *knowledge* when he groups a new tree with these previously encountered trees. And the existence of elm-like trees which are not elms in small numbers in his environment, or in large numbers outside his environment, does not prevent us from regarding a producer as knowing that a new tree is of the same kind as the previously encountered trees. The claim to knowledge extends further. For if the producer had learned in previous encounters, concerning the kind, that its members are F (e.g. that they burn well), then we shall wish to allow that he knows of the new tree that it is F too. This is, no doubt, the basis of our concern for underlying structure, for if a new instance is only superficially similar to previously encountered instances, then it will be only an accident if it too is F.

[9] This proposal is often wrongly conflated with the genuinely circular proposal: something falls into the kind referred to by 'elm' if and only if it is capable of being correctly called 'an elm'.

The precise statement of the way in which individual utterances exploit the general practices of the community must be a little complicated, because of the possibility of there being several distinct practices in the community involving the same name. If a speaker is to refer to something by using a name, then it is necessary that he manifest *which* name-using practice he intends to be, and to be taken to be, participating in.

It would be a mistake to regard this intentional element simply as the application to the case of names of the general requirement we have encountered previously (9.2), that the speaker manifest which *object* he intends to be (taken to be) referring to. It may help to grasp the point I am making if we think of individuating the words of a language not only phonetically but also by reference to the practices in which they are used. In these terms, the requirement on a speaker using a proper name is not that he indicate which *object* he intends to be (taken to be) referring to, but that he indicate which *name* he intends to be (taken to be) using. (Cf. 3.2.)

It is true that the conception which the speaker has of the referent of a name—the information which he has associated with the name—will be relevant in determining what he refers to by using the name. But this will be not by directly indicating which object he means (in the manner of a 'one-off' referential device), but by making it clear which name-using practice he intends to be (taken to be) participating in. This is why, if the speaker says (in further explanation after an utterance of 'NN is F') that NN is the ϕ, we do not necessarily conclude that by 'NN' in his utterance of 'NN is F' he meant to refer to the ϕ. We use his statement that NN is the ϕ as evidence for which name-using practice he has come into contact with, and thereby which name-using practice he intends to be (taken to be) participating in. If 'NN is the ϕ' expresses a piece of misinformation widely disseminated in a practice in which 'NN' is used as a name for x, then we shall conclude that the speaker intended to use x's name, even though x is *not* the ϕ.[10]

---

[10] We shall not conclude even that the speaker's intended referent was *that* ϕ (i.e. the source of the particular information he has received). For information from some other object may become wrongly attached to a name, as in those many cases in which legends of minor individuals have become attributed to more important figures. (We are here reminded once more of how superficial the notion of *identifying for an audience* is. See 6.4.)

It is quite easy to see how *all* the information in possession of a *consumer* may be false of the referent of the name. In fact a tremendous amount of false and quite groundless information may be circulating in the community, about NN, without there being any change in the kind of facts which determine an individual as the referent of the name. Malicious rumours, or absurdly inflated claims, equally baseless, may circulate, and such misinformation may be all that ends up associated with the name in the minds of consumers. Nevertheless, they have got hold of rumours and claims *about a particular man.* As it was used in conveying the misinformation to them, and as it is used by them in further transmitting that misinformation, the name has, and is understood by the consumers to have, a quite definite reference, provided for it by the practice of those who know some individual as NN (namely the producers). So it would be generally understood that an enquiry into the truth or falsity of those rumours and claims would require an identification of the object which is known as NN: a procedure which leaves open the possibility of the discovery that the rumours and claims are false. What would begin to undermine the link between the name-using practice and the individual is misidentification of another individual as NN by some producers, and I shall discuss this kind of change in a moment. But it is clear that wholly baseless information can end up associated with a name in the minds of consumers, without any such disturbance to the practice of calling an individual by that name.

There are two different ingredients, then, in my account of reference by names: first, an account of the mechanism whereby a *community-wide* name-using practice concerns a particular object (and hence whereby a name is endowed with a reference); and second, an account, in terms of the notion of a name's having a reference in a community, of how *individual* speakers refer by the use of the name. These two ingredients can be regarded as corresponding roughly to two elements in Saul Kripke's picture of reference by names.[11] Corresponding to the first ingredient is Kripke's idea that names are endowed with a reference by an initial baptism, or at least a decision on the part of some person or persons to initiate a practice of using a name in a certain way. And secondly, individual uses of a name are

[11] See 'Naming and Necessity'.

assigned a reference, according to Kripke, in terms of this fundamental mechanism, by an appeal to what we might call the
Recursive Principle: namely, that if someone acquires his use of
a name from a speaker (or speakers), and is speaking in causal
consequence of that acquisition, then the name on his lips will
refer to whatever was referred to by that speaker (or those
speakers) in those name-using episodes from which his use of the
name derives.[12]

This picture of Kripke's is extremely simple and elegant. In
particular, it is simpler than mine in making no appeal to the
idea of a name-using *practice*. However, I do not believe that an
appeal to this idea can be avoided. For the use we make of a
name depends upon the existence in our community of a coherent practice of using that name to refer to a particular object.
If the name-using practice in which I participate by my use of
a name has come to concern two different individuals, because
the producers now regularly confuse two men, then my use of
the name is without a referent, no matter what the facts are
about the origin of my own particular use of the name. For
example, when the name-using practice originated, it may have
concerned no one but x, and I may have been initiated into the
practice, as a consumer, at that time. Since I acquired my use
of the name from people who used the name to refer to x, Kripke
would hold that in my present uses of the name I am myself
referring to x, even if the presence of a similar looking person, y,
has, for a considerable length of time, confused the producers.
But this is surely incorrect: I cannot be insulated from the
deficiency of the practice to which I must inevitably appeal.

Kripke's Recursive Principle was designed to capture the
intuition that a *consumer* who acquired his use of the name 'NN'
by hearing remarks, 'NN is F', 'NN is G', etc., from others
would, in his subsequent uses of the name 'NN' depending upon
this initiation, refer to whichever individual those others were
referring to. Now, I have already implicitly claimed that the
Recursive Principle gives conditions too weak for reference by
name, since I have insisted that it is a necessary condition that
the speaker be able to *make manifest* which name-using practice

[12] I have eliminated from this formulation of Kripke's views the suggestion, which
must surely have been unintended, that only the first contact of the speaker with the
name-using practice matters for determining the reference of the name as used by him.

he intends to be participating in—which name he intends to use. If someone overhears a snatch of conversation, say, 'Harry Lyons was angry last night', that being the entirety of his introduction to the 'Harry Lyons' practice, then he is not in a position to use the name in order to make statements—he has not been adequately introduced into the practice. An adequate introduction must, surely, enable a speaker to go on on his own, using the name in the transmission of information to other members of the practice who are unacquainted with the particular facts of his introduction into the practice; whereas the person who picks up the name by overhearing a snatch of conversation is not an adequate link in any chain of transmission of knowledge.

This is not, ultimately, a very significant departure from Kripke, since I do not think that any support for the theories to which Kripke is opposed can be derived from it.[13] Even so, I should like to dispense with the Recursive Principle, because it seems wrong to invoke a principle specifically concerned with reference to explain the fact—which is not specifically concerned with reference—that individual speakers exploit general practices. The general principle is this: if a speaker uses a word with the manifest intention to participate in such-and-such a practice, in which the word is used with such-and-such semantic properties, then the word, as used by him, will possess just those semantic properties. This principle has as much application to the use by speakers of words like 'agronomist', 'monetarism', and the like as to their use of proper names. And it can be used to explain the intuition which the Recursive Principle was designed to explain, since it is reasonable to attribute to a speaker the intention to participate, by his use of a name, in the same practice as was being participated in by those speakers from whose use of the name the information he has associated with the name derives.

In giving an account of the mechanism whereby a name is

---

[13] To be in a position to make clear which name-using practice you intend to be participating in, it is neither necessary nor sufficient that you have a discriminating conception of the relevant object, in the sense of chapter 4. I have allowed the adequacy of information which is wholly false of the object in making one's name-using intentions clear; while sentences linking a name with a perfectly good discriminating description, like 'NN is the man my father quarrelled with last night', may not be adequate introductions to a name-using practice.

endowed with a reference, I have also found it necessary to appeal to a richer and more complicated set of facts than Kripke's initial baptism, or deliberate reference-initiating act: namely, the activities of the producers, in their practice of using the name in connection with their encounters with a particular object. One of the ways to see the importance of this range of facts in determining the reference of a name is to imagine a case in which they change: a case in which there is an alteration in the identity of the individual which the producers recognize as NN. Such a change can, at the very least, bring it about that a name ceases to have a referent in the community, and, when the circumstances are right, such a change can lead to the name's acquiring a new referent in the community. A transition of this kind can take place without anyone deciding or intending to initiate a new practice with the name. I think it worth studying such a hypothetical change in detail, for only in this way can we be sure that the two ingredients in my account of reference by names work together in a plausible and coherent way.

Let us begin, then, with a mature name-using practice, built around a core group of speakers who regularly and reliably recognize an individual, x, as NN. We may assume that they are surrounded by a group of consumers, and that information derived from their encounters with x is distributed throughout the practice. Subsequently, let us suppose, x disappears from the scene, and, at the same time, some producers begin to misidentify a different but similar looking individual, y, as NN. At this early point, of course, the name 'NN', as used by anyone who participates in this practice, still refers to x. All these uses of the name involve a manifest intention to be participating in a practice which undeniably concerns x, since the previous and well-established use of the name by the producers in the practice determined x as the referent of the name in that practice. This will remain the case even if, as we shall suppose, the mistake spreads to a large number of the producers. Someone can discover what has gone on, and report his discovery by referring to y and saying 'This is not NN'.

Suppose now that the substitution of y for x goes unnoticed,[14]

---

[14] If the proper names are names for persons, then, in order to tell a plausible story of this kind, we must explain why y does not himself point out the error. Perhaps y is suffering from amnesia.

and that y is recognized by the producers of the practice as NN for as long a period as x formerly was. Information from y is now disseminated around the practice, and, given the normal operation of human memory, such information is likely (though not certain) to outweigh information derived from x, though, presumably, a good deal of that information remains. At this point, I think we can say that the name 'NN', as used in this practice, no longer has a referent. The persistent identification of y as NN has undermined the connection which tied the name uniquely to x. It is certainly no longer possible to report what has happened by referring to y and saying 'This is not NN.' Indeed, such a remark will not have any definite truth-value.

Somewhat artificially, we can think of progress to this midpoint in the history of the name-using practice as consisting in a sequence of uses of the name, $u_1, u_2, \ldots, u_n$, commencing at the disappearance of x. Each u_i can be thought of as involving the manifest intention to be participating in the practice to which the previous utterances belonged. In the normal course of events, this would mean that each u_i would have the same referent as the previous uses. But the course of events we have described is not normal, for the practice is changing in precisely the respects which endow the name it concerns with a referent. The practice with which u_n associates itself, comprising, as it does, many uses of the name in consequence of identification of y as NN, is not one which uniquely concerns x, as did the practice with which u_1 associated itself. We must remember that a use of a name by a producer has two aspects. One is the purely semantical aspect—enquired into by the question 'To what does this use of the name refer?' The other might be described (very vaguely) as an epistemological aspect: it is enquired into by the question 'Which object's identification as NN underlies this use?' Now my account of the reference of a name in a practice makes it dependent upon the *second* of these two aspects. I do not say that the reference of a name in a practice is a function of the *reference* which the name had in prior uses by producers; this principle is a recursive principle which would preclude precisely the kind of change which I am attempting to describe. What I say is that, although those early mistaken uses, $u_1, u_2, \ldots$, etc. involved reference to x, they were beginning, by their second, epistemological aspect, to undermine the semantical connection between the name and x, which has, by the point we are describing, finally snapped.

Although the name has, by this mid-point, ceased to refer to x, I do not think that we can yet say that it has become a name for y. A good many of the producers will retain information from their encounters with x—will remember x—and so will be prepared to acknowledge (if the facts come out) that their use of the name involves some confusion. And, even if we imagine the gradual replacement of producers who knew x with new members of the practice, introduced into it as producers by reference to y, so that a point is reached at which only people who are thinking unconfusedly of y are producing members of the practice, still it does not seem to me to follow that the name has become a name for y. For there may remain, embodied in the practice, a good deal of information derived from x, and these are traces of the practice, in the past, of using the name to refer to x.[15] So long as any serious quantity of these traces remains, the practice can still reasonably be said to embody a confusion: facts about the past use of the name to refer to x will not be of purely etymological significance. This explains why a change in the reference of a proper name is so much more difficult than a change in the extension of a natural-kind term; for natural-kind terms carry with them relatively little information about the kind.[16] It also explains why a change in the reference of a name for a place is so much easier to imagine than a change in the reference of a name for a person.[17]

Nevertheless, there is no theoretical obstacle to the loss of all information derived from x; and when this happens, the name may finally be regarded as a name of y. There is a group of

[15] Misinformation retailed about x but without any source will not be relevant.

[16] Some examples of changes in the reference of natural-kind terms: 'albatross' derives from the Spanish 'alcatraz' ('pelican'); 'buffalo' is from a Greek word for a North African antelope; 'daffodil' is from 'asphodel', but the daffodil does not grow in Greece; 'turkey' was originally applied to the guinea fowl, which was brought to Western Europe via Turkey—the bird we now call 'turkey' is native to the New World; 'birch' derives from a word meaning 'white, bright tree', originally applied to the mountain ash; 'oil' derives from a word for the olive tree; 'grouse' was once applied to bustards; 'apple' was formerly used for all fruit other than berries, and 'cobra' for all snakes.

[17] These considerations do not necessitate any substantial change in our description of the mechanism whereby a name is endowed with a reference. They simply suggest that the group of producers whose use of the name is relevant should include both such contemporary producers as there are and also those producers whose identification of something as NN has left a trace upon the practice.

speakers who call *y* 'NN'—who know *y* as NN—and no group of speakers who know anything else as NN is relevant any longer. From the point of view of the users of the name, it is as though the previous practice—the one concerning *x*—had never existed. If someone attempts at this point to say, of *y*, 'This is not NN', there is nothing in the practice itself to which he can appeal. All he can do is tell a story about how *y* got his name.

11.4 THE LATE PHASE OF A PRACTICE

Let us now consider the last phase of the life of a name-using practice, when all the participants are consumers. This phase will exist for any length of time only in the case of names for persons whose lives give them some claim upon general interest; most of us will be forgotten soon after our deaths, and the practice of using our names will cease. However, we can think of many name-using practices in which this last phase has persisted for a great length of time, as generations of consumers introduce later generations into the practice as consumers. (Actually, this description is more appropriate to a purely oral tradition than for most of the names for historical characters which have been discussed in the literature. Most names which we use for historical characters, whether they are Biblical characters or characters in the history of Ancient Greece or Rome, or in more recent history, are preserved in documents, and every modern user of these names either is introduced to them by reading such documents, or is but a short chain away from someone thus introduced. This has the effect of short-circuiting the historical tradition involving the name, and our contemporary use of 'Moses', for example, does not significantly depend upon the two thousand years of the practice which preceded it.)[18]

Let us begin by considering the early stages of this phase of a name-using practice; we might focus upon the modern use of a name like 'Dr Livingstone'. Every participant has been introduced to the practice by hearing such sentences as 'Dr Livingstone was a great explorer of Africa' and 'Dr Livingstone was against the slave trade'. Now, subject to certain qualifications that will emerge shortly, it seems reasonable to regard the use of

[18] There are mixed cases as well, in which ancient documents record still more ancient traditions.

the name by such speakers in exactly the same way in which we would regard its use by *contemporary* consumers, that is, consumers who co-existed with producers. I emphasized (11.2) that a consumer who uttered a sentence like 'Dr Livingstone was against slavery' would be making, and would take himself to be making, a remark about someone called 'Dr Livingstone' (i.e. known as Dr Livingstone) and that the evaluation of the remark would depend upon discovering which individual this was—a procedure which leaves open the possibility that everything which this, and indeed all other, consumers are prepared to assert using the name might be discovered to be false. The disappearance of the producers, and the passage of time, do not appear to give any reason for taking a different view of the use made of the name by modern consumers, provided, of course, that they do not take a different view of the use themselves. The contemporary consumer possessed, in the sentence 'Dr Livingstone is F', not merely information that there was something which was F, but also information as to *which* individual was F—a cheque for identification that could be cashed by discovering the use of producers. The passage of time makes it more difficult to cash this cheque (though the producers can leave a great many traces of their use), and it may even become impossible. Nevertheless, the use of the name surely continues to be conditioned by the thought that the name is an identification-cheque drawn upon an earlier group of speakers, so that the claims embedded in the practice still constitute substantial, and falsifiable, hypotheses about a particular historical character *known to those speakers as 'Livingstone'*. Just as we would regard contemporary consumers as referring to Livingstone in virtue of using a name which had the property of referring to Livingstone (because of the use that was made of it by producers), so we shall regard the modern users of the name as referring in the same way. In this case, as opposed to the case we discussed in 11.3, reference is preserved as the practice persists, because the new uses have no relevant epistemological aspect; the consumers simply repeat what they have heard. And so there exists now a practice of using the name 'Livingstone' with Livingstone as referent, even if almost everything which is embodied in the practice as 'information about Livingstone' is false, perhaps as the result of myth and hagiography.

Later consumers manifest the intention to be participating in this practice, and, using a name which, in the practice, refers to Livingstone, themselves refer to Livingstone. Thus the practice is maintained with a constant reference, perhaps for very long periods of time.

I have told the story in such a way that a user of the name at *t* associates himself with the practice with the name which is *in existence at t*, rather than directly with the earlier practice, in order to take account of the fact that the name involved may gradually change as it is transmitted down the ages, so that it would be unrecognizable to the earlier speakers. There may not have been a practice involving the name 'NN' in existence at the earlier time: in particular, the referent of the name may not have been known as NN. In a certain sense, the name 'NN' may be 'our' name, rather than the name of the contemporary speakers. Nevertheless, we did not endow it with its reference; it has the reference it has because an antecedent name had the reference it had, and so on, ultimately back to the original speakers. A single practice of referring to something by name has been preserved despite the change in the form of the name.[19]

Thinking of the later participants in the name-using practice in this way, we can easily understand why it might be maintained that everything which is associated with the name by the community might be false of the referent. For example, the sentence 'Homer wrote the *Iliad* and the *Odyssey*' might be false. We think of some poet known to his contemporaries as Homer (or known by some name from which 'Homer' descends), and we think of the claim 'Homer wrote the *Iliad* and the *Odyssey*' being made as a substantial hypothesis about the authorship of the poems. Suppose the hypothesis was false. A contemporary Greek who was introduced into the practice by hearing this claim, and nothing else, had certainly got hold of a *false* claim about the authorship of the poems. This bit of misinformation might pass into the tradition, and end up being the only thing that modern speakers associate with the name. And if we think of ourselves in the same way as we think of the contemporary

---

[19] Relevant here are cases in which a name-using practice continues with a different name as a result of a deliberate change, as when missionaries change the name 'Jesus' into something more easily pronounceable, or when the Greeks changed the names of Trojans. [See the Appendix for some second thoughts.]

Greek consumer, it remains a bit of misinformation *about the poet whom the practice originally concerned.*

No position on the use of names for remote historical characters is going to strike us as impressively correct. The issue concerns the notion of *what is said*, which can float quite free of any substantial empirical concerns. It is quite striking how little it matters what we decide. We can proceed only by pressing analogies from other cases, in which reference, truth, and so on are more closely tied down. The position which I have been presenting so far in this section results from pressing one particular analogy: an analogy between modern users of a name for a remote historical personage and contemporary users of that name in a similar state of information. The analogy is a natural one, and the position we end up with by pressing it is not insupportable, but there remains something more that should be said.

It is pointless to deny that there can be important differences between the use of a name in the mature phase of a name-using practice and its use in the later phases. As time passes, the information about the bearer of the name embodied in the practice diminishes, and everyone who is given an adequate introduction to the practice acquires substantially the same body of information. Everyone who is introduced to the 'Homer'-practice nowadays learns 'Homer was the author of the *Iliad* and the *Odyssey*'; and everyone who is introduced to the 'Robin Hood'-practice learns more or less of the legend: the bandit in Sherwood forest who used a longbow, who robbed the rich to give to the poor, and so on. These facts, which are of course known to speakers, make possible the general use of such a name with an intention other than the simple intention of using it to refer to whatever is the referent of a name in a given practice. It is generally the case that a user of a name, at any stage in the life of a practice, intends to induce in his audience an information-based thought; and it is not uncommon for people who know each other fairly well to use a name with the manifest intention of inducing a thought embodying *specific* information. But in the later stages of a name-using practice, when it is common knowledge between participants in the practice what information they associate with the name, the presence of such additional manifest intentions is the rule rather than the exception. Thus, inside the long-lived practices of using the name 'Homer' and 'Robin Hood', there develops, so to speak, a secondary practice of using the name *as if* it were governed by the stipulation 'Let us use the name "Homer" to refer to the author of the *Iliad* and the *Odyssey*', or the stipulation 'Let us use the name "Robin Hood" to refer to that bandit who . . .'. I do not count the use of the name to repeat the information which has become associated with it as evidence of this secondary practice; indeed, as we shall see, the use of the name in such sentences is evidence of the persistence of the primary practice. It is the further uses which people make of the name—building on what they know to make new assertions ('Homer was a master of narrative'), to express desires and wishes ('I wish I had met Homer'), to give commands ('Write out a page of Homer's poetry'), to make jokes, and so on—which provides the evidence of this secondary practice.[20]

What should we say about these cases? If our modern use of the name 'Homer' derives from a practice in which a Greek poet was known by that name, but was a poet to whom the authorship of the *Iliad* and the *Odyssey* was wrongly attributed, should we say that the universal modern practice of using the name with the manifest intention of referring to the author of the *Iliad* and the *Odyssey* has brought it about that the name has changed its reference—and that it is now 'our' name for that author? Although I think that the answer to this question is 'No', I think that it is not a silly question, and it is not answered simply by pointing to the fact that a *contemporary* consumer who had got hold of the sentence 'Homer was the author of the *Iliad* and the *Odyssey*' would have got hold of a falsehood. His utterance was not part of a general practice of using the name with the intention characteristic of the secondary practice, and it needs to be argued that the existence of the secondary practice cannot endow a name with a (new) reference.[21]

[20] I do not think such a secondary practice has grown up with the name 'Goliath', despite the common knowledge that everyone associates with the name only the information 'Goliath was the Philistine slain by David'. Similarly with the name 'Sherwood Forest'.

[21] I think Kripke goes much too quickly from his obviously correct conclusion that no modern utterer of the sentence 'Gödel discovered the incompleteness of arithmetic' would be speaking the truth, in Kripke's hypothetical circumstance in which the proof was devised by someone called 'Schmidt', to the less obviously correct (though still correct) conclusion that 'Homer wrote the *Iliad* and the *Odyssey*' would not be true, in the circumstance envisaged in the text.

The main reason why I do not believe that 'Homer' has become our name for the author of the *Iliad* and the *Odyssey* is that we would not so regard it ourselves. Our use of at least personal proper names is governed by a picture of how they are endowed with a reference—the picture I have tried to describe—and this means that we would simply not think of saying, if asked to defend our assertion 'Homer was the author of the *Iliad* and the *Odyssey*', that 'I was under the impression that "Homer" was just the name we gave to the author of the *Iliad* and the *Odyssey*'. Given that we are not prepared to make such statements—given that we suppose that any association of name with information must be capable of defence—we must have at the back of our minds the idea that some individual was called 'Homer', or known as Homer (or known by some ancestor of that name), and that the discovery of which individual that is, and what his characteristics were, are germane to what we say with the use of *his* name. This general understanding of the kind of expression a personal proper name is keeps us in a position of permanent *deference*—sensitive to information which we ourselves do not possess about the person whose name we are using.[22]

It is important to remember the complexity of the intentions with which names may be used, and, in particular, the sorts of intention which make it plausible to speak of the secondary practices. I think recognition of the existence of these more complex intentions is necessary if we are to understand the usual purpose of negative existential statements involving names. I stressed, earlier (1.9, 11.2), the great diversity there can be between the information which a speaker associates with a name and the information which a hearer associates with it; but negative existential statements with names frequently presuppose a *common* background of information. For the purport of a negative existential statement, 'NN does not exist', is frequently taken to include what would be asserted by saying 'That ϕ does not exist', where 'that ϕ' is a testimony demonstrative adverting to some information generally associated with the name. Some-

---

[22] If we discover that the expression we use as a name for the author of a certain work was not in fact originally a name at all (as is the case with 'Malachi', used as a name for the author of the Book of Malachi), then our reservations about regarding it as *our* name for the author of that work lapse, and that is just what it can be regarded as being.

one who discovered that the story about the bandit in Sherwood Forest was a myth might communicate this discovery by saying 'Robin Hood did not (really) exist'; and I do not think it is clear that we can say that what he says is *false*, when it is discovered (this seems in fact to be what the historians suggest) that there really was someone to whose name this myth became attached. The name has entered a stage in its history at which I do not think it is clear what we should say.

In general it seems to me that people who use names in negative existential statements do intend to invoke specific information; they intend, at least as part of the point, to convey what might also be conveyed by a statement of the form 'That ϕ does not exist'. This is why we should normally want to insist that in such a statement the name is *used*: there is something that counts as *understanding its use*, namely bringing to bear appropriate information associated with the name. In the case of fiction, the name and the information are typically bound together in such a way as to be inseparable (for example, one learns the name 'Emma' by reading the Jane Austen novel). What happens in the different kind of case where the information is groundless, so that 'That ϕ does not exist' would be true, but it has become attached to the name of someone who really existed, is, in my opinion, just *unclear* (as can be seen from the uncertain practice of historians).

When there is no specific body of information which is generally associated with a name (as in the case of a mature name-using practice), the negative existential statement does not have a clear sense. (It certainly is not appropriate whenever a name lacks a referent: we could not appropriately report the discovery that a name-using practice involving 'NN' concerned two or more individuals simply by saying 'NN does not exist'.) If someone said 'Ronald Reagan does not exist', I should not know what to make of it. If the remark is intended to have a content such that it is true if and only if 'Ronald Reagan', as used in a certain name-using practice, does not refer, then I cannot conclude from its truth anything about the information I associate with the name, since for all that the remark, so understood, tells me, that information could still constitute knowledge about some individual. And if I can conclude nothing about the information from the remark, it is not clear how I can sensibly do anything with the information in understanding the remark—as would be required if I were to understand the remark as involving a *use* of the name. (It would be safe to say 'Ronald Reagan does not really exist', or 'Ronald Reagan is a hoax', only if almost all the information disseminated in the name-using practice were suspect. But what about the people who have been introduced to someone under that name?)

There are *thin* uses of names in existential statements. For example, I may book a flight in a false name, and then the next day telephone the airline and say 'Look, Agatha Hermer does not exist', or 'Agatha Hermer is not a real person'. Here there is no background information which is either such that I intend to invoke it, or such that the use of the name might eventually be linked with it. (Hence it is not clear that we need insist that the name is used and not mentioned.) All that the receptionist need conclude is that when I uttered the name previously, I referred to nothing. And in understanding the original utterances, e.g. 'Agatha Hermer needs a first-class flight to Baltimore tomorrow', nothing more was required of the receptionist than the thought 'Someone named "Agatha Hermer" needs . . .'. For understanding utterances containing names it is normally required that one pass beyond a thought of this sort; but not always.

11.5 UNDERSTANDING PROPER NAMES

Our question now is 'What is it to *understand* a use of a proper name?' I have been trying to give as naturalistic an account as I can of the conditions under which a participant in a name-using practice can *use* a name to make a reference to a particular object. But I have repeatedly stressed (see 4.1, 6.4) that the notion of using a term to refer is a less fundamental notion than the notion of understanding a term in such a use; it is a perfectly intelligible possibility, occasionally realized, that someone can use an expression to refer without being himself in a position to understand the reference.

We have seen the importance, at least in the case of proper names of the kind we are concerned with, of an object's being *called* '*NN*' or being *known as NN* by a certain group of speakers (the producers): something is determined as the referent of the name by its satisfying that property. But I think it will be universally acknowledged that understanding a use of a proper name requires one to go beyond the thought that the speaker is referring to *some person known as NN*, and to arrive at a thought in the thinking of which one actually thinks of the object in question.[23] The reason for this is not the one that is usually given, namely that the property of being known as NN is semantical in character,[24] but rather, a consideration of the same sort as I brought to bear in the case of, say, 'you' (see 9.2). One does not understand a remark of the form 'You are *F*', addressed to oneself, just by knowing that the speaker is saying that the person he is addressing is *F*; one must go beyond the referential feature and identify the person as oneself. Similarly, if one has a dossier of information associated with the name 'NN', and fails to bring it to bear in understanding 'NN is *F*', going no further than the thought 'Someone named "NN" is *F*', one has surely failed to do what it was the point of the utterance that one should do.[25]

But is there any particular *way* in which one must think of the object?

It would appear not. Even if we refuse to acknowledge the great diversity in ways of thinking of the referent that are likely to be found among the consumers in a mature name-using practice, there are undeniable differences between a producer, who knows an individual whom he can recognize as NN (so that he can use the name to express thoughts of the kind discussed in chapter 8), and a consumer, who does not. Now, when we discussed referential communication involving the one-off devices, in chapter 9, we noticed quite considerable restrictions on the ways in which hearers must think of referents in order to understand remarks. We traced those restrictions to the requirement that the hearer, if he is to understand, must *know* of some object that it is the referent. But we observed that this source of restriction would lapse if there were other participants in the communicative transaction, on whom hearers could rely to tell them which individual a speaker is referring to (though the fact that one-off referential communication does not exploit

---

[23] Discounting cases like the 'Agatha Hermer' example at the end of 11.4.

[24] See, e.g., Searle, *Speech Acts*, p. 171.

[25] This is not meant as a knock-down argument: simply an expression of a naturalistic view of the point of using names to refer.

such a mechanism is not an accident). Proper names, however, are precisely not one-off referential devices; and we can think of the person (or persons) who introduced the audience to the name in question, and reinforced his pattern of use of it, as just such an authoritative third party—letting the audience know (something that can be done in countless different ways) which individual a speaker is referring to. When we contemplate the fact that different audiences think of the referent in a variety of different ways (which may be quite different from the way in which the speaker thinks of it), we do not necessarily have to conclude that the audiences do not know what the speaker is referring to. This argument does not show that there are *absolutely no* restrictions upon the way in which an audience may think of the referent in understanding a remark containing a name; but it does neutralize the main reason we might have had for supposing that the situation will be like the situation we found in the case of the one-off devices.

It would appear, then, that the single main requirement for understanding a use of a proper name is that one think of the referent.

Now, it seems to me to follow that many of those who are in a position to *use* a name to refer (those who have, in that sense, been introduced to the practice in question) cannot themselves properly *understand* utterances involving the name (including their own). Indeed, one can imagine the practice of using a name propagated exclusively by people who cannot understand it—people who do not know what they are talking about. For as we saw earlier (11.3), it is consistent with being able to use a name (as a consumer) that one have wholly baseless information associated with it. If the information derives from nothing at all, then someone who interprets a use of the name by invoking the information is thereby thinking of *nothing*; and those who associate with a name of *x* only a story (widely disseminated) of the doings of *y* are thinking of *y* when they interpret uses of the name by invoking this information.

I think this conclusion, that one can be in a position to use a name without being able to understand uses of it, would be contested by many. I have in mind people who would agree that understanding a use of a proper name requires thinking of the referent, but would argue that extreme misinformation of the kind we have been discussing does not prevent a subject from thinking of the referent. We are here brought back to the discussion of Russell's Principle.

I have conceded (3.3, 4.1, 4.6) that there are uses of the idioms 'believes that' or 'thinks of' which might appear to support these views; although, as I have insisted throughout, these linguistic data cannot by themselves be taken to settle anything.

Suppose that someone, accepting the standard story associated with the name 'NN', uses the name in the sentence 'NN is F'; suppose further that 'NN' is a name of x, but that the standard story records the doings of y. Now, it is true that one could sensibly say 'He must be *thinking of x*'. (Indeed, his acceptance of the standard story is positive evidence for this attribution, given that that information is widely disseminated in the name-using practice.) But this would be equivalent to 'He *means x*' on the kind of interpretation discussed in 5.3; that is, it registers that it is the practice of using x's name which the speaker aims to be participating in (a purpose which can be attributed to him without crediting him with the capacity to entertain thoughts about x).

It is also true that such a person could be sensibly described as *believing that NN is F*, and this seems to involve attributing to him a belief (and hence a thought) about the referent of the name. But it seems to me that this sort of belief-ascription is very closely tied to the speaker's disposition to *say* that NN is F (attributable to him in part in virtue of his disposition to say 'NN is F', manifesting the intention of participating, with the use of the name, in the appropriate practice). And this leaves the substantive question, whether the speaker can entertain thoughts about the referent, in the sense which concerns us, untouched. Given that it is at least intelligible to maintain that a speaker can sincerely utter a sentence he does not himself fully understand, there is always the possibility of uses of 'believes that ...' which do not genuinely entail that the subject is even capable of entertaining the thought expressed by the embedded sentence.

We can argue, then, rather on the lines of 5.3, that the way in which people employ the notion of *thinking of* an object, and the notion of *the object of thought*, when proper names are involved, is confused, because of a failure to distinguish two notions of the intended referent of a use of a name: one in which the intended referent is determined by determining which name-using practice a speaker manifested the intention of participating in (the intended referent is the referent of the name as used in that practice); and one in which the intended referent is the object which the speaker is *aiming at* with his use of the name. Full understanding of a use of a name requires that the referent of the name be an object of the subject's thought in the *second* sense. The idioms which motivate resistance to the conclusion that one can be in a position to use a name without being able to understand uses of it show only that, in the sorts of cases we have considered, the referent of the name can be an object of the subject's thought in the *first* sense; and that is irrelevant.

Suppose someone is maliciously introduced into the practice of using the name 'Harold Macmillan' by being told 'Harold Macmillan is a bachelor, was leader of the Conservative Party, plays the organ, took Britain into the Common Market, has a yacht'. It would surely not be supposed that this person understands the name 'Harold Macmillan', because in interpreting uses of it he would be thinking of Edward Heath. Suppose now that the misapprehension that Harold Macmillan is Edward Heath becomes widespread. In that case it becomes possible to say (if someone, for instance, includes 'Harold Macmillan' on a list of unmarried British statesmen), 'Oh, you mean *that* Harold Macmillan'. But it remains the case that the person is thinking of Edward Heath: the identity of the object of his thought cannot be affected by how widely disseminated his mistaken association of information with a name happens to be.[26]

I have, in effect, been using the apparatus of 5.3 in order to undermine resistance to the claim that one can be in a position to use a name without being able to understand its use. But even if the arguments carried conviction in chapter 5, where they were expressly restricted to examples not involving proper names, the resistance may persist in the present case precisely

---

[26] We must come to terms with the idea that one and the same dossier can support the attribution of beliefs and thoughts concerning different things, depending upon how it is *used*—it will not do to say that whenever the dossier is activated, the thought concerns the same thing. Nevertheless, in the case cited in the text, it is surely reasonable to say that the subject is thinking *of Edward Heath*, and falsely believes that 'Harold Macmillan' is his name.

because of the presence of proper names in the examples. It cannot be denied that a proper name itself has some individuative force. There is thus a powerful temptation to argue that, if someone is competent in the *use* of a proper name (and hence able to function as a link in a chain by which information about its referent can be transmitted), then his acquisition of that competence must itself have put him in a position to entertain thoughts about its referent. Putting the matter in terms of Russell's Principle, as interpreted in 4.1, the suggestion is that we should recognize mastery of the use of a proper name as, so to speak, an autonomous way of satisfying the requirement that one have discriminating knowledge of the objects of one's thoughts.

In order to lessen this temptation, I should like to suggest the possibility of distinguishing communication, which requires understanding, from something which is in many ways like communication (we might call it 'kommunication'), which does not. We can regard someone who associates a wholly misleading dossier of information with a name as engaging in kommunication (receiving kommunication from others, and kommunicating with others). He is a viable participant in the name-using practice, and in the social situation he can serve as a link in a chain of information-transmission. But this is fully compatible with saying that he does not come to a proper understanding of what is said in remarks using the name. He can identify the referent of those remarks for a suitably primed audience, but he cannot identify the referent *simpliciter*.

Why should we say he does not understand what is said? That is to say he does not know the truth-conditions of, e.g., 'NN is *F*'. Now of course there is a thought which he can entertain as true just in case 'NN is *F*' is true, namely the thought that the person known as NN (in this use of the name) is *F*. But this thought sticks at the referential feature (cf. 9.2); whereas full understanding (here as in the one-off cases) requires that one move beyond the referential feature and entertain, as expressed by the speaker, a proposition of the form $\ulcorner a$ is $F \urcorner$, where a is an adequate Idea of the referent. Those who resist my claim, if they concede this much, must hold that any adequate introduction to a name-using practice equips one with an adequate Idea of the object which is its referent. But what reason is there

to accept this? At any rate the linguistic data to which I believe
proponents of this position would appeal (the fact that we would
naturally say such things as 'He means *x*' or 'He is thinking of
x') constitute, as we have seen, no reason in favour of the
position.[27]

[27] [Evans planned to continue by discussing, in connection with examples like 'Hesperus' and 'Phosphorus', the question whether there are any restrictions on how one
may *think of* the referent if one is to be credited with a full understanding of the use of a
proper name. (Cf. 1.9.) There are some notes towards such a discussion, but I am
unable to reconstruct their drift with confidence, so I simply register a lacuna.]

Appendix

Evans planned to rewrite 11.4 with a more sophisticated treatment of various aspects of the late phase of a name-using practice.

11.4 suggests that it suffices, for a present user of a name for a person in the remote past, to make it clear which *present* practice he intends to be participating in. But this involves a disanalogy with the case of a consumer in the mature phase of a name-using practice, who is able to make it clear which *producers* are relevant to his use. And it has undesirable consequences. Suppose there were in fact eight emperors of China called 'Chan', and there is a modern practice of using the name 'Chan' as if for an ancient emperor of China: the modern practice in fact derives from the use of the name for one in particular of the eight emperors, though no participants in the modern practice can distinguish that one from any of the seven others. Here, making it clear which modern practice one is participating in hardly seems to be enough to make it clear that one is speaking of that emperor in particular. If we want to retain anything of the idea that the reference of a name is fixed by uses of it by producers, it seems that we must understand the requirement that one manifest which practice one intends to be participating in in terms of an individuation of practices which does not merely concern the present, but involves an indication of who the relevant *producers* were. Or, to put it another way: if we want to use the idea that the reference of a name on our lips is fixed by the fact that we have taken over (a version of) a name by which someone was known, then we must impose the requirement that we be able to give some indication as to *who* knew the person in question by (a version of) that name. (On this view, our possession of something reasonably close to the name that was used when the person was alive *is* important. Homer is presumed to have changed Trojan names into invented Greek names; the upshot is that the usual mechanism whereby our use of a name for a historically remote character is secured a reference cannot be operative in the case of our use of, say, 'Hector', even supposing the story of the *Iliad* is substantially factual.)

Bibliography

G. E. M. Anscombe, 'The First Person', in Samuel Guttenplan, ed., *Mind and Language*, pp. 45–65.

—, *An Introduction to Wittgenstein's Tractatus* (Hutchinson, London, 1959).

D. M. Armstrong, *A Materialist Theory of the Mind* (Routledge and Kegan Paul, London, 1968).

J. L. Austin, *Sense and Sensibilia* (Clarendon Press, Oxford, 1962).

A. J. Ayer, 'Names and Descriptions', in A. J. Ayer, *The Concept of a Person and Other Essays* (Macmillan, London, 1964), pp. 129–61.

—, *The Problem of Knowledge* (Penguin, Harmondsworth, 1956).

Alan D. Baddeley, *The Psychology of Memory* (Harper and Row, New York, 1976).

George Berkeley, *A New Theory of Vision and Other Writings* (Dent, London, 1910).

Jorge Luis Borges, *Labyrinths* (New Directions, New York, 1962).

T. G. R. Bower, 'Infant Perception of the Third Dimension and Object Concept Development', in L. B. Cohen and P. Salatapek, eds., *Infant Perception from Sensation to Cognition*, vol. 2: *Perception of Space Speech and Sound* (Academic Press, New York, 1975), pp. 33–50.

Tyler Burge, 'Belief *De Re*', *Journal of Philosophy* lxxiv (1977), 338–62.

—, 'Reference and Proper Names', *Journal of Philosophy* lxx (1973), 425–39.

—, 'Truth and Singular Terms', *Nous* viii (1974), 309–25.

Susan Carey and Rhea Diamond, 'From Piecemeal to Configurational Representation of Faces', *Science* 195 (1977), 312–14.

Hector-Neri Castañeda, ' "He": a Study in the Logic of Self-Consciousness', *Ratio* viii (1966), 130–57.

—, 'Indicators and Quasi-Indicators', *American Philosophical Quarterly* iv (1967), 85–100.

R. M. Chisholm, 'Identity Through Time', in Howard E. Kiefer and Milton K. Munitz, eds., *Language, Belief, and Metaphysics* (SUNY Press, Albany, 1970), pp. 163–82.

—, 'Reply to Strawson's Comments', ibid., pp. 188–9.

Noam Chomsky, 'Questions of Form and Interpretation', *Linguistic Analysis* i (1975), 75–109.

Alonzo Church, 'Intensional Isomorphism and Identity of Belief', *Philosophical Studies* v (1954), 65–73.

C. A. J. Coady, 'Testimony and Observation', *American Philosophical Quarterly* x (1973), 149-55.

Christopher Coope, Peter Geach, Timothy Potts, and Roger White, eds., *A Wittgenstein Workbook* (Blackwell, Oxford, 1971).

Arthur C. Danto, *Sartre* (Fontana/Collins, Glasgow, 1975).

Donald Davidson, 'Truth and Meaning', *Synthese* xvii (1967), 304-23.

—, and Gilbert Harman, eds., *Semantics of Natural Languages* (Reidel, Dordrecht, 1972).

—, and Jaakko Hintikka, eds., *Words and Objections* (Reidel, Dordrecht, 1969).

Richard Dawkins, *The Selfish Gene* (Clarendon Press, Oxford, 1976).

Daniel C. Dennett, 'Where am I?', in Daniel C. Dennett, *Brainstorms* (Harvester, Hassocks, 1978), pp. 310-23.

Michael Devitt, 'Singular Terms', *Journal of Philosophy* lxxi (1974), 183-205.

Keith S. Donnellan, 'Proper Names and Identifying Descriptions', in Donald Davidson and Gilbert Harman, eds., *Semantics of Natural Languages*, pp. 356-79.

—, 'Reference and Definite Descriptions', *Philosophical Review* lxxv (1966), 281-304.

—, 'Speaking of Nothing', *Philosophical Review* lxxxiii (1974), 3-31.

Michael Dummett, *Frege: Philosophy of Language* (Duckworth, London, 1973).

—, 'Frege's Distinction between Sense and Reference', in Michael Dummett, *Truth and Other Enigmas*, pp. 116-44.

—, *Truth and Other Enigmas* (Duckworth, London, 1978).

—, 'What is a Theory of Meaning?', in Samuel Guttenplan, ed., *Mind and Language*, pp. 97-138.

—, 'What is a Theory of Meaning?' (II), in Gareth Evans and John McDowell, eds., *Truth and Meaning*, pp. 67-137.

Gareth Evans, 'The Causal Theory of Names', *Aristotelian Society Supplementary Volume* xlvii (1973), 187-208.

—, 'Identity and Predication', *Journal of Philosophy* lxxii (1975), 343-63.

—, 'Pronouns', *Linguistic Inquiry* xi (1980), 337-62.

—, 'Pronouns, Quantifiers, and Relative Clauses' (I), *Canadian Journal of Philosophy* vii (1977), 467-536.

—, 'Reference and Contingency', *The Monist* lxii (1979), 161-89.

—, 'Semantic Structure and Logical Form', in Gareth Evans and John McDowell, eds., *Truth and Meaning*, pp. 199-222.

—, 'Things Without the Mind', in Zak van Straaten, ed., *Philosophical Subjects: Essays Presented to P. F. Strawson* (Clarendon Press, Oxford, 1980), pp. 76-116.

—, 'Understanding Demonstratives', in Herman Parret and Jacques

Bouveresse, eds., *Meaning and Understanding* (De Gruyter, Berlin and New York, 1981), pp. 280-303.
—, and John McDowell, eds., *Truth and Meaning* (Clarendon Press, Oxford, 1976).
Jerry A. Fodor, *The Language of Thought* (Harvester, Hassocks, 1976).
—, 'Methodological Solipsism Considered as a Research Strategy in Cognitive Psychology', *The Behavioural and Brain Sciences* iii (1980), 63-73.
S. J. Freedman and J. H. Rekosh, 'The Functional Integrity of Spatial Behavior', in S. J. Freedman, ed., *The Neuropsychology of Spatially Oriented Behavior* (Dorsey Press, Homewood, Illinois, 1968), pp. 153-62.
Gottlob Frege, *The Basic Laws of Arithmetic*, translated by Montgomery Furth (University of California, Berkeley and Los Angeles, 1967).
—, *Logical Investigations*, edited by P. T. Geach (Blackwell, Oxford, 1977).
—, *Philosophical and Mathematical Correspondence*, edited by Gottfried Gabriel, Hans Hermes, Friedrich Kambartel, Christian Thiel, and Albert Veraart, abridged for the English edition by Brian McGuinness, and translated by Hans Kaal (Blackwell, Oxford, 1980).
—, *Posthumous Writings*, edited by Hans Hermes, Friedrich Kambartel, and Friedrich Kaulbach, and translated by Peter Long and Roger White (Blackwell, Oxford, 1979).
—, 'The Thought', translated by A. M. and Marcelle Quinton, in P. F. Strawson, ed., *Philosophical Logic* (OUP, Oxford, 1967).
—, *Translations from the Philosophical Writings of Gottlob Frege*, P. T. Geach and Max Black (Blackwell, Oxford, 1952).
P. T. Geach, 'Intentional Identity', in P. T. Geach, *Logic Matters*, pp. 146-53.
—, *Logic Matters* (Blackwell, Oxford, 1972).
—, *Mental Acts* (Routledge and Kegan Paul, London, 1957).
—, 'The Perils of Pauline', in P. T. Geach, *Logic Matters*, pp. 153-65.
J. J. Gibson, *The Senses Considered as Perceptual Systems* (George Allen and Unwin, London, 1968).
Nelson Goodman, *Languages of Art* (OUP, London, 1969).
Richard E. Grandy, 'A Definition of Truth for Theories with Intensional Definite Description Operators', *Journal of Philosophical Logic* i (1972), 137-55.
H. P. Grice, 'Vacuous Names', in Donald Davidson and Jaakko Hintikka, eds., *Words and Objections*, pp. 118-45.
Samuel Guttenplan, ed., *Mind and Language* (Clarendon Press, Oxford, 1975).

Gilbert H. Harman, 'How to Use Propositions', *American Philosophical Quarterly* xiv (1977), 173–6.

—, *Thought* (Princeton University Press, Princeton, 1973).

Martin Heidegger, *Being and Time*, translated by John Macquarrie and Edward Robinson (Blackwell, Oxford, 1962).

David Hume, *A Treatise of Human Nature* (Dent, London, 1911).

Immanuel Kant, *Critique of Pure Reason*, translated by Norman Kemp Smith (Macmillan, London, 1929).

David Kaplan, 'Demonstratives' (unpublished), Draft no. 2, mimeo, UCLA, 1977.

—, 'Quantifying In', in Donald Davidson and Jaakko Hintikka, eds., *Words and Objections*, pp. 206–42.

Saul A. Kripke, John Locke Lectures (Oxford, 1973), unpublished.

—, 'Naming and Necessity', in Donald Davidson and Gilbert Harman eds., *Semantics of Natural Languages*, pp. 253–355.

—, 'Speaker's Reference and Semantic Reference', in Peter A. French, Theodore E. Uehling, Jr., and Howard K. Wettstein, eds., *Contemporary Perspectives in the Philosophy of Language* (University of Minnesota Press, Minneapolis, 1979), pp. 6–27.

Karel Lambert, 'Existential Import Revisited', *Notre Dame Journal of Formal Logic* iv (1963), 288–92, at p. 290.

David K. Lewis, ' Attitudes *De Dicto* and *De Se*', *Philosophical Review* lxxxviii (1979), 513–43.

—, *Counterfactuals* (Blackwell, Oxford, 1973).

—, 'Truth in Fiction', *American Philosophical Quarterly* xv (1978), 37–46.

P. H. Lindsay and D. A. Norman, *Human Information Processing* (Academic Press, New York, 1972).

John McDowell, 'On the Sense and Reference of a Proper Name', *Mind* lxxxvi (1977), 159–85.

—, 'Truth-Value Gaps', forthcoming in the proceedings of the Sixth International Congress for Logic, Methodology, and Philosophy of Science.

J. L. Mackie, 'The Riddle of Existence', *Aristotelian Society Supplementary Volume* l (1976), 247–67.

—, *Truth, Probability and Paradox* (Clarendon Press, Oxford, 1973).

Michael McKinsey, 'Names and Intentionality', *Philosophical Review* lxxxvii (1978), 171–200.

Gabriel Marcel, *The Mystery of Being*, vol. 1 (Gateway Editions, South Bend, Indiana, 1978). (Originally published by Harvill Press, London, 1950.)

Benson Mates, 'Descriptions and Reference', *Foundations of Language* x (1973), 409–18.

George A. Miller and Phillip N. Johnson-Laird, *Language and Perception* (CUP, Cambridge, 1976).

G. E. Moore, *Commonplace Book 1919–53*, edited by Casimir Lewy (George Allen and Unwin, London, 1962).

—, 'Is Existence a Predicate?', *Aristotelian Society Supplementary Volume* xv (1936), 175–88.

—, ' "Real" and "Imaginary" ', in G. E. Moore, *Lectures in Philosophy*, edited by Casimir Lewy (George Allen and Unwin, London, 1966), pp. 20–43.

—, 'Some Judgments of Perception', *Proceedings of the Aristotelian Society* xix (1918–19), 1–29.

—, 'Wittgenstein's Lectures in 1930–33' (III), *Mind* lxiv (1955), 1–27.

Thomas Nagel, 'Brain Bisection and the Unity of Consciousness', in Thomas Nagel, *Mortal Questions* (CUP, Cambridge, 1979), pp. 147–64.

—, *The Possibility of Altruism* (Clarendon Press, Oxford, 1970).

John O'Keefe and Lynn Nadel, *The Hippocampus as a Cognitive Map* (Clarendon Press, Oxford, 1978).

Derek Parfit, 'Personal Identity', *Philosophical Review* lxxx (1971), 3–27.

Christopher Peacocke, *Holistic Explanation* (Clarendon Press, Oxford, 1979).

—, 'Necessity and Truth Theories', *Journal of Philosophical Logic* vii (1978), 473–500.

—, 'Proper Names, Reference, and Rigid Designation', in Simon Blackburn, ed., *Meaning Reference and Necessity* (CUP, Cambridge, 1975), pp. 109–32.

John Perry, 'Frege on Demonstratives', *Philosophical Review* lxxxvi (1977), 474–97.

—, 'The Problem of the Essential Indexical', *Nous* xiii (1979), 3–21.

George Pitcher, *A Theory of Perception* (Princeton University Press, Princeton, 1971).

Henri Poincaré, *The Value of Science* (Dover, New York, 1958).

A. N. Prior, *Objects of Thought*, edited by P. T. Geach and A. J. P. Kenny (Clarendon Press, Oxford, 1971).

Hilary Putnam, 'The Meaning of "Meaning" ', in Hilary Putnam, *Mind, Language and Reality* (CUP, Cambridge, 1975), pp. 215–71.

W. V. Quine, 'Epistemology Naturalized', in W. V. Quine, *Ontological Relativity and Other Essays*, pp. 69–90.

—, 'Natural Kinds', in W. V. Quine, *Ontological Relativity and Other Essays*, pp. 114–38.

—, *Ontological Relativity and Other Essays* (Columbia, New York, 1969).

—, 'Quantifiers and Propositional Attitudes', *Journal of Philosophy* liii (1956), 177–87.

—, *Word and Object* (M.I.T. Press, Cambridge, Mass., 1960).

A. M. Quinton, 'Spaces and Times', *Philosophy* xxxvii (1962), 130–47.

Thomas Reid, *An Inquiry into the Human Mind*, edited by Timothy Duggan (University of Chicago Press, Chicago, 1970).

Bertrand Russell, 'On Denoting', in Bertrand Russell, *Logic and Knowledge*, pp. 41–56.

—, 'Knowledge by Acquaintance and Knowledge by Description', in Bertrand Russell, *Mysticism and Logic* (George Allen and Unwin, London, 1917), pp. 152–67.

—, *Logic and Knowledge*, edited by R. C. Marsh (George Allen and Unwin, London, 1956).

—, *The Philosophy of Logical Atomism*, in Bertrand Russell, *Logic and Knowledge*, pp. 177–281.

—, *The Problems of Philosophy* (OUP, Oxford, 1912).

Jean-Paul Sartre, *Being and Nothingness*, translated by Hazel E. Barnes (Methuen, London, 1969).

Stephen Schiffer, 'The Basis of Reference', *Erkenntnis* xiii (1978), 171–206.

Rolf Schock, *Logics without Existence Assumptions* (Almquist and Wiksell, Stockholm, 1968).

Dana Scott, 'Existence and Description in Formal Logic', in Ralph Schoenman, ed., *Bertrand Russell: Philosopher of the Century* (George Allen and Unwin, London, 1967), pp. 181–200.

John R. Searle, *Speech Acts* (CUP, Cambridge, 1969).

Sydney Shoemaker, 'Persons and Their Pasts', *American Philosophical Quarterly* vii (1970), 269–85.

—, *Self-Knowledge and Self-Identity* (Cornell University Press, Ithaca, 1963).

—, 'Self-Reference and Self-Awareness', *Journal of Philosophy* lxv (1968), 555–67.

Hans D. Sluga, review of Frege, *Nachgelassene Schriften*, *Journal of Philosophy* lxviii (1971), 265–72.

P. F. Strawson, *The Bounds of Sense* (Methuen, London, 1966).

—, 'Identifying Reference and Truth-Values', in P. F. Strawson, *Logico-Linguistic Papers*, pp. 75–95.

—, *Individuals* (Methuen, London, 1959).

—, *Logico-Linguistic Papers* (Methuen, London, 1971).

—, 'On Referring', in P. F. Strawson, *Logico-Linguistic Papers*, pp. 1–27.

—, review of Ayer, *The Problem of Knowledge*, *Philosophy* xxxii (1957), 302–14.

—, *Subject and Predicate in Logic and Grammar* (Methuen, London, 1974).

Richard Swinburne, *Space and Time* (Macmillan, London, 1968).

Charles Taylor, 'The Validity of Transcendental Arguments', *Proceedings of the Aristotelian Society* lxxix (1978–9), 151–65.

Richmond H. Thomason, 'Modal Logic and Metaphysics', in Karel Lambert, ed., *The Logical Way of Doing Things* (Yale University Press, New Haven and London, 1969), pp. 119-46.

—, and Robert C. Stalnaker, 'Modality and Reference', *Nous* ii (1968), 359-72.

G. N. A. Vesey, ed., *Body and Mind* (George Allen and Unwin, London, 1964).

John Wallace, 'Only in the Context of a Sentence do Words have any Meaning', in Peter A. French, Theodore E. Uehling, Jr., and Howard K. Wettstein, eds., *Contemporary Perspectives in the Philosophy of Language* (University of Minnesota Press, Minneapolis, 1979), pp. 305-25.

Kendall L. Walton, 'Fearing Fictions', *Journal of Philosophy* lxxv (1978), 5-27.

—, 'Pictures and Make-Believe', *Philosophical Review* lxxxii (1973), 283-319.

L. Weiskrantz, E. K. Warrington, M. D. Saunders, and J. Marshall, 'Visual Capacity in the Hemianopic Field following a Restricted Occipital Ablation', *Brain* xcvii (1974), 709-28.

A. N. Whitehead and Bertrand Russell, *Principia Mathematica*, vol. I (CUP, Cambridge, second edition 1927).

David Wiggins, 'On Being in the Same Place at the Same Time', *Philosophical Review* lxxvii (1968), 90-5.

—, *Identity and Spatio-Temporal Continuity* (Blackwell, Oxford, 1967).

—, 'Identity, Designation, Essentialism and Physicalism', *Philosophia* v (1975), 1-30.

Bernard Williams, 'Imagination and the Self', in Bernard Williams, *Problems of the Self* (CUP, Cambridge, 1973), pp. 26-45.

N. L. Wilson, 'On Semantically Relevant Whatsits: A Semantics for Philosophy of Science', in Glenn Pearce and Patrick Maynard, eds., *Conceptual Change* (Reidel, Dordrecht, 1973), pp. 233-45.

Ludwig Wittgenstein, *The Blue and Brown Books* (Blackwell, Oxford, 1958).

—, *On Certainty*, edited by G. E. M. Anscombe and G. H. von Wright, and translated by Denis Paul and G. E. M. Anscombe (Blackwell, Oxford, 1969).

—, *Philosophical Investigations*, translated by G. E. M. Anscombe (Blackwell, Oxford, 1953).

—, *Tractatus Logico-Philosophicus*, translated by D. F. Pears and B. F. McGuinness (Routledge and Kegan Paul, London, 1961).

—, 'Wittgenstein's Notes for Lectures on "Private Experience" and "Sense Data"', *Philosophical Review* lxxvii (1968), 271-320.

Index